Global Accountabilities

Accountability is seen as an essential feature of governments, businesses, and NGOs. This volume treats it as a socially constructed means of control that can be used by the weak as well as the powerful. It contributes analytical depth to the diverse debates on accountability in modern organizations by exploring its nature, forms, and impacts in civil society organizations, public and intergovernmental agencies, and private corporations. The contributors draw from a range of disciplines to demonstrate the inadequacy of modern rationalist prescriptions for establishing and monitoring accountability standards, arguing that accountability frameworks attached to principal–agent logics and applied universally across cultures typically fail to achieve their objectives. By examining a diverse rage of empirical examples and case studies, this book underscores the importance of grounding accountability procedures and standards in the divergent cultural, social, and political settings in which they operate.

Alnoor Ebrahim is a Visiting Associate Professor in the Hauser Center for Nonprofit Organizations at the John F. Kennedy School of Government, Harvard University and the Wyss Visiting Scholar at the Harvard Business School. He is also an Associate Professor at Virginia Tech.

Edward Weisband holds the Diggs Endowed Chair Professorship in the Social Sciences in the Department of Political Science at Virginia Tech.

Global Accountabilities

Participation, Pluralism, and Public Ethics

Edited by
Alnoor Ebrahim and Edward Weisband

CAMBRIDGE
UNIVERSITY PRESS

CAMBRIDGE UNIVERSITY PRESS
Cambridge, New York, Melbourne, Madrid, Cape Town, Singapore, São Paulo

Cambridge University Press
The Edinburgh Building, Cambridge CB2 8RU, UK

Published in the United States of America by Cambridge University Press,
New York

www.cambridge.org
Information on this title: www.cambridge.org/9780521700115

First published 2007

Printed in the United Kingdom at the University Press, Cambridge

A catalogue record for this publications is available from the British Library

Library of Congress Cataloging-in-Publication Data

Global accountabilities : participation, pluralism, and public ethics / Alnoor
Ebrahim and Edward Weisband, editors.
p. cm.
Includes bibliographical references and index.

ISBN-13: 978-0-521-87647-6 (hardback)
ISBN-10: 0-521-87647-8 (hardback)
ISBN-13: 978-0-521-70011-5 (paperback)
ISBN-10: 0-521-70011-6 (paperback)

1. Non-governmental organizations – Evaluation. 2. International business
enterprises – Evaluation. 3. Performance standards. I. Ebrahim, Alnoor.
II. Weisband, Edward, 1939- III. Title.
JZ4841.G56 2007
338.8′8–dc22
2007007750

ISBN 978-0-521-87647-6 hardback
ISBN 978-0-521-70011-5 paperback

To Joan Elizabeth and Maria,
Sine Quibus Non

Contents

Tables

Figures

Acknowledgments

We wish to thank a number of individuals and organizations for their support of this edited volume. A seed grant from the ASPIRES Program at Virginia Tech in 2001–2 enabled us to explore the emergent area of accountability, to bring together a group of scholars from diverse disciplines and international experiences, and to create a program for its research and study, now housed in the Institute for Policy and Governance. This work was also supported by the School of Public and International Affairs and the Department of Political Science. We would like to thank our colleagues Minnis E. Ridenour, John Randolph, Ilja A. Luciak, Timothy W. Luke, Jim Bohland, and Joseph V. Rees for their intellectual contributions and support of this work from its earliest stages, and Max O. Stephenson and Russ Cargo for their ongoing collaboration. Numerous graduate students have also contributed their energy and excitement along the way: Matthew Bond, Rachel Christensen, David P. Dansereau, Elana DeLozier, Kalen Harvey, Taylor Horne, Nicholas J. Kiersey, David Moore, Ramya Ramanath, Courtney Irene Powell Thomas, and Ian Watson.

For their personal and institutional engagement, we wish to thank Mark Moore at Harvard University's Hauser Center for Nonprofit Organizations, and Steven Heydemann at Georgetown University's Center for Democracy and Civil Society. We are also indebted to a number of scholars and practitioners: Angela Bies, Lisa Berlinger, Joseph Galaskiewicz, Steve Herz, Sarah Lister, Adil Najam, Owen Pell, and Susan Sanow.

At Cambridge University Press, we wish to convey a special thanks to our editor, John Haslam, as well as to Chris Harrison. The Press' anonymous reviewers provided us with exceptionally insightful and generous feedback.

Finally, we have learned over the course of this project that not all accountabilities are equal and must be prioritized. For this, our most profound gratitude is to our families, and especially to our spouses, Maria Speck and Joan Elizabeth Weisband.

Contributors

L. David Brown is a lecturer in Public Policy and director of International Programs at the Hauser Center for Nonprofit Organizations, Harvard University.

Coralie Bryant is director of the Program in Economic and Political Development at the School of International and Public Affairs, Columbia University.

Alnoor Ebrahim is a visiting associate professor at Harvard University, in the Hauser Center for Nonprofit Organizations at the John F. Kennedy School of Government, and is the Wyss visiting scholar at the Harvard Business School. He is also an associate professor at Virginia Tech.

Randall D. Germain is an associate professor of Political Science at Carleton University.

Anne Marie Goetz is a research fellow at the Institute of Development Studies, University of Sussex.

Rob Jenkins is a professor of Political Science in the School of Politics and Society, University of London, Birkbeck.

Lisa Jordan is deputy director of the Governance and Civil Society Unit at the Ford Foundation.

David Lewis is a reader in Social Policy at the London School of Economics.

Kate Macdonald is a tutorial fellow in the Government Department at the London School of Economics. She is also a research fellow at the Centre for Applied Philosophy and Public Ethics at the Australian National University.

Michael R. MacLeod is a visiting assistant professor in the Department of Humanities & Social Sciences at Clarkson University.

Ian Smillie is an international development practitioner and writer based in Ottawa. He was a founder of the Canadian nongovernmental development organization Inter Pares, and was director of one of Canada's largest NGOs, CUSO.

Edward Weisband holds the Edward S. Diggs Endowed Chair Professorship in the Department of Political Science at Virginia Tech, and is a senior research fellow at the Institute for Policy and Governance.

Ngaire Woods is a fellow in Politics and International Relations at University College, Oxford and is director of the Global Economic Governance Programme at the Department of Politics and International Relations and Centre for International Studies of the University of Oxford.

1   Introduction: forging global accountabilities

Edward Weisband and Alnoor Ebrahim

Accountability is a confusing term, one that readily confounds efforts at precise definition or application. On one hand, its implementation is regarded as a kind of panacea with respect to the need to prevent and, whenever necessary, to punish unethical, illegal, or inappropriate behavior by public officials, corporate executives and nonprofit leaders. The refrain is by now familiar: act against sham deals, accounting tricks, securities fraud, personal use of charitable and public funds, exchange of political favors and monies, and so on. The "problematics" of accountability are accordingly framed in terms that underscore the ever-present risks of deliberate malfeasance perpetrated by individuals acting to aggrandize themselves. The commonly espoused "solution" is predictable: better oversight through tougher regulation, combined with harsh penalties as a deterrent. The magic wand of accountability is similarly seen to be at play in instances of global and state governance, where it is regarded as a supervening force able to promote democracy, justice, and greater human decency through the mechanisms of transparency, benchmarked standards, and enforcement.

In recent years, however, the analytical domains of accountability have become so extended that the very precision once conveyed by the concept has become eroded. This has generated widespread concern that the term will become devalued or incapacitated through overuse. "Appropriated by a myriad of international donor and academic discourses," write Newell and Bellour (2002, p. 2), "accountability has become a malleable and often nebulous concept, with connotations that change with the context and agenda." Other observers add further skepticism, finding the term to be "slippery," "chameleon-like," and suffering from "notorious ambiguity," with little correspondence in linguistic systems or cultures other than English, or to the complexities of management in democratic settings (Dubnick and Justice, 2004; Mulgan, 2000; Romzek, 2000). Perhaps more significantly, it is not at all clear that efforts in the name of accountability actually achieve their purported aims. The Cambridge philosopher Onora O'Neill brought

1

this point home in a series of BBC lectures, where she spoke about the "new accountability" among professions:

Unfortunately I think [accountability] often obstructs the proper aims of professional practice. Police procedures for preparing cases are so demanding that fewer cases can be prepared, and fewer criminals brought to court. Doctors speak of the inroads that required record-keeping makes into the time they can spend finding out what is wrong with their patients and listening to their patients. Even children are not exempt from the new accountability: exams are more frequent and time for learning shrinks. In many parts of the public sector, complaint procedures are so burdensome that avoiding complaints, including ill-founded complaints, becomes a central institutional goal in its own right. We are heading towards defensive medicine, defensive teaching and defensive policing. (O'Neill, 2002, pp. 49–50)

So it behooves us to take stock of this phenomenon. Certain sets of questions tumble one to the other. What is accountability? Why has it recently emerged as so central a concept in relation to the predominant issues of local and global governance, organizational behavior, and politics? How is it created, sustained, and nurtured? What influences a willingness to implement accountability procedures, regimes, and standards where none had existed before? Is more accountability necessarily better, or is there a danger of introducing "too much" accountability into the dynamics of organizational and social life? What are the real "effects" of accountability, as compared to its rhetoric and normative assumptions? How do cultural factors, social relations, and institutional forces affect accountability practices and outcomes? What are appropriate analytical metrics and measures in evaluating the impacts or influences of accountability regimes and structures?

In light of these and related questions, this volume pursues two primary objectives. The first is to problematize accountability, that is, to seek to understand the concept and its applications without taking prototypical normative assumptions for granted. The contributing chapters have been selected in order to bring a diverse set of disciplinary and empirical perspectives to bear on the problem of framing accountability. The task assumed by the authors is to muddy the waters, to develop their own definitions and perspectives, and thus to add both depth and diversity to commonly held understandings of the concept. The result is, in part, a challenge to dominant assumptions concerning accountability, especially those characterized by rationalist and principal–agent logics, in ways that stress the current value-laden and technocratic underpinnings of the concept, and so to prepare the way for a new set of heuristic propositions. In so doing, we seek to contribute to the development of what might become a "second-generation" perspective on accountability. In this sense, our approach tends to be interpretive and hermeneutic, one that anticipates future conceptual reconsiderations of accountability. This is designed to emphasize the shifting sands of discursive meanings that arise and come into play whenever and wherever the language of accountability is applied to purported realities shaped by institutional or cultural dynamics.

Our approach may be disconcerting for those readers looking for an all-encompassing and rationalist accountability framework. The chapters in this book suggest that the reality of accountability is far more ambiguous – that it is a socially embedded, politicized, pluralistic, and value-heavy construction – thus defying broad generalizations and universal theorizing. This does not mean that we cannot draw cautious conclusions among seemingly incommensurable frameworks or aim for normative ideals. A dose of skepticism, however, seems warranted.

The second related aim of this book is to observe accountability as a form of participatory praxis, and thus to identify its impacts on social relations and on the configurations of power. Accountability does not operate in a vacuum; it is a means of social control used by the weak as well as the powerful. In order to observe its actual effects in practice, the chapters rely on empirical experience and case studies where possible. The contributions thus draw on a wide range of settings seen through a number of analytical lenses, with cases from the local to the global, the North and South, and including nonprofit or nongovernmental organizations (NGOs), intergovernmental organizations (IGOs), and private sector firms. Our overriding intent, therefore, is to examine accountability by comparing and contrasting how it operates within various cases of governance and social interaction. We seek to understand it as a social phenomenon shaped by and reflective of alternating alignments of politics, cultures, social norms and institutional expectations. In this, the chapters seek to dramatize the techniques of control and the methods of articulation used by practitioners of accountability in multiple cultural and institutional settings. We do this to illustrate and, to the extent possible, to elucidate the institutional problematics and participatory practices that attend attempts to forge global accountabilities.

Framing accountability in public and global institutions

Numerous authors who have sought to portray the nature of accountability find it necessary to define what it is. The "problem of accountability" is frequently cast in technocratic terms; it is a problem of poor oversight and inadequate representation, amenable to correction through stringent regulation, more representative electoral and decision-making processes, and backed up by punitive measures. A veritable slew of definitions emerge from attempts to frame accountability in these terms, such as "the process of holding actors responsible for actions" (Fox and Brown, 1998, p. 12), or "the means by which individuals and organizations report to a recognized authority (or authorities) and are held responsible for their actions" (Edwards and Hulme, 1996, p. 967), or "the capacity to demand someone engage in reason-giving to justify her behavior, and/or the capacity to impose a penalty for poor perfor-mance" (Goetz and Jenkins, 2002, p. 5). Each of these definitions points to a "core sense" of accountability which Mulgan (2000, p. 555) identifies as having a set of three key features:

a. It is *external*, in that the account is given to an outside authority;
b. It involves *social interaction and exchange*, with one side seeking answers or rectification, while the other responds and accepts sanctions; and,
c. It implies *rights of authority*, where those calling for an account assert rights of superiority over those who are accountable.

This is essentially a principal–agent view of accountability, in which the lead actor or principal sets goals and employs agents to accomplish them. The primary accountability problematic thus lies in constraining the opportunistic behavior of agents. The logic of accountability flows from this. For Mulgan (2000, p. 557), this "original core of accountability" is premised on external scrutiny, supported by justification, sanctions, and control. In public institutions, particularly in modern democracies, such forms of accountability can be applied to two broad sets of relations: between citizens who, as principals, elect candidates to office as their agents; and, between those elected politicians who oversee the work of public administrators and other bureaucrats who act as their agents and, by extension, as agents of the public.

This view of public accountability is also widely shared among scholars of global governance and international politics. Discussions of account-ability in public institutions at the global level, have frequently centered on the "democratic deficits" of intergovernmental organizations such as the World Bank, the International Monetary Fund, the United Nations, the World Trade Organization, etc. (Nye, 2001). Definitions here likewise refer to authority of some actors over others, for example, "that some actors have the right to hold other actors to a set of standards, to judge whether they have fulfilled their responsibilities in light of those standards, and to impose sanctions if they determine that those responsibilities have not been met" (Grant and Keohane, 2004, p. 3). The literature further identifies four core components of accountability in global governance (e.g., Coleman and Porter, 2000; Oakerson, 1989; Woods, 2001):[1]

> Transparency – collecting information and making it available and accessible for public scrutiny
>
> Answerability or Justification – providing clear reasoning for actions and decisions, including those not adopted, so that they may reasonably be questioned
>
> Compliance – monitoring and evaluation of procedures and outcomes, combined with transparency in reporting those findings
>
> Enforcement or Sanctions – imposing sanctions for shortfalls in compliance, justification, or transparency

Because each of these components builds on the others (with transparency being necessary for compliance, and enforcement depending on all), accountability relies on the presence of all four. But for numerous observers, what underlies the power of accountability mechanisms is enforceability. Goetz and Jenkins (2001, p. 5) envision accountability as a discursive space between *answerability* and *enforceability*; they regard both "equally important," but recognize that "neither is sufficient." Answerability invites a conversation moored to reasons, reflections, excuse giving. It requires justifications for decisions and a rational basis for behaviors, both before and after the fact. To the extent that an accountability framework inheres in reasons given, it engages in answerability. But only enforceability and rectification produce "strong forms" of accountability. This requires the application of sanctions. Or, as Mulgan (2003, p. 9) puts it, "[t]he principal must be able to have the remedies or sanctions imposed on the agent as part of the right of authoritative direction that lies at the heart of the accountability relationship," and that accountability "thus involves an element of retributive justice in making the guilty pay for their wrongdoing."[2]

---

[1] This list of core components is adapted from a review of various analyses of accountability summarized in Herz and Ebrahim (2005). For example, Woods (2001) identifies the three "elements" of transparency, compliance, and enforcement. The component of "justification" draws from Coleman and Porter (2000, p. 380) who note that "The concept of accountability includes the idea that political leaders will explain to citizens how their actions have addressed the articulated wants and preferences of the 'people' " and from Oakerson (1989, p. 114) who writes that "To be accountable means to have to answer for one's action or inaction, and depending on the answer, to be exposed to potential sanctions, both positive and negative."

[2] Many authors who examine the issues of answerability and enforcement in accountability refer to Day and Klein (1987).

For Goetz and Jenkins, as well as for Mulgan, the key to effective forms of accountability rests in a form of *role reversal*. In the space between answerability and sanctions, or what they call the "account-ability drama," the *objects* of accountability (those upon whom the call to account is both incumbent and punishable) and the *agents* of account-ability (those empowered to seek answers and to level punishments) must and on occasion do play out their roles in reverse.[3] "Many public bodies," they observe, "are both objects *and* agents of accountability. Legislators are accountable to voters, but are also legally empowered to hold executive agencies to account" (Goetz and Jenkins, 2001, p. 5).[4] In such a manner, those armed with power and the capacities of decision-making become themselves subjected to the authority of the rectification procedures they previously applied. As Mulgan concludes, "Account-ability is incomplete without effective rectification." Seen in this light, accountability becomes the morality play of principals and agents, objects and subjects, dramatized by role reversals in the exercises of that power and authority. It is this reversibility of roles, of subjectivities and ontologies that embeds the ultimate promise of enforceability or sanctions and grounds their legitimacy in terms of public ethics.

In considering how accountability might be operationalized in prac-tice, Goetz and Jenkins (2001, p. 7) offer two further distinctions. First, *vertical accountability* refers to mechanisms in which citizens and their associations can directly hold the powerful to account, such as through elections in which voters select representatives and also hold incumbents to account. It also includes the lobbying of governments by citizen organizations, and involves demands for explanations both through potential sanctions such as negative publicity and through formal pro-cedures such as freedom of information legislation. Second, *horizontal accountability* refers to inter-institutional mechanisms or checks and balances (Goetz and Jenkins, 2001, p. 7; Woods, undated, p. 4). In the public sector, this typically includes the oversight of executive agencies

---

[3] Note the difference in use of terminology here. What we have called principals and agents, Goetz and Jenkins respectively call agents and objects. This is because the agent of a goal (i.e., someone tasked with achieving a goal) becomes the object of accountability. Similarly, the principal who sets that goal becomes the agent of accountability when he or she seeks to exercise oversight.

[4] Goetz and Jenkins (2001, p. 5) also note that "divisions of labor" in accountability processes can become complicated so that the role reversals are not always direct. "Those entitled to demand answers from power holders," they write, "are not necessarily the same as those put in charge of deciding on and doling out penalties." Several authors that address the tensions between answerability and enforceability or sanctions in accountability systems, as in this present instance, refer to Schedler (1999, pp. 14–17).

by legislatures, the use of quasi-independent review bodies such as auditors-general and anti-corruption commissions, as well as assessment by the judiciary of adherence by public actors to laws and legal norms, and so on. Constitutional divisions of power among the executive, judiciary, and legislative branches of government further enable such forms of accountability.

Vertical and horizontal mechanisms such as these have proven much more difficult to apply at the global level because of the absence of the "political infrastructure" that would support oversight in nation-states, such as geographically bounded political communities, direct election of representatives, and formalized relations between political, adminis-trative, and judicial bodies (Grant and Keohane, 2004; Herz and Ebrahim, 2005; Nye, 2001). As a result, some observers of global public institutions such as the World Bank and World Trade Organization have concluded that these institutions are unlikely to ever be much more than venues for bureaucratic bargaining between elites (Dahl, 1999, p. 19; as cited in Herz and Ebrahim, 2005, p. 55; Kapur, 2002, p. 75).

Conceptualized another way, a question of legitimacy and norms arises in discourses over accountability with respect to authority, power, and control mechanisms. "Accountability presupposes a relationship between power-wielders and those holding them accountable," write Grant and Keohane (2004, p. 3, emphasis added), "where there is *a general recognition of the legitimacy* of 1) the operative conditions for accountability and 2) the authority of the parties to the relationship." They stress the relevance of consensus or common understanding by adding that the very concept of accountability, "implies that the actors being held accountable have obligations to act in ways that are *consistent with accepted standards of behavior*" (Grant and Keohane, 2004, p. 3). If accountability is embedded in accepted standards of behavior, and if it is this factor that endows it with legitimacy, then the struggle for account-ability at the global level is a battle over how to establish and enforce such standards or norms of behavior. Mechanisms of vertical accountability (such as elections and right-to-know legislation) and horizontal accountability (such as legislative oversight and judicial checks) typically associated with democratic societies do not necessarily enjoy broad legitimacy at the global level. Efforts to impose them from abroad are frequently characterized as infringements on state sovereignty. Even where broad norms are accepted in rhetoric and even formalized in treaties or declarations (such as the Kyoto Protocol and the Universal Declaration on Human Rights) their enforcement remains problematic despite procedural structures designed to ensure the enunciation of guidelines.

As a consequence, this discussion suggests that calls for accountability in global public institutions are likely to pursue three general directions: 1) improving vertical accountability by reforming representation in existing governance structures, and thus making it possible for principals (i.e., member governments and their citizens) to hold their agents (i.e., the managers and directors of those institutions) to account; 2) improving horizontal accountability through quasi-independent oversight mechanisms, separation of powers, ombudspersons, judicial review, and conflict management procedures; and 3) establishing new approaches to decision-making that are less well charted and constrained by the binary distinctions of principal–agent and vertical–horizontal dichotomy, but which are more pluralistic, on the grounds that this can improve both legitimacy and effectiveness.

The chapters in this book contribute insights into each of these arenas. Goetz and Jenkins examine the limitations of both horizontal and vertical accountability mechanisms in the context of municipal and state governance in India, and draw on local experiments to forge "hybrid" mechanisms developed by citizens and civil society groups. Woods and Germain each examine mechanisms currently used in institutions of global finance and trade, and point to the need for new participatory approaches and logics. But while Woods emphasizes a need for better monitoring and enforcement, Germain proposes a shift away from a "logic of compliance" towards a "logic of participation."

The chapters also go beyond evaluation of the mechanisms in order to develop new ways of conceiving accountability and its frameworks. The predominant principal–agent perspective, while no doubt useful, is nonetheless constrained in its ability to explain how accountability functions in practice, particularly in settings where distinctions between principals and agents are ambiguous, shifting, and interdependent. The chapters by Brown, Ebrahim, and Macdonald examine the limitations of analyses shaped by the rationalist assumptions intrinsic to principal–agent formulations. Brown compares principal–agent accountability to representative accountability and presents a third model – *mutual accountability* – based on his experience with multiparty social action initiatives. Ebrahim builds on Brown's use of principal–agent theory, by showing how organizations such as development NGOs act as both principals and agents in their relations with funders, regulators, and communities. This dual role creates tension and ambiguity in accountability relations, with actors vying to establish authority through mechanisms of control. Macdonald, too, provides a critique and alternative framework, through her analysis of transnational supply chains in the garment industry. She articulates a *plurilateral accountability* framework that more accurately describes the interdependence among the key players: Southern workers, transnational firms, producer states, consumer states, and non-state actors in transnational advocacy networks. In this last category, she observes that while Northern NGOs play crucial roles in raising the profile of workers' issues, they often dominate decision-making in advocacy campaigns and thereby demonstrate little direct accountability to Southern workers. She argues for a reconceptualizing of accountability based on the idea of "complex reciprocity" in networks rather than on simple binary relationships. The analytical significance of networks is revisited by Weisband in his concluding chapter to this volume in order to emphasize the need to problematize the role and impacts of accountability regimes within theoretical frameworks that combine the discursive character of public ethics to efficiencies in participatory action.

Framing accountability in organizations

Attention to accountability has, of course, not been limited to public institutions, be they governmental or intergovernmental. In the business world, corporate social responsibility and transparency have become ubiquitous terms. This is a result not only of highly visible cases of corporate malfeasance and whistle-blowing, but also from a growing recognition of the diverse interests and values of corporate stakeholders (e.g., Braithwaite and Drahos, 2000; Gundlach et al., 2003; Halal, 2001; Weaver and Agle, 2002; Zadek et al., 1997). In the world of nonprofit or nongovernmental organizations, previously buffered by their reputations as "do-gooders," board members and key officers have been accused of wrongdoings ranging from mismanagement of resources and use of funds for personal gain to sexual misconduct and fraud. In the United States, for example, scandals have been reported at well-known organizations such as the United Way of America, Goodwill Industries, Head Start, the American Cancer Society, and the American Red Cross. Concerns at these and other organizations of inappropriately high executive compensation, high costs of administration, operation, and fundraising, wealth accumulation, commercialization, and failure to reach the poor, have all contributed to an erosion of public confidence in nonprofit organizations (Gibelman and Gelman, 2001; Young et al., 1996).

Discussions of accountability in the organizational behavior literature have largely focused on organizational ecology, resource dependence, and stakeholder theories. The organizational ecology literature has suggested that accountability provides a sense of stability in organizational relations by maintaining the commitments of members and clients. Accountability, as such, involves the production of internally consistent – but not necessarily truthful – accounts of how resources have been used by an organization, as well as about the decisions, rules, and actions that led to them (Hannan and Freeman, 1989, pp. 73–4, 245). Social selection processes tend to favor organizational forms with high levels of such accountability and reliability. This suggests that accountability practices have value in creating stability and assuring public confidence, but not necessarily in promoting ethical behavior.

The resource dependence literature concentrates more explicitly on the problems of establishing stability in the face of asymmetries in resources, and thus power. Much of this literature has focused on private sector firms (e.g., Pfeffer and Salancik, 1974; 1978), although its characteristic forms of analysis are equally applicable to relationships among nonprofit organizations and their funders. Indeed, NGO concerns about accountability to donors have often centered on asymmetries in resources that result in excessive conditionalities or onerous reporting requirements attached to funding. Accountability mechanisms, such as annual project reports and financial statements, are used not only by funders to keep track of NGO spending, but also by NGOs to leverage funds by publicizing their projects and programs. Thus there is a resource interdependence (albeit often asymmetric) in which NGOs rely on donors for money, and donors rely on NGOs for their reputations in development activities. Studies of resource dependence potentially offer much insight on accountability, especially by revealing the kinds of mechanisms used by organizations to leverage responsiveness (e.g., Hudock, 1999; Smith, 1999). This theme is developed in several chapters below that deal with issues of development and accountability.

Accountability relationships within organizations tend to become complicated by virtue of the fact that organizations must often deal with competing demands. Stakeholder perspectives evolving from the organizational behavior literature point directly to subsequent predicaments. Much of the early work in this field is credited to Edward Freeman's (1984) writing on a "stakeholder approach" to strategic management among private sector firms, in which stakeholders are defined to include not only stockholders but also other individuals and groups who can affect, or are affected by, a particular business. This work, in turn, has fed into a burgeoning literature on corporate social responsibility, performance, and ethics (e.g., Clarkson, 1995; Hummels, 1998; Jawahar and McLaughlin, 2001; Soule, 2002; Wheeler and Sillanpää, 1997; Wicks et al., 1994), which has become increasingly relevant in the wake of corporate accounting scandals. Private firms are thus not only accountable to stockholders, but now also face demands by customers and communities with respect to social and environmental criteria. Similarly, a number of observers of nonprofit organizations have noted that they are accountable to multiple actors: upwards to patrons, downwards to clients, and internally to themselves and their missions (Edwards and Hulme, 1996; Kearns, 1996; Lindenberg and Bryant, 2001; Najam, 1996). Some scholars have even suggested that there are as many types of accountability as there are distinct relationships among people and organizations (Lerner and Tetlock, 1999, p. 256). At the very least, it seems that accountability is not the simple and clear social panacea that its advocates might pitch, but rather a complex and somewhat ambiguous construct even when applied to fixed corporate realities.

What sense, therefore, is one to make of these varied but related discussions on accountability in organizations? Within the context of institutional or agency dynamics, the problematics of accountability center on two sets of issues, the first dealing with power asymmetry, the second dealing with learning and benchmarking. As to the first, since accountability frameworks include organizational or agency actors embedded in structural arrangements, asymmetric relationships among stakeholders are likely to result in modes of accountability skewed or distorted in ways that satisfy the interests of dominant actors. *In other words, accountability is about power, in that asymmetries in resources become important in influencing who is able to hold whom to account.* Or, to borrow a stronger characterization, accountability *is* a relationship of power (Goetz and Jenkins, 2001, p. 5). Thus whether one adopts an analytical lens based in organizational ecology, resource dependence, or stakeholder theories, one must deal with the relationships, demands, and power plays among actors.

This leads some authors to characterize the problematics of accountability as political theatre — where relationships among actors are sometimes tightly scripted and cast, and at other times improvised and experimental. In the chapter by Jordan, for example, this theatrical stage is internal to organizations. Based on the experiences of ActionAid and the Humanitarian Accountability Project, she proposes a new model of accountability that casts organizational mission in the leading role. On the other hand, a sense of dramatic political interaction among organizational actors permeates many of the case studies in this volume. In the chapter by Lewis, which examines the social embeddedness of NGOs in Bangladesh, the accountabilities of actors are bounded by culture and values where power asymmetries shape the forms of political confrontation and define the contexts of struggle. For Smillie, who looks at efforts by NGO networks to ban "blood diamonds," there is a sense of constant improvisation in order to build a collective or networked accountability among NGOs, states, and transnational corporations. Therefore, power asymmetries, institutional structures and arrangements and inter-organizational dynamics all combine in alternating episodes and modalities to produce multiple sets of accountability relationships and in a sense multiple accountabilities and accountability problematics. These accountabilities are contingent upon context and on the relationships. No single form of accountability predominates the field. The overall result is that we live in a world in which numerous types of accountability battle for recognition and legitimacy.

A second central feature of accountability in organizations concerns the balance, or perhaps tension, between internal organizational learning and external standards and benchmarking. On the one hand, measurable parameters standardized across organizations are necessary for purposes of legitimation: they send signals of appropriate behavior and possibly of quality. On the other hand, is it not plausible that a "strong unified accountability will be at the expense of diversity and innovation" (Cnaan, 1996, pp. 223–4) in organizations? Observers of the nonprofit sector have noted that there is "a delicate balance between enough regulation to protect legitimate social interests in preventing diversion of charitable assets to private pockets . . . and enough regulation to squelch the qualities our society has most valued in the charitable sector" (Chisolm, 1995, p. 149) such as creativity and independence of thought and action (Young et al., 1996, p. 348).

But is accountability really possible without externally verifiable benchmarks? How important are internal processes of learning for accountability? Several of the contributors to this volume examine these questions, with all agreeing on the critical need to integrate external benchmarking with internal learning. They differ, however, in emphasis. In Part III of the book, Ebrahim identifies a set of "accountability myopias" common among NGOs and nonprofits that are an effect of external benchmarks and short-term targets – and which have a chilling effect on organizational learning. This theme is developed empirically in the chapters by Jordan and Bryant, both of which point to the need for more reflective forms of accountability among NGOs and donors, and which are driven by mission and internal learning processes rather than external demands. But the chapters in Part IV, on corporate social responsibility, advocate on behalf of a greater emphasis on external benchmarks as part of this delicate balancing act. Weisband, in particular, suggests that the absence of externally verifiable benchmarks is what renders corporate social responsibility (CSR) inadequate as a form of corporate accountability. Drawing on seven different CSR frameworks, he argues that while CSR fosters internal learning, it falls short of providing the recursive forms of feedback benchmarked to external standards that are essential, indeed, the sine qua non necessary to ensure genuine global corporate accountability.

The dilemmas of accountability at the organizational level are clearly numerous: multiple and competing accountabilities, asymmetries in resources and power among actors, and the difficulties of balancing internal learning and innovation with external benchmarking and standards. These challenges are not altogether different from those faced by global and public institutions. While the literature on accountability in global institutions speaks of the inadequacy of vertical and horizontal mechanisms for enabling citizen influence, this is similar to problems of resource asymmetries and interdependence in the organizational literature. And where observers of IGOs point to the problems of weak enforcement and rectification in accountability systems, students of NGOs and private firms frame this as a problem of integrating externally benchmarked standards with internal processes of organizational learning. Although these accountability challenges may not be identical, since public institutions seek to compensate for democratic deficits, the problematics are sufficiently similar to prod us to explore them collectively in this book.

The approach in this volume: accountability as sign and symbol

Whether one considers accountability at the level of single organizations such as for-profit and nonprofit firms, or in institutions of public governance at the state and intergovernmental levels, one is confronted with a common analytical dilemma: the rift between how accountability is imagined and how it actually operates. As Goetz and Jenkins (2001, p. 5) put it, "Accountability is often derided as a cure-all development buzzword: a fit subject for exhortation, but something that in most parts of the world is rarely achieved because it demands too much compassion of the powerful and too much undiluted civic virtue from ordinary citizens." This disjuncture poses an analytic problem that must be addressed if we are to better understand the concept – that definitions and framings of accountability tend to be driven by normative agendas rather than by empirical realities. Such an approach tends to proceed formulaically: specify the agents; identify the principals; enumerate the objectives; define the standards; review the mechanisms; locate the sectors or the policy domains and issue areas. This treatment tends to devolve into a format comprised of the following: "who," "to whom" "why," "for what," and "how."

This approach leaves out what Clifford Geertz once called, "thick description" – empirical observation and interpretation that might enable us to better understand how accountability actually operates, how it is appropriated and manipulated, how it varies across social and cultural contexts, and with what effects. In this spirit, Dubnick and Justice (2004, pp. 14, 20) argue for a socially constructed analysis of the concept, cautioning that "Any effort to categorize, measure, or model accountability must be guided by the qualities of the construct, magnitude or 'reality' it is intended to represent" and further advising that "students of accountability must be prepared to deal with alternative and shifting manifestations of the concept depending on the issue and arena being examined." Theirs is a decidedly postmodernist outlook on accountability, one that confronts the discontinuities between discourse and reality (Dubnick, 1998; 2002; Dubnick and Justice, 2004). For them, the word "accountability" serves to cover, conceal, and mask disparate meanings and realities precisely because so much semantic freight is conveyed by it. It is a "semiotic sign," one that acts as a "symbol," or stand-in for other terms, including transparency or answerability[5] and as an "indicator" of desired conditions such as bureaucratic efficiency, organizational effectiveness, equity or fairness in social relations, due process, and democracy in political order. And, perhaps most powerfully, the word accountability serves as an "icon" that stamps an imprimatur of legitimacy on a whole range of activities on the assumption that agents, processes, and structures are being held to account.

Such an assessment of accountability must be nested within an analysis of the positions and relations of actors, standards, and mechanisms within broader configurations of power. Here, Dubnick and Justice point us to the work of the French social theorist and historian Michel Foucault. They argue that what matters in examining accountability is *perspective*, that is, an emphasis on how actions and events are the effects of power and knowledge. In an especially revealing passage, they explain:

The term "perspective" is not used lightly when related to Foucaultian analysis. Those who apply Foucault's approach explicitly refuse to regard it as a theory or paradigm or method, but instead put it forward as an "effect": the making visible, through a particular perspective in the history of the present, of the different ways in which an activity or art ... has been made thinkable and practicable. (Burchell et al., 1991, p. ix, as cited in Dubnick and Justice, 2004, p. 17)[6]

---

[5] Newell and Bellour (2002, p. 2) list the following as synonymics: surveillance, monitoring, oversight, control, checks, restraint, public exposure, and punishment.

[6] The Foucauldian analytical methods adopted in the analysis of governmentality and perspectivism require investigation into the origins of knowledge/power; such a methodological process is referred to in terms of genealogical excavation or historical

To examine accountability in "perspective," one cannot take for granted its normative assumptions, particularly the notion that more accountability is necessarily better. Scholars must instead seek to uncover the effects of accountability: how and to what extent its mechanisms and techniques serve to reinforce existing relations of power, or under what circumstances they result in reconfigurations. This is a skeptic's view, and one in which the tools of the trade – disclosure and surveillance, standards and regulation, monitoring and compliance, sanctions and deterrents – are more likely to serve the interests of the powerful than the weak through the control of those very tools and expertise employed to validate them. In Foucauldian terms, accountability may thus be seen as part of a new set of disciplinary knowledges or *savoirs*, with its attendant forms of measurement, monitoring, auditing, and punishment. Accountability, in this sense, is a subset of "governmentality," which Foucault has described as an "ensemble formed by the institutions, procedures, analyses and reflections, the calculations and tactics that allow the exercise of this very specific albeit complex form of power" (Foucault, 1991, p. 102). This does not mean that accountability mechanisms cannot be agents of social change, but rather that one must look to the effects of those mechanisms to understand their impacts and operations, rather than the rhetoric that motivates and accompanies them. A central point here is that the discourse of accountability is a reflection of broader social norms, and assumptions at work in our society.[7] In other words, accountability discourse is a manifestation of more pervasive forms of social mistrust, marketized measurement, and control that have emerged and come to characterize our worlds, thereby influencing our individual relationships, our organizations, and our governance systems.

For students of accountability, this discussion can be summarized as pointing to two general sets of analytical assumptions that in philosophical terms reveal both modernist and postmodernist themes and predilections. As indicated above, accountability discourses are frequently framed as a technocratic or administrative issue where problems are relatively identifiable, e.g., mismanagement of financial resources for personal gain, fraud, and other forms of malfeasance. The solutions that follow from this form of "problem framing" tend to be fairly straightforward, e.g., tougher regulation, codes of conduct, sanctions. Such an

ontology. For an account of the historical origins of accountable governance, see Dubnick (1998; 2002).

[7] For a discussion on the term "discourse" see Edwards (1996, p. 34) and Gardner and Lewis (1996, p. xiv).

approach to accountability is common in managerial and public policy discussions involving private corporations, nonprofit organizations, the public sector, and intergovernmental organizations. This may be classified as a positivist and modernist view of accountability where it is assumed that more information and transparency can reveal the "truth" about behavior, thus making corrective action or rectification possible. As a line of inquiry, this approach leads to questions such as: What standards or measures are indicative of good, or poor, behavior and performance? How can such behavior be monitored? What penalties for noncompliance will deter such behavior in the future?

A second and more skeptical approach to accountability treats it as a social phenomenon, in which its actual impacts are a result of relationships of power and interplays among actors. The method is empirical, based on observations of the effects of accountability discourses and mechanisms on actors, their relationships, and their relative positions in society. Within this context, Dubnick and Justice (2004, p. 20) offer three clusters around which the concept can be framed and analyzed: a) social relationships which serve as the context for action; b) "normative points of reference to which accounted-for actions are compared"; and c) the actual processes or mechanisms through which accountability plays out. Such an approach to accountability seeks to understand how specific knowledges and mechanisms influence (or are influenced by) shifting configurations of power. This can be both a structuralist and/or a postmodern view of accountability. It is pluralistic rather than universalizing, and leads to questions such as: What kinds of knowledge are considered legitimate or valid in designing and implementing accountability systems? Whose interests are served and validated by systems of accountability and the specialized forms of knowledge embedded in them? What kinds of information, knowledge, expertise are devalued in this system? How do the mechanisms of accountability serve to reproduce, or alter, existing configurations of power?

The cases in this book and many of the chapters here mark a transition from the first mode of inquiry to the second, from modernist forms of certainty and universalism to postmodernist forms of skepticism and particularism. Most of the contributors straddle both worlds, hoping for clear and replicable models of accountability guided by normative ideals, while skeptically viewing the effects of past or current efforts to generalize in universalistic or globalist terms. While we are able to draw thematic generalizations from these chapters – on the prevalence of accountability myopias, on logics of participation, and on the tension between externally benchmarked standards and internal organizational learning – our central aim is to illustrate the multileveled, pluralistic, and contested nature of the terrain of accountability.

Table 1.1 *Levels of accountability analysis*

Level of analysis	Primary accountability concerns
1. Individual	• personal integrity, morality and responsibility • personal and professional ethics
2a. Organization (private, nonprofit)	• control of self-interested behavior and malfeasance • fiduciary/legal requirements concerning disclosure and reporting • organizational reputation, risk, and performance • externally benchmarked standards • internal organizational learning
2b. Public organization (state and intergovernmental)	• democratic deficits in governance, representation, and decision-making • transparency, answerability, compliance, and enforcement
3. Network	• interdependence among actors • creation of "mutual," "plurilateral," or "tripartite" forms of accountability
4. Structure (regime, social, cultural)	• social control through relationships and configurations of power, and through knowledge systems, expertise and professional norms • legitimating behavior through socially accepted standards of behavior

It becomes useful, therefore, to situate the contributions in a simple typology of levels of analysis. Table 1.1 identifies four basic levels at which the scholars in the chapters that follow have engaged the accountability debate: individual, organizational (private, nonprofit, state, intergovernmental), network, and structural. Units and levels of analysis shift according to case, culture, and setting in ways that permit us to clarify how accountability relationships differ instance to instance and with what effects.

Admittedly, the individual level of analysis receives limited attention in this volume. There is an established literature dating back to at least the 1940s, in fields such as public administration and ethics, that examines the relationship between professionalism and personal morality (e.g., Finer, 1941; Friedrich, 1940), and which Mulgan (2000, p. 557) sees as extending beyond the "core sense" of accountability. Nonetheless, questions of personal integrity and responsibility do permeate organizational life and, as Dobel (1999, p. xi) has argued, "institutions could be made more effective by placing public integrity at the core of their strategies." As such, issues of personal integrity, morality, and responsibility are addressed in the following chapters only to the extent that they shed light on organizational approaches to accountability. This link is especially apparent in the chapter by Jordan which stresses the importance of mission and purpose, and in Weisband's concluding chapter, in which he proposes embedding accountability within a postmodern public ethics grounded in value-pluralism.

Most of the chapters in this book focus on the organizational level of analysis. The nature and scale of organizations examined varies substantially, ranging from highly localized NGOs to corporations and multilateral institutions. Yet, commonalities in accountability constraints and concerns do arise and appear to be significant. The distinction between the organizational and public governance levels is somewhat artificial, since the analysis still focuses on the organization, except that the latter is distinguished by explicit attention to questions of "democratic governance" and "democratic deficits" in especially large and complex organizations. Most of the chapters in Parts I, II, and III of this book examine particular organizations and relationships among organizational actors.

The third level of analysis involves networks and fields of organizations. The case material for such analysis necessarily centers on interdependence among diverse sets of actors and examines the development of what Brown calls "mutual accountability" or Macdonald terms "plurilateral accountability" – in contexts as diverse as development advocacy campaigns in the Philippines and cooperation among competitors in the US semiconductor industry (Brown), multiparty negotiations to develop product certification systems for diamonds (Smillie), transnational supply chains in the garment industry (Macdonald), and tripartite multilateralism in the International Labour Organization (Weisband). Networks offer a potentially powerful mechanism for increasing both efficiency and effectiveness in complex policy domains in which resolution of social problems requires collaborative forms of interdependence among actors.

The final level of analysis is structural, alternately called the accountability "regime" or the "social" level of analysis.[8] A handful of the chapters venture into a discussion of social relations and configurations of power as a means of reflecting on the social and cultural substrata on which their cases are built. Macdonald's piece, in particular, captures the essence of a structural exploration of accountability. In her look at the highly politicized and globalized setting of the global garment industry, she examines not only existing accountability structures, but also the

---

[8] The authors are grateful to Steven Heydemann and Mark Moore for conversations on these terms. A regime is "emergent" in that it reflects the ongoing tensions that surround the diffusion and adoption among organizations of the norms, regulations, and practices that constitute it.

efforts by networks of actors radically to transform them, as well as the counter-responses of states and firms to protect the existing account-ability regime. Such structural contextualization is also a feature of Lewis' analysis of the role of politics and culture in shaping accountability dis-courses and, to some degree, of MacLeod's constructivist description of corporate social investment. In this vein, Ebrahim's essay at the end of Part III revisits some of the preceding chapters in order to identify deeply rooted logics of accountability that dominate and constrain the nonprofit and NGO sector. And Weisband's analysis of tripartite multilateralism provides an inventory of the major frameworks of corporate social responsibility, with an eye to identifying their limitations as accountability mechanisms.

Taken as a collection, this book cannot help but communicate a normative agenda. As scholars, we seek to describe, analyze, and frame alternative discourses of accountability, their assumptions, realities, and purported effects. But as privileged inhabitants of a world characterized by pervasive forms of inequity and poverty, we also recognize our niches in those structures where we trade in the production of knowledge, of expertise, and where we are active participants in its legitimation. In the spirit of accountability, it would be appropriate for us to attempt to acknowledge our normative agenda. This agenda is, in part, to inject skepticism into current accountability debates, which are heavily technocratic, modernist, and binary in orientation. Accountability is a social phenomenon, reflective of relationships of power in society. One can thus expect the instruments of accountability to reproduce those relationships rather than overturn them.

And yet, as the cases in this book show, accountability as a battle cry for participatory practice also possesses enormous transformative potential. On the basis of the empirical insights presented throughout this book, it becomes reasonable to seek external benchmarks of beha-vior that can effectively be integrated with internal dynamics of learning. In multiparty settings, it is possible to envision and devise inter-dependent forms of accountability (what our contributors have variously labeled mutual, plurilateral, and tripartite). But this requires a vision of what is important in social and political development, and a perspective on the interconnected nature of normative expectations in a world that is both global and local. Such normative accountability is thus a public endeavor, in the broad and inclusive sense of promoting an ethic of societal betterment, rather than in the narrow and exclusive sense of oversight, punishment, and control. This normative agenda is further elaborated in the closing chapter to this volume, in what Weisband titles a "Prolegomena to a Postmodern Public Ethics." It marks a beginning rather than an end and, in this sense, is part of a process of forging global accountabilities based on the recognition that empowerment requires reciprocity and mutuality. This is a vision of public ethics that resists the temptation to offer a meta-narrative of accountability, offering instead a landscape of value-pluralism, and grounded in participatory practices that nurture trust, learning, and civility in collective action.

References

Braithwaite, J. and P. Drahos (2000) *Global Business Regulation*. Cambridge University Press.

Burchell, G., C. Gordon and P. Miller (eds.) *The Foucault Effect: Studies in Governmentality*. University of Chicago.

Chisolm, L. B. (1995) "Accountability of Nonprofit Organizations and Those Who Control Them: The Legal Framework," *Nonprofit Management and Leadership* 6(2), 141–56.

Clarkson, M. B. E. (1995) "A Stakeholder Framework for Analyzing and Evaluating Corporate Social Performance," *Academy of Management Review* 20(1), 92–117.

Cnaan, R. (1996) "Commentary," *Nonprofit Management and Leadership* 7(2), 221–5.

Coleman, W. D. and T. Porter (2000) "International Institutions, Globalisation and Democracy: Assessing the Challenges," *Global Society* 14(3), 377–98.

Dahl, R. A. (1999) "Can International Organizations be Democractic? A Skeptic's View," in I. Shapiro and C. Hacker-Cordon (eds.) *Democracy's Edges*. Cambridge University Press.

Day, P. and R. Klein (1987) *Accountabilities: Five Public Services*. London: Tavistock.

Dobel, J. P. (1999) *Public Integrity*. Baltimore and London: The Johns Hopkins University Press.

Dubnick, M. J. (1998) "Clarifying Accountability: An Ethical Theory Framework," in *Public Sector Ethics: Finding and Implementing Values*. NSW, Australia: The Federation Press/Routledge.

Dubnick, M. J. (2002) "Seeking Salvation for Accountability," Paper presented at the annual meeting of the American Political Science Association, Boston, MA (29 August–1 September).

Dubnick, M. J. and J. B. Justice (2004) "Accounting for Accountability," Paper presented at the annual meeting of the American Political Science Association, Chicago (2–5 September).

Edwards, M. and D. Hulme (1996) "Too Close for Comfort? The Impact of Official Aid on Nongovernmental Organizations," *World Development* 24(6), 961–73.

Edwards, P. N. (1996) *The Closed World: Computers and the Politics of Discourse in Cold War America*. Cambridge, MA: MIT Press.

Finer, H. (1941) "Administrative Responsibility and Democratic Government," *Public Administration Review* 1, 335–50.

Foucault, M. (1991) "Governmentality," in G. Burchell, C. Gordon, and P. Miller (eds.) *The Foucault Effect: Studies in Governmentality*. University of Chicago.

Fox, J. A. and L. D. Brown (eds.) (1998) *The Struggle for Accountability: The World Bank, NGOs, and Grassroots Movements*. Cambridge, MA: MIT Press.

Freeman, R. E. (1984) *Strategic Management: A Stakeholder Approach*. Boston: Pitman.

Friedrich, C. J. (1940) "Public Policy and the Nature of Administrative Responsibility," in C. J. Friedrich and E. S. Mason (eds.) *Public Policy*. Cambridge, MA: Harvard University Press, pp. 3–24.

Gardner, K. and D. Lewis (1996) *Anthropology, Development and the Post-Modern Challenge*. London: Pluto Press.

Gibelman, M. and S. R. Gelman (2001) "Very Public Scandals: Nongovernmental Organizations in Trouble," *Nonprofit and Voluntary Sector Quarterly* 12(1), 49–66.

Goetz, A. M. and R. Jenkins (2002) "Voice, Accountability and Human Development: The Emergence of a New Agenda," Background paper for the Human Development Report 2002. New York: United Nations Development Programme.

Grant, R. W. and R. O. Keohane (2004) "Accountability and Abuses of Power, in World Politics," International Law and Justice Working Paper. Institute for International Law and Justice, New York University School of Law.

Gundlach, M. J., S. C. Douglas and M. J. Martinko (2003) "The Decision to Blow the Whistle: A Social Information Processing Framework," *Academy of Management Review* 28(1), 107–23.

Halal, W. E. (2001) "The Collaborative Enterprise: A Stakeholder Model Uniting Profitability and Responsibility," *Journal of Corporate Citizenship* 1(2), 27–42.

Hannan, M. T. and J. Freeman (1989) *Organizational Ecology*. Cambridge, MA and London: Harvard University.

Herz, S. and A. Ebrahim (2005) *A Call for Participatory Decision Making: Discussion Paper on World Bank–Civil Society Engagement*. Civil Society Members of the World Bank–Civil Society Joint Facilitation Committee (JFC): ActionAid International, Amnesty International, Association for Women's Rights in Development, Caribbean Policy Development Centre, CIVICUS: World Alliance for Citizen Participation, Europe and Central Asia NGO Working Group, Global Movement for Children, InterAction, International Confederation of Free Trade Unions, Transparency International, World Confederation of Labour, World Conference of Religions for Peace, World Council of Churches, WWF: The International Conservation Organization, World Young Women's Christian Association, Worldwide Initiatives for Grantmaker Support. Available at www.civicus.org/new/media_World_Bank_Civil_Society_Discussion_Paper_FINAL_VERSION.pdf and at http://siteresources.worldbank.org/CSO/Resources/World_Bank_Civil_Society_Discussion_Paper_FINAL_VERSION.pdf.

Hudock, A. (1999) *NGOs and Civil Society: Democracy by Proxy?* Cambridge, MA: Blackwell.

Hummels, H. (1998) "Organizing Ethics: A Stakeholder Debate," *Journal of Business Ethics* 17, 1403–19.

Jawahar, I. M. and G. L. McLaughlin (2001) "Toward a Descriptive Stakeholder Theory: An Organizational Life Cycle Approach," *Academy of Management Review* 26(3), 397–414.

Kapur, D. (2002) "The Changing Anatomy of Governance of the World Bank," in J. R. Pincus and J. A. Winters (eds.) *Reinventing the World Bank*. Ithaca, NY: Cornell University Press.

Kearns, K. P. (1996) *Managing for Accountability: Preserving the Public Trust in Nonprofit Organizations*. San Francisco: Jossey-Bass.

Lerner, J. S. and P. E. Tetlock (1999) "Accounting for the Effects of Accountability," *Psychological Bulletin* 125(2), 255–75.

Lindenberg, M. and C. Bryant (2001) *Going Global: Transforming Relief and Development NGOs*. Bloomfield, CT: Kumarian Press.

Mulgan, R. (2000) "'Accountability': An Ever-Expanding Concept?," *Public Administration* 78(3), 555–73.

Mulgan, R. (2003) *Holding Power to Account: Accountability in Modern Democracies*. Hampshire, UK: Palgrave Macmillan.

Najam, A. (1996) "NGO Accountability: A Conceptual Framework," *Development Policy Review* 14 , 339–53.

Newell, P. and S. Bellour (2002) "Mapping Accountability: Origins, Contexts and Implications for Development," IDS Working Paper 168. Sussex: Institute of Development Studies.

Nye, J. S. (2001) "Globalization's Democratic Deficit: How to Make International Institutions More Accountable," *Foreign Affairs* 80(4 (July/August)), 2–6.

Oakerson, R. J. (1989) "Governance Structures for Enhancing Accountability and Responsiveness," in J. L. Perry (ed.) *Handbook of Public Administration*. San Francisco: Jossey-Bass, p. 114.

O'Neill, O. (2002) *A Question of Trust: The BBC Reith Lectures 2002*. Cambridge University Press.

Pfeffer, J. and G. R. Salancik (1974) "Organizational Decision Making as a Political Process: The Case of the University Budget," *Administrative Science Quarterly* 19(2 [June]), 135–51.

Pfeffer, J. and G. R. Salancik (1978) *The External Control of Organizations: A Resource Dependence Perspective*. New York: Harper and Row.

Romzek, B. S. (2000) "Dynamics of Public Sector Accountability in an Era of Reform," *International Review of Administrative Sciences* 66(1), 21–44.

Schedler, A. (1999) "Conceptualizing Accountability", in A. Schedler, L. Diamond and M. F. Plattner (eds.) *The Self-Restraining State: Power and Accountability in New Democracies*. Boulder, CO: Lynne Rienner.

Smith, S. R. (1999) "Government Financing of Nonprofit Activity," in E. T. Boris and C. E. Steuerle (eds.) *Nonprofits and Government: Collaboration and Conflict*. Washington, DC: Urban Institute Press, pp. 177–210.

Soule, E. (2002) "Managerial Moral Strategies – In Search of a Few Good Principles," *Academy of Management Review* 27(1), 114–24.

Weaver, G. R. and B. R. Agle (2002) "Religiosity and Ethical Behavior in Organizations: A Symbolic Interactionist Perspective," *Academy of Management Review* 27(1), 77–97.

Wheeler, D. and M. Sillanpää (1997) *The Stakeholder Corporation: The Body Shop Blueprint for Maximizing Stakeholder Value*. London: Pitman.

Wicks, A. C., D. R. Gilbert and R. E. Freeman (1994) "A Feminist Reinterpretation of the Stakeholder Concept," *Business Ethics Quarterly* 4 (4), 475–97.

Woods, N. (2001) "Making the IMF and the World Bank More Accountable," *International Affairs* (January).

Woods, N. (undated) "Accountability, Governance, and Reform in the International Financial Institutions," unpublished paper.

Young, D. R., N. Bania and D. Bailey (1996) "Structure and Accountability: A Study of National Nonprofit Associations," *Nonprofit Management and Leadership* 6(4), 347–65.

Zadek, S., P. Pruzan and R. Evans (1997) *Building Corporate Accountability*. London: Earthscan.

Part I

Public accountability: participatory spheres from global to local

The following chapters explore accountability in public institutions, with special attention to intergovernmental or multilateral organizations. Ngaire Woods leads the section by introducing the reasons for public disaffection with multilateral institutions. The challenge of accountability, as she sees it, is twofold: how to make global institutions more effective and more legitimate. She is critical of reform efforts that seek to increase effectiveness by insulating the institutions from politics (by strengthening the roles of independent experts). Instead, her analysis suggests that political pressures are inescapable, and that a more legitimate process – built on carefully structured forms of participation and representation – could also improve effectiveness and implementation. For participation to have impact, however, it must also be buttressed by enhanced forms of transparency, monitoring, and judicial-style accountability.

In the ensuing chapter, Randall Germain builds on this argument, examining a "hard case" of accountability: the highly specialized agencies and networks that constitute global financial governance. He proposes a rethinking of accountability away from a core emphasis on monitoring and compliance and towards mechanisms that "internalize accountability" within key governance institutions in ways that ensure "dissent and a critical engagement across a range of politically contentious issues are allowed to occur *within these institutions themselves.*" He calls this a "logic of participation" rather than a "logic of compliance." While this is no small task among the tight expert circles of central banks, treasuries, and regulators, he provides evidence that the basis for such a rethinking already exists. Where Woods and Germain especially agree is on a need for more structured forms of participation to enable greater public influence in decision-making among global institutions. But their reviews of the landscape of global governance do not offer many concrete details of how this might be accomplished.

Hence, the third contribution, by Anne Marie Goetz and Rob Jenkins, turns to cases of citizen activism in the public sector in India where gains in accountability through participation have been achieved. Their cases demonstrate the "logic of participation" in practice. And while there is a need for caution in extending Goetz and Jenkins' local-level findings to the global sphere, they demonstrate that citizen oversight of complex public policies and processes is indeed possible.

2   Multilateralism and building stronger international institutions

Ngaire Woods

International institutions are facing a double challenge of effectiveness and legitimacy. Many dissatisfied or disenfranchised governments and groups are deeply affected by global governance yet feel governance is poorly executed and that they themselves are inadequately represented. As global governance expands, few can hold those who exercise power to account. The implications for democracy are profound. Within the boundaries of the state people enjoy at least a *potential* to hold their governments to account through elections, ombudsmen, court actions, nongovernmental agencies, and the media. Yet increasingly, govern ments are delegating or ceding control over such decisions to inter- national organizations, networks or other actors. This means that even in democracies, governments cannot be held to account for a widening range of decisions.

The institutions of global governance are mostly intergovernmental. They are constructed to represent member states and to provide a forum for discussion, agreement, and multilateral cooperation. In global gov- ernance, no actor can claim to have been directly elected by voters. Nor are many institutions subject to the normal restraints or checks and balances of public office. Multilateral organizations grapple with an unwieldy structure of government representation behind which most decisions are made by a small group of powerful states using a com- bination of formal and informal influence. As a result, accountability in global governance is complex and difficult to achieve.

The most deeply affected or disenfranchised are peoples in developing countries. In international organizations, developing country govern- ments have little power and influence to wield in decision-making in these organizations and just as little power in holding these agencies to account. For these reasons, the strengthening of international institu- tions and enhancing of their accountability – especially with reference to developing countries – is vital.

The aim of this chapter is critically to consider the principles which are underlying current attempts to enhance and strengthen international institutions. In the first section, the chapter discusses the growing disaffection with multilateral organizations. Subsequently, the main part of the chapter examines how the twin challenges of improving effectiveness and legitimacy are likely to be affected by: independence, participation, enhanced transparency, and enhanced accountability.

The growing disaffection with multilateral organizations

Recent years have highlighted a growing contradiction in world politics. Traditional multilateral organizations are being asked to take on ever wider responsibilities in maintaining global security and economic order. Yet they command inadequate respect, support, and compliance from their powerful member states in order to fulfill these ambitions. They face a twin challenge: how to be more effective, and how to be more legitimate.

The new expansion of intergovernmental decision-making takes international institutions into areas previously considered the preserve of national governments. In the security realm since 1990 international institutions and security alliances have been called upon to intervene in order to contain ethnic and intrastate conflicts, to stabilize the regional threat they pose and to alleviate the humanitarian catastrophes which result. The UN in particular has been called upon to assist in peace-making, peace-building and peace enforcement *within* states. In Kosovo, Afghanistan, and Iraq, international arrangements have been put in place to govern countries in the wake of external intervention. Yet, as presciently described in a US Commission in 1999, the major powers are still struggling "to devise an accountable and effective institutional response to such crises" (USCNS, 1999).

The "responsibility to protect" idea extends intervention further than most other proposals for international cooperative action. The principle was laid out in 2001 by an International Commission on Intervention and State Sovereignty (partly funded by the Canadian government). Although the primary responsibility to protect citizens lies with those citizens' own government, the Commission argued that where a government fails or is unwilling to protect its citizens, then the international community has responsibilities to intervene (ICISS, 2001).

In the international financial system, a new intrusiveness has also emerged in response to the challenges of globalized capital and financial markets. In the wake of financial crises in the 1990s, policy-makers desperate to contain the risks and vulnerabilities involved in highly mobile, globalized capital markets have sought ways to strengthen and stabilize the system. An early response by the G7 was to call upon the IMF to ensure "forceful, far-reaching structural reforms" in the economies of their members in order (among other things) to correct weaknesses in domestic financial systems and ensure growth and poverty alleviation (IMF, 1998). The World Bank was expected to follow suit. This epitomizes two decades of dramatic rewriting of the role of the multilateral organizations whereby by the 1990s they had doubled the conditionality they demanded of borrowers and expanded their remit into the areas of the rule of law, judicial reform, corruption, and corporate governance (Kapur and Webb, 2000).

In international trade a similar picture emerges. Since 1986 international trade rules have expanded to cover *domestic* or *national* rules on foreign direct investment, the entry of foreign personnel, intellectual property rights (TRIPS), trade-related investment measures (TRIMs), sanitary and phytosanitary measures, technical barriers to trade, anti-dumping, subsidies, and countervailing duties (WTO, Multilateral Agreement on Trade in Goods). This list is now expanding to include issues such as competition policy and government procurement. The international limitations being imposed on national governments are stark. A simple example is that a government wishing to maintain a high standard of food safety or environmental protection is now limited by strict international rules as rulings on beef hormones and the use of dolphin-safe fishing nets have shown (Hoekman and Kostecki, 2001). For some, the failure in 2006 to reach agreement on the Doha Round of trade talks is at least in part a "blowback" from the expansion of issues achieved in earlier rounds.

The implication of the analysis so far is that global governance is being pushed to rely on deeper cooperation among states not just in terms of interstate rules but equally in upholding standards in respect of states' domestic arrangements. Yet the UN Security Council, the IMF, the World Bank, and the WTO do not have an inherent or autonomous authority over other global actors. They depend for compliance on the support of their most powerful members. And just as they are being pressed to take on more responsibilities, so too some of their most powerful members are eroding their authority.

Most obviously, the actions in Iraq of the United States and the United Kingdom (and subsequently the coalition of the willing) were taken without the support of the UN Security Council even after that body had apprised itself of the issue of Iraq and taken those actions which its membership as a whole thought were appropriate. Previously the Security Council had already been circumvented when NATO was used to undertake enforcement actions in Bosnia and then in Kosovo. These actions are widely perceived as undermining the multilateral system. When powerful states turn their back on multilateral procedures and institutions and pursue goals through private–public alliances, "coalitions of the willing," or regional or unilateral means this creates a sense of injustice on the part of countries and groups required to "play by the multilateral rules." It undermines the credibility and authority of the multilateral institutions. This is as true in the world economy as it is in global security.

In the global trading system, while multilateral negotiations fail, both the United States and the European Union fall back on bilateral and regional trade agreements through which they secure agreements from countries to comply with a yet more comprehensive list of conditions than are permissible within the WTO. For example, the US–Jordan Free Trade Agreement signed on 24 October 2000, eliminates duties and commercial barriers to bilateral trade in goods and services originating in the United States and Jordan (USTR, 2000). It also provides for intellectual property right protection, trade and the environment, labor, and electronic commerce and side letters concerning marketing approval for pharmaceutical products, and trade in services. These additional elements represent interests the US has been unable to negotiate in the WTO and demonstrates the way the US can seek to achieve trade goals without recourse to multilateral negotiations. The European agreements (EPAs) push forward governance-related conditionalities into relations with trade partners.

What does this mean for global governance? Bilateralism and regional arrangements offer all states an alternative to purely multilateral regimes. However, the states who benefit most from such arrangements are those with the largest market access to offer, the largest security umbrella to share, and the greatest capacity to threaten negative consequences from noncompliance or exclusion. The European Union and the United States have huge trade markets to offer. This means that in negotiations with any one state or small combination of states, negotiations are asymmetrically weighted towards EU or US preferences and policies. However, for both the US and the EU there is a real limit to bilateralism as a global strategy. Bilateral agreements are costly and time-consuming to negotiate, and it is not clear that they can extend beyond small or historically close economies to encompass larger trading partners with whom the US and EU need stable trade arrangements.

Although powerful states are pursuing economic and security strategies outside of multilateral institutions, it is clear that they continue to depend on the efficacy and legitimacy of global agencies. For this reason both the EU and the US are deeply engaged in thinking about how to strengthen international institutions. In this debate several core principles have come to the fore.

The debate about strengthening multilateral organizations

The argument above is that the legitimacy of most international institutions has been outpaced by an expansion in their mandates. In trade, aid, finance, and security, international institutions are being expected to intervene in ways well beyond the dreams of their founders. The result is not just a problem of effectiveness but equally a problem of legitimacy. Most multilateral organizations still have the governance structures with which they were born. The result is a serious gap between what they are now attempting to do, and what they are perceived as having the legitimacy to do. Most are criticized for insufficiently representing their member states or for not permitting adequate participation by wider stakeholders, as well as for being ineffective. The result is a wide-ranging debate about how to enhance the legitimacy and effectiveness of international organizations.

Legitimacy and effectiveness: no clear trade-offs

Strengthening the legitimacy of international institutions is difficult not least because of a widespread belief that there is a trade-off between enhancing effectiveness and improving legitimacy. Effective institutions are assumed to enjoy "hard power" which means they have a coercive capacity to make rules and to enforce them. At the extreme this implies institutions run by powerful states with little restraint. By contrast, legitimate institutions are assumed to spend too much time ensuring representation and participation, reducing themselves to talking shops.

Legitimacy and effectiveness might be seen as opposite ends of a spectrum.

A false dichotomy	
Legitimate but ineffectual: ————————	**Effective but unrepresentative:**
(Participatory, representative and inclusive such as well-run Parliaments or the United Nations General Assembly)	(Non-participatory and often strictly hierarchical such as a central bank or military command structure)

The logic which pits effectiveness against legitimacy, has led to some proposals for improving global governance by making institutions less representative of member states and less accountable to a wider political constituency.

Bolstering the independence of institutions – what implications?

One set of arguments about reforming international institutions proposes that they should be more independent of governments and run by experts so as to avoid the problems, vested interests, and contradictions which arise from domestically rooted intergovernmentalism. Part of the argument has been elegantly expressed by Ernst-Ulrich Petersmann in the following terms: "governments risk to become prisoners of the sirene-like pressures of organized interest groups unless they follow the wisdom of Ulysses (when his boat approached the island of the Sirenes) and tie their hands to the mast of international guarantees" (Petersmann, 1995, p. 166). Away from the hurly-burly of domestic politics, policy-makers (we are led to believe) can come to more rational and selfless conclusions. Four examples from the late 1990s illustrate this reasoning.

After the financial crises of the late 1990s, in April 1999 the G7 formed a Financial Stability Forum (FSF) to promote international financial stability through information exchange and international cooperation in financial supervision and surveillance (see Germain, below, ch. 3). The new network was self-consciously selective, bringing together experts from the most important players in the international financial system including national authorities responsible for financial stability in significant international financial centers, international financial institutions, sector-specific international groupings of regulators and supervisors, and committees of central bank experts. There was no sense that the FSF should represent all countries or regions of the world. Rather its goal was to coordinate the efforts of various bodies in order to promote international financial stability, improve the functioning of markets, and reduce systemic risk (FSF, 2001).[1]

At the same time as the FSF was formed, a proposal surfaced for making the IMF "truly independent and accountable" so as "to permit it to focus more efficiently on surveillance and conditionality" (De Gregorio et al., 1999). It was argued that the IMF's Executive Directors should be discouraged from taking advice from their governments. Like a central bank, the IMF should be permitted to work in a more technical, independent way with its accountability ensured through transparency and a different kind of oversight by member governments. The rationale was that just as independent central banks have proven better

---

[1] That said, the G7 soon found it necessary to expand its membership to include representatives from Hong Kong, Singapore, Australia, and the Netherlands (FSF, 2001).

at fighting inflation, so too an independent world authority would better protect international financial stability.[2]

In the European Union a similar "effectiveness-first" argument was put in 1999 by Romano Prodi: "At the end of the day, what interests them [i.e., people living in the EU] is not *who* solves these problems, but the fact that they are being tackled" (Prodi, 1999). Several years before, this efficiency rationale had led to the European Monetary Union (EMU) and more specifically in the nature and structure of the European Central Bank (ECB) which lies at the heart of EMU. The ECB is an independent and unaccountable body (e.g., compared to its counterparts in the UK, USA, and Japan, all of which publish formal voting records of their decisions), whose legitimacy rests on its technical and expert nature rather than a potential representativeness or democratic accountability.

The World Trade Organization (WTO) offers a final example of an argument for a more effective, less representative organization – here made in legal terms. One argument has been to constitutionalize the WTO, providing a written constitution as "a contractual means by which citizens secured their freedom through long-term basic rules of a higher legal rank" (Petersmann, 1995). Like the argument for a more independent IMF, constitutionalizing the WTO is seen as a way of protecting the application of sensible "long-term basic rules" for trade which might otherwise be shipwrecked on the ragged shores of national politics.

The counter to each of the arguments for more independent governance is that political forces and pressures are inescapable. Delegating power or authority to international institutions does not supersede politics. It simply delivers it into a new and different arena in which different pressure groups and actors will have more power. This can be seen in each of the cases mentioned above. Yet more importantly, in every one of the above-mentioned cases, representation is essential to effectiveness. Most simply put, without the buy-in of key stakeholders, the institution cannot be effective.

Soon after the Financial Stability Forum was created, its participants decided it could not be effective unless it extended its membership. If it were effectively to enhance information exchange and international cooperation in financial supervision and surveillance, it needed to include more members. Hence, in short order it expanded its membership to

---

[2] The proposal also argued for making the IMF more accountable through: 1) increased transparency with the publication of voting records, Executive Board minutes and performance evaluations; 2) the strengthening and bolstering of an oversight committee comprising Finance Ministers; and 3) a requirement that Executive Directors justify their actions in terms of an explicit mandate such as "to advance economic and financial stability" and face dismissal by the oversight committee if they failed.

include Hong Kong, Singapore, Australia, and the Netherlands (FSF, 2001). Furthermore, the G7 Finance Ministers grouping which created the FSF had itself found its membership too narrow to be effective. In the wake of the East Asian Crisis, the G7 found it needed to hear – and have buy-in – from those countries most affected by the crisis and central to contagion and its containment. Hence they created a wider more representative G20 group of Finance Ministers to consider global institutional reform – although critics would also point to the G20's lack of legitimacy as a representative of all countries (Helleiner, 2001).

The proposal to make the IMF more independent has in part been driven by a weariness with the political bargaining, influence, trade-offs, and compromises which underpin some of the organization's work (these are elaborated in Woods, 2006). Like independent central banks, a stronger IMF would be insulated from political pressures. However, the IMF is involved in advising on a broader range of policies than any central bank. It advises on policies which involve ranking and prioritizing the rights and obligations of different groups of people. It monitors and reports on economic policies and decisions in all of its member countries. Its judgments necessarily involve interpretations about which there are different perspectives among its members – and different interests at stake. This is why the process of decision-making in the IMF is unavoidably one which has to include a process – accepted by all – for adjudicating among different alternatives.

In respect of the European Central Bank and the EU's other institutions, political legitimacy has emerged as a vital issue, leading to a wide debate about institutional reform not just spurred by the exigencies of enlargement, but by the need to ensure the confidence of the public in existing member countries. As European Commissioner Michel Barnier put it in 2001, European policy-makers need to go beyond negotiating the "necessary technical adaptations" to institutions and to consider how to reinforce the democratic legitimacy of the European Union (Barnier, 2001). The anatomy of more legitimate EU institutions was one of the goals of those who participated in the debate and construction of the (failed) Constitution for the EU (see Nicolaidis, 2004).

A more independent WTO raises similar problems. WTO rules encroach more into the national realm, affecting issues of welfare, the environment, labor rights, and intellectual property protection. Effective implementation of such rules requires an acceptance by participating governments that the rules are legitimate. They will not be seen as legitimate because some claim that they reflect some higher legal truth. Rather they are seen as reflecting deeply political priorities and choices over which citizens expect to have some say. This is not a simple contest between economists who favor liberalization versus NGOs pushing human rights and other values. The outcomes involve subtle adjudications over priorities, means, and ends. Should one form of environmental protection be privileged over another? Should one species of dolphin be protected more than another? Most importantly of all, who should decide and to whom should they be accountable?

For all these reasons, the relationship between representation and efficiency is more complex than the simple spectrum with which we started. International institutions cannot simply be made more independent in order that they might be more effective. A more useful depiction of the relationship between representation and efficiency must at least begin with a recognition that different institutions derive their legitimacy from different sources. A central bank's legitimacy may derive from its fulfillment of narrowly specified and monitorable targets in a transparent way – not from its representativeness. By contrast, a Parliament's legitimacy derives precisely from its representativeness, not from its efficacy in achieving specified and monitorable goals. In each case the source of legitimacy reflects why stakeholders accept the decisions of the institution – making effectiveness possible. Typically legitimacy becomes an issue for institutions when coercion is too costly, too time-consuming, or simply ineffectual.

One way some institutions have sought to bolster legitimacy while enhancing their independence has been through an embrace of "participation." This deserves examining. But first let's examine the broader argument for making international institutions more participatory.

Making institutions more participatory

Participation has become a powerful aspiration in global governance. It is embraced as a way to overcome three challenges in global governance. First, it is forwarded as at least a partial solution to the narrowness or limited representativeness of international organizations. Dialogue with global civil society – or more accurately put, nongovernmental transnational advocacy organizations (and the difference between NGOs and global civil society is a significant one for this debate) – opens organizations to more views without having to add seats or further representatives to the decision-makers' table. Second, participation is embraced as a way to enrich global debates by adding a wider set of views and values to the debate. Enthusiasts go further, arguing that "the right way to defeat bad ideas is with better ideas. Just as national democracy entails participation and debate at the domestic level, so too does democratic global governance entail participation by transnational NGOs" (Charnovitz, 2000).

Finally, "participation" is advocated as a way to make international organizations more effective. Put simply, the aspiration is not just that greater participation would result in better informed policy with greater feedback from those affected by the policies of institutions, but that a wider group of "stakeholders" will help institutions implement policy.

Are the governance-improving aspirations for participation well founded? Can an engagement with nongovernmental groups make international organizations more legitimate or effective? And in areas where there is no formal international governance, can global nongovernmental organizations be part of a viable alternative?

The most visible and vocal NGOs in global governance are large transnational nongovernmental organizations based in industrialized countries who lobby for particular principles or issues such as debt relief, environmental protection, and human rights such as Amnesty International, the World Wildlife Fund, or Oxfam. It is worth noting immediately that these groups do not claim to represent countries or geographical groups nor do they represent particular commercial interests (although they are accountable to their donors and members and many are also in the business of delivering aid or similar goods). Their stake in the arena of global governance is more of a deliberative one. They bring principles and values to the attention of policy-makers. They also play a role in monitoring global governance, analyzing and reporting on issues as diverse as the Chemical Weapons Treaty, negotiations on global climate change, world trade, and the actions of the IMF, World Bank.

Multilateral institutions have engaged directly with NGOs in consultations about their work. For example, the World Bank has a formal NGO–World Bank committee and as I have detailed elsewhere, in the 1990s vociferous NGO action led the IMF and World Bank to revise their debt strategy (see Woods, 2006, chapter 6) and move towards greater transparency and accountability (as will be further discussed below). International donor institutions across the board are now also committed to enhancing "participation" on the ground in countries (World Bank, 1989; 1992; 1994; 1996; 1999 and cf. IMF, 1997; 2000).

A further way in which international organizations are leveraging participation is less direct – involving corporate self-regulatory codes and NGOs. The United Nations, for example, is actively trying to leverage self-regulation by corporations increasingly concerned about being branded in their main consumer markets as using "sweatshops" or peddling "blood diamonds." The UN Global Compact initiative was created to bring together private companies, governments, multilateral organizations, and NGOs to advocate and promulgate nine core principles drawn from the Universal Declaration of Human Rights, the ILO's

Fundamental Principles and Rights at Work, and the Rio Declaration on Environment and Development.

Nongovernmental organizations are crucial to these multilateral attempts to bolster and expand private sector self-regulation. They have pushed corporations to act in the wake of campaigns and consumer boycotts. For example, after NGOs publicly accused large oil companies such as BP and Royal Dutch/Shell of colluding in human rights violations in countries such as Colombia and Chad-Cameroon, these companies adopted human rights policies strongly endorsing the UN Universal Declaration of Human Rights. The companies also offered to work more closely and openly with NGOs (British Petroleum, 2001; Shell, 2001). In a similar vein, diamond companies such as De Beers have reacted to bad publicity linking them to the mining of "blood" and "conflict" diamonds in countries where the industry funds and perpetuates brutal civil wars such as Sierra Leone (see Smillie, below, ch. 6). In their *Annual Report 2000* De Beers wrote of the "threat to the entire legitimate diamond industry" posed by the "effect of conflict diamonds on consumer confidence" (De Beers, 2000). To ward off this threat, the diamond industry created a World Diamond Council based in New York to develop, implement, and oversee a tracking system for the export and import of rough diamonds to "prevent the exploitation of diamonds for illicit purposes such as war and inhumane acts" (World Diamond Council, 2001). A further example of a self-regulatory code is that promulgated by chemical companies in the wake of the Bhopal incident. The "Responsible Care" code was launched in 1988, requiring members to continually improve their health, safety, and environmental performance; to listen and respond to public concerns; to assist each other to achieve optimum performance; and to report their goals and progress to the public. In 2001 the code had been adopted in some forty-six countries, representing over 85 percent of the world's chemical production (ACC, 2001).

However, critics point to the limitations of casting the new politics of "participation" as a solution to inadequate representation or effectiveness. They argue that NGOs cannot resolve and should not obscure the gaps in representation in the system. In particular, developing countries are inadequately represented in the formal governance of the IMF and World Bank, as well as in the informal processes which underpin negotiations in the WTO and in dispute settlement proceedings (Bown and Hoekman, 2005). The politics of "participation" pose three questions: who is being represented, through what processes, and with what impact?

The inclusion of NGOs in the discussions around the WTO will not necessarily redress the failure of the WTO adequately to represent some countries and groups while it over-represents others. Indeed, inclusion might exacerbate rather than redress the lack of voice and influence suffered by developing countries. For instance, of the 738 NGOs accredited to the Ministerial Conference of the WTO in Seattle, 87 percent were based in industrialized countries. Enthusiasts of inclusion need to consider more carefully how NGOs might be included without further distorting the underrepresentation of developing countries and peoples in the WTO.

A second problem arises in the broader nongovernmental sector which is how and who from the private sector the new "participation" embraces. There is a high politics to participation in global governance. For example, it is simply wrong to assume that a constitutionalized WTO would side-step the vested interests which "distort" trade policy at the national level. Even a cursory examination of private sector participation in existing WTO negotiations reveals their powerful influence. Groups such as the US Coalition of Services Industries (CSI, 2001) and International Financial Services, London (IFSL, 2001) were deeply involved in negotiations on the General Agreement on Trade in Services and the WTO Basic Telecommunications and Financial Services Agreements. The Financial Leaders Group – a private sector group of North American, European, Japanese, Canadian, and Hong Kong financial leaders – publicizes its role as "a key player in securing the 1997 Financial Services Agreement and continues its work in the current WTO services negotiations" (FLG, 2001). Naturally, representatives of private sector organizations bring a high level of expertise and ideas to the negotiating table. However, they represent, indeed they have a duty to represent, the narrow sectoral and material interests of their members. It distorts reality to propose that their inclusion necessarily ensures that public interests will be better served.

As NGOs begin to take a part in global governance the question of who chooses which NGOs to include or consult in national or international negotiations becomes crucial. Equally important is how they are included and to what degree their input is influential. In choosing NGO interlocutors, international organizations become powerful gatekeepers and shapers of "global civil society." Furthermore, in designing rules and processes for engaging civil society, international institutions also greatly influence the impact of NGOs. While the "new participation" has opened up decision-making and implementation to a wider range of stakeholders in some spheres, in others it is little more than a public relations exercise.

Proponents of participation argue that international organizations and large multinational private actors today perceive a need to respond not just to global markets but to global social and political pressures: "as markets have gone global, so, too, must the idea of corporate citizenship and the practice of corporate social responsibility. In this new global economy, it makes good business sense for firms to internalize these principles as integral elements of corporate strategies and practices" (UN Global Compact, 2001). So too, international organizations themselves have a rationale for opening up. But in answering "open to whom" we are taken back to core principles of multilateralism.

Structuring participation

The need to structure participation, so as to create an effective process, takes us back to existing multilateral organizations which, for all their imperfections, are the best approximation of institutionalized representation and voice at the global level.

Enhancing transparency and monitoring

Transparency refers to the recording, reporting, and publishing of information about the processes, decisions, and outcomes of an institution. The rise of both the internet and public expectations about transparency have created a quiet revolution in global governance whereby institutions such as the United Nations Security Council, the IMF, the World Bank, and the WTO can and do post documentation about their activities in an instantaneous way. That said, government members in each of these institutions have blocked opening them up further to public scrutiny. Crucial decisions are still taken in private. Individual government positions are often still kept secret. The result is that citizens of member countries stand little chance of holding their own government to account for its actions in international organizations, let alone the international agency itself. This opens up an important way in which institutions could be strengthened – in terms of both their effectiveness and their legitimacy.

Most international institutions are under constant pressure from shareholders and members, as well as outside NGOs and critics, to evaluate their operations and effectiveness in a more thorough, effective, and public way. The new expectation that institutions conduct and publish critical evaluations of themselves was highlighted by the UN's publication of a very critical independent examination of UN policy in Rwanda, commissioned by the Secretary General in May 1999 (UN, 1999). Similarly the Executive Board of the IMF created an Office of Independent Evaluation in 2000 the objectives of which included: to improve policy by better learning from past experience; to enhance Board oversight; and to build public understanding and external credibility by undertaking objective evaluations in a transparent manner. The World Bank has now renamed its operations evaluation department – now the Independent Evaluation Group – with similar goals in mind.

The lessons about monitoring and accountability also point to the need for citizens and outsiders not just to access information but to be able to use it effectively. This particularly affects developing countries where typically there is very little capacity to absorb, publicize, and act on information. In industrialized countries, NGOs, the media, politicians, Parliaments and others at the national level all play a role in picking up and publicizing information and translating concerns into pressures on international organizations (see Eggers et al., 2005). Among developing country governments, the perception that transparency works to the advantage mainly of industrialized country NGOs and governments has led to regular opposition to increased transparency and monitoring in international agencies. Regrettably such opposition cuts off an important longer-term goal of holding these institutions better and more equitably to account. People in developing countries stand to gain if NGOs push for the kind of transparency and openness which exposes and reduces a bias against the key concerns and priorities of the less privileged. What developing countries need to ensure is better institutionalized consultation and monitoring which structure participation to give key groups a voice.

Using judicial-style accountability

A further strengthening of the responsiveness of institutions can be achieved through more active judicial-style accountability which usually refers to tribunals, ombudsmen, or other processes of redress. The object is to ensure that organizations act within their powers and in keeping with their own operational rules. Judicial-style panels or actors examine specific actions or decisions taken by an institution in order to adjudicate whether or not some breach has occurred. Often in the case of courts, tribunals, or ombudsmen there are few direct powers positively to direct a wrongdoing institution to take some alternative course of action. Rather the process draws attention to a breach of rules and can result in agencies being asked at least to reconsider their decision.

Two unprecedented steps in global governance have been taken in this regard in the World Bank Group. In 1993 an Inspection Panel was created by the Executive Board of the World Bank to service the IBRD and IDA. The Inspection Panel can receive complaints from any group able to show that: 1) they live in the project area (or represent people who do) and are likely to be affected adversely by project activities; 2) they believe that the actual or likely harm they have suffered results from failure by the Bank to follow its policies and procedures; 3) their concerns have been discussed with Bank management and they are not satisfied with the outcome. A three-person Inspection Panel has powers to make a preliminary assessment of the merits of a complaint brought by a group, taking into account Bank management responses to the allegations. Subsequently, the Panel can recommend to the Board that a full investigation be undertaken, and make recommendations on the basis of such a full investigation. The Executive Board retains the power to permit investigations to proceed, and to make final decisions based on the Panel's findings and Bank Management's recommendations.

It is worth noting that this form of accountability requires institutions to develop and publish detailed operating principles and procedures for which they can subsequently be held to account. It exists in a different form in another part of the World Bank Group.

A different model of judicial-style accountability was created in 1999 to service two other agencies within the World Bank group: the International Finance Corporation (IFC) and the Multilateral Investment Guarantee Agency (MIGA). A Compliance Adviser/Ombudsman's office (CAO) was set up after consultations with shareholders, NGOs, and members of the business community. The aim is to find a workable and constructive approach to dealing with environmental and social concerns, and complaints of people directly impacted by IFC, and for MIGA-financed projects. The CAO or ombudsman and her staff are independent of the Bank and IFC and report directly to the President of the World Bank. The emphasis of the office's work is on dialogue, mediation, and conciliation. The CAO has the power to make recommendations but not to act as "a judge, court or policeman."

There are several obvious limits to judicial-style accountability. First, not everyone is in an equal position to use the procedures available, not just in bringing formal complaints but in ensuring that the threat of such actions keeps officials of an institution within their powers and rules. In many cases people in developing countries have relied on Northern NGOs to assist in funding and presenting their case.

Critics allege that the role of NGOs risks skewing the work of accountability tribunals in favor of issues and areas of most concern to people within industrialized countries, as expressed through Northern NGOs, leaving unserviced those people in the developing world who have not attracted the attention of such NGOs. A further risk is that the outcomes of a formal process, such as the Inspection Panel, may well end up being shaped more by the needs of Northern NGOs to garner publicity through confrontation and showdown, rather than by quiet measures which more modestly improve the lives of those directly affected.

A second limitation on judicial-style accountability is that the process can be used to attack good decisions which suffer a minor technical flaw in respect of the rules. It can also be long, costly, and time-consuming, diverting resources away from the central purposes of the institution. For this reason the threshold or cause for complaint which can spark a full inspection or action is crucial.

A final important limitation in judicial-style accountability is that the process examines whether an institution has adhered to its existing policies and operational rules. It does not examine or adjudicate the quality or purposes of those policies or rules. Judicial-style accountability does not substitute or offer recourse against the responsibility of decision-makers to make good policy or rules. It cannot prevent or call to account bad decisions being made within the rules. This means that accountability for the quality of the rules themselves has to be achieved through some other means.

New forms of accountability could usefully expand the scope for holding decision-makers in global governance collectively to account through the recognition of minority or developing country shareholders' rights. It might also hold officials acting in a professional capacity to account for the quality and diligence of their work. Still untouched however are a large range of substantive policy decisions made by international organizations in which people in developing countries have little input in decision-making. Here a real capacity to hold decision-makers to account requires adequate participation in the processes of priority setting, policy-making, resource allocations, and implementation.

Conclusions

Global governance stands accused of being inadequately effective and legitimate to cope with the demands of globalization. The accusation is not altogether unfounded. This chapter has described the erosion of authority in multilateral institutions even as they are expected to perform more tasks and manage more problems. At the same time, it has examined the principles which underpin the debate about how best to reform institutions. Independence does not offer a solution to either the legitimacy gap or the lack of effectiveness of organizations. Rather, a scrutiny of the arguments for independence in the end returns us to the need for better representation, more responsiveness, and stronger accountability. Participation, by contrast, has a clear value in spotlighting gaps and problems in global governance, and in bolstering partial solutions. That said, the structure and nature of participation depends in itself on the rules of pre-existing multilateral institutions.

International organizations need to be strengthened and improved. At the core of better institutions is a structure of representation which gives all members a minimum degree of confidence in the organization – so that they will effectively delegate to it. In turn this requires an effective corporate governance structure which gives voice to the members but at the same time permits strategic objectives, operational decisions, review, and audit to be undertaken independently of one another. This, combined with the principles of transparency, monitoring, and judicial accountability, can assist in building better international institutions.

References

ACC or American Chemistry Council (2001) *Responsible Care* at www.cmahq.com.

Barnier, Michel (17 October 2001) *L'urgence européenne* (*Note personelle*). Brussels: European Commission. Also at: http://europa.eu.int/comm/commissioners/barnier/document/171001_fr.pdf.

Bown, Chad P. and Bernard Hoekman (2005) "WTO Dispute Settlement and the Missing Developing Country Cases: Engaging the Private Sector," *Journal of International Economic Law* 8(4), 861–90.

British Petroleum (2001) *Human Rights Policy* at www.bp.org.

Charnovitz, Steve (2000) *On Constitutionalizing the WTO: A Comment on Howse and Nicolaidis* at www.ksg.harvard.edu/cbg/trade/charnovitz.htm.

CSI or US Coalition of Services Industries (2001) Documentation at www.uscsi.org.

De Beers (2000) *De Beers Annual Report 2000*. London: De Beers.

De Gregorio, Jose, Barry Eichengreen, Takatoshi Ito, and Charles Wyplosz (1999) *An Independent and Accountable IMF*. ICMB, CEPR.

Eggers, Andrew, Ann Florini, and Ngaire Woods (2005) "Democratizing the IMF: The Role of Parliaments," in Barry Carin and Angela Wood (eds.) *Accountability of the International Monetary Fund.* Burlington, VT: Ashgate and IDRC, pp. 38–61.

FLG or Financial Leaders Group (2001) Documentation, membership and description available at www.uscsi.org/groups/finLeader.htm.

FSF or Financial Stability Forum (2001) Documentation at www.fsforum.org.

Helleiner, Gerald (2001) *Developing Countries, Global Financial Governance and the Group of Twenty: A Note*. Toronto: University of Toronto at www.globaleconomicgovernance.org/docs/Helleiner%20on%20G20.pdf.

Hoekman, Bernard M. and M. M. Kostecki (2001) *The Political Economy of the World Trading System*. Oxford: Oxford University Press.

ICISS or International Commission on Intervention and State Sovereignty (2001) *The Responsibility to Protect*. Ottawa: ICISS.

IFSL or International Financial Services London (2001) Documentation at www.bi.org.uk.

IMF (2000) *A Guide to Progress in Strengthening the Architecture of the International Financial System.* Washington, DC: IMF.

IMF (1998) *External Evaluation of the ESAF.* Report by a Group of Independent Experts. Washington, DC: IMF.

IMF (1997) *Good Governance: The IMF's Role.* Washington, DC: IMF.

Kapur, Devesh and Richard Webb (2000) *Governance Related Conditionalities of the International Financial Institutions.* G-24 Discussion Paper Series 6:3.4. New York and Geneva: UNCTAD and Center for International Development, Harvard University, August.

Nicolaidis, Kalypso (2004) "We, the Peoples of Europe ...," *Foreign Affairs,* November/December, 97–110.

Petersmann, Ernst-Ulrich (1995) "The Transformation of the World Trading System through the 1994 Agreement Establishing the World Trade Organization," *European Journal of International Law* 6(2), 161–221.

Prodi, Romano. (21 July 1999) Speech to the European Parliament as President-Designate of the European Commission.

Shell or Royal Dutch/Shell (2001) *Human Rights Policy* at www.shell.org.

UN (15 December 1999) *Report of the Independent Inquiry into the Actions of the United Nations during the 1994 Genocide in Rwanda.* New York: United Nations. Also at www.un.org/News/dh/latest/rwanda.htm.

UN Global Compact (2001) *Updates* at www.unglobalcompact.org.

USCNS or US Commission on National Security in the 21st Century (15 September 1999) *New World Coming: Major Themes and Implications.* The Phase 1 Report on the Emerging Global Security Environment for the First Quarter of the 21st Century.

USTR or United States Trade Representative (24 October 2000) *The US–Jordan Free Trade Agreement.* Washington, DC: USTR. Also at www.ustr. gov/regions/eu-med/middleeast/US-JordanFTA.shtml.

Woods, Ngaire (2006) *The Globalizers: The IMF, the World Bank, and its Borrowers.* Ithaca, NY: Cornell University Press.

World Bank (1999) *Annual Review of Development Effectiveness.* Washington, DC: World Bank.

World Bank (1996) *The World Bank Participation Source Book.* Washington, DC: World Bank.

World Bank (1994) *Governance: The World Bank's Experience.* Washington, DC: World Bank.

World Bank (1992) *Governance and Development.* Washington, DC: World Bank.

World Bank (1989) *Sub-Saharan Africa: From Crisis to Sustainable Growth.* Washington, DC: World Bank.

World Diamond Council (2001) *About WDC* at www.worlddiamondcouncil.com.

3   Global financial governance
     and the problem of accountability:
     the role of the public sphere

Randall D. Germain

Recent developments concerning the international financial architecture have drawn attention to the problem of accountability within the structure of global financial governance. Some progress has been achieved in outlining the scale of the problem in terms of multilateral economic institutions such as the International Monetary Fund (IMF) and World Bank (see Woods, above, ch. 2). But little progress has been made with regard to the vexed question of how to address – either conceptually or practically – the problem of accountability in the myriad of other institutions actually involved in global financial governance. This is unsurprising. Most of the institutions and agencies involved in global financial governance are either national in scope or less formalized in their levels of institutionalization than are the IMF and World Bank. Moreover, they are by their very nature highly specialized agencies concerned with technical issues that require a certain level of expertise before meaningful oversight can be achieved. In order to advance lines of accountability in the absence of traditional democratic links between decision-making institutions and the public, I argue that accountability has to be better internalized within the context of a strengthened global financial public sphere, where norms of inclusion and publicness can be established and instantiated.

Accountability as a 'problem'

Accountability within the broader structure of financial governance needs to be problematized precisely because of the way it forms part of the general ensemble of governance concerns.[1] It should be seen as part

---

[1] Other governance concerns would include legitimacy, justice, representation, and effectiveness. As an *ensemble* they are also mutually constitutive, meaning that any consideration of the "governance problematic" that ignores their interaction risks being

of the broader discourse now underway over democracy and economic governance at the global level (Dahl, 1999; Bohman, 1999b; Scholte, 2002a). So far, this debate has highlighted the ownership and inclusion deficits of financial governance – especially with respect to emerging markets and the Third World more generally – and has thrown into sharp relief the peculiar barriers standing in the way of making the governance structures of finance more accountable to those who must carry out and bear the costs of financial reform (Armijo, 1999; Germain, 2001; Porter, 2001; Stiglitz, 2002). Three barriers are especially significant for this discussion.

The first barrier to strengthening accountability at the global level is broadly political, namely the primacy of vertical over horizontal accountability. That is, the agencies that exercise financial governance are in every case national authorities, and they are responsible to their national governments either directly or through the operation of their mandates. There is simply no such thing as horizontal accountability among central banks, treasuries or regulators, even if on many occasions there are strong social bonds and sympathetic connections between them.

The second barrier is linked to the above, but can be understood more narrowly as a matter of law. Many of the agencies responsible for financial governance are in fact statutorily independent from central government. The best-known case is that of central bank independence, which has gained ground as one of the key architectural conditions of modern financial systems (Gill, 2003). But regulatory agencies are increasingly becoming independent as well. One of the key problems this raises for a globalized form of accountability is therefore legal: simply put, the legislation that established many of the agencies involved in *global* financial governance places their global responsibilities in a subservient relationship to their *national* responsibilities. Even where governments might be inclined to emphasize global responsibilities, central banks may be more reticent.

The final barrier to strengthening accountability is the high degree of specialist knowledge demanded from those who participate in and contribute to the practices and debates of financial governance. Nearly all of the practitioners involved in financial governance are trained economists or bankers, and the socialization of these skills requires either advanced educational achievements or long years operating in banking and capital markets. Additionally, in terms of both education

---

incomplete. However, given the theme of this book, I focus specifically on the problem of accountability at the expense of other concerns.

and practical experience, it is rare for these not to include significant stints in America or Britain. Thus American (or British) advanced degrees and/or experience in New York or London markets are virtually essential prerequisites for an entrée into the rarified circles of (global) financial governance. In this sense there is a cultural context at work which shapes the way in which the problem of accountability is viewed.

In this chapter I explore how these barriers may be attenuated within the context of the newly emergent framework of international decision-making, using two examples to demonstrate how accountability might take a more progressive direction. Even though global financial governance may be a "hard case" in terms of strengthening accountability, it need not be a lost case. Although the barriers to better accountability are real and clear, there are good reasons to argue that they do not define entirely the accountability problematic. What needs to be more consistently pursued, I argue, is a strategy for more viably internalizing the mechanisms of accountability within the institutions of global financial governance. In particular, just as some argue that a neoliberal form of discipline has been instantiated into the constitution of global capitalism (e.g., Hardt and Negri, 2000), a strong case can be made for instantiating a more effective and progressive sense of accountability within the broader ensemble of financial governance. I call this new sense of accountability a logic of participation rather than a logic of compliance.

How we can think about participation

The call for a shift in the logic of accountability from compliance to participation rests on two presumed social facts about the organization of finance that are often undervalued. By "social fact" I refer to a shared or inter-subjectively recognized attribute that enables collective human activity by providing meaning and interpretive certainty to specific forms of social relations. Social facts such as a belief in a particular kind of human spirit or nature, or in the definitive existence of a racial or ethnic group, or in the sanctity of a particular institutional form, enable collective action to occur because of the belief that this form of social organization is legitimate and/or preordained. Human behavior is in this sense guided (or enabled) by the existence of "social" facts. And while social facts may be cognitive in their origin, they always also have material and institutional foundations. I will claim in this context that they are the building blocks of collective social order.[2]

[2] In a short chapter such as this I can do no more than assert the importance of social facts. They are associated with what I have elsewhere called the "historical mode of thought."

The first social fact upon which the case for a more progressive logic of accountability rests is the role of institutions in mobilizing, allocating, and regulating finance. If finance is understood as a resource,[3] its creation and allocation are guided by incentives that are produced by the interaction of multiple institutions that are usually identified as "markets." Such "markets" stand over and above individual institutions precisely because they provide the collective incentives to which each institution must respond. If we look closely at the production of these incentives, however, it is more accurate to insist that it is the complex interaction of these institutions – together with their concomitant organizational structures, ideational dynamics, and personnel mixes – that produces the precise formulation of incentives at any one point in time. In other words markets are nothing other than institutions organizing information and other advantages in particular ways (Perraton, 2000). And for institutions to be part of an effective and legitimate ensemble of governance, they need to be linked into sets of mutually accountable relations that encourage ownership and responsibility to be shared. In other words the institutional basis of what I have elsewhere called the "international organization of credit" (Germain, 1997) provides the substrata upon which all appeals to accountability rest. It is precisely because credit is organized through institutions that we can even speak about the necessity of accountability as participation in the first place.

The second social "fact" of finance concerns the deployment of direct coercion within financial relations. The organization of credit rests upon the way in which institutions pursue their interests in line with the prevailing structure of incentives. Coercion cannot play an overdetermining role in the construction of incentives, since a) they are nonmaterial values whose precise meaning varies between institutions; and b) they are values to which institutions may commit to differing extents. Crucially, the "reach" of coercion is itself dependent upon a number of variables or factors that weigh differently on institutions in accordance with their own individual conditions. For example, the fungibility of credit undercuts the effectiveness of certain levers of coercion (such as taxation levels or capital

The intellectual lineage of this formulation is provided by historically informed scholars writing in traditions of inquiry that are located mainly outside of the disciplines of international relations and international political economy (the acknowledged intellectual "home" of this author). They include Vico (1968/1744), Sorel (1950/1908), Collingwood (1946), and in a more contemporary vein Carr (1961) and Cox (1981; 1983). See Germain (1997; 2000) for a discussion of some aspects of the historical mode of thought.

[3] I prefer to call this resource "credit," on the basis that it must be mobilized before it can be utilized. In this sense finance or credit is a resource to which individual and collective agents *have access* under certain conditions (Germain, 1997).

controls), while the necessity of ownership of rules and standards under-cuts their direct imposition by the strong on the weak or underdeveloped. This is not to say that power and influence are absent within either the global financial system or financial institutions, merely that their exercise as direct coercion is ambiguous. This ambiguity lends to the organization of credit – global finance – a contingency that is malleable and unpredictable.

The way in which these two social facts interact means that for governance to occur within the global financial system, an institution-alized framework must exist in which incentives for behavior can be formulated, codified, and used as barometers against which best practice can be developed and measured. Historically, such an institutionalized framework has been associated with either a highly centralized and interlinked set of financial markets or with a financial hegemon. We no longer live in the shadow of a single financial hegemon or under the wing of a highly centralized financial system. For financial governance to actually exist and be exercised, some mechanism is required through which competing sets of incentives can be debated, negotiated, and advanced in terms of institutionalized practice (consistent of course with the operational prerequisites of today's complex form of financial capitalism). Today, this mechanism – or institutionalized framework – is the public sphere, and I argue that using this framework as our depar-ture point provides the basis for a viable strategy of strengthening accountability within financial governance in a progressive direction.

Internationalized decision-making and the public sphere

How can we argue today that financial governance in the global context both exists and is improving? At a basic empirical level it exists because the modalities of governance are everywhere in evidence. All states with functioning financial systems of course have the full panoply of gov-ernance agencies, usually a combination of treasury ministry, central bank and financial regulator(s). But beyond this there has been an explosion of recent initiatives at the global level to better coordinate governance and address regulatory gaps, including most importantly the formation in 1999 of the Financial Stability Forum (FSF) and the G20. Regional level initiatives also have their place, for example EMEAP in Asia.[4] Alongside established mechanisms of financial governance such

---

[4] EMEAP, the Executives' Meeting of East Asia Pacific Central Banks, dates back to early 1991, when the heads of central banks met at the instigation of the Bank of Japan to discuss the exchange of information on regional market developments (Yam, 1997).

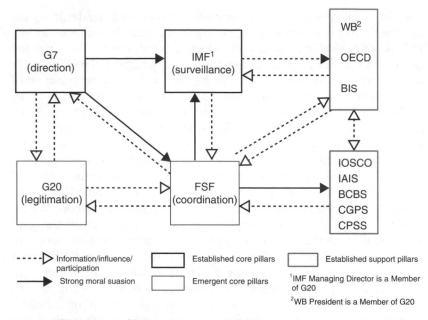

Figure 3.1 Global architecture of financial governance (From *Global Governance: A Review of Multilateralism and International Organizations*, 7(4), Copyright © 2001 by Lynne Rienner Publishers, Inc. Used with permission.)

as the IMF and G7, these new bodies have been developing standards, codes, and benchmarks that offer guidance and direction to public authorities at the national level. In other words, there has been both an enhanced institutionalization of governance and a signal development in the incentive structure at the heart of global financial transactions. On this basis we can argue that financial governance has become more genuinely global and interlinked over the past half-decade. Figure 3.1 schematically represents what I have elsewhere called the emerging global architecture of financial governance (Germain, 2001).

By broadening out the decision-making process, we can assert that the structure of financial governance has become more globalized. Two noteworthy aspects of this increasingly globalized governance structure are especially significant in terms of the argument about accountability. The first point to note is its increased "publicness." Previously, financial governance at the global level was confined primarily to elite-level deliberations among a select set of relatively opaque institutions, such as the G10, the OECD's Working Party 3 (where codes of liberalization were first discussed), and the Bank for International Settlements (BIS).

Today, however, even though the actual meetings of the FSF and the G20 (and indeed many of the more specialized agencies such as the Basel Committee on Banking Supervision, or BCBS) are closed to immediate public scrutiny, the results of these meetings are published and an extensive system of outreach has been put in place to ensure a dialogue occurs among as wide a cross-section of the public as possible. For example, the FSF conducts regular meetings with nonmembers to ensure communication and foster dialogue about the regulatory issues with which it is concerned. The BIS makes similar outreach efforts, and has recently opened offices in Hong Kong and Mexico City to strengthen its regional presence. Taken together, these efforts are an indication of the extent to which official debate and dialogue on matters of financial governance have become increasingly "public" over the past several years.[5]

The second noteworthy aspect to the increasingly globalized structure of financial governance is its consensual nature. The turn towards a more consensual decision-making structure has been prompted by the emergence of a specialized division of labor within the international financial architecture between the G7, IMF, FSF, and G20. At one level, we might observe that the G7 provides signals for the general direction of financial governance; the IMF provides surveillance on behalf of the international community; the FSF provides coordination among regulatory agencies; and the G20 provides political legitimacy for the broader process through its inclusion of emerging market economies.[6] At another level, however, this structure of governance brings together in different ways the overlapping parts of public authority that together constitute financial governance. Central banks, who are in the main responsible for the stability and soundness of domestic financial systems, work primarily through the FSF and G20, where central banks from the most systemically significant financial markets (developed and emerging) are represented. Treasury ministries work in part through the G20 and FSF, but the larger share of their efforts is directed through the IMF and, where they are members, the G7 and/or OECD. National regulatory authorities for financial institutions and associated services (accounting, insurance, stock exchanges) work through the FSF and other specialized institutions like the International Organization of Securities Commissions (IOSCO), which feed into discussions and debates at the BIS and IMF as well.

---

[5] This new level of "publicness" extends also to the increased involvement of civic organizations and other elements of what may be identified as civil society (Scholte, 2002b).

[6] I provide a fuller account of these different functions in Germain (2001).

This complex division of labor actively discourages coercion and encourages consensus as a key hallmark of international decision-making. An example of this is the recent overture by the IMF (and US Treasury) to further investigate the problem of sovereign debt rescheduling (Krueger, 2002; cf. Eichengreen, 2002). Although in the past this has been fiercely resisted by successive American administrations, the American financial community, and even the IMF, concerted and persistent international pressure from German, British, and other governments has finally succeeded opening up an official multilateral dialogue that is structured around the search for consensus rather than the imposition of a particular framework rooted entirely around a single state's preferences. The formulation of many of the standards and codes by the FSF and BCBS has followed a similar consensual pattern in terms of being the products of widespread international consultation.[7] In terms of the operation of the new global architecture of financial governance, then, consensus appears to be one of its most important cornerstones.

This is not to downgrade some of the more problematic aspects of consensual decision-making, such as the acceptance of a widely diffused ideational framework (in this case a refined version of free-market neo-liberalism), the continued centrality of the US and its financial community for all decisions, the constrained nature of emerging market participation, and the continued exclusion of important participants and issues from the dialogue that consensus promotes. It is also the case that consensus can sometimes shade into coercion. Nevertheless, we should acknowledge the significant progress in terms of developing the effectiveness and legitimacy of financial governance which this development represents. Consensual decision-making demands and requires a certain kind of discourse for its very existence, one that looks to evidence, argument, and reason as the guiding precepts of dialogue. And even though consensual decision-making cannot ignore the material constraints that shape the flow of dialogue and act as barriers to the realization of whatever goals are mutually agreed, looking to the use of a very public form of reasoning for verification, authentication, and legitimation is a tremendous progressive step in the history of financial governance at the global level. It helps to promote ownership and inclusion among both decision-makers and decision-takers, thereby enhancing the effective implementation of decisions on a broader scale.

---

[7] One might argue that the formation of the FSF itself, and possibly the G20, was also the product of such a consensual approach, although they met different national interests as well.

All decision-making occurs within a context however, and what is interesting about the new global financial architecture is that it has emerged alongside another significant development: a global financial public sphere. James Bohman has defined a "public sphere" as an institutionalized arena of discourse and dialogue where issues of public concern are considered and addressed within a context of specific audiences able to engage in social, cultural, and political criticism, and in which a certain form of public reasoning holds sway (Bohman, 1998; 1999a).[8] This definition adapts the understanding of the public sphere made prominent by Jürgen Habermas and critically extended by others (Calhoun, 1996).[9] Its chief utility for our purpose lies in helping to explain how governance is actually achieved in a global financial system marked by decentralized globalization and the absence of a single financial hegemon. The signal advantage of the idea of a "public sphere" for the global sphere is that it illuminates some of the key mechanisms through which decision-making is pursued under conditions of decentralized consensus formation, which I have elsewhere argued is precisely the contemporary condition of the global financial system (Germain, 1997; 2002).

We may identify the global financial public sphere as an enabling environment anchored by the interaction of four key globally institutionalized configurations of power. It is important to recognize that none of these configurations of power exist in and of themselves solely within a public sphere; rather the public sphere is constructed out of their many and multiple interactions. I would identify these configurations of power as a government-led institutional framework at the global level, the global operation of financial markets, a global media, and what many now call civil society (Scholte and Schnabel, 2002). It is within this environment that the principal operational features of a global financial public sphere are becoming instantiated, namely clear modes of public reasoning, a plurality of participants, and a growing critical reciprocity between participants. Figure 3.2 schematically represents the global financial public sphere as an interactive set of institutionalized configurations of power. I will take each element of the public sphere in turn.

---

[8] There are many other foundational elements central to the consolidation and operation of a "public sphere," such as equality among participants, nonuse of force, indefinite audiences, etc. For purposes of space I will touch on these only as required for the argument (for extended discussions, see Bohman, 1999a; Fraser, 1996; Cochran, 2001).

[9] I am for the moment ignoring the republican and pragmatic formulations of the public provided by Hannah Arendt and John Dewey (see Cochran, 2001; Hohendahl, 1996; Benhabib, 1996).

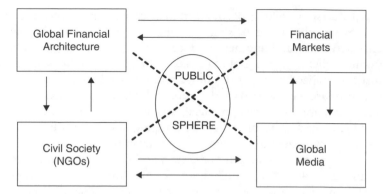

Figure 3.2 The structure of financial governance (Figure originally published in the journal *Global Society* 18(3), by Taylor & Francis, 2004. Used with permission.)

The global financial public sphere is anchored in the first instance around a complex institutional framework that enables dialogue and communication to occur within the context of policy development. This institutional framework has been identified in Figure 3.1, and comprises the key institutions that transform what might otherwise remain simply a public "space" – a space purely for dialogue, or a *weak public* in Nancy Fraser's terminology (Fraser, 1996, p. 132) – into an operational sphere where actual decisions are made. The complex division of labor at the heart of the global architecture of financial governance – which encompasses the key public authorities in their individual and collective formulations (i.e., as the US *and* the G7, for example) – both debates and makes policies. It is a "strong public" (Fraser, 1996, pp. 132–6) insofar as this is where the major discussions about the future shape and operational imperatives of global finance develop.

This "strong public" is further anchored in the second instance around the operation of global financial markets. Why should we think of financial markets as part of the public sphere? The first part of our answer is that markets are important channels of information with regard to issues that are central to financial governance. They are often also "public" channels of information, so that in effect they provide information which can be used to help evaluate competing claims about the scope and impact of actually existing financial governance. Markets provide important clues to the effective achievement of financial governance. The second part of our answer is that markets help to produce and shape the organizations which are the objects of governance. They produce the actors that governments are in fact trying to govern. As such, markets have a crucial role to play in the evolution of the financial institutions that form in effect the terrain of governance. These institutions in turn attempt to shape and direct the exercise of financial governance, and in many ways are active participants in the government-led institutional framework outlined in Figure 3.1.

The third anchor point for the global financial public sphere is the global media. The media (principally television, radio, and print, but increasingly also internet-based outlets) is one of the key mechanisms promoting communication and exchange within the public sphere. Significant here is the growth in the interest in and reporting of financial issues, among both the financial press and the more broadly focused popular press. The widespread impact of financial crises together with the sheer number of near-meltdowns since the 1992 ERM debacle, as well as the consequences of high-profile bankruptcies like Enron and WorldCom, have brought home to the general public the stake they have in the general health of the financial system. It is important to note, however, that the media on its own does not necessarily promote a public sphere (Bohman, 1999a). Rather, it both makes possible a wider audience and helps to educate that audience by making it more financially literate. In this sense the media is crucial in the dissemination of a mode of public reasoning which subjects established views to critical engagement. And while we must be alert to the place of the media within the contours of the material interests of the global economy (most media outlets are owned by transnational corporate interests such as that controlled by Rupert Murdoch, for example), the sheer diversity of media outlets does enable contestation and struggle to inform a broader public debate. In other words the media in all its forms is a key medium through which debate about financial governance proceeds.

The final configuration of power around which the global financial public sphere is anchored might be termed civil society, or more exactly the organizations which many have identified as belonging to civil society (Scholte and Schnabel, 2002). These are organizations that neither fall formally under the rubric of government nor are fully active in markets. Rather they are non-state and noncommercial actors that – starting from a variety of motivational purposes – attempt to influence the arrangements of financial governance in directions that are consistent with their core principles.[10] They range from those formally linked to religious organizations to organizations of conscience to broad-based social

---

[10] I use the term noncommercial rather than non-market because some associations that are usually categorized as civil society organizations represent commercial firms even if

movements to oppositional organizations that exist in contest with either government agencies or market-based institutions (Scholte, 2002a). These organizations engage in the debate over financial governance primarily either by seeking to influence governments and intergovernmental institutions directly or through mass protest, or sometimes both. They contribute to the anchoring of a public sphere precisely because they have become part of the intended audience of the world's financial discourse.[11]

By embedding the officially led financial architecture into this broader ensemble of governance, we obtain a representation of decision-making which illustrates both the increased *publicness* of financial governance and the ambiguous role of coercion in financial arrangements. Accountability emerges as a significant attribute of decision-making precisely because under a consensus-dominated system of decision-making the accountability of rule-makers to rule-takers is a key factor in the ownership of rules by makers and takers alike. Simply put, making rules for all without their input into the process of rule-making compromises the legitimacy of the established rules. It is within this context that strategies for strengthening accountability can be discussed.

Strengthening accountability

Enabling trajectories

The previous discussion of the structure of global financial governance establishes that we have a newly emergent governance structure which both builds upon the historical legacies of the Bretton Woods era and takes the financial system in new directions. The decision-making mechanisms at the heart of governance today are more internationalized than in the past. The different agencies involved – at both the national and multilateral level – are more clearly aware of where their jurisdictions overlap and where they remain distinct. And the role of financial institutions in the broader economy, in particular what constitutes healthy or prudentially run institutions, is much more advanced now than it was prior to the Asian crisis. Each of these developments – more inclusive decision-making, better communication between agencies, and a clearer understanding of the prerequisites of healthy financial systems – allows for the pursuit of certain kinds of strategies to strengthen accountability.

---

the organizations themselves do not engage in commercial activities, such as business associations for example.
[11] This point has been corroborated among a wide set of interviews across G7 and emerging market institutions.

The extension of interstate cooperation with the formation of the Financial Stability Forum and the G20, for example, has brought emerging markets into some of the key consensus-formation institutions of global finance, those that help to determine the broad structure of incentives that guides all individual financial institutions. For the first time emerging market economies have a formalized input into the construction and creation of standards and codes which the wider community uses as key international benchmarks.[12] This access should not of course be misconstrued as veto power, or anything other than a formal seat at the negotiating table, but neither should it be completely dismissed as irrelevant or tangential (cf. Strange, 1998; Gill, 2003). In the longer term the development of a more inclusive decision-making structure will enable the accountability of developed economies to emerging markets and their particular needs and demands to be strengthened, even if only slowly (Stiglitz, 2002).

The development of better levels of communication concerning financial matters has had the benefit of clarifying who does what at the global level. Successive financial crises have sharpened the lines of responsibility among regulators and others, enabling them to more clearly ascertain the ongoing financial health of commercial institutions. This of course should not be overstated, insofar as commercial institutions will always be one or two steps ahead of regulators, and unanticipated developments always have at least the potential to overwhelm governments. Nevertheless, lines of communication both among public authorities and between them and their populations are today much better developed, enabling a higher level of debate about relevant issues to occur. Accountability in such a world is more easily traced and placed under careful examination, simply because there are fewer dark corners in which to hide. Put quite starkly, from an historical perspective, more is known today about decisions taken by public authorities than ever before. The contribution of the public sphere to this development should not be underestimated, since it is the very publicness of financial debate today that helps to enable a broader consensus to develop.

Finally, the state of knowledge about both sound financial systems and prudentially run financial institutions is more advanced today than even five years ago. The debate over capital-account liberalization, for example, has clearly been resolved in favor of careful sequencing, while the level of prudential supervision is now recognized as crucial to the

---

[12] These include Singapore, Hong Kong, and Australia in the case of the FSF, and in the case of the G20 it includes Argentina, Australia, Brazil, China, India, Mexico, Russia, Saudi Arabia, South Africa, South Korea, and Turkey.

overall health of the financial system. Furthermore, in part due to the existence of better systems of communication, this knowledge is increasingly widely diffused. This development has been reinforced through the drive of many civic organizations, who have helped to focus their expert knowledge on important issues such as the ongoing effects of sovereign debt, or the catastrophic consequences of clinging to an overvalued fixed exchange rate (Scholte, 2002b). The diffusion of knowledge means that the workings of the financial system are more clearly visible, and that expertise paradoxically is more widely shared among all contributors to financial debates. This enables those in positions of power to be more clearly held to account for their actions (or inactions); in other words it provides a tool for strengthened accountability.

Taken together, a more inclusive decision-making structure, more visible lines of communication, and a more widely diffused knowledge about the organization of credit have created an environment within which the possibility of strengthening accountability within the broader ensemble of global financial governance has become a very real possibility. But it is equally clear that such accountability cannot role back vertical lines of accountability in favor of horizontal lines of accountability, and that it cannot undo the newly developed statutory independence of regulatory agencies. Instead, strategies are required that work within existing knowledge parameters to strengthen in a practical way the delivery of accountability among those institutions that actually govern finance. But at the same time it must be an accountability that neither privileges elites at the expense of more popular forces nor erodes basic democratic claims at the national level. In other words, it must be an accountability organized around a logic of participation rather than a logic of compliance. Within the context of present circumstances, two strategies suggest themselves.

Practical strategies

The first strategy is to more clearly "internalize accountability" within the institutions that govern finance. There are two aspects to this strategy. First, the accountability which institutions have to the broader population can be strengthened if a broader cross-section of those populations were able to be represented within the decision-making levels of these institutions themselves. For example, more sociologists and political scientists should be on the research staff of central banks, or industrialists and psychologists on the research staff at regulatory agencies. The point here is to provide mechanisms for broader points of view to be engaged with at the point of decision-making itself – to internalize debate within institutions in order to help make them more accountable to broader currents of thought and points of view. In this way important institutions cannot so easily be captured by the vested interests they regulate. Similarly, international institutions like the IMF, World Bank, or Bank for International Settlements could also internalize dissent in a more proactive manner, forcing a wider engagement upon those maintaining established views.[13]

Regular outreach programs would also be a helpful corollary to the above departure. Accountability is compromised when the debate and negotiation upon which it is based lacks a critical reciprocity between contending parties. While it may be true that to a certain extent all decisions create winners and losers, where losers understand their input to have been unfairly treated and not genuinely accepted, acquiescence or acceptance is grudging and compromised. Outreach can help to defray that sense of being shut out, and also hold out the possibility of helping to influence change via contributions to a genuinely rational debate. Internalizing accountability more thoroughly within those institutions that govern finance does hold out the prospect of helping to address the accountability deficit within the broader ensemble of financial governance.[14]

A more important strategy for strengthening accountability, however, lies in consolidating the emergent global financial public sphere. This can be accomplished via a number of means. One means is to extend the growing transparency of information concerning public finances to the private sector, so that institutional involvement in speculative financial transactions is more readily apparent. While critics of transparency have rightfully focused on the asymmetrical pressures that transparency can produce, they have at the same time downplayed the utility of increased transparency for the monitoring of private sector developments, and have perhaps unfairly confused a desire for information with neo-liberal disciplining (Best, 2003; Gill, 2003). Disciplining and its internalization

---

[13] In advocating this strategy I am not saying that these institutions are permanently closed to outside, non-mainstream views; rather that they stand to benefit significantly from internalizing dissent in a more proactive manner.

[14] The BIS has created a strong outreach program by establishing resident offices in Hong Kong and Mexico City, and by undertaking regular consultations with member central banks on a regional basis. The IMF and World Bank offer similar outreach programs. The suggestion here, however, is to take this outreach program one step further and involve in a systematic and meaningful way civic organizations and affected parties, those whose consensual involvement in the development of policies would enable ownership and inclusion to become more widespread and deep-rooted.

can work in two directions, and transparency can be made into a weapon of power in the hands of the weak.

Another means by which the public sphere can be strengthened requires concerted government action, namely to create clear forums in which dissent and contestation of established views can take place. One of the most important features of a public sphere is its reliance on public modes of reasoning to build consensus behind decision-making (Bohman, 1999a). One of the most powerful arguments concerning the deplorable state of contemporary global governance is its capture by vested commercial and class interests, most notably American (Strange, 1998; Pauly, 1999; Underhill, 2000; Gill, 2003). The pernicious element of such "capture" can be both exposed and addressed through a well-functioning public sphere, precisely because the publicity attendant to the public sphere can make visible the distribution of costs and benefits within the existing international organization of credit. Without a public sphere this distribution is less visible, harder to expose, and therefore more enduring.

Such public forums could initially at least take one of two forms. The "town hall" model would establish rotating meetings of concerned parties to create and maintain a dialogue on issues that public authorities would have to respond to in order to justify their stances within the prevailing structure of governance. These would be organized, funded, and run by national governments, but with the input and support of concerned parties. Public justification is a key element of the public sphere, and where this justification is itself open to engagement and criticism – to a public mode of reasoning – a more genuinely participatory system has a greater chance of emerging.

The appointment of a dedicated commissioner or other-named officer to canvass and mobilize public opinion on global financial matters – much in the tradition of Commissioners for children or for human rights – is another model to follow. This officer would be charged with creating and maintaining public debate on global financial issues to inform and engage with government policy. As with the previous model, such an office would become a crucial part of the infrastructure of a financial public sphere. Such an office would have to be independent of the executive, however, in order to have the authority and stature to provide government with contrary advice on its policies.

With either model, a public sphere that enables those with a stake in the financial system to engage in debates that shape the structure of incentives to which financial institutions respond becomes more clearly instantiated. This will have knock-on effects in terms of the broader ensemble of governance, helping to make a participatory governance structure more possible. And where genuine participation increases, there also follows a more robust sense of accountability. It is in this sense that participation, accountability, representation, and legitimacy are in the long term linked.

Rethinking accountability?

There is without doubt an accountability gap within the structure of global financial governance. It exists not only within formal multilateral institutions but also more broadly across the entire fabric of financial governance. Furthermore, the barriers to stronger horizontal accountability will not disappear; indeed, the trend towards granting those institutions responsible for financial regulation increased statutory independence will strengthen them in important ways. What is needed therefore is to rethink the logic of accountability, shifting its central core from a logic of monitoring and compliance to one of participation and reciprocity.

The basis for this rethink already exists. The governance structure of finance is now more inclusive than at any time prior to 1999, with emerging market economies and their public authorities increasingly involved in a genuine manner across a broader range of consensual incentive-building activities. These activities and their consequences are more widely communicated both to the authorities involved and to a larger and more financially literate cross-section of the population. Such extended communication facilitates a wider and deeper debate about the core principles around which financial systems and their incentives are structured. And finally the state of knowledge about finance more generally is more advanced than pre-1997. The evidence of that catastrophic experience has been accepted as genuine by all major participants in these debates, and has helped to shape a new baseline from which discussions concerning capital mobility, capital account liberalization, and prudential supervision proceed.

Thinking about accountability in terms of participation and reciprocity, however, demands that the enabling foundation for participation be deepened. Governments must therefore move to consolidate the emergent global financial public sphere that has enabled a more genuine participation of emerging market economies and civic organizations to occur. This means helping to internalize accountability within key governance institutions by ensuring that dissent and a critical engagement across a range of politically contentious issues are allowed to occur *within these institutions themselves*. It also means that participation must be based upon adequate representation of those with a genuine stake in the consequences of decision-making. Without such representation it is unlikely that the norms and principles produced by international decision-making mechanisms will be internalized outside of the mature financial systems of the developed world. This will lead to declining legitimacy for the governance structure as a whole.

Some might argue that global capitalism is of course incapable of developing a more progressive structure of financial governance. The ideational homogeneity of the Washington consensus itself acts as a barrier to achieving even the modest reforms offered above. This is a powerful argument, but it is weakened both by adopting an historical perspective and by following through on the logic of the public sphere. In historical terms, global capitalism has on more than one occasion demonstrated its unique capacity to embrace reform, not only to prevent its demise but more importantly to bring in a wider set of stakeholders and to distribute its rewards among a broader cross-section of the world's population (Maddison, 2001). More significantly, the deepening of the public sphere and the strengthening of the debate over financial issues which this makes possible, will help to partially decouple the exercise of power from the deployment of language and reason. In other words strengthening the public sphere will further instantiate what Bohman (1999a) identifies as a public mode of reasoning. In this circumstance the specialist financial knowledge – which has heretofore acted as a barrier to accountability – might possibly be turned on its head and diffused to a wider set of stakeholders better able to deploy argument and reason in pursuit of their own interests and needs. The need for specialist knowledge remains, but its diffusion through the public sphere unlocks its potential and makes it an enabling rather than a disabling tool of financial governance.

We are once again therefore faced with the impossibility of separating accountability concerns from the broader problematic of governance at the global level. Adequate accountability without representation is not possible, and justice without representation is difficult to conceive. Governance without either representation or justice would not be legitimate, and history demonstrates that illegitimate governance will inevitably collapse because its effectiveness cannot be maintained over the long term. The link between all of these elements of governance is adequate levels of participation to ensure that those with a stake in the proceedings feel themselves to be genuine participants in the process. Global financial governance therefore needs to more clearly pose the question of how such participation can be rendered so that genuine and adequate accountability is served. This is a key agenda for the twenty-first century, and one that all institutions involved in financial governance must address.

References

Armijo, Leslie Elliott (ed.) (1999) *Financial Globalization and Democracy in Emerging Markets*. London: Palgrave.

Benhabib, Seyla (1996) "Models of Public Space: Hannah Arendt, the Liberal Tradition, and Jürgen Habermas," in Calhoun (1996).

Best, Jacqueline (2003) "The Politics of Transparency: Ambiguity and the Liberalization of International Finance," in James Busumtwi-Sam and Laurent Dobuzinskis (eds.) *Turbulence and New Directions in Global Political Economy*. London: Palgrave.

Bohman, James (1999a) "Citizenship and Norms of Publicity: Wide Public Reasoning in Cosmopolitan Societies," *Political Theory* 27(2), 176–202.

Bohman, James (1999b) "International Regimes and Democratic Governance: Political Equality and Influence in Global Institutions," *International Affairs* 75(3), 499–513.

Bohman, James (1998) "The Globalization of the Public Sphere," *Philosophy and Social Criticism* 24(2/3), 199–216.

Calhoun, Craig (ed.) (1996) *Habermas and the Public Sphere*. Cambridge, MA: MIT Press.

Carr, E. H. (1961) *What is History*. London: Penguin.

Cochran, Molly (2001) "Conceptualizing International Public Spheres," Paper delivered to the annual conference of the International Studies Association, Chicago (USA).

Collingwood, R. G. (1946) *The Idea of History*. Oxford: Clarendon Press.

Cox, Robert (1983) "Gramsci, Hegemony and International Relations: An Essay in Method," *Millennium* 12(2): 162–75.

Cox, Robert (1981) "Social Forces, States and World Orders: Beyond International Relations Theory," *Millennium* 10(2), 126–55.

Dahl, Robert (1999) "Can International Organizations be Democratic? A Skeptic's View," in Ian Shapiro and Casiano Haker-Cordón (eds.) *Democracy's Edges*. Cambridge University Press.

Eichengreen, Barry (2002) *Financial Crises and What to do About Them*. Oxford University Press.

Fraser, Nancy (1996) "Rethinking the Public Sphere: A Contribution to the Critique of Actually Existing Democracy," in Calhoun (1996).

Germain, Randall (2002) "The Emerging Structure of Financial Governance: The Value of an Historical-Institutionalist Perspective," Paper delivered to the annual meeting of the British International Studies Association, London, 16–18 December.

Germain, Randall (2001) "Global Financial Governance and the Problem of Inclusion," *Global Governance* 7(1), 411–26.

Germain, Randall (2000) "E. H. Carr and the Historical Mode of Thought," in Michael Cox (ed.) *E. H. Carr: A Critical Appraisal*. London: Palgrave.

Germain, Randall (1997) *The International Organization of Credit*. Cambridge University Press.

Gill, Stephen (2003) *Power and Resistance in the New World Order*. London: Palgrave.

Hardt, Michael and Antonio Negri (2000) *Empire*. Cambridge, MA: Harvard University Press.

Hohendahl, Peter Uwe (1996) "The Public Sphere: Models and Boundaries," in Calhoun (1996).

Krueger, Anne (1 April 2002) "New Approaches to Sovereign Debt Rescheduling: An Update on our Thinking," Address given to conference on "Sovereign Debt Workouts." Institute for International Economics. Available at www.iie.com/papers/krueger0402.htm.

Maddison, Angus (2001) *The World Economy: A Millennial Perspective*. Paris: OECD.

Pauly, Louis W. (1999) "Good Governance and Bad Policy: The Perils of International Organization Overextension," *Review of International Political Economy* 6(4), 401–24.

Perraton, Jonathan (2000) "What are Global Markets? The Significance of Networks of Trade," in Randall D. Germain (ed.) *Globalization and Its Critics*. London: Palgrave.

Porter, Tony (2001) "The Democratic Deficit in the Institutional Arrangements for Regulating Global Finance," *Global Governance* 7(4), 427–39.

Scholte, Jan Aart (2002a) "Civil Society and Democracy in Global Governance," *Global Governance* 8(3), 281–304.

Scholte, Jan Aart (2002b) "Civil society and the Governance of Global Finance," in Scholte and Schnabel (2002).

Scholte, Jan Aart and Albrecht Schnabel (eds.) (2002) *Civil Society and Global Finance*. London: Routledge.

Sorel, Georges (1950/1908) *Reflections on Violence*. Trans. T. E. Hulme. New York: Collier Books.

Stiglitz, Joseph (2002) *Globalization and Its Discontents*. New York: W.W. Norton and Company.

Strange, Susan (1998) *Mad Money*. Manchester University Press.

Underhill, Geoffrey (2000) "The Public Good Versus Private Interests in the Global Monetary and Financial System," *International and Comparative Corporate Law Journal* 2(3), 335–59.

Vico, Giambattista (1968/1744) *The New Science of Giambattista Vico*. Trans. T. G. Bergin and M. H. Fisch. Ithaca, NY: Cornell University Press.

Yam, Joseph (1997) "Asian Monetary Cooperation," *BIS Review*, at www.bis.org. Accessed 28 November 2002.

4   Citizen activism and public accountability: lessons from case studies in India [1]

Anne Marie Goetz and Rob Jenkins

A central problem of accountability in public institutions is how to structure citizen participation so that it is meaningful, rather than token, and so that it extends beyond the exercise of "voice" and towards concrete influence over decision-making and enforcement. Both of the preceding chapters in this book closed with an invocation for greater participation. Woods pointed to the need for people in developing countries to have more influence in setting development priorities, and Germain suggested that a key challenge for institutions of financial governance in the twenty-first century will be to operationalize participation in order to achieve "genuine" accountability.

This chapter begins to address this challenge by presenting two cases of citizen activism in India where notable gains in public accountability through participation have been achieved. These are municipal and state-level experiences, and thus cannot easily be translated into implications for global institutions for reasons already elaborated in this volume. However, if accountability is to be built from the bottom up, these cases provide an empirical opening.

Introduction

Aid and development organizations have in recent years funded a large number of anti-corruption commissions, auditors-general, human rights machineries, legislative public-accounts committees, and sectoral regulatory agencies in developing countries. They are institutions of "horizontal accountability" – state agencies that monitor other organs of the state. Their reform has been a central concern of contemporary "good governance" policies. Low levels of public confidence in horizontal mechanisms of accountability in most developing countries have

---

[1] This chapter is an updated and abridged version of an article that appeared in *Public Management Review* (2001), 3(3), 363–83. Used with permission. Taylor & Francis Ltd, www.tandf.co.uk/journals.

persisted alongside growing dissatisfaction with limitations on the effectiveness of "vertical" forms of accountability, which include both the individual citizen's exercise of electoral choice and the collective exertion of pressure by civil society organizations. Vertical accountability systems suffer from many shortcomings, among which is their tendency to blunt the impact of citizen "voice."

To date, efforts to rectify problems of horizontal and vertical accountability have proceeded independently of one another. The focus has been on strengthening the performance of each axis, based on a fairly clear division of labor between the two. Thus, development organizations have supported horizontal accountability by reorganizing audit and account mechanisms, and worked towards improvements in vertical accountability by funding electoral reform and voter-awareness initiatives, as well as encouraging consultation in policy formulation that allow civic groups greater access to decision-making processes. This has had the unintended effect of preserving the specialized and distinct roles to which political convention has assigned vertical and horizontal accountability systems.

It is in this context that this chapter explores two cases of civic activism in India that challenge the vertical–horizontal dichotomy around which accountability is usually conceived. The two organizations at the center of these case studies adopted approximations of the methods normally associated with official state institutions of horizontal accountability, before initiating dialogue with different arms of the state in an effort to insert themselves more directly into this horizontal axis. This chapter argues that the work of these civic groups represents a hybrid form of accountability that bridges the vertical–horizontal divide – a form of direct citizen engagement that both mimics and prods improvements to intrastate accountability functions.

The first of our two cases is the Rationing Kruti Samiti (RKS), a coalition of NGOs and other social action groups working mainly among slum-dwellers in the Indian city of Mumbai (formerly Bombay). Since 1992, the RKS has been mobilizing people to pressure officials to improve the operation of the city's Public Distribution System (PDS), a network of privately operated but publicly subsidized and supplied "ration shops" through which a range of mainly food items are made available to poorer citizens. Acting as a form of collective pressure on the state, the RKS in many respects pursued conventional channels of vertical accountability. But the RKS realized early on that protest action was insufficient given the scale and complexity of corruption in the PDS. Official monitoring systems – the mechanisms of horizontal accountability – were manifestly failing. Through a partnership with a network of reform-minded officials, the RKS responded by, for a time, inserting its network of grassroots associations directly into official processes of oversight through which corruption in the PDS is supposed to be curbed. The RKS experience is based not only on the belief, common to many organizations representing marginalized social groups, that improved systems of vertical accountability require more organizational activity among the poor, but more importantly, on a conviction that responsive service delivery requires people's access to conventionally closed bureaucratic systems of horizontal accountability.

The second case study centers on the work of the Mazdoor Kisan Shakti Sangathan (MKSS), which like the RKS seeks to insert citizens and their associations directly into oversight functions – in this case relating to financial auditing – that have long been performed exclusively by government entities, such as the Comptroller and Auditor General of India. Beginning in the mid-1990s, the MKSS conducted participatory audits of local-government projects based on official expenditure records obtained informally from bureaucrats. It then succeeded in getting the state government to change the Local Government Act to include local residents directly in auditing official development schemes.

These and other cases of citizen activism represent a shift towards augmenting the effectiveness of civil society's watchdog function by breaking the state's monopoly of key oversight functions such as financial auditing and project appraisal. While we do not contend that this phenomenon of citizen engagement in horizontal accountability institutions is particularly widespread, the case studies explored here offer insights into how citizens might prompt more satisfactory performance from state authorities – or even encourage enforcement action against officials who engage in manifestly poor decision-making or outright corrupt behavior. We conclude with a reflection on the daunting obstacles to this new hybrid form of accountability, including the state's tendency to neutralize citizen efforts to engage in horizontal accountability processes by offering civic groups opportunities for *ex ante* consultation as a substitute for the ability to engage in *ex post* accountability.

The place of civil society in accountability institutions

It is widely agreed that contemporary democracies,[2] North and South, face a "crisis of accountability." The World Bank's massive "Consultations

[2] We restrict this discussion to democracies. Accountability problems are of course much more blatant in authoritarian regimes. In this chapter we begin with states that have formal

with the Poor" exercise concluded that "[f]rom the perspectives of poor people world wide, there is a crisis in governance ... State institutions, whether represented by central ministries or local government are often neither responsive nor accountable to the poor ... Poor people see little recourse to injustice, criminality, abuse and corruption by institutions" (Narayan et al., 2000, p. 172).[3] In both the North and South, short-comings in conventional accountability systems – secrecy in auditing, ineffective legislative oversight mechanisms, electoral systems that fail to reflect voter preferences, excessive delays in courts, and inadequate sanctions for administrative abuses – have fueled demands for improved channels of vertical information flows and stronger accountability relationships between state agents and citizens.

Accountability can perhaps best be thought of as a relationship between two actors that is characterized by *answerability* (the requirement that one actor justify his actions) and *enforcement* (the right granted to the other actor to impose penalties if these actions, or the justification thereof, are deemed unsatisfactory) (Schedler, 1999). Accountability is often seen as operating along two dimensions, the vertical and the hor-izontal. The "vertical" relationship between citizens and the state can be either formal (through electoral systems) or informal (though lobbying and public advocacy by civic associations). The "horizontal" relationship involves one public authority scrutinizing the activities of another – for instance, legislative oversight of executive agencies, or the judiciary checking that public authorities have not exceeded their legal mandates. Alternatively, horizontal accountability can involve specialized autho-rities (ombudsmen, anti-corruption agencies, auditors-general) investi-gating charges of malfeasance, and if necessary triggering enforcement action (O'Donnell, 1999).

A deeply entrenched convention in this separation of "vertical" and "horizontal" systems of accountability is a differentiation between the types of actors who may legitimately demand accountability and participate in formal accountability processes. In "vertical" channels of accountability, citizens – as voters or participants in civic associations – are the designated seekers of accountability. Horizontal channels of accountability, on the other hand, limit participation to state actors: the judiciary, civil servants, elected politicians, officially appointed auditors. This convention supports a principle common to all horizontal accountability functions: the main-tenance of the public sector worker's remoteness from citizens and

---

vertical and horizontal institutions for accountability, and in which civil society has relative freedom to engage critically with the state. This implies democracy of some kind.
[3] We are indebted to John Gaventa for bringing this quote to our attention.

associations, and indeed disregard of information not obtained through the procedures stipulated in the legislative acts under which they operate. Bureaucrats, auditors, and judges are insulated from citizens and politicians precisely to guard against too much responsiveness to particular interests. However, the protestation that public servants must remain "neutral" is often an excuse for restricting public scrutiny of their actions and denying responsibility for their mistakes. The formal and informal institutions that insulate officials from citizens, such as official secrecy laws, the use of non-vernacular or impenetrably technical languages, or the physical distance of government offices from ordinary people, also helps to conceal the abuse of public office for private gain.

Of course, direct citizen engagement in official accountability processes is not without precedent. In long-established constitutional democracies, such as India and the USA, citizens have used their right to litigate to, in some cases, obtain rulings which serve to break down the vertical–horizontal accountability divide and bring citizens directly into what were once closed official processes (Grant, 1997). Of particular note is the experience of Public Interest Litigation (PIL), sometimes referred to as Social Action Litigation in the Indian context. Since the early 1980s, the number and visibility of PIL cases has expanded enormously. A series of landmark decisions by India's Supreme Court established the principle that the judiciary was morally required and constitutionally mandated to increase its responsiveness to citizen requests for investigative (and, if warranted, remedial) action in relation to the detailed performance of specific government agencies, including the police, service-delivery ministries, and pollution-control boards.

Public-interest litigation itself represents a kind of template for the activism that has driven the creation of hybrid forms of accountability. While the judiciary is clearly an institution of public oversight, operating in the mode of horizontal accountability, when adjudicating public-interest cases brought by members of the public, the judiciary's orientation shifts to allow it to act as a mediator between the otherwise incommensurable vertical and horizontal axes of accountability. It is through judicial proceedings that citizens can begin entering the horizontal process of in-depth monitoring of government: using the tools available through litigation, individual citizens and activist groups become, in effect, part of an official fact-finding process. Discovery motions, for instance, lead to the availability of government-held information that can incriminate officials who never expected such detailed scrutiny of their decisions.

Now a familiar feature of India's institutional landscape, PIL has substantially legitimized the notion of direct citizen engagement with issues of executive oversight. PIL has shown that it is possible for citizen-litigants to engage directly – and indeed monitor the performance of – horizontal accountability institutions. Citizens and their associations thus become active demanders of answerability in a forum that carries the weight of enforcement. This combination of answers and sanctions is precisely what most citizen-initiated approaches to hybrid account-ability aim to achieve.

There are, however, daunting barriers to the effective use of PIL, particularly by poor people. These barriers include cost, time, biases in the courts, and the near-impossibility of having favorable decisions implemented by a hostile bureaucracy. The cases discussed in this chapter demonstrate citizen efforts to engage with accountability pro-blems at the level of service delivery. The RKS has inserted itself into oversight of the performance of the Public Distribution System, while the MKSS has sought to substitute for failing official financial accountability mechanisms which should, in theory, be monitoring local development spending. Both cases are notable for involving poor people themselves in the process of scrutinizing how state agencies, *and the official bodies responsible for monitoring them*, have performed. This chal-lenges the widespread assumption that socially marginalized people lack either the skills or the capacity for collective action necessary to demand improvements in the quality of governance.

Mobilizing for food security: citizen-initiated vigilance committees in Maharashtra

The Rationing Kruti Samiti (RKS), or Action Committee for Rationing, based in Mumbai, was created in the wake of the widespread (mainly) Hindu–Muslim rioting that shook the city in December 1992. Its objec-tive was to improve the capacity of the Public Distribution System (PDS) – a national program to supply subsidized food and a few other basic commodities (notably kerosene) – to the poor. In Mumbai's enormous low-income, or slum, settlements, the PDS is a critical resource for the food security of the poor, particularly women, who manage house-hold food supplies. The PDS, despite its many successes in different parts of India, has over the years manifested a broad array of problems. It suffers from chronic management shortcomings concerning: the extent and timing of procurement, poor forecasting capacity, antiquated logis-tical systems, inappropriate product offerings, cost inefficiencies, poor-quality food grain, harassment of consumers at the point of client interface, and exclusion of large numbers of the poor from the system entirely.

Above all, there is the problem of "leakage" of grains supplied by the Food Corporation of India to the shop owners licensed by the state government's ministry of food and civil supplies to trade, at a stipulated profit, the commodities supplied at government-determined prices to holders of government-issued "ration cards." The illegal diversion of grain to the open market, through a highly institutionalized network of agents and middlemen, is a common practice, and severely undermines the capacity of the system to serve the needs of the poor. Widespread theft of supplies by the workers and managers who operate the vast network of PDS warehouses and fair-price shops means that poor consumers are faced with chronic shortages. Those products that are available are often adulterated to cover up leakages from stocks. In many areas, in order to obtain 5 kilograms of grain, consumers must agree to sign a shop register recording that they had received 10 kilograms. This again helps to fix the otherwise out-of-balance books produced by the shopkeepers' (and government supply agencies') continued theft of supplies. With such systemic problems plaguing the PDS it is not surprising that one of the RKS's main objectives was to plug these "leaks."

The RKS has lobbied and agitated for improved norms and procedures relating to the issuing of ration cards. To obtain a ration card, which should be provided free of charge, requires the payment of a substantial bribe. People are willing to pay for their ration card even though the cost sometimes exceeds the financial payoff in terms of subsidized food, because it also provides access to basic citizenship rights. Possession of a ration card is widely demanded by officials to verify identity and domicile. Without this form of identification, many public and private services would be unavailable. Seeking a ration card is thus a major preoccupation of many poor families.

To provide even a minimal food-security safety net in a vast city like Mumbai is an expensive proposition. Unwilling to devote resources from the state budget, as other state governments have done, to offset funding cuts created by the central government's de facto reduction in the per capita food subsidy during the 1990s, the Maharashtra government slowly chipped away at the universality of the system. Beginning in the mid-1990s, the system of ration-card allocation was "targeted" to eliminate access for middle-class families. In 1997, the government introduced a policy of issuing color-coded ration cards to different income groups, providing varying levels of rights to purchase cheap commodities. Yellow cards provided the greatest range of subsidies, but were also the hardest to obtain, as they required applicants to provide documentary proof that they fell below the poverty line. The discretion exercised by local rationing officials in issuing these cards is, of course, an important source of illicit income.

The PDS is, in theory, monitored and "performance audited" by official Vigilance Committees, chaired by the elected representative of the municipal ward in question, augmented by "concerned citizens." This arrangement bears a surface similarity to the idea of hybrid accountability introduced in the first two sections of this chapter. But these committees have been plagued by several defects. Appointment to the committees through a process of official selection increases the possibility of capture by the very political organizations that benefit from the forms of leakage outlined above. Moreover, committees have little access to information. And since many ration shops can function only thanks to the "protection" of local politicians, who themselves sit on the committees, citizen-members have little incentive to remain eternally vigilant. Shopkeepers also often sit on these committees, and do their best to undermine any monitoring initiatives.

One of the RKS's critical decisions as an advocacy organization – especially one built by already overburdened activists, heavily involved in managing clinics and childcare centers and helping slum-dwellers to avoid eviction – was to form parallel *informal* vigilance committees. These were composed of five women for each ration shop. These women were all PDS clients, and their concern was to track the amount and quality of subsidized commodities that arrived in their shops, and to monitor their sale to determine how much of the commodities had been illegally diverted to the private market by the shop owners and their accomplices. The RKS's initial strategy was to use its negotiating strength as a collective to establish a constructive relationship with public sector officials. Its success on this front peaked in an eighteen-month period between 1992 and 1994, during which an unusually reform-minded bureaucrat held the post of Regional Controller of Rationing (RCR). This senior position gave him a huge degree of influence over the system. The Controller granted the RKS's vigilance committees access to information about PDS deliveries, and established monthly meetings between the RKS and officials involved in the PDS. The RKS used these meetings as a means of informing officials about specific cases of malpractice that had been uncovered by its vigilance committees. The regular meetings, which systematically reviewed progress on various aspects of reform, were also used to push successfully for simplification of procedures at the shop level and the introduction of new products.

The partnership between the RKS and the officials responsible for the functioning of the PDS also led to new measures to improve product quality, including a requirement that distribution agents attach a sealed transparent sample of each commodity for each new delivery. This sample would indicate the quality of commodities *at the time of delivery*.

The purpose was to counter the practice of adulteration by shopkeepers or other intermediaries, in which kerosene is diluted, or rice mixed with sand, to disguise the theft of some portion of the original consignment. Physical evidence about the quality of the sample was important because it enabled illiterate consumers to identify differences between the quality of the original consignment from the government warehouses and the commodity that actually made it to the PDS sale counter. Official auditors could be alerted to these cases, and could then perform a more detailed probe of the shop's operations.

Under the system developed collaboratively between the then Regional Controller of Rationing, the RKS, shop owners' associations, and lower-level ration inspectors, each shopkeeper was required to post information about deliveries and the updated prices of commodities on a notice-board in the shop. This data would be reproduced in the official delivery register through which shops report to the rationing bureaucracy's internal oversight processes. Finally, the sales register – in which shopkeepers record transaction details next to the ration-card number of each purchaser – was made available for inspection by ordinary PDS customers. In principle these reforms meant that the RKS's informal vigilance committees could monitor the incoming commodities against what was sold. Access to records of actual sales was of particular importance, since shopkeepers disguise their sales to the open market by recording sales against nonexistent (or defunct) ration-card numbers, or (as noted above) by overstating the amount sold to an individual consumer. Many consumers have little choice but to conspire in this form of fraud for fear of souring their relationship with the shop owner, which could prove very costly for families on the economic margin.

The RKS's success during the early 1990s owed much to contingent factors: its actions coincided with a political crisis in which the bureaucracy needed to be seen to be responding to the poor after the 1992 riots, and with the appointment of a sympathetic Controller of Rationing. The Controller was able to use the RKS's activities to support much-needed reforms in this notoriously corrupt and under-resourced government service. He combined efforts to improve transparency, efficiency, and probity in the delivery and sale of subsidized commodities with efforts to improve working conditions for all staff, and to build a commitment to service delivery among the famously corrupt PDS staff. However, the reformist momentum was arrested when the Controller was transferred to another post, reportedly at the behest of politicians with an interest in returning to the status quo ante.

After the departure of this Controller in 1994, the relationship between the PDS bureaucracy and the RKS deteriorated, moving from "continued cooperation, through disinterest and opposition to down-right rejection of the credibility of the RKS as a networking group" (UNRISD, 1998, part II). The RKS continued to try to enforce the transparency-related changes achieved during the 1992–4 era, but without official support, the RKS's women's committees found it difficult to monitor PDS shops effectively. Interestingly, few of the reforms instituted by the previous Controller were formally rescinded. Records of deliveries to each shop remained available, but only for a fee, and the format in which the data was presented made it useless to the RKS vigilance committees, whose literacy and numeracy skills were in any case weak. Shopkeepers found it easy to evade rules requiring them to post information on the quantity, quality, and price of deliveries, and blamed suppliers for not including the necessary transparency sample pouches.

In the end, this participatory monitoring partnership between civil society and the state was undermined by politics. Politicians were infuriated that their control over the PDS had been undermined by a bureaucrat and a group of CBOs. Without official support for its work, the RKS had to return to more conflictual but rather ad hoc tactics, such as citywide protest actions and sustained community pressure on individual shopkeepers. The RKS experience is at best a limited "success story." CBOs were able to coordinate their actions, mobilize ordinary people, against great odds, and in some localities even spur temporary improvements in the quality of service. The RKS also probably helped to forestall further destruction of the PDS by the reckless and incompetent government that ruled Maharashtra during the second half of the 1990s. Moreover, the RKS experience – particularly its pattern of engagement with issues, and its development of new methods – reveals three noteworthy features of citizen efforts to hold government agencies accountable.

First, a huge increase in resources for operational costs will be required in order to improve the effectiveness of citizen monitoring of an entity as large and diverse as India's PDS, which encompasses the public and private sectors and operates through agencies of the local, district, state, and central administrations. The slum-dweller women who served on the informal vigilance committees had plenty of incentive to try to make the PDS more effective. Their main problem – in addition to the power of patronage politics – was a dearth of resources, particularly the time needed to continuously monitor the PDS stores to check for the arrival of commodities. Women slum-dwellers often lack the technical skills for monitoring and audit. They lack the literacy and accounting skills needed to make sense of PDS records so as to track inconsistencies between amounts of goods delivered and sold. All the talk of self-help aside, it is hard to imagine these kinds of committees making any sustained impact without some kind of official assistance, whether from Indian charitable trusts, development agencies, or publicly budgeted funds. The latter would, of course, imply a further "officialization" of the civil society's engagement with mechanisms of direct oversight, a point to which we return in the conclusion.

Second, an initiative such as this one requires a corresponding effort to create incentives for the "street-level bureaucrats" – in this case the shopkeepers – to improve their performance. The RKS had not engaged seriously with the problem of raising incentives to shopkeepers for better performance. This is not very surprising, given the ill will between consumers and shop owners, some of whom have physically attacked customers who raise grievances or seek information (see Bhatt, 2000). But refusing to entertain the legitimate complaints of shop owners may be a tactical misjudgment. In late 2000, for instance, the RKS opposed a government proposal to double shopkeepers' commissions on the sale of subsidized goods to 10 percent (Bhatt, 2001, p. 8). This underlines the danger that civil society activism can "harden" in steadfast opposition to potentially workable solutions when a service-delivery system has undergone persistent, systematic decline.

Finally, to return to the theoretical plane, this case supports the proposition that efforts of citizens and their associations to participate in conventionally closed institutions of horizontal accountability help to support their work in the more traditional channels of vertical accountability, through which associations press for change in the operation of public services. The RKS's protest actions could mobilize large numbers of people mainly due to the RKS member-organizations' experience of participatory monitoring, which had galvanized public discontent and provided first-hand evidence of specific cases of malfeasance. In this sense, the RKS shares a key feature with the protagonists of the second case study under discussion.

We're all auditors now: the Rajasthan experience of public hearings

The management of public accounts tends to be a highly secretive affair because of the great political sensitivities involved in identifying sources of government revenue, collecting it, establishing expenditure priorities, and allocating funds to specific budget heads. But what comes after the budgeting and spending of funds – formal auditing – gets even less public attention, largely because the multiple levels of auditing are not fully grasped by most people. One form of auditing is to determine whether, according to government records, funds were indeed spent under the stipulated budget heads. For a more thorough assessment of government performance, however, auditors must also review financial records and investigate a sample of individual expenditure transactions, contacting recipients of funds to verify the amounts received, identifying other data sources that could corroborate or falsify the government's own record, and inspecting the physical assets allegedly created under public sector works programs. These are very time- and labor-intensive tasks.

Because these auditing functions concern the epicenter of corruption – where it is linked to operational fraud – it is normally closed to citizen involvement. Citizens have a great direct interest in how national and local funds are spent. But almost nowhere are citizens or their associations given access to information on, let alone a more substantive role in, formal auditing processes. Indeed, even in the far less sensitive area of expenditure *planning*, there is just a handful of experimental cases worldwide encouraging citizen involvement.[4] Citizen *auditing* strikes at the heart of bureaucratic discretion and the political power underlying it. Secrecy in the management of public expenditure – especially the audit function – helps to mask the use of public funds for personal advantage.

However, the experiment in popular auditing initiated by the MKSS in the state of Rajasthan focused on intimate details of specific transactions in public works schemes, and stressed the importance of direct citizen engagement in local-level auditing of public spending.[5] Citizen auditing is almost unheard of anywhere for several reasons. First, few countries offer citizens a statutory right to government-held information that is wide-ranging enough to provide access to the financial records of state agencies that detail ground-level public expenditure activity. Second, because citizen auditing can expose corruption and networks of privilege between bureaucrats and local elites, it is strongly resisted by administrators and politicians. It can, therefore, be a highly risky activity

---

[4] The most important of these are the participatory budgeting initiatives in Brazil (see next footnote). They should be distinguished from the gender-, poverty-, or environment-sensitive budget analysis methods that have been taken up with great vigor in, among other places, South Africa (see Budlender, 2000) and Canada, and have inspired similar efforts in Jamaica, Tanzania, Uganda, and Mozambique (Esim, 2000).

[5] This distinguishes it from the better-known examples of direct citizen participation in local expenditure planning, in particular the experiments with participatory budgeting in Brazil, where reviews are conducted by looking at aggregated data on expenditure. See Abers, 1998, and Avritzer, 2000.

for ordinary citizens, jeopardizing carefully cultivated patronage relationships they may have nurtured with people in positions of authority. Third, a minimum level of expertise in financial accounting is required to make sense of government budget documents. Finally, for citizen auditing to be effective, a capacity for generating independent information on government spending is needed if individual transactions buried within official accounts are to be verified or falsified.

The Rajasthan experiment in public audits of spending on local development works, led by a 1,000-person-strong self-defined "non-party political movement" called the Mazdoor Kisan Shakti Sangathan (MKSS), or Workers' and Farmers' Power Association, addresses each of these constraints on citizen auditing. It spearheaded a successful national campaign for the creation of a statutory right to information to enable citizens to access most non-defense-related documents held by government, including of course records of expenditure transactions. The MKSS also developed tools for analyzing accounts and making them accessible to illiterate people, while also establishing the importance of mobilization and solidarity to support the process of investigating and exposing specific instances of corruption.

The main tools for expenditure analysis and audit used by the MKSS are their dramatic, but infrequent public hearings (*jan sunwai*), which have been held periodically since 1994 in villages around the organization's base in Rajsamand district, located in the central part of the state. These hearings are the culmination of a methodology for reviewing local government accounts and determining whether funds were spent in the manner indicated in official records. Meticulous research is conducted in the weeks prior to the public hearing. The first step is to procure government expenditure accounts, including receipts for building materials purchased and employment-wage registers. Sometimes this information is given willingly by sympathetic bureaucrats; at other times, filching by low-level clerks connected with the MKSS has proven effective. The MKSS's implied threat of agitation and protest creates an incentive for at least some officials to cooperate.

The MKSS's team of activist "auditors" compares records of ostensible expenditures with hard evidence of actual spending. This evidence is gathered through interviews with workers and contractors on public-works schemes, as well as villagers who observe poor-quality work – such as excessive sand in cement, violations of building codes – or the complete absence of works promised. This is a painstaking process: citizen auditors must verify, for instance, that all day-laborers listed on an employment register for a particular public work were indeed involved in the work. The individuals listed on the daily registers are contacted and asked to recollect the number of days they worked on a particular project, the amount of work they accomplished, and what (or even whether) they were paid. Some workers have developed, with the help of the MKSS, methods for recording their work schedules for precisely this reason. Suppliers are asked to show their accounts and attest to the quality of materials supplied, the quantity supplied, and the amounts they were paid. Dossiers are compiled on every public work under investigation. These virtually reconstitute government accounts from scratch. This direct and intimate form of public audit enables a much more accurate investigation of local accounts than is possible in massive "paper" audits. Because the latter focus only on consistency within the documentation, and do not cross-check documentary sources against physical evidence or the testimony of local people, they cannot uncover the many small diversions of funds at the local level which can mean so much to poor people's livelihoods.

At the MKSS's public hearings, held in large cloth tents in village squares and town markets, the relevant details of questionable public-works schemes are read aloud to the largely illiterate assembly. For each work under examination, individual local residents identified in the pre-hearing research phase as having relevant testimony are invited by the MKSS moderators to inform the meeting of whether their own experience, observation, or knowledge of a specific transaction is at variance with the officially recorded version. For instance, did each of the workers on the drainpipe installation project on the main road get paid Rs 50 per day, as stated in the employment register signed by the foreman and approved by junior officials in the relevant administrative agency? The names of individual laborers listed on these registers are read aloud, and those present will often step forward to recount the actual payments received. The mainly women workers on drought-relief public-works programs, on which the MKSS's auditing work has focused, often discover that the portion of their wage which they had been denied on the grounds of insufficient public funds had in fact been divided between the head of the village council (the *sarpanch*) and the junior engineer and supervisor overseeing the schemes on behalf of the department of public works. Others may discover that they had been listed as beneficiaries of anti-poverty schemes but had never received the job opportunities or subsidized housing which was their due. Or the collective may discover that names of nonexistent or dead villagers had been used to pad out the beneficiary lists of anti-poverty schemes to create a reserve to be drained by village politicians and bureaucrats.

This very public, and collective, form of speaking out – into a microphone in front of hundreds of people, some engrossed and others milling around the nearby tea stalls – can act as a spur to others, some of whom will reveal information leading to unexplored cases. The accused officials are sometimes in the audience, and at times appear markedly sheepish at revelations of the gap between what they were paying the workers and what they claimed from the state government for their wage bill. The officials' earlier excuses for underpayment are sarcastically reprised by the very irate workers, both individually in their testimonials and in the audience-reaction chatter.

In fact, local officials (including the District Collector, a post reserved for members of the elite Indian Administrative Service, or IAS) are invited to attend the hearings, and sometimes do. On several occasions, an exposed *sarpanch* has pledged to return stolen monies. In the early phases of this experiment in popular auditing, a major constraint was the absence of a statutory right to information (that is, access to government-held documents) about local-government spending. During the 1990s, the MKSS and its supporters in other social movements – most notably the women's movement – launched high-profile public protests to demand the right to information about government accounts. In 1996 and 1997, extended protest actions in the state capital and in other small towns generated widespread public backing, and resulted in Rajasthan's chief minister promising to change regulations such that ordinary people would be granted the right to photocopy local-government accounting documents. These promises were never fully implemented, but sustained pressure, and the opportunities created by the installation of a sympathetic state government in late 1998, resulted in the passing of a state-level Right to Information Act by the Rajasthan state assembly in May 2000.

The other major constraint on the public-hearing method was the lack of mandatory legal action to ensure that cases of corruption or malfeasance highlighted through such open processes were acted upon by the investigative agencies, police, courts, and other organs of the state government. Neither the identification of accounting discrepancies clearly worthy of further investigation, nor even admissions of guilt from local officials at the MKSS's unofficial public hearings, were sufficient in most cases to force the state police to initiate follow-up action. Nor have other state agencies been cooperative. For instance, the Rajasthan local-government ministry, responsible for monitoring the performance of elected local-government bodies, has been largely unresponsive when the MKSS has brought prima facie evidence of misconduct to its attention, even when the discrepancies between data in official documents and the physical evidence on the ground could easily be verified through an official inspection.

In response to this persistent obstacle, the MKSS, alongside its efforts to promote right to information legislation, successfully campaigned for amendments to Rajasthan's local-government law (the Panchayati Raj Act) to create mandatory legal procedures for the investigation of corruption and to institutionalize the participatory-audit/public-hearing method at the village-assembly (Gram Sabha) level. The amended Act legally empowers (indeed, requires) village assemblies to conduct collective participatory audits of the development activities initiated by their elected local councilors (the ward *panches* and the *sarpanch*) and by local bureaucrats – particularly the *gram sevak* (the village-development worker), the junior engineer (who oversees and signs off on all public works), and the *patwari* (the lowest-level land registry official). Under the amended Act, the Gram Sabha forwards cases of what it believes to be misuse of funds to higher-level officials, such as the Sub-Divisional Officer (SDO); the latter are legally obliged to register these cases, constitute an inquiry committee, and eventually report back to the Gram Sabha (Mander, 2000, p. 27).

Prospects for the proliferation of hybrid forms of accountability

Clearly, what makes these two cases of citizen activism noteworthy is their exceptional nature rather than their representativeness. There are other groups in India engaged in similar work – especially in mobilizing people to demand fuller information from bureaucrats processing applications for industrial projects financed by multinational corporations. While there has been considerable national interest in the MKSS's participatory-audit/public-hearing method,[6] there is not a huge amount of evidence of comparable action to support a claim that the MKSS approach has been widely replicated. The RKS is more or less sui generis as well.

One reason for the dearth of similar efforts to clean up official oversight institutions is the enormous risk involved, particularly for poor people, in confronting power-holders in the ways described above. This is especially so where the poor rely on officials to turn a blind eye (often for a price) to illegal activity that poor people routinely engage in to survive, such as squatting on city pavements, encroaching forest lands,

---

[6] The MKSS has participated in a nationwide learning process involving other social movements and some NGOs working to improve local-government accountability. In March 2000 the MKSS hosted a large assembly of representatives of these groups in Dev Dungri, its village base, and organized a public hearing for the panchayat of Bhim as a demonstration of its methods.

making use of child labor, and so forth. Moreover, members of the RKS and MKSS have had to face tremendous hostility, including physical harassment, from politicians and bureaucrats for the obvious reason that efforts to clean up official oversight processes directly challenge the material interests of these officials. This is a basic political problem that confronts any citizen group pushing for better government performance, and can only be resolved through organizational strength, a point stressed by both RKS and MKSS activists. Another option is to enter the political arena, which the MKSS has done in a small way by running candidates in local-government elections (occasionally even winning some seats). But other recent efforts to build political alliances around the social movements of the poor, such as the National Alliance of People's Movements, spearheaded in the mid-1990s by the anti-Narmada Dam activists, have not assumed the profile many had hoped.

Beyond this central constraint to generalizing citizen engagement in the state's internal oversight functions, there are two other problems worth noting here. The first is the tendency for the state to resist citizen poaching on its exclusive oversight domain. An increasingly popular means of reasserting state control over the accountability agenda is for the state to pre-empt the emergence of new forms of citizen participation in oversight institutions by introducing similar-seeming initiatives of its own. New hybrid forms of accountability thus face stiff competition from the state itself. State elites, eager to justify their evasion and emasculation of intrastate (horizontal) mechanisms of accountability, argue that their own reform initiatives are geared towards modified forms of (vertical) accountability that link the state directly to citizens and their groups. These are typically unproductive means of obtaining citizen "input," or else forums for citizen "complaint." They are pale imitations of the RKS and MKSS methods,[7] which are themselves, ironically, a conscious mimicking of state process. State substitutes for direct citizen engagement in auditing functions – citizens' juries, consultative forums, focus groups, and citizens' charters – may amplify the "voice" of certain previously excluded groups, but they almost never supply participants with statutory rights to a response or explanation

---

[7] Indeed, a measure of the impact of the MKSS in Rajasthan was a borrowing of the public-hearing method by the state government in 1999, when its State Planning Board invited comment upon its progress in implementing its development programs, particularly in health care, rural electrification, and social welfare services. Public meetings were held at panchayat samitis, but only elected local politicians, not the general public, were invited to participate "Rajasthan Launches Panchayat Samiti Evaluation Meetings," *The Hindu*, 22 October 1999; "Review to Verify Development Statistics," *The Hindu*, 7 December 1999.

from officials, let alone with obligations on the state to provide recompense for citizens' grievances.

Such state-initiated measures tend to fail on five key prerequisites that must accompany any official effort to incorporate people and their associations within formerly closed channels of horizontal accountability: 1) legal standing for nongovernment participants; 2) regular and continuous presence for these non-state actors; 3) clear procedures for conducting meetings; 4) an ironclad right to information; and 5) the right for non-state actors to issue a dissenting report to legislative bodies on the conduct of auditing activities. State-driven accountability experiments are designed to create the impression of a government willing to listen, and they do at times inform officials about public perceptions of government behavior. But they require neither an answer from officials, nor impose sanctions for poor performance – the two litmus tests for any accountability initiative. By virtue of working with NGOs, these state-initiated programs give the appearance of blurring the vertical/horizontal distinction. But state-led efforts are based on motivations that bear little resemblance to those that have animated the work of the RKS or the MKSS, and their presence can even constrain the ability of more radical experiments, initiated by people's organizations themselves, to proliferate more widely into arenas where they could be profitably pursued, such as within regulatory bodies.[8]

The second constraint on the proliferation of mechanisms for formally including ordinary citizens in official oversight processes is the problem of scaling up. Both of the case study organizations discussed in this chapter operate at very local levels. And the one example that involves formal institutionalization – the Gram Sabha reforms in Rajasthan – is actually a part of the local-government structure. Any move beyond the level at which ordinary people's personal experience and knowledge can

---

[8] Indeed, an expanded definition of horizontal accountability agencies would include regulatory agencies, to the extent that they oversee not just private sector entities, but also other government departments and parastatal organizations. The Telecom Regulatory Authority of India, for instance, regulates competition between private and public sector providers, as well as the government department responsible for devising and implementing policy in the sector. Some of these agents of horizontal accountability have greater investigative powers than others; some have greater enforcement power. The MKSS has itself moved in the direction of regulatory issues. In November 1999 it organized a public hearing on "Transparency in Power Sector Reforms." While the immediate intention was to assert that "people have a right to know what is happening in the power sector and how it is going to affect their lives," the broader issue was a consistently articulated demand that decision-making take place on the basis of equal access to quality information made available on a systematic basis (that is, as part of an information regime) to nonpartisan experts who could cross-examine officials ("Rajasthan Cautioned against Power Riots," *The Hindu*, 23 November 1999).

convincingly contradict the state's account of its transactions increases the risk that citizen-auditors will succumb to the same practical difficulties as normal auditors: how can one verify things that one does not know about? In fact, civil society watchdogs face an additional problem of legitimacy when their representatives are elevated to official observer status within auditing institutions: there is always a suspicion that such figures may sell out the people on whose behalf they are ostensibly acting.

This last point underscores the limitations of citizen-initiated accountability efforts, particularly those that end up establishing scrutiny processes parallel to, rather than in partnership with, official horizontal accountability institutions. In different ways, both the RKS's informal vigilance committees and public protests and the MKSS's people's audits have functioned as surrogate courts. In adopting, almost mimicking, legal processes, these cases reflect the influence of Public Interest Litigation on Indian social movements and politics. This influence has taken the form of procedurally complex public hearings, where voluntary groups and NGOs fill the space vacated by authorities that fail to provide information or consult with citizens. This is particularly true for controversial infrastructure projects likely to have damaging environmental or financial impacts, such as the Enron power project in coastal Maharashtra. The logistical arrangements surrounding the collection of evidence, both for one-off hearings as well as for the researching of faux-official "status reports" on incidents of police violence, or (as in the RKS case) tracking the leakage of subsidized commodities onto the black market, are formidable and represent a "legalization" of social action. Instead of demanding an inquiry, such activist-led initiatives conduct inquiries themselves, and if sufficiently successful in conveying their evidence to a larger constituency, are sometimes in a strong position to demand at least ex-officio inclusion in official investigations.

But the proliferation of these do-it-yourself investigations, hearings, and even mock trials brings serious risks that they will be used as forums for score-settling. The MKSS itself has been accused of this by its detractors, who complain that the MKSS has no democratic mandate, no obvious processes or institutions through which it can be held accountable even by its own constituency, and that there is no "objective" external monitor of its work, save for the panels of eminent people from within and outside the local area who sit as panelists at the MKSS-organized public hearings. The MKSS relies for its credibility and legitimacy on the reputation of its core leadership group for incorruptibility and modest living. But the MKSS's increasing prominence beyond Rajasthan has raised questions about legitimacy and representation, and is behind debates within the organization about whether and how to enter the political process, and whether to move to a more formal organizational structure.

The substitution of citizens' informal institutions for state accountability institutions inevitably runs into problems of legitimate authority, controls on power, and at the same time, limited impact. Where such institutions function as, in effect, surrogate courts, without a democratic mandate and with, in the end, rather limited resources for investigating official wrongdoing, some miscreants may evade prosecution, while others may become scapegoats. It is precisely for this reason that the MKSS stages its public hearings infrequently, and with great care, and is now seeking means of incorporating its techniques within the procedures used by official institutions.

References

Abers, Rebecca (1998) "From Clientalism to Cooperation: Local Government, Participatory Policy, and Civic Organising in Porto Alegre, Brazil," *Politics and Society* 26(4), 511–38.

Avritzer, Leonardo (2000) "Civil Society, Public Space and Local Power: A Study of the Participatory Budget in Belo Horisonte and Porto Alegre," Report for the IDS/Ford Foundation project *Civil Society and Democratic Governance*. Unpublished mimeo, IDS, Sussex.

Bhatt, Mayank (2001) "Report for October – December 2000: Monitoring Developments with Rationing Kruti Samiti and Girni Kamgar Sangharsh Samiti," Field notes prepared for the DFID-funded research project *Grassroots Anti-Corruption Initiatives and the Right to Information in India*. Mimeo, IDS, Sussex.

Bhatt, Mayank (2000) "Report for July – September: Monitoring Developments with Rationing Kruti Samiti and Girni Kamgar Sangharsh Samiti," Field notes prepared for the DFID-funded research project *Grassroots Anti-Corruption Initiatives and the Right to Information in India*. Mimeo, IDS, Sussex.

Budlender, Debbie (2000) "Review of Gender Budget Initiatives," Community Agency for Social Enquiry, South Africa, December.

Esim, Simmel (2000) "Impact of Government Budgets on Poverty and Gender Equality," Draft paper presented at the Interagency Workshop on Improving the Effectiveness of Integrating Gender into Government Budgets. Commonwealth Secretariat, Marlborough House, London, 26–27 April.

Grant, D. S. (1997) "Allowing Citizen Participation in Environmental Regulation: An Empirical Analysis of the Effects of Right-to-Sue and Right-to-Know Provisions on Industry's Toxic Emissions," *Social Science Quarterly* 78(4), 859–73.

Mander, Harsh (2000) "Direct Democracy and Gram Sabhas in India: Of Rancid Hopes and Embattled Territories," Mimeo.

Narayan, Deepa, Robert Chambers, Meera Kaul Shah, and Patti Petesch (2000) *Voices of the Poor: Crying Out for Change*. Oxford University Press.

O'Donnell, G. (1999) "Horizontal Accountability in New Democracies," in A. Schedler et al. *The Self-Restraining State: Power and Accountability in New Democracies*. London: Lynne Rienner.

Schedler, A. (1999) "Conceptualising Accountability," in A. Schedler et al. *The Self-Restraining State: Power and Accountability in New Democracies*. London: Lynne Rienner.

UNRISD (1998) "For a Handful of Grain," Occasional paper case study by YUVA and the Action Committee for Rationing (RKS), Geneva.

Part II

Experiments in forging NGO accountability: mutuality and context

The contributions in this section focus their attention on accountability problematics among development organizations, particularly NGOs. David Brown offers a critique of existing accountability models, based in principal–agent theory and democratic representation, arguing that neither are adequate for multiparty initiatives that rely on negotiation and reciprocity among actors. He thus offers a third framing, what he calls "mutual" accountability, elaborated through two examples of civil society and private sector networks.

The workings of such accountability are also forcefully demonstrated in Ian Smillie's chapter which documents the global campaign against "blood diamonds." Smillie was an insider in the campaign, having worked with a pioneering NGO in the conflict as well as for a UN Security Council Expert Panel to track the connection between diamonds and Sierra Leone's grisly civil war. His analysis is thus activist and applied in tone rather than theoretical, and lends further empirical weight to Brown's mutual accountability framework. It also shows, however, that for certain accountability problems such as diamond certification, mutual accountability is not enough and must be backed by regimes of monitoring and enforcement.

The final chapter in this section, by David Lewis, emphasizes the socially constructed nature of accountability, and the centrality of cultural context in grounding an analysis of it. Drawing from the experiences of a large and successful Bangladeshi NGO, Lewis explores the positioning of accountability "within wider fields of power and social networks." He argues that one can acquire, at best, only a partial understanding of accountability through analysis of the formal bureaucratic and managerial systems of NGOs encapsulated in the "audit culture" that dominates the discourse. One must instead view organizational systems – and therefore accountability processes – as *social* systems that are subject to localized forms of control and tension, patron-clientelism, and interpretations of appropriate behavior. As such, Lewis provides confirmation of the tensions between rationalistic or technocratic conceptions of accountability and socially constructed or postmodern ones.

5   Multiparty social action and mutual accountability [1]

L. David Brown

Accountability in multiparty initiatives is an issue for many actors, from governments to businesses to civil society organizations. This chapter focuses on multiparty social action initiatives that seek solutions for complex, uncertain, and changing social problems.

The accountability problem is particularly acute for cause-oriented civil society organizations, both because they are inherently obligated to many stakeholders (Kanter and Summers, 1987; Brown and Moore, 2001) and because they must often combine with other actors to gain resources and leverage (Edwards and Hulme, 1992; Uvin et al., 2000). As civil society actors have become increasingly important in social action initiatives, they have also been increasingly subject to demands to articulate and meet their own accountabilities (Brown and Moore, 2001; Edwards, 2000).

The concept of "multiparty social action initiatives" may be illustrated by two examples, one focused on influencing government and international policies and the other focused on solving business and industry problems:

The campaign against the Mount Apo thermal plant

In the early 1980s the Philippines government proposed to build a geothermal plant on Mount Apo. The project generated strong resistance from local, regional, national, and international coalitions of dozens of civil society organizations, including indigenous peoples groups, farmer associations, environmental and development NGOs,

[1] Earlier versions of this paper were presented to the Program on Nonprofit Organizations Seminar at Yale University, the Work in Progress Seminar at the Hauser Center for Nonprofit Organizations at Harvard, and the Association for Research on Nonprofit Organizations and Voluntary Action (ARNOVA). I am particularly grateful for feedback from Takayoshi Amenomori, Bob Behn, Brent Coffin, Alnoor Ebrahim, Jim Honan, and Mark Moore. I also want to express my appreciation to the Sasakawa Peace Foundation for a grant that partially supported work on this paper.

church groups, and human rights organizations. The campaign sought to influence government agencies and courts in the Philippines as well as World Bank support for the project. It focused on environmental impacts of the proposed plant and on its siting on land sacred to local indigenous groups. Eventually the campaign was governed by a series of "national solidarity councils" that brought together local, regional, and national coalition participants. Those councils worked with the Philippine Development Forum, a network of Filipino and international NGOs, to make their case to the World Bank. The campaign eventually blocked construction of the plant by terminating support from the World Bank and other outside sources as well as reducing political support within the Philippines. It was able to organize a coalition across local, regional, national, and international boundaries and coordinate activities among actors who were very diverse in wealth, culture, power, and expectations (Royo, 1998).

The semiconductor manufacturing technology (SEMATECH) consortium

In the late 1980s the US semiconductor industry was in catastrophic decline. The SEMATECH consortium brought together fourteen US firms, many with long histories of bitter competition, to try to improve US market share in the industry. The consortium used resources from participating companies and matching funds from the US government for cooperative research, development, and testing projects. Although it was initially unclear as to how this goal could be accomplished, the consortium evolved through early disorder and ambiguities to create a "moral community" among its members that grew from clear commitment and unselfish sharing of resources by corporate leaders in spite of their competitive histories. SEMATECH enabled rapid improvements in industry infrastructure, manufacturing processes, and factory management. In its first five years the consortium contributed to achieving a 46 percent US share of the market instead of the predicted 20 percent share, and it significantly changed the way the industry and its firms understood and managed their work (Browning et al., 1995).

These initiatives had different goals and participants, but they both depended on mobilizing the resources of parties who regarded each other with suspicion and distrust to deal with a complex set of challenges that members could not solve by themselves.

This chapter will argue that the most common conceptual models for understanding and ensuring accountability are not very helpful in organizing and governing such initiatives, and it will argue that a third model – mutual accountability – offers more leverage for understanding such initiatives. Since multiparty initiatives appear to be on the increase, it is important that the ramifications of this alternative model be explored in more detail.

The chapter first describes two widely used models of accountability – agency accountability and representative accountability. Then it examines how the attributes of multiparty initiatives present problems for these models. The fourth section discusses mutual accountability as a model that is better adapted to handling multiparty initiatives. After comparing the characteristics of the three models, the paper explores approaches to building mutual accountability systems. Finally the paper discusses models of accountability as socially constitutive patterns – promoting behaviors and social experience that reinforce the model – and the implications of that constitutive impact for the agendas underlying social action campaigns.

Existing models of accountability

Two conceptual models underlie much of the research and discussion of organizational accountability: agency theory and representative theory. Each has roots in a larger theoretical tradition, and they reflect different assumptions about the key challenges posed to actors and the stakeholders to whom they are accountable.

Agency theory

Agency theory focuses attention on the relations between principals and their agents and in particular an agent's accountability to the interests and goals of a principal. The model is grounded in neoliberal economic theory (Walker, 2002, pp. 64–6). Its central concern is with restraining the opportunism of an agent whose goals may conflict with those of the principal (Jensen and Meckling, 1976; Cutt and Murray, 2000). Performance expectations are defined by contracts that articulate expectations and create legally enforceable obligations. Contract provisions create incentives for agents to act for the interests of principals. Boards of directors, for example, develop compensation packages for chief executives to encourage them to attend to the interests of stockholders. The assumption is that these incentives will induce the agent to act in accordance with the letter and spirit of the contract. The more explicit the contracted outcomes the more easily the principal can hold the agent accountable.

At its simplest, agency theory provides clear mechanisms by which principals can hold agents to implementing their objectives. Sanctions available for agent nonperformance include incentives and disincentives written into the contract. In practice agency contracts can focus agent attention on serving the interests of their principals. But agency contracts may also have perverse effects, such as encouraging CEOs to maximize short-term shareholder interests to enhance CEO compensation rather than fostering long-term corporate viability. Contracting for performance also assumes that the parties can define good performance, so uncertainties about problem definition or outcome assessment do not hamper contracting. Agency theory has been widely used in economic and management theory to describe superior–subordinate relations (e.g., Jensen and Meckling, 1976; Walker, 2002). It has also been invoked to define civil society obligations to donors that provide financial support.

Representative theory

Representative theory, in contrast, focuses attention on the accountability of officials to their constituents. This model has roots in democratic theory (Walker, 2000, pp. 66–9; Behn, 2001; Weber, 2003). It focuses on the responsibilities of elected officials responsible directly to voters, and bureaucrats responsible to those officials, for carrying out constituent mandates and for meeting standards of financial management, operational procedures, or organizational performance. If representatives fail to implement this mandate, stakeholders can hold them accountable at the next election. If representatives violate established standards, they can be sanctioned by the media and other watchdog mechanisms. The activities and outcomes specified by mandates are often quite general, but the standards of financial practice and operational procedures may be quite detailed. The ability of constituents to monitor representative performance varies considerably, though the presence of an active media helps to identify deviations.

In essence representative theory offers a frame for assessing the responsiveness of politicians and bureaucrats to their constituents. At its best it provides a vehicle for constituents to hold representatives to voter mandates. But sanctioning politicians by voting them out of office is a blunt instrument for holding them accountable, and the rates of incumbent re-election suggest it is seldom employed effectively. Often constituents are not organized well enough to exert effective voice. Other mechanisms for holding public representatives accountable focus on deviations from established practices. These challenges can deter egregious abuses of the public trust, but their use may also encourage public agencies to avoid the risks of innovating or improving performance (Behn, 2001). Growing specialization also offers opportunities to ignore problems that do not fit neatly into assigned responsibilities (Weber, 2003). Representative theory is likely to be invoked with respect to civil society organizations when they challenge or critique government agencies. When agencies ask, "Who do you represent?" they invoke representative accountability as the primary basis for legitimate influence.

Multiparty social action

The agency and representative models of accountability have been most well developed in the for-profit and the public arenas, respectively, though there have been – particularly in recent years – many efforts to apply them across institutional realms (Cutt and Murray, 2000; Behn, 2001). From the point of view of multiparty social action initiatives, such as the Mount Apo campaign and SEMATECH consortium, there are several drawbacks to these models.

First, the representative and agency models are focused on two party relationships: representatives are accountable to constituents, and agents are accountable to principals. Clarity about these roles greatly simplifies the negotiation of accountability in their relationship.

Multiparty social action initiatives, in contrast, *involve many parties in poorly defined relationships*. At the start of the SEMATECH consortium, for example, many actors with quite diverse agendas were potential members; some invited parties did not show up, and others came with grave reservations about participating. The Mount Apo campaign brought together dozens of dissimilar actors – indigenous peoples' organizations, farmers' movements, environmental and development NGOs, churches – in a campaign that had little coherence about its members' resources or roles at the start. Many multiparty initiatives bring together a confusing array of actors with diverse perceptions of why and how they might work together. This variety often creates multiple accountabilities rather than a single clearly defined relationship.

Second, the representative and agency models are grounded in a shared hierarchical relationship that defines major flows of influence. Agents accept the authority of principals to define goals and activities; representatives accept the legitimacy of constituent definition of mandates. This is not to say that agents and representatives are without influence in the relationship – their control over information, for example, gives them a great deal of influence over principals and constituents. But the basic conception for both models is an asymmetrical relationship in which one party's interests prevail over the other's.

For multiparty social action initiatives, however, the parties *have no shared organizational or hierarchical bases* that set common expectations about whose interests prevail. Multiple accountabilities and ambiguous power relations characterize many multi-organization initiatives. The struggle to stop the Mount Apo thermal plant, for example, involved dozens of organizations – some local, some regional, some national, and some international – with no shared organizational or institutional hierarchies. The SEMATECH initiative involved fourteen corporations and the federal government, none of whom would accept subordination to the interests of the others. So the existence and directionality of accountabilities become a matter of negotiation and the resulting obligations may involve many diverse parties and expectations.

Third, the representative and agency models assume that contracts and mandates will define substantive expectations for accountability relations from the start of the relationship. Agency contracts in particular may be quite detailed about expected performance, incentives for meeting goals, and sanctions for failure. Representative mandates are typically more general, though they are also implicitly set at the time the representative takes office.

For multiparty social action initiatives, however, *definitions of tasks and associated accountabilities evolve* as the parties develop better understanding of problems and shared goals. Defining tasks may require much analysis, and party roles may continue to evolve with that analysis. In the Mount Apo case, for example, national solidarity meetings brought together representatives of local, regional, and national coalitions to make joint decisions about strategy and tactics. But those meetings were not developed until halfway through the struggle. Agreements about responsibilities evolved from experience with influence targets like government agencies, courts, and the World Bank. The SEMATECH consortium drew on member resources to identify strategies for building better semiconductors, gradually identifying key capacities and setting norms that encouraged members to contribute their best efforts to the initiative. For multiparty initiatives on novel problems, the information required to negotiate clear expectations about roles and responsibilities often does not exist at the start, so mandates or contracts that clearly define roles, expectations, and accountabilities are not an option at early stages.

Fourth, agency and representative models assume that parties have the capacities needed to carry out the activities required. Agents and representatives would not be recruited or elected if their principals and constituents did not believe in their capacities to carry out the needed contracts and mandates.

In multiparty initiatives, the *capacities of actors often evolve substantially* and so alter early assumptions about roles. These changes are particularly likely when initiatives occur over long periods of time and parties expand their capacities. The Mount Apo campaign, for example, shifted its emphasis from environmental concerns to violations of indigenous rights to take advantage of growing international concerns and increasing capacities of indigenous alliances members. The SEMATECH consortium focused attention on building the capacity of industry suppliers in early years, and then shifted emphases as those initial efforts bore fruit. The consortium developed norms that encouraged members to contribute resources as they became needed, and those norms enabled members to take on more responsibility as their special resources became relevant. Growing capacities within the initiative can fundamentally change activities that might be constrained by detailed contracts or firm mandates.

In short, multiparty initiatives present demands that strain the agency and representative models of accountability: many parties in undefined relationships rather than clearly defined roles; few shared organizational or hierarchical bases that define those relationships; poorly defined tasks that hamper setting accountability expectations; and evolving capacities of parties as challenges become better understood. These issues raise the possibility of an alternative to the representative and agency models of accountability. We turn now to exploring the rudiments of one such alternative: mutual accountability.

Mutual accountability

Concern about the adequacy of existing models of accountability is not new. Investigators in the business sector have challenged the value of agency theory (e.g., Perrow, 1986) and suggested a "stewardship" alternative (e.g., Davis et al., 1997). Public sector analysts have criticized representative conceptions and argued for a "shared compact" view that includes multiple actors (e.g., Behn, 2001; Weber, 2003). Analysts of civil society organizations have suggested that "negotiated" or "mutual" accountability concepts better explain relations among social service actors (Ospina et al., 2002; Goodin, 2003) or partnerships between Northern and Southern NGOs (Ashman, 2001). Concern with existing models of accountability is particularly common when initiatives coordinate multiple actors.

Mutual accountability can be defined as *accountability among autonomous actors that is grounded in shared values and visions and in relationships of mutual trust and influence.* Mutual relationships involve some degree of shared goals, identifications and interests among the parties (Brinkerhoff, 2002). Thus agency contracts or representative mandates are replaced by commitments to shared values and visions and by relationship bonds. Such "compacts" bind members in terms of social aspirations and identities rather than by economic or political interests (Behn, 2001). Sanctions for violating such compacts are rooted in the loss of valued relationships, social status, and personal identifications rather than in economic incentives and legal sanctions or in public embarrassment and voter rejection.

Since mutual accountability compacts depend on value commitments and relationships, their creation requires investment in building shared commitments and mutual relationships – particularly if the actors have histories of significant conflict, as in the SEMATECH example. Constructing mutual accountability compacts may be difficult, though shared goals and mutual trust have been built even where there is a substantial history of distrust and conflict in the past (e.g., Browning et al., 1995; Gricar and Brown, 1981).

On the other hand, once such commitments have been developed, the parties can flexibly respond to rapid change. When the issues are poorly understood, the ability to act quickly and innovatively in response to emerging issues can be critical. Articulating general standards of "responsibility" may be more important for such circumstances than setting specific standards of accountability (Jordan and van Tuijl, 2000). Social action alliances that share values and mutual trust can respond effectively to such challenges (Ring and van de Ven, 1992). In retrospect the effectiveness of the SEMATECH consortium depended in large measure on the willingness of its members to contribute critical information and resources as needed rather than according to a careful "balancing of the books" across corporations. Constructing such alliances can set the stage for inter-organizational learning and innovation that is difficult under the constraints of agency or representative accountability (Behn, 2001). Responding to the shifting political discourse on the rights of indigenous peoples in the Philippines and the World Bank during the Mount Apo campaign was critical to the campaign's success; early commitment to an environmentally focused strategy could have foreclosed the later emphasis on indigenous rights.

In other models, the emphasis is on delivering performance defined at the outset. For many multiparty initiatives, however, early definition of tasks and roles can undermine effective action. The initiative can itself be an important occasion for inter-organizational learning, in which the parties develop understanding of the issues and enhance their capacities for solving them (Brown and Ashman, 1999; Social Learning Group, 2001). Over the course of the Mount Apo campaign, the capacities of grassroots alliances to take cohesive initiatives and to influence the

World Bank grew substantially. Mutual accountability, with its opportunities for flexible response within shared values and visions, can foster considerable initiative learning and innovation.

The sanctions for failing to live up to expectations of mutual accountability compacts are reputation- and relationship-based. Parties who do not perform may lose their credibility as actors for alliance values and visions; they may undermine their relationships with the other parties; and they may erode their own conceptions of themselves as social actors. Some see such sanctions as being feeble in comparison to the financial and legal incentives associated with agency theory or the threats to office associated with representative theory. But commitments to values, relationships, and identities can be sources of powerful sanctions, as the police and firemen who died in the World Trade Center as well as the terrorists who created the catastrophe have demonstrated. People are sometimes willing to pay high prices to defend their aspirations, their social identities, and their relationships to important others.

Comparing the models

Table 5.1 compares the three models. This stylized presentation simplifies the models to highlight their underlying differences. It is important to note that the boundaries of these models can be blurred in practice. Agency contracts can specify responsibilities and constraints for both parties and so set accountability expectations for both parties. But an agency contract founded on financial and legal incentives enforceable in courts is quite different from a mutual accountability compact grounded in mutual trust, shared values and goals, and moral obligations. The differences in the three models suggest that they may be appropriate in different situations.

It is not surprising that the principal–agent model has been used extensively by theorists concerned with market transactions, or that the representative model has been applied most often to democratic political systems. The mutual accountability model has been most often described in the context of civil society actors, such as social movements or nonprofit actors, who often organize around shared values and visions.

But the alternative models are *not* exclusively relevant to any single sector. Civil society organizations, for example, are often expected to account for financial resources and program outcomes as agents of donor principals (Lindenberg and Bryant, 2001). Civil society actors that seek to influence public policy are frequently questioned about their legitimacy under the representative model ("Who elected you?").

Table 5.1 *Three models of accountability*

	Agency	Representative	Mutual
Parties	Agent accountable to principal	Representative accountable to constituents	Multiple actors accountable to each other
Core concern	Accomplish principal's goals and constrain agent opportunism	Represent constituent interests while enabling representative flexibility	Accomplish shared goals while respecting interests of parties
Relationship character	Hierarchical context where principal's goals take priority	Democratic system in which representatives respond to constituents	Collegial peer relations that emphasize trust and mutual influence
Definition of performance	Formal contracts specify goals, indicators of success, incentives to perform	Political mandates describe directions; financial and procedural standards define good practice	Informal compacts describe shared values, relationships, and general responsibilities
Sanctions for failure	• Economic incentives • Legal obligations • Court oversight and enforcement	• Voter support • Watchdog agencies criticize • Media oversight and publicity	• Relationship pressure • Moral obligations • Personal identity and responsibility • Network oversight

Strengths	• Efficient action on principal's goals • Constraints on agent opportunism	• Effective voice for constituent interests • Preserves flexibility of representative role	• Multiparty action on shared concerns • Capacity to adapt to novel problems
Weaknesses	• Assumes outputs can be specified • Agent focused on contract incentives, not larger interests	• Requires ongoing voter organization • Emphasis undermines performance • Specialization narrows response	• Large investment in building compacts • Sanctions depend on values, relationships, and identity
Appropriate situations (normative)	• Shared hierarchy of authority • Agent capacity to accomplish goals • Task is well defined and measurable	• Democratic political system • Representative can carry out mandate • Constituents are organized for voice	• Shared values and goals • Multiparty capacity required for action • Situation requires flexible, evolving response

So agency and representative models are relevant to civil society actors as well as to business and government agencies.

On the other hand, government and business actors are increasingly concerned about issues for which mutual accountability may be appropriate. The SEMATECH example reflects government and corporate concern with problems for which a multiparty alliance was needed. Other companies operating in environments characterized by rapid change have developed networks for interorganizational collaboration and mutual accountability (e.g., Powell, 1996). Government actors have recognized the importance of partnerships with other actors over whom they have little or no direct authority, and so turned to negotiated agreements and mutual accountability (Gray and Hay, 1986; Susskind et al., 1999). Multisectoral ecosystem management arrangements that have grown out of intense conflict, for example, utilize shared values and informal norms to provide the basis for mutual accountability (Weber, 2003).

In short, the appropriateness of accountability models may be determined by situation more than by the sectoral origins of the parties, though parties from different sectors may be more adept at different models. The challenge to many actors in an increasingly interdependent world is to diagnose the requirements of a situation so they can employ the appropriate model.

Building mutual accountability

While the technologies for creating agency and representative accountability systems are well developed, constructing systems for mutual accountability requires attention to different issues. In the past two decades investigators have paid increasing attention to the challenges of bringing together diverse parties for action on complex social problems (Gray, 1989; Susskind and Cruikshank, 1987; Susskind et al., 1999; Weber, 2003). The creation of accountability systems across diverse parties involves at least five elements: 1) negotiating shared values and visions; 2) creating relationships of mutual influence and trust; 3) refining strategies and complementary expectations; 4) assessing performance and rendering mutual accounts; and 5) fostering joint learning in face of changing circumstances. We will consider each briefly, drawing on the Mount Apo and SEMATECH cases for illustrations.

Negotiating shared values and visions

The foundation for mutual accountability compacts is agreement on values and visions for the issue at hand, rather than organizational or institutional contexts. Shared visions can create motives that are as or more powerful than economic or political incentives for accountability, as demonstrated by Christian martyrs, Al Qaeda terrorists, or military heroes from many traditions. Discussions of problem definitions and interpretations can create a context for joint action by otherwise autonomous parties. Without that shared perspective it is difficult for independent actors to agree on strategies, responsibilities, or bases for accountability to each other.

Developing shared agreements about values and visions is not easy, especially when the parties have little prior contact that creates credibility (Gray, 1989; Susskind and Cruikshank, 1987). In practice the development of such agreements may take considerable time and exploration, particularly when initial engagements involve conflict (Weber, 2003). Real agreement may emerge only after struggles that demonstrate the high costs of continued conflict, though approaches exist for identifying common ground (e.g., Weisbord et al., 1992; Susskind et al., 1999). Diverse resources and perspectives offer potential for expanding joint capacities of the alliance – but they also contain the seeds for disagreement and conflict.

For some situations, problem definitions and shared strategies evolve over time, even when the parties begin with agreement on values. In the Mount Apo case, for example, the campaign brought together indigenous tribes, local farmers, environmental NGOs, Catholic church activists, and other civil society actors concerned about the impact of the thermal plant. Early activities focused on both environmental impacts and desecration of sacred lands. The campaign had been underway for several years when the national solidarity councils built a shared strategy and framing of the problems.

When the parties have histories of competition or conflict, creating shared visions may require special leadership. In constructing the SEMATECH consortium, the parties were initially more attuned to their decades of competition than to their shared stake in the global market for computer chips. The creation of a joint initiative depended heavily on the willingness of highly visible corporate leaders to sound the alarm about the industry's decline and to explicitly subordinate some of the interests of their firms to act for the industry as a whole. These "altruistic acts" enabled others to take seriously the possibility of building a shared vision of the future in spite of the history of competition.

So the joint construction of a shared vision that enables working together is central to mutual accountability. This articulation may require that key actors invest time, energy, and resources to define problems and strategies for solving them.

Creating relationships of mutual influence and trust

Relationships are at the center of mutual accountability. But creating relationships of trust and mutual influence that link diverse actors is no small matter. Trust involves positive expectations about another's motives in circumstances of risk (Boon and Holmes, 1991). Research has identified several forms of trust: calculus-based trust is grounded in incentives and disincentives; knowledge-based trust grows out of interaction that builds understanding and predictability; and identification-based trust comes from understanding and acceptance of the other's desires and intentions (Lewicki and Bunker, 1996). Calculus- and knowledge-based trust are probably quite common in agency and representative models of accountability; identification-based trust is particularly relevant to mutual accountability. Identification-based trust can be fostered by committing to shared values, by joint action for shared goals, by continuing interaction, and by developing a collective identity – but its creation demands more time and investment than the other two forms (Lewicki and Bunker, 1996, pp. 123–5; see also Vangen and Huxham, 2003).

Mutual influence involves recognition of the parties' capacities to advance or retard each other's interests. When parties begin with perceptions of unequal power, some rebalancing of power (though not necessarily full equality) may be required to enable mutual influence. Systems of mutual accountability may involve organizing the parties for effective voice with each other, recognizing each other's interests in mutual influence, and managing differences in ways that enable them to hear and respond to each other (Brown and Fox, 1998; Gaventa and Cornwall, 2001).

In the Mount Apo campaign, for example, the national solidarity councils brought together coalition members in face-to-face meetings to build a shared strategy. The councils' decision-making and the resulting strategies recognized the influence and contributions of many parties. Accountability relationships with the Philippine Development Forum in Washington involved a series of face-to-face meetings among Forum leaders, leaders of the national campaign, and elders of the indigenous groups. At the heart of the campaign's mutual accountability was a series of relationships that supported roles for local, regional, national, and international actors.

In the SEMATECH consortium, initial caution about sharing sensitive information was gradually replaced by recognition of their interdependence for maintaining the industry. Existing relationships among corporate leaders, their willingness to share sensitive information, initiatives by consortium leaders to create trust, and accumulating evidence that parties were committed to mutual influence all contributed to building a "moral community" among consortium members.

When the parties to a coalition have histories of conflict and mistrust, creating mutual accountability may take considerable time and cautious experimenting to create new expectations. Once created such relationships may be reused: Research on transnational civil society coalitions suggests that network relationships may be reused for new initiatives (Brown and Fox, 1998). The trust and mutual influence that buttress mutual accountability is more easily destroyed than created, and lapses may require much time and attention to repair. The difficulty of constructing such relationships may make individuals and organizations with widespread credibility the key to constructing new initiatives, since they can bridge differences among potential collaborators.

Refining strategies and redefining expectations

Convening parties with shared values and visions does not automatically create shared action strategies and responsibilities. While agency contracts and constituent mandates are often clear about performance expectations at the start, multiparty social action initiatives often deal with poorly defined or novel problems that require reshaping strategies and performance expectations as understanding evolves (e.g., Gricar and Brown, 1981). Initial expectations may be revised and made more specific, and so clarify or redefine performance expectations and accountabilities (Jordan and van Tuijl, 2000). Shifting expectations require ongoing negotiation among the parties to adjust to the demands of emerging problems and evolving strategies. It may also require shifting indicators and standards for performance as problems and expectations change.

The national coalition involved in the Mount Apo campaign, for example, initially focused on both environmental impacts and indigenous rights. As the momentum of the campaign built, both the commitment of indigenous peoples and the resistance of government agencies increased. The national solidarity councils and the Philippine Development Forum recognized that concerns with the rights of indigenous people within the Philippines and at the World Bank created special influence opportunities. So they shifted strategy to emphasize the protection of indigenous rights. This shift changed member roles and responsibilities, as indigenous representatives and alliances with indigenous movements became more important bases of influence.

The hallmark of the initial phases of the SEMATECH consortium was disorder and ambiguity that reflected the chaotic state of the industry, the varying agendas of consortium members, and the challenges of organizing actors from fourteen companies. Central to the creation of shared strategies and organization for the consortium was the commitment of leaders from member companies and the gradual adoption of norms and systems from leading companies. The consortium adopted practices for managing meetings from Intel, for example, that fostered face-to-face discussion, sharing sensitive information, and cooperative problem-solving. Those meetings created and reinforced expectations for cooperation and mutual accountability.

Accountability systems evolve with changing analyses of the problem, refinement of action strategies, and shifting capacities and resources of campaign participants. Mutual accountability systems provide strategic and organizational flexibility for adapting to emerging needs in situations that are fluid and poorly understood at the outset.

Assessing performance and rendering accounts

The evolving character of problem definitions and strategies presents difficulties for assessing performance and holding actors accountable. Initial expectations about joint work are often vaguely defined, while specific responsibilities and performance expectations cannot be defined until shared goals and strategies have been negotiated. Decisions about indicators of performance, collecting and interpreting evidence, communicating interpretations and results, and hearing and responding to each other's reactions are all subject to revision as initiatives evolve.

As initiatives clarify expectations, they create the base for identifying performance responsibilities and indicators. For many multiparty initiatives, assessment and learning involve face-to-face engagements to reflect on emerging indicators, assess performance, sanction failures to meet expectations, and learn from shared experience. These activities place high demands on these face-to-face meetings and the individuals who manage them. But they also provide opportunities for relationship building and maintenance – for exercising mutual influence and reinforcing trust – that are essential to mutual accountability (Powell, 1996; Vangen and Huxham, 2003).

The Mount Apo campaign depended on the national solidarity councils to share information about progress and to assess strategies for dealing with opposition actions, such as efforts to undercut the credibility of indigenous leaders. The councils offered opportunities to engage national members about their performance. The councils did not include the international allies in the Philippine Development Forum, however, so monitoring their performance and accountability depended on electronic communications and on travel by key actors for face-to-face meetings.

The SEMATECH consortium was founded to expand market share and reestablish the infrastructure of the US semiconductor industry, so the most basic measure of success was market share. Members renewed the consortium charter when the industry more than doubled its predicted market share after five years. The consortium organization offered a forum for constant engagement and assessment of impacts, and developed norms for assigning high-quality staff that could quickly respond to emerging needs: When crises called for new resources, members would recognize "It's our turn" and respond. So SEMATECH staff had the skills to create plans, milestones, assessments, and review procedures that could hold key actors accountable to the overall campaign.

The Mount Apo and SEMATECH initiatives varied in how much their members had experience with assigning responsibilities, collecting and interpreting assessment data, and holding one another accountable. In both cases, however, member relationships evolved that were characterized by mutual trust and influence, and organizational arrangements reinforced those relationships. Continuing engagement offered opportunities for assessing their progress and validating their organizational arrangements. Complex problems made prior specification of responsibilities difficult, but agreement on general values and goals, relationships, and organizational arrangements held the alliance together and enabled articulation of more specific expectations as time passed.

Fostering joint learning

Mutual accountability enables substantial flexibility for innovation and experimentation as well as the mobilization of a wide range of resources. Compacts for mutual accountability can be particularly useful when ambiguity and uncertainty call for innovation and joint learning (Powell, 1996; Weber, 2003). In recent years there has been considerable attention to the challenges of organizational learning (e.g., Argyris and Schon, 1978; Senge, 1990; Ebrahim, 2003, 2005). Inter-organizational learning, on the other hand, is a less-explored area (Knight, 2002; Ring and van de Ven, 1994). But it will become increasingly important as more multiparty systems are organized to deal with complex and poorly understood issues.

Network learning can alter the cognitive and behavioral capacities of multiparty systems, reshaping their shared schemas for understanding events, their strategies and tactics for pursuing their goals, the network structures and systems that guide their activities, or their repertoires of activities (Knight, 2002). Some learning enhances the capacities of parties to act on substantive problems. Insights into the World Bank's priorities from its international allies enabled the Mount Apo campaign to influence the Bank and the government of the Philippines. Close relations within SEMATECH enabled the consortium to influence its members' research, to adopt effective practices from some members, to set standards across the industry, and to provide support to national suppliers.

Network learning capacity can be enhanced by the development of processes and structures that allow exploration of differences, creation of new knowledge, dissemination of ideas and results across the network, and retention of useful learning (Brown, 1999). SEMATECH drew on the experiences of its members to foster learning about the technical issues facing the industry. The Mount Apo campaign used its learning capacity to respond to changes in the strategies and tactics of its influence targets by creating a variety of committees and councils to develop campaign ideas.

It is probably not coincidental that both these initiatives responded to crises that posed high potential costs to their members and demanded novel strategies and network learning. Mutual accountability is not inexpensive to create, though once created it may be relatively inexpensive to maintain. It is particularly valuable, however, when rapid and effective network learning – with its demands for flexibility, inventiveness, and mutual trust – is critical.

Accountability models and social construction

I have argued that three models of accountability – agency accountability, representative accountability, and mutual accountability – are useful in designing systems that encourage interdependent parties to keep their promises. These models vary in their utility for different purposes. Agency accountability is useful for organizing to accomplish a principal's goals while constraining agent opportunism. Representative accountability helps to secure the interests of constituents while preserving representative flexibility. Mutual accountability helps to accomplish shared visions and goals for multiple parties facing complex and changing problems. While the models have roots in different sectors and intellectual disciplines, they are applicable across sectors and problems.

The models may resonate differently with different cultural contexts. Agency theory dominates much of the discussion of accountability in the United States, in keeping with its cultural emphasis on individualism and free-market forms of economic interaction. In Japan, however, cultural values on cooperative relationships and collective responsibility are more resonant with mutual accountability. Choosing among the models may turn in part on the cultural contexts in which the actors operate.

It is important to recognize that accountability models can be both *regulative* and *constitutive* of social interaction. They are regulative in the sense that they constrain and shape the behavior of actors that are subject to them. So agency contracts shape the activities of agents, voter mandates shape the activities of representatives, and shared goals and compacts shape the activities of mutually accountable network members.

The models are also constitutive in a deeper sense in that they shape the experience of actors and the social systems in which they are embedded (Berger and Luckmann, 1971; Giddens, 1984). Accountability models offer frames for social interaction that focus the attention of actors on some features of the interaction more than others. Agency theory, for example, focuses attention on individual agent responsibility and economic incentives, and so fosters conceptions of self as an individual driven by economic rewards. The regulative and constitutive impacts of agency models are mutually reinforcing, as meeting agency contractual expectations also supports societal frames and expectations about relationships as following the principal–agent model. The combination of regulative and constitutive impacts can strengthen the effectiveness of principal–agent relations, but it can also create over-reliance on the model, as in the "commodification" of all relationships or in promoting agent opportunism that the model seeks to control (Roberts, 2001).

The regulative and constitutive impacts of representative accountability can encourage representative adherence to constituent mandates and active citizen participation processes. But the same systems may create an "accountability as punishment" (Behn, 2001) climate that encourages risk avoidance at the expense of flexibility or innovation, and poll-watching at the expense of political courage. When elections are widely spaced and constituents are loosely organized, representative accountability can create diffusion of constituent responsibility and permanent incumbents who are not accountable to constituents.

The regulative impact of mutual accountability creates agreements about values and visions, and emphasizes operations rooted in mutual trust and influence. The constitutive impacts of mutual accountability may create experience and expectations of interdependence across a community of formally autonomous actors and encourage participants to understand themselves as responsible to that larger community.

The "moral community" created in the SEMATECH consortium, for example, pressed members to put aside competitiveness to innovate for their common industry. The community encouraged long-term cooperation over the short-term competitiveness that dominated prior relations, and the success of that cooperation reinforced and reconstituted community norms. The shared commitments of the Mount Apo campaign supported creative policy influence activity; and those experiences reinforced and invigorated its members' understanding of and commitment to their interdependence. Research on multiparty management of ecosystems indicates that shared visions for ecosystem viability can regulate ecosystem use as well as constitute experience, perceptions, and long-term engagement of many constituents (Weber, 2003).

Mutual accountability can also be expected to have a dark side, like the other models. Mutual accountability compacts may fail to regulate the behavior of some participants, and so leave other parties feeling betrayed and exploited. Parties to mutual accountability compacts are particularly likely to interpret violations as betrayals of core values and to have highly charged reactions as a result. The emphasis on constituting communities of mutually accountable members may also encourage framing nonmembers in negative terms, and so foster conflict with outsiders even while community members are embracing interdependence with insiders. But on the whole it seems that an accountability model that emphasizes the interdependence of many actors to solve complex problems will be valuable for many current problems.

All three approaches to accountability are relevant in many settings, though mutual accountability has received less attention than agency and representative accountability. For some kinds of problems – such as those facing the Mount Apo campaign and the SEMATECH consortium – mutual accountability offers advantages over the other models. While mutual accountability is more easily launched among like-minded actors, the model can be used to negotiate cooperation in conflict situations when the parties begin to recognize their interdependence (see Smillie, below, ch. 6, and Weber, 2003).

More important in the long run, the constitutive impacts of mutual accountability on individuals, organizations, and the larger society may be crucial for an increasingly interdependent world. It is important to recognize that mutual accountability may not be feasible in situations where actors are insufficiently organized or distinct, where the possibilities for identifying and negotiating shared interests are limited, and where the incentives for more atomized behavior are high. But the choice of accountability model affects both immediate responses to problems and the constitution of the people and social systems involved.

Systems grounded in mutual accountability or in combinations of accountability models are needed to enable effective problem-solving and to develop individual attitudes and organizational capacities to meet the challenges of growing global interdependence.

References

Argyris, C. and D. Schon (1978) *Organizational Learning: A Theory of Action Perspective*. Reading, MA: Addison-Wesley Publishing.

Ashman, D. (2001) "Strengthening North–South Partnerships for Sustainable Development," *Nonprofit and Voluntary Sector Quarterly* 30(1), 74–98.

Behn, R. (2001) *Rethinking Democratic Accountability*. Washington, DC: Brookings Institution.

Berger, P. and T. Luckmann (1971) *The Social Construction of Reality*. Harmondsworth: Penguin.

Boon, S. D. and J. G. Holmes (1991) "The Dynamics of Interpersonal Trust: Resolving Uncertainty in the Face of Risk," in R. A. Hinde and J. Groebel (eds.) *Cooperation and Prosocial Behavior*. Cambridge University Press, pp. 190–211.

Brinkerhoff, J. M. (2002) *Partnership for International Development: Rhetoric or Results?* Boulder, CO: Lynne Rienner.

Brown, L. D. (1999) "Social Learning in South–North Coalitions: Constructing Knowledge across Social Chasms," in D. Lewis (ed.) *International Perspectives on Voluntary Action: Reshaping the Third Sector*. London: Earthscan, pp. 39–59.

Brown, L. D. and D. Ashman (1999) "Capital, Mutual Influence and Social Learning in Intersectoral Problem-Solving in Africa and Asia," in D. L. Cooperrider and J. E. Dutton (eds.) *Organizational Dimensions of Global Change: No Limits to Cooperation*. Beverly Hills, CA: Sage, pp. 139–59.

Brown, L. D. and J. Fox (1998) "Accountability within Transnational Coalitions," in J. Fox and L. D. Brown (eds.) *The Struggle for Accountability: NGOs, Social Movements, and the World Bank*. Cambridge, MA: MIT Press, pp. 439–84.

Brown, L. D. and M. H. Moore (2001) "Accountability, Strategy and International Nongovernmental Organizations," *Nonprofit and Voluntary Sector Quarterly* 30(3), 569–87.

Browning, L. D., J. M. Beyer and J. C. Shetler (1995) "Building Cooperation in a Competitive Industry: SEMATECH and the Semiconductor Industry," *Academy of Management Journal* 38(1), 113–53.

Cutt, J. and V. Murray (2000) *Accountability and Effectiveness Evaluation in Nonprofit Organizations*. London: Routledge.

Davis, J. H., F. D. Schoorman and L. Donaldson (1997) "Toward a Stewardship Theory of Management," *Academy of Management Review* 22 (1), 20–47.

Ebrahim, A. (2005) "Accountability Myopia: Losing Sight of Organizational Learning," *Nonprofit and Voluntary Sector Quarterly* 34(1), 56–87.

Ebrahim, A. (2003) *NGOs and Organizational Change*. Cambridge University Press.

Edwards, M. (2000) *NGO Rights and Responsibilities: A New Deal for Global Governance*. London: The Foreign Policy Centre.

Edwards, M. and D. Hulme (eds.) (1992) *Making a Difference*. London: Earthscan.

Gaventa, J. and A. Cornwall (2001) "Power and Knowledge," in P. Reason and H. Bradbury (eds.) *Handbook of Action Research*. London: Sage, pp. 70–90.

Giddens, A. (1984) *The Constitution of Society*. Cambridge: Polity.

Goodin, R. E. (2003) *Democratic Accountability: The Third Sector and All*. Cambridge, MA: Hauser Center for Nonprofit Organizations.

Gray, B. G. (1989) *Collaborating: Finding Common Ground for Multiparty Problems*. San Francisco: Jossey-Bass.

Gray, B. G. and T. M. Hay (1986) "Political Limits to Interorganizational Consensus and Change," *Journal of Applied Behavioral Science* 22(2), 95–112.

Gricar, B. G. and L. D. Brown (1981) "Conflict, Power and Organization in a Changing Community," *Human Relations* 34(10), 877–93.

Jensen, M. and W. Meckling (1976) "Theory of the Firm: Managerial Behavior, Agency Costs, and Capital Structure," *Journal of Financial Economics* 3, 305–60.

Jordan, L. and P. van Tuijl (2000) "Political Responsibility in Transnational NGO Advocacy," *World Development* 28(12), 2051–65.

Kanter, R. M. and D. V. Summers (1987) "Doing Well While Doing Good: Dilemmas of Performance Measurement in Nonprofit Organizations and the Need for a Multiple-Constituency Approach," in W. W. Powell (ed.) *The Nonprofit Sector: A Research Handbook*. New Haven: Yale University Press, pp. 154–67.

Knight, L. (2002) "Network Learning: Exploring Learning by Interorganizational Networks," *Human Relations* 55(4), 427–54.

Lewicki, R. J. and B. B. Bunker (1996) "Developing and Maintaining Trust in Work Relationships," in R. M. Kramer and T. R. Tyler (eds.) *Trust in Organizations: Frontiers of Theory and Research*. Thousand Oaks, CA: Sage, pp. 114–39.

Lindenberg, M. and C. Bryant (2001) *Going Global: Transforming Relief and Development NGOs*. Bloomfield, CT: Kumarian Press.

Ospina, S., W. Diaz and J. F. O'Sullivan (2002) "Negotiating Accountability: Managerial Lessons from Identity-Based Nonprofit Organizations," *Nonprofit and Voluntary Sector Quarterly* 31(1), 5–31.

Perrow, C. (1986) *Complex Organizations*. New York: Random House.

Powell, W. W. (1996) "Trust-Based Forms of Governance," in R. M. Kramer and T. R. Tyles (eds.) *Trust in Organizations: Frontiers of Theory and Research*. Thousand Oaks, CA: Sage, pp. 51–67.

Ring, P. S. and A. H. van de Ven (1994) "Developmental Processes of Cooperative Interorganizational Relationships," *Strategic Management Journal* 19(1), 483–98.

Ring, P. S. and A. van de Ven (1992) "Structuring Cooperative Relationships between Organizations," *Academy of Management Review* 13, 483–98.

Roberts, J. (2001) "Trust and Control in Anglo-American Systems of Corporate Governance: The Individualizing and Socializing Effects of Processes of Accountability," *Human Relations* 54(12), 1547–72.

Royo, A. (1998) "Against the People's Will: The Mount Apo Story," in J. A. Fox and L. D. Brown (eds.) *The Struggle for Accountability: NGOs, Social Movements and the World Bank*. Cambridge, MA: MIT Press.

Senge, P. M. (1990) *The Fifth Discipline: The Art and Practice of the Learning Organization*. New York: Doubleday.

Social Learning Group (2001) *Learning to Manage Global Environmental Risks*. Vol. I. Cambridge, MA: MIT Press.

Susskind, L. and J. Cruikshank (1987) *Breaking the Impasse: Consensual Approaches to Resolving Public Disputes*. New York: Basic Books.

Susskind, L., S. McKearnan and J. Thomas-Larmer (eds.) (1999) *The Consensus Building Handbook*. Thousand Oaks, CA: Sage Publications.

Uvin, P., P. Jain and L. D. Brown (2000) "Think Large and Act Small: Toward a New Paradigm for NGO Scaling Up," *World Development* 28(8), 1409–19.

Vangen, S. and C. Huxham (2003) "Nurturing Collaborative Relations: Building Trust in Interorganizational Collaboration," *Journal of Applied Behavioral Science* 39(1), 5–31.

Walker, P. (2002) "Understanding Accountability: Theoretical Models and their Implications for Social Service Organizations," *Social Policy and Administration* 36(1), 62–75.

Weber, E. P. (2003) *Bringing Society Back In: Grassroots Ecosystem Management, Accountability and Sustainable Communities*. Cambridge, MA: MIT Press.

Weisbord, M. et al. (1992) *Discovering Common Ground*. San Francisco: Berrett-Koehler.

6   Not accountable to anyone? Collective
     action and the role of NGOs
     in the campaign to ban "blood diamonds"

Ian Smillie

This chapter examines the NGO campaign on "conflict diamonds," sometimes known as "blood diamonds." It reviews efforts by a handful of self-appointed NGOs to press governments into the creation of an international regulatory system for the sale and purchase of rough diamonds, and it looks at NGO activities which aimed to force the world's entire diamond industry to change the way it has done business for more than a hundred years. This is not an objective, academic review of the subject. In 1995 I wrote a book about NGOs entitled *The Alms Bazaar* (Smillie, 1995). I subsequently worked on the diamond campaign myself for several years, seeing it from the inside, and from the beginning. I have worked with one of the pioneering NGOs on conflict diamonds – Partnership Africa Canada (PAC). I also worked for a UN Security Council Expert Panel, tracking the connection between diamonds and weapons in Sierra Leone's horrific civil war, and I have been an active participant in the Kimberley Process, a series of meetings that began in 2000 in an effort to deal with the problem. I therefore bring a variety of personal perspectives to bear on the story, and on the question of NGO accountability.

The contribution of this chapter to the broader themes of this book is thus more empirical than theoretical. The Kimberley Process, which I detail below, required not only the building of "mutual" accountability among actors (in the sense elaborated by Brown, above, ch. 5), but remains dependent on a still emerging regime of monitoring and sanctions, enforceable through external oversight (in the sense outlined by Woods, above, ch. 2).

In highlighting the central role played by NGOs in this process, I also examine concerns about representative accountability raised by critics of NGOs. "Do NGOs represent a dangerous shift of power to unelected and unaccountable special-interest groups?" This question was the centerpiece of a lengthy article in *The Economist* in 1999, not long after the first anti-WTO riots, also known as the "battle in Seattle." The article concluded that the answer was at least maybe, although it ended with an economist's standard two-handed conclusion: "Some will celebrate [growing NGO political influence] as the advent of the age when huge institutions will heed the voice of everyman. Others will complain that self-appointed advocates have gained too much influence. What is certain is that a new kind of actor is claiming, loudly, a seat at the table" (*The Economist*, 1999).

Conflict diamonds

Conflict diamonds were first brought to the world's attention late in 1998 by a small British NGO called Global Witness. Global Witness had been started only five years earlier by three environmentalists who had previously worked on issues such as banning the ivory trade in order to protect elephants in Africa. They had seen that environmental and human rights problems were complex and interrelated and, in order to solve them, the source of the problem rather than public exhortation needed to be addressed. They began to look at the role of resources in fueling conflict. Their first issue was timber exploitation in Cambodia. Their concern was not timber or forests but what the exploitation of forests by unscrupulous logging firms was doing to the security of Cambodia and Cambodians. The firms, mostly Thai, were in the thrall of the Khmer Rouge, and the funds – as much as $20 million a month at its height – were being used to buy weapons and to fuel a brutal, rearguard Khmer Rouge struggle, long after it had disappeared from the headlines. The evidence of commercial and official cupidity exposed by Global Witness was irrefutable. It forced both governments and aid agencies, in particular the World Bank, to take action, which in due course cut off the Khmer Rouge money machine and helped in its final demise.

In 1998, Global Witness turned its attention to the war in Angola, and found that diamonds were fueling the UNITA war machine. UNITA, which had long before lost any moral or political justification for its twenty-year war effort, and which had lost the Cold War rationale needed for American backing, was funded now almost exclusively through the sale of diamonds. In a December 1998 report entitled *A Rough Trade*, Global Witness reported that between 1992 and 1998, UNITA controlled between 60 and 70 percent of Angola's diamond production, generating $3.7 billion to pay for its war effort (Global Witness, 1998). Half a million Angolans died, and many more were displaced, their lives ruined.

A year later in January 2000, a Canadian NGO, Partnership Africa Canada, released its own report on diamonds: *The Heart of the Matter: Sierra Leone, Diamonds and Human Security* (Smillie et al., 2000). That report told the story of Sierra Leone's Revolutionary United Front (RUF), a rebel movement devoid of ideology, without ethnic backing or claims to territory. Charles Taylor, the Liberian warlord, had financed the early stages of his brutal fight for power by selling timber. As Global Witness had shown in Cambodia, the market for tropical hardwood is lucrative, and once Taylor secured a seaport, he had both the supply and the means to export. But diamonds would prove to be even more lucrative. Taylor backed Sierra Leone's fledgling Revolutionary United Front, giving it a Liberian base, weapons, and an outlet for whatever it could steal in Sierra Leone. The RUF trademark was grisly: they chopped the hands and feet off civilians, often small children, a terror technique aimed at clearing the country's alluvial diamond fields.

The Heart of the Matter traced Sierra Leone's diamond story from its decline into corruption in the 1970s through to 1999, when formal diamond mining had come to an almost complete halt. By then, there were no government-supervised diamond exports, while across the border in Liberia, diamond exports were thriving. Between 1994 and 1999, more than $2 *billion* worth of diamonds were imported into Belgium from Liberia. Liberia, however, is a country with almost no diamond production of its own. Partnership Africa Canada's report exposed diamond fraud of massive proportions. It accused the diamond industry at large of complicity. And it charged the Belgian authorities in particular, of closing their eyes to massive corruption, in part to protect the Antwerp diamond trade which had been diminished in recent years by competition from Israel and India.

Between them, Global Witness and Partnership Africa Canada put the diamond industry on notice, and they also singled out the giant De Beers conglomerate for special attention. De Beers has traditionally controlled about 80 percent of the world's trade in rough diamonds.[1] In its annual reports in the mid-1990s, it boasted about its ability to keep mopping up diamonds from Angola, despite the unsettling business of war. In addition to diamonds from its own mines in Southern Africa, De Beers bought diamonds on the "open market" and maintained offices in Guinea, the Democratic Republic of Congo (DRC), and elsewhere, taking whatever was on offer, no questions asked. Control over supply was key to sustaining the high price of diamonds in a world where more

---

[1] The figure has dropped to approximately 60 percent in recent years.

and more gem-quality finds were occurring. Antwerp and De Beers were the largest entrepôts for diamonds, but they were not alone in failing to see the damage that their product was doing in Africa. Israel represents about a quarter, by value, of all the rough diamonds that are cut and polished in a year. The equivalent Indian figure is more than 40 percent. The United States consumes more than 40 percent of all diamond jewelry sold every year. Russia produces about 20 percent by value of all the world's rough diamonds while more than 25 percent are produced in Botswana. Australia, Namibia, and South Africa are also significant producers. None of these countries or their diamond industries had anything to say about conflict diamonds until the issue was exposed by NGOs.

The problems of Sierra Leone and Angola were not unique. While Mobutu Sese Seko was President of Zaire (now the DRC), formal diamond production fell from 18 million carats in 1961, to 12 million in 1970, finally leveling off at about 6.5 million carats in the 1990s. But these are only the figures that were recorded. Mobutu "informalized" much of the diamond industry, bringing it and its profits under his own control and that of his cronies. Miners and middlemen devised a simple way to avoid his rapacious appetite and a heavy system of informal taxation (otherwise known as "bribery"). They simply smuggled their product across the river to Brazzaville. Records of Belgian diamond imports from Brazzaville are, in fact, a relatively good barometer of war and corruption in the DRC. In 1997, when the DRC was undergoing its chaotic transfer of power from Mobutu to Laurent Kabila, Belgium imported $454.6 million worth of diamonds from Brazzaville. By 1999, however, when things had settled down, and when it looked as though Kabila might actually sweep away the corruption and cronyism of the past, Belgium imported only $14.4 million worth of diamonds from Brazzaville, and there was growth in imports from the DRC. By 2000, however, things had reverted to form, and the volume from Brazzaville soared to $116.6 million, almost doubling again in 2001 to $223.8 million.[2] The human cost of this level of corruption, and of the resource-based war that followed Kabila's takeover, was enormous. In 2001, the International Rescue Committee, an American NGO, reported that 2.5 million more people had died in the Congo during the second half of the 1980s, than would otherwise have died, had the resource wars not occurred (IRC, 2000).[3] In 2003 they revised the

---

[2] Figures compiled from various reports of the Diamond High Council, Antwerp, and *Diamond Intelligence Briefs*, Tel Aviv.
[3] The story of conflict diamonds in the DRC is detailed in Dietrich (2002).

figure upwards to 3.3 million (IRC, 2003). It is probably safe to say, therefore, that more than 3.5 million people died during the 1990s as a result of wars fueled in part, or in whole, by diamonds.

The UN steps in

The United Nations Security Council withdrew its UN peacekeeping force from Angola in 1998. There was no peace to keep, and the rebel UNITA movement had repeatedly broken UN arms embargoes with impunity, paying for light weapons, tanks, rocket launchers and ground-to-air missiles with the millions it derived from diamonds. In 1999, the Security Council Sanctions Committee on Angola, chaired by Canada's UN ambassador, Robert Fowler, fielded an "expert panel" to examine the connection between diamonds and weapons, first exposed several months earlier by Global Witness. When they reported to the Security Council in March 2000, they also had the benefit of the PAC report. Unable to ignore what the NGOs had already shown, for the first time a UN report named sitting heads of government as accomplices in the breaking of UN sanctions. The Presidents of Togo and Burkina Faso were named as both diamond and weapons traffickers.

A Security Council ban was placed on any Angolan diamonds not certified as clean by the Angolan government, although as subsequent reports would show, very little changed. During the first half of 2000, however, something did change: the attitude of the diamond industry. De Beers, spooked by the Global Witness report, had closed all of its buying offices in Africa in 1999, now taking diamonds only from its own mines and from known companies with which it had a formal mining arrangement. Worried that growing NGO awareness and publicity might spiral out of control, the government of South Africa called a meeting of interested governments, NGOs, and the diamond industry in May 2000. The meeting, held in the town of Kimberley, where South African diamonds had been discovered 135 years before, was ground-breaking, not least because of the eclectic mix of people. NGOs were able to talk for the first time directly with the Belgian Foreign Minister; De Beers was able to have a direct conversation with its accusers. Many diamond officials had their first encounters with NGOs. The meeting reached no conclusions, but the participants did decide to hold another meeting at which the issues could be explored further.

This was the beginning of what became known as the "Kimberley Process," and it eventually culminated, a dozen meetings and thirty months later, at Interlaken, in Switzerland. The road from Kimberley to Interlaken was a bumpy one, with more than a few false starts. To its credit, the diamond industry had realized by the summer of 2000 that if it didn't take the NGO charges seriously, it faced a public relations disaster that could turn into a devastating commercial problem. It was not just NGO lobbying and a UN report that alarmed them. In May 2000, a peace deal in Sierra Leone fell apart. With its back to the wall militarily, the government of Sierra Leone had accepted an arrangement brokered by the United Nations and the United States. Rebel leader Foday Sankoh had been brought into the government as head of a mineral resources commission and given the status of Vice President. A UN peacekeeping force was then sent to Sierra Leone, but the RUF resisted its attempts to move peacekeepers into rebel-held diamond areas. Then, without warning, more than 500 United Nations peace-keepers were kidnapped by the RUF. Some were killed and the rest were held for ransom.

The UN operation went into a tailspin. Panicky Sierra Leoneans, fearful of being left to the devices of the RUF, organized a massive public demonstration outside Foday Sankoh's house in Freetown. It turned violent when his guards shot and killed seventeen civilians. Suddenly, the entire concept of UN peacekeeping was thrown into question, and active thought was given to abandoning Sierra Leone to its fate. Journalists flocked to Freetown, and for a moment, the "CNN effect" – so long absent from this brutal and forgotten war – came into play.

Diamond industry initiatives

In the end, the hostages were released, and the UN was given a stronger mandate. But in the process, Partnership Africa Canada's report, *The Heart of the Matter*, now five months old, found a new audience. Sebastian Junger, author of *The Perfect Storm*, understood the issue and, in a lengthy feature story for *Vanity Fair*, he highlighted RUF thuggery and the diamond connection (2000). That issue of *Vanity Fair* appeared in July, on the eve of the Antwerp World Diamond Congress. The Congress, a biannual gathering of the most important companies and individuals in the diamond world, was devoted almost completely to the issue of conflict diamonds. There was concern that the conflict diamond issue, now airing in the diamond heartland, was getting completely out of control. The NGO antagonists were invited to the World Diamond Congress, and were allowed into most of the meetings. Despite the danger they represented, they were treated cordially. The diamond industry was moving rapidly from a position of denial to one of engagement.

One of the outcomes of the congress was the creation of a World Diamond Council, representing a range of companies and nationalities, and designed to get a grip on the issue before it went any further. By now, other NGOs had become involved. Fatal Transactions, based in the Netherlands, was formed by a coalition of five European NGOs to act as a focal point on the conflict diamond issue. Oxfam International had become involved and participated in the Antwerp meeting, as did Amnesty International and World Vision. Global Witness and PAC had done the research, understood the details and led in the discussions, but they were small organizations and didn't have name-brand recognition. Oxfam, Amnesty, and World Vision did, and their representatives came with the backing of a growing coalition of European and American NGOs, including several church organizations. The head of one had suggested that if a boycott was wanted, he could activate the 30,000 ministers in his church, all of whom officiated over at least one wedding a week if not many more.

A boycott was what the industry feared most. Images of the earlier fur boycott loomed large in their thinking. De Beers Chairman Nicky Oppenheimer spoke about how destructive a boycott would be, not just to a legitimate industry, but to an industry that provided jobs and income in countries untainted by conflict diamonds. Diamonds are a major part of the economies of South Africa, Namibia, and Botswana. They are important to the economies of Russia and Australia; they are the largest economic force in Canada's Northwest Territories. And in India almost a million people work in the diamond cutting and polishing business. Nelson Mandela made a speech in South Africa denouncing irresponsible talk about a boycott.

The boycott discussion was interesting, because it was mainly industry leaders who talked about it. NGOs rarely mentioned a boycott. First, they didn't have to; the industry was doing all the talking. Second, and more importantly, NGOs did understand the economic importance of diamonds beyond the wars they fueled. The purpose of the growing campaign was never to hurt the industry; it was to stop conflict diamonds. That said, there would be several occasions in the long months ahead when NGOs would ask themselves whether negotiation was the right approach. Nobody could reasonably make an equation between Sierra Leonean lives and jobs in Namibia or India.

The Kimberley Process

The essential key to the Kimberley Process, however, was not the diamond industry. A blanket intergovernmental agreement was the only real answer, backed by national legislation in the countries that produce and trade rough diamonds. Through the last half of 2000 and in 2001, the Kimberley Process gathered steam. More and more governments joined the debate, realizing that their mining industry, or their processing or trade in diamonds, would be affected as the discussions focused more and more on a possible agreement aimed at solving the problem. As new governments arrived, the basic concept became more complicated. The core idea was that there should and could be a global certification system for all rough diamonds.[4] Under such a system, each diamond-producing country would undertake to ensure that no conflict diamonds entered the pipeline between the mine and the point of export. In other words, the government of each producing country would guarantee that its diamonds were conflict free.

The second part of the emerging system related to the transportation of diamonds from one country to another. If an agreement could be reached, it would include provisions for standardized, tamper-proof parcels, and confirmation of receipt would be acknowledged by the importer back to the exporter. The third part of the system concerned countries like Belgium, the United States, and Israel, where rough diamonds are sorted and many, if not most, are reexported. How could there be any assurance that the reexports were clean, when it was common practice for smugglers to unload millions of dollars' worth of undeclared goods on Pelikanstraat or 47th Street with impunity?

Essential to a comprehensive agreement would be an undertaking by the governments of these countries to issue a reexport certificate ensuring that the diamonds were clean. The more difficult problem would be to ensure that the diamonds actually *would* be clean. A partial solution was offered by the diamond industry. The World Diamond Council offered to develop what it called a "chain of warranties" within the industry, which would require diamonds to be tracked, by value and weight, as they moved from one dealer to another. This would give the exporting authority the assurance that conflict diamonds had not entered and contaminated the system.

Many issues, of course, arose. Kimberley meetings were held in London, Brussels, Luanda, Pretoria, Moscow, and Gaborone. They were two-day affairs which got bigger as time passed, losing the informality of the early events. Governments arrived with official statements professing gratitude at the wonderful hospitality of the host country and a determination to end the scourge of conflict diamonds

---

[4] Discussions about marking diamonds or in some way identifying their physical characteristics arose, but made little headway. Markings can be changed, copied or cut off a diamond, and the technology for physical "fingerprinting" has not yet developed into a practical application.

forthwith. And then they would raise objections at virtually every turn. Statistics were a problem. The shape of the actual Kimberley Certificate and the font to be used in printing it occupied several hours during various plenaries. At one meeting there was a ninety-minute debate on the wording of the final communiqué: had there been "significant progress" in the meeting, or just "an emerging consensus" about the design of the certificate? It turned out to be the latter because some governments had come with a mandate to block "significant progress."

The WTO became an issue. Would regulation of rough diamonds be, in some way, an infringement on the free and open trade of goods? NGOs insisted that the issue of conflict diamonds was a security issue, not a trade issue, pointing out that the 1994 General Agreement on Trade and Tariffs contained appropriate human security provisions which supported the Kimberley Process. A lawyer hired by ActionAid was the first to recognize this provision as a way forward, although some governments, notably Canada, the United States, and Japan, kept raising the need for a formal WTO waiver. Statistics were another stumbling block. Diamond production and trade statistics were notoriously unreliable, or simply nonexistent. Without good statistics, however, a certification system could never hope to function effectively. At the Kimberley meeting in Moscow in July 2001, PAC presented a paper on the need for reliable diamond production and trade statistics, and this particular logjam finally started to break. But the greatest NGO contribution, perhaps, was the continuing pressure on governments and the industry to act quickly and decisively on an overall agreement.

At the September 2001 meeting in London, NGOs presented a petition signed by over 200 civil society organizations in Europe, North America, Europe, and Asia, demanding more decisive action. The document – first distributed in photocopy form because a printed version had not arrived – was quickly dismissed. When the final version arrived from the printers, however, in bright red with a 300-point headline – STOP BLOOD DIAMONDS NOW! – it created a considerable stir. Amnesty International mimicked a De Beers television advertisement, and placed a dramatic action cartoon on its website showing rebels hacking the hand off a civilian in order to get at diamonds. American NGOs worked with two dedicated Congressmen, Tony Hall, a Democrat, and Frank Wolf, a Republican, in sponsoring a congressional "Clean Diamond Bill" that aimed to ban conflict diamonds from the United States. The US diamond jewelry industry, worried about the provisions of the bill but understanding the demand for better regulation, worked with a Senator, Judd Gregg, on softer legislation. In June 2001, World Vision bought some air time as the credits were rolling on the last episode of the popular television program, *The West Wing*. In the program, Martin Sheen plays a likeable American President. The World Vision promo showed film of Sierra Leonean children without hands. The voice of Martin Sheen told viewers that diamonds were contributing to such atrocities, and if they wanted to stop them, they should ask their Congressman to support the Hall/Wolf bill.

Within days the Gregg bill had disappeared, and the US industry made peace with the NGOs and the Clean Diamond Bill. NGOs worked the media. They worked closely with all the major international television networks; with national and international radio; with print journalists and the internet. Feature articles appeared in *Esquire*, *National Geographic*, *USA Today*, the *New York Times*, *Der Spiegel*, and *Jornal do Brazil*. Feature programs were shown on television in Britain, Canada, Japan, and in the United States. *60 Minutes* (and *60 Minutes II*) ran the story, working closely with NGOs on the background. Conflict diamonds were twice used as a plot device on the popular American television drama, *Law and Order*; they were the leitmotif in the 2003 James Bond film, *Die Another Day*, and they featured large in a major 2005 film, *The Lord of War*. In 2006, *Blood Diamond*, starring Leonardo DiCaprio, was released.

In addition to material about conflict diamonds produced for their supporters and the general public, NGOs also produced policy-related documents, op-ed articles and background research. Early in the debate Global Witness produced a detailed description of what a certification system might look like (2000). Partnership Africa Canada produced research papers on diamonds in Guinea, Canada, and India. It produced a follow-up report on Sierra Leone which examined the role of the Lebanese diaspora in the illicit diamond trade, and it reviewed other international agreements for their provisions on monitoring.

The NGO coalition and its allies

The NGO coalition was an interesting one. It was never a formal grouping; there were no regular meetings; no chair; no "members." There was no "leadership" as such, although because Global Witness and Partnership Africa Canada had dedicated resources and people to the issue, they tended to be more active and informed on day-to-day issues. Other key players were the British NGO, ActionAid, Oxfam International, the Amsterdam-based Fatal Transactions, World Vision and Amnesty International. Important participants also included two African NGOs representing broad coalitions in their own countries: the Network Movement for Justice and Development in Sierra Leone, and

CENADEP in the Democratic Republic of Congo. This coalition was supported and backed by a loose grouping of 200 other NGOs around the world, including an important coalition of American NGOs. Altogether, it was an eclectic grouping: development and human rights NGOs; NGOs in the North and the South; very big NGOs and very small NGOs; faith-based NGOs and activist campaigning NGOs. While there were occasional disagreements, there was never anything like a dispute. Each organization carried out its own activities, but there was regular sharing of information by e-mail, frequent telephone conference calls, and meetings before and after each Kimberley session. The coalition's strength appeared to derive from its informality and the broad range of interests, and from a willingness to share, to listen, and to cooperate when common stands were required. In this sense, the NGO coalition demonstrated many of the characteristics described in Brown's model of mutual accountability – shared goals, relations of trust and mutual influence, network oversight, and a dependence on moral obligations rather than overly formalized procedures.

However, the accountability relations were not limited to like-minded NGOs. The NGOs had four sets of allies through the Kimberley Process. Ironically, and in an odd way, the first was the diamond industry. The relationship was frequently adversarial, and the industry wanted little more than for the NGOs to go away. But for this to happen, the NGOs would need to be satisfied that an effective agreement was in place. Although the industry balked and kicked at each NGO demand, there was little disagreement by the time of the Interlaken meeting in November 2002. This, however, would not have been obvious to the casual observer. Only a week before Interlaken the diamond industry had held its second World Diamond Congress since the issue had emerged, this time in London. But this time the NGOs were not inside, they were outside demonstrating. A bomb threat cleared the building at one stage, and among the demonstrators were a remarkably good Marilyn Monroe look-alike and four actors in top hats and tails, acting out scenes from *Gentlemen Prefer Blondes*. A year earlier, NGOs had pressed the industry to ensure that its proposed "chain of warranties" would be open to public scrutiny, in the form of government-supervised audits. An initial refusal had given way to an agreement. But by the time of the London meeting, no details of this chain of warranties had been released. The Marilyn Monroe look-alike, in a tight pink dress and long white gloves, was not demanding diamonds, she was demanding commercial transparency. A week later at Interlaken, outside the main Kimberley meeting, the NGOs and industry representatives had a private discussion, marked at first by shouting and recrimination, and then by a more reasoned discussion about how to carry remaining issues forward into 2003. The dynamic was an interesting one, because by then all the industry and NGO participants had struggled through a dozen Kimberley meetings together; all were on a first-name basis; and there were regular phone and e-mail contacts between meetings. Although they were often at each other's throats, they now shared a common interest: stopping conflict diamonds. And they shared common frustrations as well, such as government delegations at Kimberley meetings harping on tiny issues and refusing to come to grips with substantive problems. But it was the shared goal, and a process that remained focused on it, that made mutual accountability possible among unlikely allies.

The second NGO ally was the United Nations. The first UN Expert Panel report on Angola in March 2000 had changed the nature of the debate. It was no longer "just" an NGO campaign; the Security Council itself now had its own study confirming what NGOs had said. Sanctions-busting governments were "named and shamed." Other Expert Panels followed: Sierra Leone, the Democratic Republic of Congo, Liberia. These, and a continuing Angola panel, issued several reports between 2000 and the end of 2002, confirming and reconfirming the connection between war, weapons, and diamonds. Interestingly, all the panels took advice and information from NGOs, and NGO personnel were seconded to serve on some of them.[5] In December 2000 the UN General Assembly passed a unanimous resolution endorsing the Kimberley Process, urging it to reach an effective conclusion, and asking it to report back in a year. Once this happened, the Kimberley Process had a new form of legitimacy, and a time frame. This helped many of the participating delegations explain the urgency and the importance of the issue to their governments.

The third ally in the process, and perhaps the most important, was the government of South Africa. Without a governmental champion for the process, it would certainly have taken a very different turn in its early stages. In fact the thing most feared by the industry and South Africa – an NGO boycott – might well have come to pass, in the absence of any alternative. South Africa called the first Kimberley meeting, and it chaired the process throughout the following months. It gathered and disseminated information, it did the background preparations for all the meetings and hosted three itself, and it chaired all of them. It was

---

[5] The author left his work with Partnership Africa Canada to serve for six months on the Sierra Leone Expert Panel in 2000. Other panels included individuals seconded from Human Rights Watch in London and the International Peace Information Service in Belgium.

instrumental in getting the UN General Assembly Resolution drafted and passed, and when all about them were losing their heads – which happened on more than one occasion – the South Africans who had stayed with the process from its beginning, never once appeared to lose patience, interest, or heart.

A fourth ally was a community of academics and research institutions that began to take an interest in the economics of civil war, just as the NGO campaign was gathering strength. The World Bank began a program to study the economics of civil wars, crime, and violence in 1999. In 2000, the International Peace Academy published an edited volume on economic agendas in civil wars – *Greed and Grievance* – drawing attention to the work of several academics on the generic issue (Berdal and Malone, 2000). Informed by the NGO work on diamonds, these institutions and others helped to publicize the issue in new ways, and to new audiences. Between 2000 and 2003, across Europe, North America, and Africa, there was a spate of academic conferences on the subject, at which NGO campaigners were invited to speak and present papers.

It may be instructive to compare the Kimberley Process briefly with the campaign that led to the international convention to ban landmines. The comparison is useful because the landmine campaign also demonstrated characteristics similar to the Kimberley Process and of mutual accountability at a global scale. Like the diamond accord, the landmine agreement dealt with a complex and sensitive issue; it appeared to reach international consensus in a short space of time; and it involved governments and NGOs working together rather than as antagonists. In the early 1990s, several NGOs began to coordinate the many existing initiatives aimed at banning antipersonnel landmines, eventually creating the International Campaign to Ban Landmines (ICBL) which brought together hundreds of organizations. In October 1996, Canadian Foreign Minister Lloyd Axworthy addressed an Ottawa strategy conference on landmines, and proposed something dramatic and unexpected: he called on all the nations of the world to negotiate a mine ban treaty and asked them to return to Ottawa in fourteen months to sign it. That it actually happened is no small miracle, not least because the protagonists were charting completely new waters in reaching an international agreement. Among the reasons for success, as described by two Canadian participants:

- there was an open-ended, dynamic, and continual expanding community of self-selected, like-minded states;
- there was an "intimate" partnership between governments, international organizations, and NGOs;

- a wide range of tools – diplomatic, public, political and technological – were used to generate public and political will;
- a credible political process and a negotiating forum were established where discussions could take place;
- legitimacy and credibility of the final instrument was ensured by placing it within a UN context for long-term custodianship (Gwozdecky and Sinclair, 2000).

A conscious, two-track approach was used. On one hand, a massive public campaign was undertaken, mainly by the growing number of NGO participants, to create public support and political will. On the other, a formal negotiating process was established to create a forum where an agreement could be debated and concluded. More than a dozen meetings were hosted by as many governments, in Asia, Africa, Europe, Australia, and Canada, at which the issue was treated not as a weapons issue, but as a humanitarian issue.

The Kimberley Process was very similar, in an unconscious way. The willingness of the government of South Africa to champion the cause and chair the process from the start was essential to its success. The NGO coalition was probably smaller and less formal. And unlike the "intimate" partnership of the landmine campaign, the relationship between the four sectors in the Kimberley Process – industry, governments, NGOs, and international institutions – was often difficult, although all developed a healthy respect for one another and all managed to work creatively and (mostly) cordially through the process. The involvement of the private sector made Kimberley both different and probably more complex than the landmine agreement. Fewer governments were involved in Kimberley, but the seventy-odd participants certainly represented every political color of the rainbow.

Both the Kimberley system as it stood in mid-2003, and the landmine agreement as signed, had weak enforcement mechanisms. NGOs combined to form a new organization, "Landmine Monitor" – supported by twelve governmental signatories – to evaluate international compliance with that agreement, publishing annual reports of a thousand pages or more. No such system had been agreed within the Kimberley Process.

The agreement

In March 2002, a make-or-break Kimberley Meeting was held in Ottawa. Depending on who was counting, it was either the twelfth or thirteenth meeting in the series. As the hours passed, most of the insoluble problems melted away, and by the end, only one remained. NGOs had insisted from the outset that the system would only be credible and effective if there was regular, independent inspection of all national control systems. If all countries were eligible to join, there was an obligation that all be subject to regular inspection. Why would more rules be any more effective than existing laws against theft, murder, sanctions busting, and human rights abuse? The draft Kimberley agreement, however, left monitoring vaguely to decisions that would be made at annual plenary meetings, and then to take place only in cases of "indications of significant non-compliance."

For NGOs, monitoring was a fundamental requirement if the system was to be effective. And those NGOs present at the Ottawa meeting had to decide at the eleventh hour whether they would endorse the agreement as far as it had gone, or dig in. If they were to dig in, they feared that several delegations would withdraw from the process and the Kimberley Process might very well collapse. India, China, Russia, and Israel had all spoken against regular monitoring. While some governments were favorably inclined, at least privately, none spoke in favor of the NGO position in the plenary discussions. The issue threatened to turn septic. NGOs held their ground against a withering attack from several governments. They were said to be bargaining in bad faith; they were even called "deplorable," by one government delegation – oddly harsh language in a diplomatic forum where tempers rarely flared. The World Diamond Council pleaded for reconsideration. In the end, and without enthusiasm or even full agreement among themselves, the NGOs agreed to endorse the Kimberley system as developed to that point. They reserved the right to speak publicly about the monitoring issue, however, and they said that they would not let the issue drop as the system moved forward.

Between March and November 2002, governments worked to ensure that the required regulations and legislation would be in place to enable a launch of the Kimberley Process in January 2003. And they came together at Interlaken to review progress and tie up whatever loose ends might remain. On the opening day, the South African Chair asked each delegation whether or not it would be ready to implement on 1 January. There were a few holdouts – Japan and Thailand said they might be ready "later," not seeming to understand that if they were not in the system, their diamonds would be banned from world trade. Cyprus, Malta, and Ukraine said they were working towards compliance as quickly as possible. Most of the others were, they said, ready, willing, and able.

A few problems remained. The system for gathering and monitoring statistics had still not been worked out, although this was gradually put in place after 2003. Some governments continued to express concern about WTO compliance. And the major NGO concern remained regarding the lack of regular independent monitoring of all national control mechanisms.

These issues notwithstanding, several important changes took place in the diamond world on 1 January 2003. First, several countries that had been laundering diamonds were forced to stop immediately. These included Gambia, Zambia, Rwanda, Uganda, and others. These countries, all entrepôts for conflict diamonds as well as the wider trade in illicit goods, represented hundreds of millions of dollars' worth of rough diamonds, if not more. Second, all Kimberley Process participating governments were now required to issue certificates of legitimacy for rough diamonds leaving their borders. Even if there was no clear monitoring process, they would now be on record as authenticating their exports. And in February 2003, the WTO provided the Kimberley Process with the long-anticipated waiver.

Other changes and improvements were to follow. At the end of 2003, negotiations among NGOs, the World Diamond Council, and Israel resulted in the acceptance by the Kimberley Process of a voluntary "peer review mechanism." The idea was that a participating country might *invite* a peer review of its internal diamond controls. Although purely voluntary, several countries quickly issued invitations and a procedure was soon established using teams comprised of representatives of three governments and a representative each from NGOs and industry. These reviews and their reports became an effective way of tightening internal controls and of measuring the capacities of new KP applicants. Following a review in 2004, the Republic of Congo (Brazzaville) was expelled from the Kimberley Process because it could not demonstrate convincingly where it had obtained the diamonds it had exported – a demonstration of the system's new teeth.

By mid-2006, thirty reviews had been conducted, and only five countries had not invited one, a significant advance on the opening position where regular reviews of any kind had been deemed politically unacceptable. There were other significant outcomes, not least a huge increase in the volume of legitimately traded diamonds. In 2004, the DRC officially exported more diamonds than in any other year since their discovery. In 2005, Sierra Leone exported $142 million worth of diamonds, up from less than $2 million only a few years earlier. The Kimberley Process was serving not only to curtail *conflict* diamonds, it was now curtailing illicit diamonds as well.

The system was not without its continuing weaknesses, many of them regularly exposed by the two NGOs – PAC and Global Witness – that had been there from the beginning. A 2005 PAC report, for example, revealed massive corruption in Brazilian diamond controls, corruption that would not likely have been found by the Kimberley Process alone. The exposé resulted in a series of arrests and the complete suspension of all Brazilian diamond exports for several months in 2006. The Brazil case demonstrated that there remained a role for NGOs, not just as participants in the Kimberley Process, but as watchdogs to ensure its effectiveness.

Conclusion

In summary, there are at least three accountability issues in this story. The first concerns the potentially powerful global impacts of mutual accountability arrangements. These are complex negotiated processes, both among and within organizations. In the case of the conflict diamonds campaign, the shared goals of the NGO coalition had to be weighed against individual organizational aims and concerns. A question that arose for several NGOs related to the potential danger for their field staff in Africa if they became associated with a public campaign critical of governments or rebel movements. There were also informal responsibilities to coalition members who did not want the overall effort derailed by individual cowboyism. Should ActionAid have hired the Marilyn Monroe impersonator to demonstrate outside the World Diamond Congress meeting in October 2002? It was a stunt, and it was bound to get publicity – none of it likely to be bad for the NGO. But would it persuade the diamond industry to produce details of its long-awaited chain of warranties, or would it annoy industry leaders so mightily that it could actually be counterproductive? The NGO coalition debated these issues and maintained coordination on broad brushstrokes of the campaign through regular e-mail contact, frequent transatlantic conference calls, and meetings at least two or three times a year. In addition, there were smaller NGO coalitions in Europe, Canada, and the United States. The story of mutual accountability also extended beyond these like-minded actors towards historical adversaries: the diamond industry and, in some cases, governments. What held the process together was a shared goal – to end conflict diamonds – whether for humanitarian or public relations reasons.

There were also more traditional forms of accountability at play, between NGOs and those who funded the campaign. PAC was supported financially by a dozen other NGOs. Some supported the campaign through small unearmarked contributions, with no strings attached. Others supported specific aspects of the campaign, requiring detailed reports on precisely how the funds had been spent, and on what had been achieved. Funding from institutional donors – government departments and foundations – is always provided with clear instructions on reporting against planned activities and objectives. Such contributions may require a formal evaluation, and most contain provisions for an external audit, to be conducted at the discretion of the donor. For example, PAC received a small contribution from the Peacebuilding Fund of the Canadian Department of Foreign Affairs and International Trade and this was the subject of a surprise (and positive) audit in 2002. This could be described as classic principal–agent accountability.

The third major accountability issue in this case revolves around NGO legitimacy and representation, and the frequent critique that NGOs have no right to interfere in the affairs of governments or the private sector. A 2002 article about diamonds in the *Spectator* praised the "almost nauseating rectitude of De Beers" and attacked its critics as "anti-global-capitalists, liberal idealists and bearded, sandal-wearing Africa experts" (Delingpole, 2002). The courts offered a potential recourse for companies and governments where NGO accountability was concerned. The government of Angola initiated a lawsuit against Global Witness in 2001 for comments it had made about corruption at senior levels in the ruling party. In the end, however, the case was dropped. Perhaps the government's lawyers realized that a public court case would only draw more attention to the avalanche of corruption charges against Angola made by a small army of other organizations, ranging from Transparency International to the IMF.

It is important to recognize that the diamond industry was always considerably more than a defenseless victim under NGO siege. The diamond industry employs a legion of public relations experts. De Beers alone spends more than $200 million annually on advertising. Senior officials in many firms have been sent for training by firms in Switzerland that specialize in how to deal with NGOs. The government of Botswana hired the public relations giant, Hill and Knowlton, which had worked for Nestlé on an NGO baby food campaign. It is perhaps a measure of the quality of the NGO effort, the power of the message, and the legitimacy of the call for diamond regulation, that no government ever followed through on a threatened lawsuit, no company openly attacked an NGO, and only a handful of journalists ever questioned NGO motivation.

One might conclude that legitimacy was conferred on the NGO campaign by the fact that governments, industry, and the United Nations became involved, creating the Kimberley Process and a global certification system for rough diamonds. The campaign, however, was *activity*; the Kimberley meetings were, as the name implies, *process*; and the certification system was *outcome*. Had there been no outcome, or if the certification system were to fail, could it be argued that the campaign would have been something less than legitimate?

In the end, the issue of accountability in the conflict diamond campaign was less about NGOs than it was about an unregulated industry that had allowed itself to become badly infected by illicit behavior, thus opening the door to much worse criminality: gun running, sanctions busting, war, and the deaths of hundreds of thousands of people. To focus the issue on NGO representation loses sight of the fact that accountability is about more than procedure, and masks the real problem as to why the diamond industry had been so unaccountable – why its own leaders had never spoken out, never considered codes of conduct, never expelled a single diamond trader from a bourse anywhere in the world until NGOs exposed the issue. Not accountable to anyone? The NGO diamond campaign was, and remains, focused on accountability: in an industry which could have been the engine of development in the Congo, Angola, and Sierra Leone, but which chose instead to ally itself with corrupt politicians, joining them in a downward spiral of chaos, disintegration, and war.

References

Berdal, Mats and David Malone (eds.) (2000) *Greed and Grievance: Economic Agendas in Civil Wars*. Boulder, CO: Lynne Rienner.

Delingpole, James (20 July 2002) "Diamond Geezers," *The Spectator*.

Dietrich, Christian (2002) *Hard Currency: The Criminalized Diamond Economy of the Democratic Republic of the Congo and its Neighbours*. Ottawa: Partnership Africa Canada.

Economist (9 December 1999) "The Non-Governmental Order," *The Economist*.

Global Witness (1998) *A Rough Trade*. London: Global Witness, p. 3.

Global Witness (2000) *Possibilities for the Identification, Certification and Control of Diamonds*. London: Global Witness.

Gwozdecky, Mark and Jill Sinclair (2000) "Landmines and Human Security," in Rob McRae and Don Hubert (eds.) *Human Security and the New Diplomacy*. Montreal and Kingston: McGill-Queen's University Press, p. 31.

IRC or International Rescue Committee (April 2003) "Mortality in the Democratic Republic of the Congo: Results from a Nationwide Survey," New York: IRC.

IRC or International Rescue Committee (May 2000) "Mortality in Eastern DRC: Results from Five Mortality Surveys," Bukavu: IRC.

Junger, Sebastian (August 2000) "The Terror of Sierra Leone," *Vanity Fair*.

Smillie, Ian (1995) *The Alms Bazaar: Altruism Under Fire – Nonprofit Organizations and International Development*. London: IT Publications.

Smillie, I., L. Gberie, and R. Hazleton (2000) *The Heart of the Matter: Sierra Leone, Diamonds and Human Security*. Ottawa: Partnership Africa Canada.

Bringing in society, culture,
and politics: values and accountability
in a Bangladeshi NGO

David Lewis

Introduction

Questions of accountability have become important and difficult ones in recent years for nongovernmental organizations (NGOs) working in the development field. The rise of development NGOs during the late 1980s generated considerable expectations regarding their performance strengths and political contributions, but this was accompanied by growing doubts about their ability to maintain appropriate and effective levels of accountability to a wide range of "stakeholders" including users, funders, staff, and government (Edwards and Hulme, 1995). While this accountability critique was initially focused on the section of the NGO community rooted in industrialized countries – often known as "Northern NGOs" – there is a growing recognition that a similar set of structural and relational accountability issues are also faced by NGOs with their roots in developing country contexts.

This chapter reflects on a recent study by the author of research and advocacy work undertaken by a large Bangladeshi NGO, referred to here by a pseudonym, Association for Credit and Empowerment (ACE). The study is considered in the light of issues of accountability and the chapter discusses the complex accountability problems which face even a relatively successful Southern NGO.[1] The broader contribution of this chapter to the study of "global accountabilities" lies in its exploration of the cultural embeddedness of accountability systems. To truly understand the effects of accountability on organizations, it is useful to examine them in context: within configurations of power and

---

[1] The anthropological convention of using a pseudonym has been maintained in this paper in order to conceal the formal identities of persons involved in the issues reported here. Increasing political sensitivities became apparent in the relations between some development NGOs and the government formed by the Bangladesh Nationalist Party (BNP) since 2001.

social institutions. Accountability may be a global phenomenon, promoted worldwide by donors in terms of managerial requirements and systems, but its manifestations, effects, and tensions play out locally.

Development NGOs are a highly diverse family of organizations and there has been considerable effort expended in the research literature on the different ways in which NGOs can be categorized and labeled. It would be both unnecessary and probably unproductive to attempt to summarize such wide-ranging debates here. A useful simple definition of such NGOs is that they are "self-governing, private, not-for-profit organizations that are geared to improving the quality of life for disadvantaged people" (Vakil, 1997, p. 2060). However, the term NGO is in many ways an unhelpful one for analytical purposes. It includes a great many different types of organization, from small local groups operating on a largely voluntary and informal basis, to large private development agencies with multimillion dollar budgets and many thousands of paid, professional staff. It may include some organizations which far from being relatively independent are in fact very close to the state or the private sector. There are other organizations which call themselves NGOs which have a "bogus" character, simply finding the NGO label a convenient one to further their political or economic goals or as a means of claiming entitlements. In spite of such complexity, there is widespread agreement that there has been a rapid growth in the numbers and profile of NGOs in the past decade, both in the industrialized "North," where NGOs are concerned with poverty and social justice at home and abroad, and in the aid-recipient countries of "the South," where NGOs old and new have been identified as potential "partners" by governments and international aid agencies (Salamon, 1994; Smillie, 1995; Lewis, 2007).[2]

Alongside structural problems of accountability faced by NGOs in their relations with a wide range of stakeholders, there are also issues which need to be considered in relation to new thinking on the challenges of development work itself, and in relation to the overall context in which an NGO operates. For example, the need to link local and global agendas and constituencies within development work appears to be making accountability pressures for most NGOs grow increasingly more complex. As a result, there may be a "trend towards more diverse

----

[2] The rise of NGOs has been driven by a range of factors and these have been summarized elsewhere (Howell and Pearce, 2001; Lewis, 2002). During the past decade or so, NGOs have become established organizational actors within development policy and practice, but more critical questions are now being asked of their accountability and their performance (Edwards and Hulme, 1995; Lewis and Wallace, 2000).

and seemingly unconnected voices making requests or demands of the nonprofit organization to be accountable for different things" (Fry, 1995, p. 191). At the same time, higher levels of diversity within and between NGOs bring new challenges in terms of integrating values and managing responsibilities between NGO staff, users, and funders. In their study of South Asian NGOs, Smillie and Hailey (2001) identify "the influence of context and culture" and "balancing formality and informality" as key characteristics of successful NGOs. This chapter concludes that such problems are not simply managerial or technical ones as is frequently claimed, but instead will require *analysis within a broader contextual framework for thinking about accountability which takes into account an organization's position within wider fields of power and social networks.*

This chapter focuses on a development NGO in Bangladesh which displays a complex set of accountability problems, both in relation to the operation of its formal organizational structures and systems, and as a consequence of the embeddedness of these systems in the wider society and institutions which surround the organization. The NGO sector in Bangladesh has received considerable academic and donor attention in recent years, but there has been a stronger focus on formal accountability issues than on the nature of its embeddedness. Wider civil society in Bangladesh is strongly influenced by vertical patron–client relationships which characterize wider social structures and which also help to structure relationships between people within and between organizations (Wood, 1997; Lewis, 2004). Within many development agencies, gender inequalities too are subtly reproduced, as in cases where wider attitudes inform the construction and labeling of "gendered" programs and activities. For example, it has been common in programmatic development discourse in Bangladesh to distinguish unhelpfully between men's "employment" projects and women's "income-generating activities" (Kabeer, 2000).

The analysis of NGO accountability

Accountability is an issue which has been widely debated and theorized within the social sciences, well before the current period of heightened interest in accountability in relation to development NGOs. Within the wider tradition of thinking on accountability, it is possible to discern two central theoretical strands within the analysis of accountability. The first approach, following mainly from Weber's analysis of bureaucratic structures, has theorized accountability primarily in terms of rule-bound responses by organizations and individuals who must report to recognized authorities such as government agencies or donor organizations in order to ensure that the resources they receive are used properly and that the work they undertake is done effectively. The role of sanctions in order to maintain proper accountability is heavily emphasized in these types of accounts.

From an institutional perspective, accountability is often conceptualized as a "principal–agent" relationship such as a donor or government contracts with an NGO in order to provide a specified service (see Brown, above, ch. 5, and Brett, 1993). Such an arrangement requires that a set of checks and balances is put in place – such as mechanisms for reporting, monitoring, and evaluation – which can ensure that an NGO provides these services in a trustworthy manner and that the service is provided properly in terms of cost-effectiveness, quality, and targeting. This form of thinking also lies behind the "audit culture" of much of the "new managerialism" which has become a common feature of public life from the aid industry to higher education. O'Neill (2002) has reviewed the growth of what is often perceived to be a burdensome regime of inspection and target setting which, it is argued, may have actually undermined levels of professionalism and trust within the health and education sectors in the UK. There has also been considerable concern around these themes within British academia, where the raise of audit culture has been analyzed in neo-Foucauldian terms as part of a shift to neoliberal forms of governance which depend in large part on the role of individual agency in which "individuals, as active agents, are co-opted into regimes of power" (Shore and Wright, 2001, p. 760).

A second strand of thinking takes a more open-ended view characterized by a Durkheimian perspective of the integrative roles of organizations. This view of accountability takes as its starting point the idea that organizations are socially constructed entities. In this view, accountability can be understood as the maintenance of organizational integrity through dialogues among and between different stakeholders – such as staff, clients, governors, funders – which seek to enhance the effectiveness of an NGO. In this view, accountability processes form part of the ways in which organizations as socially constructed entities seek to construct shared systems of meanings and practices. Rather than seeing accountability issues as issues which are raised when things go wrong, accountability is instead viewed as a process which can be understood as part of the daily organizational life of an NGO (Fry, 1995). As well as emphasizing the importance of issues such as organizational learning, this view also stresses the ethical dimension of organizational accountability: it is not simply a set of controls to be imposed upon an organization from the outside, but is a set of "felt responsibilities" derived from within an organization's values, mission, and culture. This approach is also close to Biggs and Neame's (1995) thinking on NGO accountability which views the negotiations which follow from such felt responsibilities as unique opportunities for the more successful NGOs to learn and innovate.

As noted in the introductory chapter to this volume, most writers on NGO accountability draw attention to the fact that it takes on a complex, multidirectional character. For example, Najam (1996) demonstrates the ways in which an NGO is simultaneously accountable to its *patrons* such as donors, whose concerns are usually centered upon whether funds are used for designated purposes; to *clients* such as its users in the community, who are concerned with ensuring that the NGO acts in their interests, but have no clear means of ensuring this, or the government, which may contract an NGO to carry out a particular task; and finally to *itself*, in the sense that each NGO has a vision which it seeks to actualize, and staff for whom it is responsible. Najam (1996, p. 351) argues that all too often NGOs "tend to focus principally on their responsibility to their patrons, very often at the cost of their responsibility to their clients and to their own goals and vision."

The result is that for many NGOs accountability can become skewed and unbalanced. One result of this unbalanced accountability is the phenomenon of unplanned growth, where a "successful" small-scale NGO evolves into a large, hierarchical organization with many of the bureaucratic problems associated with traditional government agencies – such as a slowness to respond to problems, loss of contact with a certain part of the community, or the disappearance of a flexibility which made it possible to learn from experience. Another consequence is the problem of goal displacement, when for example an NGO drifts away from its original emphasis on education work towards credit delivery, due to the availability of donor funds for this purpose rather than from any special competence.

In the Bangladesh context, many development NGOs have drifted from quite radical roots in the transformational implications of aspects of Paolo Freire's conscientization theory, for example, towards the credit and service delivery approach in part as a result of the greater availability of donor funds for such activities (Lewis, 1997; 2004). The rise of contracting arrangements between NGOs and bilateral and multilateral donors has fueled concerns that wider NGO roles may be changing. For example, NGOs may be increasingly co-opted by states and donors into fulfilling the larger geopolitical objectives of "containing disorder" in parts of the post-Cold War world, rather than responding primarily to humanitarian needs and poverty (Fowler, 1995). Another important accountability problem has therefore traditionally concerned the unequal relationships which obtain within the "aid industry" between donors, Northern NGOs, and Southern NGOs. Many Northern NGOs have moved away from the direct implementation of projects in developing countries towards a "partnership approach" with Southern NGOs, part of which includes efforts to undertake "capacity building" work with local organizational partners in order to build greater levels of effectiveness and self-reliance, but the precise nature and terms of such partnerships often remain unclear (Lewis, 1998).

Since accountability for NGOs can be understood as involving a combination of both internal and external factors (Ebrahim, 2003), it is clear that both of the above approaches to accountability will be relevant to both the analysis and practice of NGO accountability. It is also the case that accountability has important implications for the performance of NGOs, which has come under closer scrutiny in recent years. After the initial "discovery" of NGOs as development actors in the 1980s, hard evidence of effective performance has proved elusive. Earlier assumptions made about the comparative advantages of NGOs over other kinds of organization in poverty-reduction work have been challenged. While there are many effective NGOs to be found, there are also many which lack basic management competencies and operate without a clear focus, or which exist for nondevelopmental reasons, such as building political patronage, or accumulating resources for leaders or staff. There are also questions about the management capacity of NGOs which may be motivated by ambitious objectives but which are in practice hindered by confused vision, weak administrative systems, and domineering leadership.[3]

Association for Credit and Empowerment

Bangladesh's NGO sector has become an increasingly significant and well-documented feature of the country's social and economic life. It emerged primarily in the wake of the independence struggle in 1971, as part of the efforts of both local and international individuals and organizations to establish reconstruction and poverty reduction efforts within the new state (Lewis, 1997; 2004). Bangladesh's organizations

---

[3] For example, an evaluation of Danish NGOs in Bangladesh, Nicaragua, and Tanzania presented findings that highlight a range of accountability problems (Oakley, 1999). In a comparison of four local NGOs in South Asia, Edwards (1999) suggests that the most effective development NGOs were characterized by independent thinking, clear goals, personal qualities of commitment among staff and volunteers, and a close working relationship built up with clients over a long period of time.

are considerably varied in terms of their size and scope, and some organizations such as the Grameen Bank have specialized in micro-finance
service provision, while others such as the Bangladesh Rural Advancement Committee (BRAC) offer a wide range of different services – in
addition to credit – in support of education, health, and agriculture.
Alongside service provision, there is increasing interest in advocacy work
among some NGOs, and this case study focuses on an organization which
has been seeking for the past half-decade or so to institutionalize its
advocacy function within a special unit within the NGO.

The Association for Credit and Empowerment is one of the dozen or
so large development NGOs which have now become well-established
organizational actors on the Bangladesh development scene. ACE has
been active since the mid-1970s and has steadily grown so that it now
has field offices around much of the country. ACE's general approach
has been to form a network of small groups of landless rural and urban
poor across the country in order to build economic self-reliance
through the provision of credit services and raising awareness for action
on social justice issues. Unlike many NGOs in Bangladesh which have
moved towards becoming micro-finance institutions and left behind
earlier radical roots, ACE has tried hard to retain an "activist" edge
alongside its range of service delivery programs. ACE's own accountability, at least in formal terms, is relatively clear: it is registered with
the government, which must approve its receipt of foreign funds; it has
established a donor consortium with which it agrees financial policy
and systems; and it has begun the federation of its large network of
grassroots groups which is designed to strengthen its accountability
to users.

While ACE had effectively expanded its grassroots activities steadily,
a point was reached in the early 1990s where its leaders began thinking
in more ambitious terms. A new strategy was devised to help move it
more fully into the policy-influencing sphere, and ACE's Centre for
Advocacy and Research (CAR) was established in 1994. The main aim
was to build a semi-autonomous institute which would conduct research
on policy issues for advocacy, conduct media campaigning, and
undertake training with a wider range of "civil society" organizations
and issues in order to link more fully with social movements and citizen
activism. CAR was therefore conceived as a response to a perceived
need to balance micro-level interventions with efforts to challenge
macro-level policy constraints on poverty reduction. CAR undertakes
three main types of activities in its three units. First, it develops advocacy campaigns on a range of issues, such as land rights and the abuse of
the banned chemical pesticides, and lobbies for change. Second, CAR

undertakes training work to build the capacity of the local and regional NGO sector to undertake advocacy work, basing the workshops in part on ACE's own experience. Third, CAR undertakes research in support of its campaigning work. As well as commissioning research from local specialists, it has also established an "in-house" research capacity with a team of young local researchers.

The establishment of CAR was an organizational response to a process of strategic reflection in the early 1990s on the implications of ACE's growth, learning, and experience since it began its work back in the 1970s. At the heart of this discussion was a growing recognition of the importance of the need to improve organizational capacity in support of policy advocacy, training, and research work. A new set of questions had emerged as a result of the NGO's growing development-intervention experience and the changing political context in which ACE was operating. In particular, it was felt that ACE needed to build on its grassroots work in order to communicate its work and ideas more widely with policy-makers and influence wider institutions and structures. What were the implications for ACE's work of the changing institutional landscape in Bangladesh, which shifted from a military dictatorship to a parliamentary democracy in 1991? How could ACE make use of the new democratic institutions which might offer potential opportunities for "scaling up" through policy influence? Was it possible for ACE to counter "in-house" the poor availability of relevant, critical, high-quality research and policy information accessible to development organizations?

Research into CAR's first five years of operation found significant achievements in the campaigning and advocacy fields, particularly a pioneering effort in Bangladesh which had contributed to a new emphasis on NGO advocacy work during the 1990s in the NGO sector.[4] At the same time, the study also highlighted a number of key organizational problems which were undermining CAR's performance, many of which had roots in accountability issues (Lewis and Madon, 2003). First was the finding that there were weaknesses in the ways in which advocacy and research agendas were being managed. A criticism made of CAR's work was that, despite ACE's network of more than 100,000 grassroots groups across the country, much of the advocacy agenda was driven from the

---

[4] Research within CAR was undertaken by the author as part of a review organized by ACE as an outcome of the midterm evaluation carried out by its four-donor funding consortium. Fieldwork was carried out during two fourteen-day trips to Bangladesh in early 2001, and included semi-structured interviews with a range of internal and external CAR stakeholders (staff, group members, government, wider civil society).

top – from opportunities identified by the senior Dhaka-based leadership and the director of the organization in particular. While it was seen as important to try to influence policy through maintaining good personal contacts with powerful key figures in the government "at the center," it was pointed out by some informants that opportunities to build a more participatory approach were being missed. Some field staff and group members also felt that what CAR was doing had little direct relevance to the day-to-day struggles of ordinary people. Other activists and NGOs pointed out that the great potential strength of ACE as an organization – as opposed to small urban policy think-tanks which undertake campaigning work – was to root its campaigning more directly to the needs and concerns of its beneficiaries. This was not just an issue of effectiveness but also of accountability, since ACE as an organization is committed to responding to the needs of the poorest in society and assisting them with their efforts to organize and act.

The second area of weakness concerned organizational learning, which was restricted by the absence of an effective information system with which to judge the impact of CAR's advocacy work (Lewis and Madon, 2003). What tended to happen was that campaigns or training workshops were undertaken and considered to have either met with "success" – such as a change in the implementation of the law – or with "failure" – no perceivable impact – and then were gradually replaced with new activities as other events, concerns, or opportunities presented themselves. This pragmatic approach was certainly flexible and responsive, but CAR lacked the tools with which to draw conclusions from these experiences and distil lessons which could be used to improve its programs. The fact that there was considerable activity evident overall was taken as proof that CAR was operating effectively.

During the review process, more detailed discussions helped to build a framework through which the impact of advocacy work could be assessed according to a clear set of criteria. Four types of impact were identified: 1) the immediate outcomes in terms of the aim of the campaign; 2) whether the process of policy-making has changed over the longer term or whether the result was a mere "one off"; 3) the results in terms of ACE's own learning about approaches to future advocacy work; and 4) whether wider relationships for future action among civil society actors have been strengthened, regardless of whether the campaign has been a success in terms of meeting its goals.

The importance of viewing organizational systems – and therefore accountability processes – as *social* systems can be usefully elaborated in relation to the complexity of CAR's structures, systems, and people. One of the striking findings to emerge from the review was the contrast between formal and informal advocacy work undertaken.[5] CAR has developed an internal advocacy team, which is designed to develop and undertake advocacy work on behalf of the organizations, but the reality tends to be that the senior ACE leadership plays the major role in campaigning. The leadership has moved into a prominent position on the Dhaka "civil society scene" and has constructed wider relationships with politicians and bureaucrats. There is a strong "personal" dimension to successful policy advocacy work, seen as necessary for success by some senior staff, and power is heavily concentrated at the top of the organization among the senior leadership.[6] Balancing this tension between individualized advocacy by senior staff, and grassroots-driven advocacy carried out and supported by teams at different levels of the organization, proved a major problem. It was not unusual to find grassroots ACE groups in the more remote areas of the country who were rather dismissive of work done at the center in the name of advocacy work because it could appear remote and self-serving. But from the leadership point of view, it is felt that effective political action in Bangladesh requires both mobilizing personalized networks of horizontal trust and the building of vertical patron–client linkages. It is perhaps not surprising that ACE and its leaders have embarked on both strategies.

At the same time, CAR has faced a major problem in attracting and keeping high-quality research and advocacy staff at junior and middle levels. A succession of well-qualified young researchers – many educated outside the country in British or United States universities – had joined CAR with high expectations only to leave a year or even a few months later. Partly this was a result of being tempted away by the promise of higher salaries within an increasingly competitive development agency job market, but it was also partly because they felt undervalued within CAR's overall organizational hierarchy and culture.[7] This problem helps reveal the tensions which exist between formal and informal views of human resource management. There is an ideology within ACE, propagated by its founders, that solidaristic values among staff should take precedence over financial reward, at least in the early years of

---

[5] Smillie and Hailey's (2001) book on South Asian NGOs bears out this duality between the formal and the informal as a key component of management practice within many large South Asian NGOs.

[6] This fits well with recent studies of NGOs which take an "actor-oriented approach" to organizations; that approach acknowledges that organizational boundaries are highly artificial, and personal kinship ties and informal networks may be just as influential in determining organizational behavior as formal systems, labels, and structures (Hilhorst, 2003).

[7] A detailed conceptual review of the importance of organizational culture in development agencies is provided in Lewis et al. (2003).

involvement with the organization.[8] While pay and conditions within CAR were more than adequate, they were deliberately kept a little below the level of those found in the increasingly competitive development agency sector, which is dominated by foreign organizations such as the UN and international NGOs. As a result, CAR's terms and conditions were found to be unattractive to many young foreign-educated Bangladeshi researchers faced with more lucrative opportunities in other areas of the development industry.

However, the ACE leadership was reluctant to pay higher salaries to CAR employees which could cause resentment among other sections of the staff, particularly those in remote field posts. The leadership complained that the organization was a "family" whose shared values were being challenged by a more commercially minded younger generation who were on one occasion referred to in a derogatory way as "mercenaries." Tensions between "activists" and "professionals" were also seen by the leadership as a cause of these problems – between those staff committed to the values and aims of the organization who were prepared to work for low salaries and those who saw NGO work as a career and needed a decent salary and a clear opportunity for progression in the job. The gulf between the need to reform the formal system to suit younger, specialized, in-demand recruits and the prevailing social vision – voiced through the social symbol of "the organizational family" – of the older generation of founder leaders seemed likely to prolong the problem. An organizational "culture conflict," with its roots in both internal politics and external changes, is severely weakening organizational performance.

Culture and context therefore have a significant bearing on accountability issues within ACE. Furthermore, the political environment in which NGOs in Bangladesh operate is hazardous, leading many NGOs to take on a somewhat defensive organizational form which can impede the operation of information systems. Tensions between government and NGOs are commonplace as NGOs increasingly move into roles previously occupied by the public sector. At the same time, the political nature of campaigning work challenges the position of entrenched elites,

---

[8] The key founders were mainly student activists who, within a pre-professionalized period of organization building, saw development NGOs as a vehicle for social work backed up by a strong level of ideological commitment to working with the poor. This has evolved into a powerful founding myth – essentially rooted in truth, but occasionally somewhat romanticized – which is deployed from time to time by senior managers in their discussions with disaffected junior staff. There are now quite determined efforts being made to hold on to this idea and ensure its reproduction within the organizational culture of ACE. However, as an ideology it has less appeal to the newer, younger generation of employees faced with an increasingly difficult and competitive job market.

such as rural landowners. Some of ACE's staff and members have been attacked and even killed as a result of conflicts over land. There are also occasional tensions and conflicts with religious groups who take exception to the ideology of gender equality which NGOs such as ACE seek to put into practice in their programs. Many NGOs which engage in work with women have also been criticized by conservative elements from within the religious community, some of whom view education and empowerment programs for women as an undesirable challenge to local values and customs. Finally, relations with foreign donors who fund substantial areas of the work of the NGOs can also prove problematic. While the donors themselves make strong accountability demands of the NGOs they fund, there are frequent accusations from sections of the public that NGOs' legitimacy and political integrity is compromised by the fact that they are accountable through funding relationships to powerful organizations and interests outside the country.

All these pressures can contribute to a "culture of defensiveness" in NGOs where there is a reluctance, for example, to commission research that might prove challenging to the organizational status quo and values. Added to these pressures are the prevailing patterns of patron–client relationships and social hierarchy, which within NGOs tend to internalize and reproduce significant social inequality and vertical relationships that then require high levels of deference in the management of relationships between senior and junior staff (Wood, 1997). One of the most serious results of this "culture of defensiveness" is a reluctance to confront less successful activities and initiatives, which has the effect of reducing organizational learning (Lewis and Siddiqi, 2006). From the top managers downwards, the organization is placed under constant pressure by this prevailing culture to demonstrate success but ignore failure, through sustaining an agenda of action and the addition of new activities, but there is little incentive given to find time to reflect and learn.

Growing linkages between local, national, and global levels of action are apparent from the CAR experience. While advocacy work has been undertaken with some success at the local and national levels, there is a growing awareness of the need to understand the global context of policy formulation and implementation as well as the importance of linking local priorities more effectively with wider action. Such thinking informs CAR's regional advocacy training work, and in 2000 the first regional training workshop was held with participants from all over South Asia from a range of NGOs. CAR was also part of the recent initiative, which set up an NGO working group to examine the World Bank's activities in Bangladesh, and another focusing on the consequences and implications of its structural adjustment policies. However, it was found in the review that national advocacy work tended to take an "elite" form – based on the personal values, interests, and contacts of senior staff – and often remained somewhat unconnected from the priorities of ACE's grassroots groups themselves. For example, we have seen that there were weaknesses in the ways information was being managed from the grassroots level for seeking explanations as to why particular campaigns "succeeded" or "failed," thus impairing levels of organizational learning. This then led to a growing perception among field staff that the functioning of CAR had little relevance for day-to-day struggles of ordinary people. As CAR engages more fully with complex global advocacy, a wider set of specialized knowledge and skills will be needed to maintain close ties with events "on the ground," and a key priority for the NGO continues to be the effort to connect local, national, and international efforts more coherently.

As a result of the CAR review, there has been a recognition among ACE leadership and staff more widely that attention now needs to be given to strengthening the organizational values and systems which support research and advocacy. This recognition goes well beyond technical systems towards a clearer recognition that problems related to staff skills, culture, and politics are crucial to the improvement of accountability and performance. There is now a plan to reconvene CAR's international advisory board as soon as possible – which has been more or less inactive for the past two years – in order to turn the review findings into new strategies. Within a few months of completion of the review, ACE took a decision to increase its investment in the capacity of young research staff and five were sent on appropriate overseas masters programs later that year in order to begin the strengthening process for the future. This has in part diffused the tensions which were contributing to low morale among many of the CAR staff. However, the election of the Bangladesh Nationalist Party (BNP) government shortly after the review took place has created a more difficult political environment for ACE, since it is one of a group of NGOs which are considered by the government to have identified themselves with the previous government.

Conclusion

The case study presented in this chapter suggests that NGO accountability can be only partly understood through analyzing the formal bureaucratic operation of organizational relationships and the internal systems established for activities such as advocacy, monitoring, and evaluation. While these foci are important – and at times can be seen to be quite problematic – for analyzing a development NGO, they can provide only a partial understanding of accountability processes.

To understand the organizational realities of an NGO we must go further and deeper into local social realities, evoked in Hilhorst's (2003) book on the "real world" of NGOs. NGO structures, activities, and relationships are socially embedded within institutions and power structures at both local and international levels. While accountability is increasingly a global phenomenon – with expectations for bureaucratic operation, management, auditing, and performance assessment – its impacts differ across more localized or regionalized social structures.

A number of problems described in the case study lend themselves to analysis along these lines. First, CAR's advocacy work was characterized by a strong personal dimension in the ways in which advocacy themes were identified and addressed "from the top," in many cases with relatively little discussion with grassroots users, in a style which corresponds with prevailing cultures of personalized leadership and management. The second is the importance of both formal and informal dimensions of human resource management, where culture conflict emerges as an outcome of both power asymmetries between managers – involving at least a degree of patron-clientelism in the ways that these operate – and the socially constructed nature of existing accountability systems. The third is the idea of a "culture of defensiveness" which is derived in part from the nature of these power relations and the difficult political environment in which NGOs operate, and in part as an outcome of the extreme vulnerability felt, at least by more junior managerial staff, in relation to the wider economic climate and job market in Bangladesh.

There are some accountability problems which can be addressed by building clearer communication linkages between different levels of the organization, such as creating opportunities for greater staff and group voice in the shaping of CAR's advocacy and research agendas, or linking advocacy more clearly to evaluation learning. But there are other organizational problems that are rooted in the wider context of society, culture, and politics. For example, it is constantly necessary to negotiate an appropriate relationship with government which can serve to reassure citizens that ACE is a legitimate and responsible organization, but which avoids negative interference based on political involvement in an NGO's internal affairs on party political lines. While some of the problems identified during the ACE review have generated internal discussions about trying to find solutions, there is a danger that certain "inward-looking" responses – such as the attempt to build a stronger culture of loyalty and solidarity within the organization to try to reduce rising levels of staff turnover – may not be able to address wider contextual realities in the form of increasing economic and social pressures affecting a new, younger generation of NGO staff.

It is the first of the two approaches to accountability discussed above which has taken hold most strongly both in policy circles and in public perceptions. The "audit culture" model of accountability which follows from current climates of managerialism may ultimately weaken organizations because, by creating an erosion of trust through the creation of perverse incentives, it may lead NGO staff and leaders to make arbitrary or unprofessional choices. At the same time, formal thinking on accountability does not sit well with the cultural embeddedness of organizational systems within a development NGO. O'Neill's (2002) argument for a form of trust-based "intelligent accountability," which pays more attention to the perceptions and realities of users than to endlessly detailed and complex validation documents and targets, is of potential value to development NGOs. She writes:

> Those who are called to account should give an account of what they have done and of their successes and failures to others who have sufficient time and experience to assess the evidence and report on it.

Such a view fits with the need to adjust thinking on NGO accountability to take far more account of its socially constructed aspects. While the formal structural view of accountability is still an important one, it threatens to overbalance thinking away from accountability systems which can take better account of the complexity of development work, the political realities in which NGOs operate, and the cultural relationships which both constrain and structure action.

References

Biggs, S. and A. Neame (1995) "Negotiating Room for Manoeuvre: Reflection Concerning NGO Autonomy and Accountability within the New Policy Agenda," in M. Edwards and D. Hulme (eds.) *Beyond the Magic Bullet: NGO Performance and Accountability in the Post-Cold War World*. London: Earthscan.

Brett, E. A. (1993) "Voluntary Agencies as Development Organizations: Theorizing the Problem of Efficiency and Accountability," *Development and Change* 24, 269–303.

Ebrahim, A. (2003) "Accountability in Practice: Mechanisms for NGOs," *World Development* 31(5), 813–29.

Edwards, M. (1999) "NGO Performance – What Breeds Success?," *World Development* 27(2), 361–74.

Edwards, M. and D. Hulme (eds.) (1995) *Beyond the Magic Bullet: NGO Performance and Accountability in the Post-Cold War World*. London: Macmillan.

Fowler, A. (1995) "Capacity Building and NGOs: A Case of Strengthening Ladies for the Global Soup Kitchen?," *Insitutional Development (Innovations in Civic Society)* 1(1), 18–24.

Fry, R. (1995) "Accountability in Organizational Life: Problem or Opportunity," *Nonprofit Management and Leadership* 6(2), 181–95.

Hilhorst, D. (2003) *The Real World of NGOs: Discourse, Diversity and Development*. London: Zed Books.

Howell, J. and J. Pearce (2001) *Civil Society and Development: A Critical Exploration*. Boulder, CO: Lynne Rienner.

Kabeer, N. (2000) *The Power to Choose: Bangladeshi Women and Labour Market Decisions in London and Dhaka*. London: Verso.

Lewis, D. (2007) *The Management of Non-Governmental Development Organisations*, 2nd edn. London: Routledge.

Lewis, D. (2004) "On the Difficulty of Studying 'Civil Society': Reflections on NGOs, State and Democracy in Bangladesh," *Contributions to Indian Sociology* 38(3): 299–322.

Lewis, D. (2002) "Organisation and Management in the Third Sector: Towards a Cross-Cultural Research Agenda," *Nonprofit Management and Leadership* 13(1), 67–83.

Lewis, D. (1998) "Development NGOs and the Challenge of Partnership: Changing Relations between North and South," *Social Policy and Administration* 32(5), 501–12.

Lewis, D. (1997) "NGOs and the State in Bangladesh: Donors, Development and the Discourse of Partnership," *Annals of the American Academy of Political and Social Science* 554, 33–45.

Lewis, D., A. Bebbington, S. Batterbury, A. Shah, E. Olson, M. S. Siddiqi and S. Duvall (2003) "Practice, Power and Meaning: Frameworks for Studying Organizational Culture in Multi-agency Rural Development Projects," *Journal of International Development* 15, 1–17.

Lewis, D. and S. Madon (2003) "Information Systems and Non-governmental Organisations (NGOs): Advocacy, Organisational Learning and Accountability in a Southern NGO," *The Information Society* 20(2), 117–26.

Lewis, D. and M. S. Siddiqi (2006) "Social Capital from Sericulture?: Actors, Markets and Power in a Multi-agency Project in Bangladesh," in A. Bebbington, M. Woolcock, S. Guggenheim and E. Olson (eds.) *The Search for Empowerment: Social Capital as Idea and Practice at the World Bank*. Bloomfield, CT: Kumarian Press, ch. 9.

Lewis, D. and T. Wallace (eds.) (2000) *New Roles and Relevance: Development NGOs and the Challenge of Change*. Hartford: Kumarian Press.

Najam, A. (1996) "NGO Accountability: A Conceptual Framework," *Development Policy Review* 14, 339–53.

Oakley, P. (1999) *A Review of Danish NGO Activities in Developing Countries: Synthesis Report*. Oxford: International NGO Training and Research Centre (INTRAC).

O'Neill, O. (2002) "A Question of Trust," Lecture 4, BBC Reith Lectures. Available at www.bbc.co.uk/radio4/reith2002/.

Salamon, L. (1994) *Partners in Public Service: Government–Nonprofit Relations in the Modern Welfare State*. Baltimore: The Johns Hopkins University Press.

Shore, C. and S. Wright (2001) "Reply to Maguire," *Journal of the Royal Anthropological Institute* 7(4) (December), 759–63.

Smillie, I. (1995) *The Alms Bazaar: Altruism Under Fire – Non-Profit Organisations and International Development*. London: Intermediate Technology Publications.

Smillie, I. and J. Hailey (2001) *Managing for Change: Leadership, Strategy and Management*. London: Earthscan.

Vakil, A. (1997) "Confronting the Classification Problem: Towards a Taxonomy of NGOs," *World Development* 25(12), 2057–71.

Wood, G. D. (1997) "States without Citizens: The Problem of the Franchise State," in D. Hulme and M. Edwards (eds.) *NGOs, States and Donors*. London: Macmillan, ch. 5.

Part III

Reflective accountability: new directions for participatory practices

We now turn to operational innovations for meeting the challenges identified in Part II – for reconciling the technocratic and managerial demands of accountability with the social impulses drawn from organizational mission, values, and context. Lisa Jordan leads this section by proposing a "rights-based framework" within which to build NGO accountability. She challenges NGOs and donors which promote democratic rights to practice what they preach. Drawing from the path-breaking experiences of ActionAid and the Humanitarian Accountability Project, she offers an approach to accountability that not only recognizes the importance of context, but also provides a powerful way of linking accountability to mission and values. This is accountability as strategic choice, rather than accountability as coercion or mimicry.

Coralie Bryant similarly pursues how accountability might be used to strategic advantage by several of the world's largest transnational NGOs engaged in international emergency relief work. She is especially concerned about increasing calls from donors for accountability centered on measurable "results" and cautions that this "can mean either pushing for quick fixes or insisting upon digging up the seedling to examine its roots before it can bear fruit." She thus challenges NGO leaders to refocus on long-term effectiveness achievable through better evaluation practices. A surprising insight from her cases is that those NGOs least dependent on donor funding are actually the most effective in terms of evaluation and learning.

Alnoor Ebrahim draws on the contributions of Parts II and III to articulate two themes that course through the writings: a critique of short-sighted or myopic views of accountability that currently characterize public policy discourse, and a call for new modes and logics of participation. Building on Jordan and Bryant, he charts a case for a "reflective" accountability in NGOs, characterized by two core features: a prior-itization of accountabilities based on mission, and implementation through better evaluative practice and organizational learning. He argues that such a shift would not diminish upward accountability to funders – because the very notion of accountability would be reframed in terms of valuing and measuring long-term learning and change, and multiple accountabilities to mission, clients, and donors.

8 A rights-based approach to accountability [1]

Lisa Jordan

The explosive growth of NGOs all over the world, their variety of missions and structures, and the concerns raised by government and multinational authorities about them has prompted much discussion on NGO accountability. Accountability (the obligation to report on one's activities to a set of legitimate authorities) is the basic principle of responsible practice for any institution, public, private, or NGO (Edwards, 2002). NGO accountability discussions have arisen predominantly from government or other donor sources and have led to a series of accountability mechanisms like certification systems, rating systems, infrastructure and management capacity tools, and codes of conduct. These types of accountability mechanisms can be helpful in creating a standard in particular fields but do not reflect the value-base of NGO activities and can often seem to NGOs to be quite divorced from the mission of the organization. Furthermore, they do not address the rights of NGOs to operate (for example the right to associate freely) nor the responsibilities of NGOs to a wide array of stakeholders. Lastly, the complex web of relationships that mark the role of NGOs is not reflected in many accountability mechanisms.

This chapter tackles a question frequently raised in Part II of this book: How can NGOs reconcile their missions, values, and context with the top-down operational demands of accountability? The first section of this chapter reviews the state of play of NGO accountability. The second section questions the purpose of accountability discussions and introduces a framework of rights within which to view NGO activities. The third section poses the question how important is political context in defining NGO responsibilities. The fourth section reviews types of mechanisms that speak to the complexity of NGO realities.

---

[1] Views expressed in this chapter are those of the author and do not represent those of the Ford Foundation.

151

The state of play on accountability

NGO accountability is a wildly popular topic these days for three reasons: rapid growth, attraction of more funds, and a stronger voice in shaping public policy. One, the number of NGOs worldwide is increasing rapidly. The NGO may be the fastest growing form of civic association worldwide. For example, in Indonesia it is estimated that the number of NGOs grew in the past five years from several thousand to several tens of thousands (Ibrahim, 2003). There are over 20,000 networks (comprised by NGOs) in global civil society that have arisen in the past two decades (Edwards, 2002). All the growth in the sector has not been healthy. For example, many government officials establish NGOs alongside public office in order to receive public funds. There is the phenomenon of suitcase NGOs which are NGOs made up of one person who travels from conference to conference. The unhealthy aspects of growth have attracted calls for accountability.

Two, the NGO attracts more state funding than before. Since the early 1980s an important part of liberalization has been the privatization of services. NGOs have been the darling of social service delivery, preferred by donors over state entities. The attraction of more and more funds has prompted calls for accountability mechanisms. Three, NGOs have sought to shape public policy, especially within, but not limited to, the global political arena. NGOs are widely perceived to have set many of the global public policy agendas over the past ten years including issues like unsustainable debt, environmental degradation, human rights law, landmine removal, corporate social responsibility, etc. The more vocal NGOs become in the policy arena, the louder the call for accountability from those concerned about the rising power of NGOs to set the global public policy agenda and to influence the shape of markets (Manheim 2003).

There are reams of materials available on NGO accountability. Most of it starts with mechanisms that preface operational capacity, management structure, performance measurements, and accounting practices with an emphasis on legal obligations (Ball and Dunn, 1995). Outcome tracking software has been developed to measure how many clients have been served by an individual caseworker (Anthrop, 2001). Proposals have been made to increase and improve accounting as a measure of accountability (Müller, 2003). The tools used in the development industry are riddled with accountability mechanisms like exit strategies, participatory assessments, etc. In India, commercial ratings and certification systems have arisen in droves and they are beginning to be created at a global scale as well.

What's wrong with all this activity? Plenty. There is nothing inherently wrong with these accountability mechanisms and in some circumstances they can be quite helpful. But in other circumstances they are inadequate, they do not address the needs of the NGOs, they are divorced from missions, they do not address moral obligations, they prioritize some relationships over others, they are quite often punitive and controlling in application, they are built upon some pretty powerful faulty assumptions, and often fail to recognize the context within which NGOs operate. In part the inadequacies of these mechanisms reflect the source from which they have arisen and, more worrisomely, reflect a lack of serious discourse among NGOs themselves.

NGO accountability discussions have arisen predominantly from government or other donor sources and have led to a series of accountability mechanisms that, unsurprisingly, answer questions about NGOs that donors feel need to be answered. They prioritize the needs and desires of donors and governments over those of other stakeholders within and surrounding NGOs. They do not address the rights of NGOs to operate (for example the right to associate freely) nor the responsibilities of NGOs to a wide array of stakeholders. They do not prioritize other relationships that are important to NGOs like those with beneficiaries of NGO services, the broader public, or with social movements or coalition partners. NGOs typically have relationships with at least six identifiable stakeholders of which donors and governments are two. The others are its own staff, the general public, other NGOs, social movements, beneficiaries of services, global organizations, and the private sector. Not every NGO has a relationship with each of these societal sectors, but one or more come into play with almost every NGO. Accountability mechanisms as they now exist often do not prioritize these other relationships.

As noted by Alnoor Ebrahim (2003) in a comprehensive review of accountability mechanisms, accountability in practice has emphasized "upward" and "external" accountability to donors, while "downward" and "internal" mechanisms remain comparatively underdeveloped. NGOs and funders have focused primarily on short-term "functional" accountability responses at the expense of longer-term "strategic" processes. Furthermore, accountability mechanisms that emphasize the needs of donors, donor agencies, and/or governments could jeopardize other important relationships with other stakeholders.

Accountability mechanisms often do not reflect the value-base of NGO activities and can often seem to NGOs to be quite divorced from the mission of the organization. One example of accountability mechanisms divorced from all moral obligations inherent in much NGO activity are the certification standards being proposed by the private sector to "certify" NGOs. Société Générale de Surveillance markets the "SGS Solution," based upon the "NGO 2000 Standard," to governments and donors (SGS, 2002). It appears that SGS hopes to create a market demand for ratings and certification systems among donors so as to force NGOs to undergo scrutiny. SGS suggests that all stakeholders have the same interests; that there is a baseline from which to measure acceptable practice; that efficiency is a key goal in NGO work; and essentially that an NGO is no different from a profit-driven business (and uses market terms like "suppliers" for donors and "customers" for beneficiaries). The "SGS Solution" is based upon a private sector model of independent verification that has been widely discredited over the past few years in the wake of corporate scandals.

To begin a conversation about NGO accountability with accountability mechanisms seems premature. It assumes that we all agree on a definition of accountability; that accountability has an intrinsic recognizable value that would compel NGOs to naturally take up the issue; that there are universal standards of accountability; and that the question, to whom or to what NGOs should be accountable, is easily answered. The focus on accountability mechanisms divorced from questions like "accountability to whom" and "for what purpose" has engendered negative responses from NGOs. Many do not see the purpose in taking up the issue of accountability. Jan Aart Scholte, a professor at the University of Warwick, has undertaken surveys of over 600 NGOs worldwide. He and his global team found that most NGOs had given almost no thought to the issue of their own accountability (Scholte, 2005). Arguments range from efficiency arguments (it's too expensive) to questions about the behavior of other actors in a political arena (the real accountability problem is with the government/private sector) to questioning the purpose (how is this related to our mission). Most accountability mechanisms are viewed with suspicion as controlling elements imposed by actors more powerful than the NGOs. And for good reason. Most legal mechanisms are imposed by governments that view a strong civil society as a potential threat to their power.

No one has really made a positive argument as to why NGOs should undertake a risky, expensive, difficult exercise to create meaningful and concrete accountability mechanisms. All arguments are punitive or assume the intrinsic value of accountability would be enough to compel NGOs to adopt accountability mechanisms. Arguments currently circulating include the issue of maintaining public trust (SustainAbility, 2003), the intrinsic value of accountability (Edwards, 2002), and the need to create checks and balances on growing NGO power (American

Enterprise Institute/governments). In practice, none of these arguments has been strong enough to compel NGOs as a sector in different political landscapes (national and global) to undertake complex accountability discussions and create mechanisms.

Yet, NGOs do take up the issue of accountability even without positive arguments. Why? An informal survey of twelve national NGO associations (i.e., those organizations that certify NGOs, or develop codes of conduct for the field) confirmed the suspicion that most NGOs address the issue of accountability only when the political space within which they operate is somehow threatened. Kenya, India, Uganda, and the Philippines all developed national NGO associations in order to counter legal threats from national governments which would have limited the operating environment for NGOs.

Sadly, there is no conclusive evidence that developing codes of conduct and certification schemes actually helps to broaden or protect the political space in which NGOs operate. Thus the most prominent reason for NGOs to undertake accountability issues is called into question. The closest we get to conclusive evidence is in the Philippines where the creation of a self-regulatory certification system staved off a change in the tax code that would have been unfavorable to NGOs. The relationship between political space and self-regulatory systems is an under-explored area, ripe for academic review.

A second rationale is as noted above, when donors demand it. And lastly, NGOs undertake the issue of accountability when they fail to carry out their mission. More work needs to be done to help NGOs understand the value of addressing accountability or how addressing accountability can be a strategic choice rather than a punitive process divorced from the mission of an NGO.

Why should NGOs address the issue of accountability?

As noted above, NGOs address the issue of accountability when their political space is threatened. They may also take up accountability in cases of obvious mission failure, or in situations where the political arena is changing or forming (like in states that are moving from dictatorship or in the global political arena).

I would like to introduce another reason for NGOs to take up accountability. In order to exercise what are basically democratic citizen rights in political systems that are wary of these freedoms, and to solidify the civic sphere in the global political arena, NGOs need to be able to clearly articulate to their supporters and to the public who they are, what their role is, where their support comes from, and to whom they are accountable. In other words accountability can help to solidify rights in myriad political contexts. "Rights stabilize civil society as a distinctive, autonomous sphere of social interaction. The rights to communicate, assembly and association among others constitute the public and associational spheres of civil society as spheres of positive freedom within which agents can collectively debate issues of common concern, act in concert, assert new rights and exercise influence on policy society." (Arato and Cohen, 1992).

NGOs or NGO networks assume human rights like the right to associate, the right to assemble, and the right to expression in myriad political contexts. NGOs rely on universal human rights for their very existence and operations including the right to a voice on policy decisions, the right to participate in political discourse, the right to mobilize or associate, the right to serve a public, the right to organize, and the right to dissent. These rights are universally understood and have allowed NGOs to develop a voice to influence public policy; to serve a greater public good; to define, protect, and defend the public good; to monitor government performance; to enhance government performance by aiding social service delivery; and to protect minority rights.

While rights are universally understood, they are in fact normative and their application is often far removed from a universal normative ideal. NGOs often assume universal rights in arenas where the recognition of rights by authoritarian regimes is mere lip-service. They also assume rights in the global political arena where rights are not articulated or have disappeared in the impenetrable policy and decision-making by international institutions, especially those rights that are embedded in democratic systems of decision-making, like the right to a voice, the right to participate, assemble, and express opinions, and rights which protect minorities.

To assume rights in an opaque political arena that does not operate on democratic principles is risky business. It can lead to challenges of credibility (who do you represent), to questioning the legality of actions, to disruptions at the operational level, to illegal attacks, etc. (Van Tuijl, 1997). In many nations, the NGO position is fragile because the role of NGOs is not well understood by the public. Globally, the disconnect between national and global politics often means that there is not a great public understanding or support for key NGO positions even though NGOs are one of the very few voices that articulate broad public interests.[2]

---

[2] Compounding the difficulties faced by NGOs operating in the global political sphere is the lack of acceptance of the concept of global citizenship and little attention from civil society to the responsibilities inherent to global citizenship.

Adopting a rights-based approach to accountability

A rights-based approach to accountability would begin by recognizing the importance of context, and by this I mean the political arena in which NGO operations are taking place. Then there are some key questions that have guided NGO efforts to establish accountability mechanisms from a rights-based approach. These are "To whom are we accountable (or to what) and why?" "What purpose does accountability serve for us?" And then, "How can we exercise our responsibilities towards these stakeholders?" The importance of context is illustrated below in the case of the Global Accountability Project, run by One World Trust, which attempts to define accountability of NGOs and other actors working in the amorphous global political arena.

One World Trust, a UK-based NGO, has tried to define the responsibilities of all three major actors in the global political arena (corporations, multilateral institutions, and NGOs) and then compare the relative levels of accountability of each actor in that arena (Kovach et al., 2003). One World Trust prefaces its discussion by examining accountability deficits among the three major actors as they operate in a specific arena. For example, it notes that the dynamics of globalization erode the two most powerful accountability mechanisms over the private sector: market regulation which extends only nationally, and consumer choice, which assumes wide consumer awareness and choice within the marketplace. There are over 60,000 transnational corporations that operate globally without binding accountability frameworks today. Similarly, there are over 40,000 NGOs operating globally that have varying degrees of access to policy-makers who shape the agenda within the global political arena, and often speak on behalf of various communities or issues that have no access to the global political arena. Beyond accountability to donors, which as already stated is limited to the interests of the donors, there is very little holding NGOs to account. And in the case of multilateral organizations, states are often only nominally in charge when the management of large organizations like the International Monetary Fund presents its board with decisions that can only be tinkered with at the margins.

The accountability framework employed by One World Trust has two main parameters: internal and external accountability. It compares across all three institutions the following aspects of accountability:

1) member control;
2) disclosure of information over the internet (privileging the global audience over the local audience);
3) how senior staff are appointed;

4) how evaluation is carried out and reported to a global public;

5) how external stakeholders are involved; and

6) how an organization enables those most affected by its work or actions to register complaints and how complaints are acted upon.[3]

While this work is in its preliminary stages, the approach is very interesting because it does not take national legal parameters and try to apply them to the global arena, as has been suggested by others (Riggs and Huberty, 2003). Legal frameworks were not employed simply because there are no global legal frameworks that govern the actions of global institutions. One World Trust did not equate accountability with representation as often happens, but has tried to define accountability as a dynamic and complex issue, within the context of the arena itself, i.e., what would be appropriate measures of accountability for organizations acting globally? The identification of the accountability variables in and of itself has been of great service to our understanding of the global political arena.

Beyond context

There are two global examples of NGOs and NGO Networks embracing accountability mechanisms that stem from a rights-based approach. One is ActionAid, which has adopted a rights-based approach to development, and the other is the Humanitarian Accountability Project (HAP). ActionAid operates nationally all over the world and has a presence within the global political arena as well. (It advocates for changes in global policies set by the World Bank, the IMF, and the UN.) HAP is made up of thirteen international emergency relief organizations. The important thing to note about both the ActionAid case and the organizations engaged in HAP is that all had already adopted many of the standard accountability mechanisms that are often prescribed by donors. All organizations have boards to which they are accountable, all produce audited financial reports, many are membership based and have adopted mechanisms that allow the members a certain degree of control. *However, these managerial mechanisms failed to address the missions of the organizations or protect the operating environments.*

ActionAid

In 1999 ActionAid adopted a rights-based approach to its work based upon the 1948 Declaration of Human Rights. The rights-based

---

[3] For more information on these variables see www.oneworldtrust.org.

approach goes beyond providing basic services as an act of charity. It recognizes the UN's conventions on the right to education, food, water, health, and shelter. ActionAid attempts to tackle the root causes of poverty which the organization identifies as an unjust distribution of power and resources. ActionAid now defines what it does as working with impoverished communities to help them both identify and demand their rights. While not specified in ActionAid literature, the adoption of a rights-based approach may have stemmed from a realization that child sponsorships are generally not able to stem the structural causes of poverty and do not address the context of the child's life.

The rights-based approach provided a framework for advocacy work that ActionAid felt was very important to its mission, but was not addressed adequately by any of its tools. Furthermore, ActionAid was challenged both internally by operational staff and externally by donors to justify a shift in resources from basic social service delivery to campaigning and advocacy. In order to address the challenge, ActionAid felt it had a responsibility to prove that campaigning and advocacy work is meaningful, perhaps as meaningful or more meaningful, as basic social service delivery. In 2001 it began to explore its responsibilities to the communities with which it works and how these responsibilities can be assessed in relation to advocacy work that so often seems very far away from the daily life and needs of a poor person. As they describe it:

For ActionAid impact assessment is about understanding the changes (intended and unintended) that are brought about in men, women's and children's lives as a result of our work. Understanding change is important not just to donors, or supporters, it is also crucial for ensuring that our work is constantly improving the lives of the people who are intended to benefit. We believe that a robust impact system must tell us about the things that are most important to the people with whom we work; tell us whether the work we are doing is helping or not; help us know more about other things that affect people's lives; help us learn about what we are doing; help us improve our work in the future. It should be a system which creates the possibility for honest, transparent, empowering relationships between ActionAid, its partners and the people with whom we work in communities.[4]

In 2001 Amboka Wameyo and Jennifer Chapman undertook a scoping study to find ways in which to assess advocacy. The outcome was summed up by Rosalind David, head of the impact assessment department:

During the course of putting together this Scoping Study it became clear that we, in the development community, still have some way to go in developing appropriate systems to monitor and evaluate influencing and advocacy work. The

---

[4] See www.actionaid.org.

last five years have seen a rapid change in the types of work that fall beneath this banner. Among them are "people centred advocacy" and "participatory advocacy" as well as global advocacy initiatives carried out by large and rapidly changing coalitions. The dearth of empirical analysis of local level influencing and advocacy work, or of different forms of national and international advocacy has become very clear. There is much work to be done. (Chapman and Wameyo, 2001)

Today, ActionAid is experimenting with the Accountability Learning and Planning System that has a number of important features. The rights-based approach has provided the rationale for being engaged in both service delivery and campaigning in order to serve the mission. The accountability tool identifies the primary stakeholder as the communities with which ActionAid works. ActionAid is operating in multiple political arenas and thus it could have been very tricky to identify who or what the primary stakeholder would be. Should it be the eradication of poverty? Or the British people who support ActionAid's work? Or should it prioritize the ideals of its founder? The local community stakeholder is prioritized over the donor public, foundations, and aid agencies which support ActionAid's work. Communities are also prioritized over advocacy targets like governments and multilateral institutions. Clarity about the primary stakeholder has allowed ActionAid to resist pressures from donors to concentrate on social service delivery; to answer the question "who do you represent"; and to justify its campaigning work in national, local, and global political arenas.

Second, the accountability mechanisms are tied very closely to the mission. ActionAid is very clear about why it has undertaken extensive work on accountability. The rationale is published in all of its documentation and stands as a daily reminder to all staff that assessment is about responsibilities to the mission and to the communities within which the mission is carried out. Third, it is not punitive or externally driven. Accountability mechanisms are learning tools for the organization and for its primary stakeholders.

Humanitarian Accountability Project

A second model to review is the Humanitarian Accountability Project (HAP).[5] HAP was a two-year interagency research project established by thirteen humanitarian organizations that operate globally, channel billions of dollars in emergency relief, and have increasingly experienced

---

[5] Many of the details cited here can be found at www.hapgeneva.org. Members of HAP are: CARE International, Caritas International, Danida, DFID, DRC, Fundemos, IFRC, OFADEC, Oxfam International, SLANGO, SSRC, UNHCR, and World Vision International.

violence and other problems in the field, especially but not limited to the aftermath of the Rwandan genocide. HAP was devised at a meeting in March 2000 of fifty humanitarian organizations which were contemplating to establish an ombudsman for crisis-affected populations. The thirteen organizations that ultimately established HAP identified a growing crisis in the field of humanitarian relief that is characterized by growth in the types and numbers of organizations prepared to deliver relief, a lack of defining ethics in the field, controversy surrounding the role of NGOs, mission failure, growing public scrutiny, confusion among NGO providers over their own roles, competition among agencies, and an emphasis on technical, financial, and logistical management issues over ethics, rights, and responsibilities. They noted that organizations involved in humanitarian action account to those who provide them with funds and/or who are responsible for their governance. Other primary stakeholders include staff, volunteers, partner organizations, and sometimes parliaments. Conspicuously absent from that list were crisis-affected populations. The overall mission for HAP was to develop recommendations for strengthening accountability within the humanitarian sector, and to design and constitute governance and executive management structures to oversee and administer a permanent accountability mechanism.

HAP undertook three field trials to test different kinds of accountability mechanisms to address the needs of the field (i.e., how to be accountable to the mission of humanitarian intervention and disaster-affected populations), the agency (i.e., individual organizations), and the sector (i.e., the industry of emergency relief). HAP also underwent a number of workshops to bring its members to an agreement on which stakeholders should be prioritized, published a number of articles to bring along the members on key questions and concepts, and ultimately began to establish a self-regulatory body that will govern the actions of its members.

The issue of separating out different kinds of accountability mechanisms for different stakeholders – field, agency, and sector – acknowledges the web of relationships that characterizes the reality of most NGO operations. The three field trials confirmed that some mechanisms are needed at the organizational level to support staff; some are needed at the sector level to address the partnership relationships among agencies; and some are needed at the field level to address responsibilities to the mission and to the beneficiaries. *Not all mechanisms are appropriate in all circumstances and there is no one mechanism that serves every stakeholder.*

HAP addressed five accountability questions: Who is accountable? To whom? For what? Through what mechanism? For what outcome?

The approach it adopted was to look at the context within which emergency relief operations take place, and then to look at ethics, rights, and responsibilities within that context. In order to address these issues, the staff at HAP adopted a rights-based framework to explain humanitarian action. They explicitly recognized that the most basic right of disaster-affected people is to life with dignity and that to have a right to a voice on actions that affect them constituted the first step to dignity. The responsibilities that flow from this right are the responsibility to provide relevant information to crisis-affected populations and to give those populations the opportunity for a meaningful say in actions that will affect their lives. Currently, there are no accountability mechanisms in the sector that recognize the basic rights of crisis-affected populations.

HAP answered its five accountability questions in the following way: agencies delivering emergency relief are primarily responsible to crisis-affected populations; their goal is to help those populations establish a life with dignity; that a variety of mechanisms including a self-regulatory body would be necessary to ensure accountability in the field; and the outcome envisioned is a strengthened sector.

Challenges abound within the emergency relief sector for NGOs, including USAID's insistence that US NGOs delivering emergency relief identify themselves with the foreign policy objectives of the US government. However, those members of HAP that accept contracts from USAID may be better able to withstand state pressure given the new found clarity on rights and responsibilities.

Context, rights, and accountability mechanisms

What are the implications of the experiences of ActionAid and HAP for NGO accountability more generally? NGOs that undertake a serious discourse on accountability may find that explicitly addressing a rights-based approach can help them in three ways: in sorting through a complex web of relationships inherent to NGO activity and identifying primary stakeholders; in identifying responsibilities that adhere to the mission of the NGO; and in developing accountability mechanisms that are appropriate to the context and mission. The major parameters of a rights-based approach to accountability are as follows:

1) a clearly understood mission for an organization;
2) a thorough examination of the political context, and in particular the rights afforded and assumed in that context;

Table 8.1 *Key questions on accountability*

Rights-based approach to accountability	HAP	ActionAid
To whom are we accountable?	• People we serve • Donors • Staff • Membership • Agents engaged in setting parameters for relief services, etc.	• Communities in which we operate • Membership • Donors • Governments • Board • Founder • Organization
To what are we accountable?	• Providing relief	• Poverty alleviation
What rights do we rely upon?	• International conventions being honored	• Right to association • Right to free speech, etc.
What rights are we trying to realize?	• A life with dignity • A voice	• A life free of poverty
What mechanisms do we need?	• Self-regulation • Management structures • Staff support, etc.	• Assessment for advocacy; village roundtable approaches, etc.
What outcomes do we envision?	• Strengthened sector	• Stronger communities with more resources

3) an answer (or answers) to the question "to whom (or what) are we accountable/responsible?" which should be answered by reviewing all stakeholders and ranking them in order of importance; and
4) a thorough examination of the responsibilities to different categories of stakeholders and to the mission.

These issues would be explored before creating or adopting accountability mechanisms.

HAP asked several major questions before experimenting with different accountability mechanisms. The multiple answers to the questions are provided in Table 8.1, as examples to illustrate the approach.

ActionAid developed different mechanisms than those of HAP, yet both ended up prioritizing the beneficiary as a primary stakeholder. Both operations are extremely complex works in progress and emphasize long-term strategic choices versus short-term logistical and managerial approaches. Both also genuinely grapple with the issues of NGO power, which is relative to the context and stakeholders surrounding an NGO operation. Internal and external mechanisms are noted in both examples as important. And the impact of adopting accountability mechanisms that work for NGOs cannot be underestimated. If the recommendations of HAP, for example, are fully adopted, the operational characteristics of emergency relief will undergo profound changes over the next decade. ActionAid is also seeing shifts in its operational approach as a result of its evaluative framework.

Approaching the question of accountability from a rights-based framework may not make it any easier for NGOs to develop accountability mechanisms or accountable approaches to their day-to-day operations. In many situations it is difficult to connect an assumption of rights to a clear concept of accountability, because the context is not conducive. The governance process may be opaque itself and not offer a viable model, or the role of NGOs lacks a clear foundation (legal or otherwise). Both factors may come into play as they do in the global political arena. Furthermore, the groups or issues (e.g., nature, animals) in society that NGOs often say they are supporting or protecting do not have many obvious means to articulate a demand for the NGOs' responsibility to them. Governments, international institutions, and elements in the corporate sector have a conflict of interest, because they may very well have an interest in using an accountability discussion as a means to control the influence of NGOs and limit their exercise of rights.

While many NGOs would like to improve their record on accountability, the lack of a roadmap, an unconducive political environment, and constraints from the context within which they operate, can make it difficult to define to whom and to what an organization should be responsible and from there to determine the ensuing accountability mechanisms. And there can be some political danger to addressing accountability in a context where assuming some rights and responsibilities could open one's organization or partners to agents who may want to undermine an NGO's assumption of rights. This point, where the articulation of responsibilities becomes self-defeating, is where the circle from rights to responsibilities to accountability closes. The challenge is to identify mechanisms that promote rights and accountability, by seeking ways to articulate NGO responsibilities that do not endanger the political space for the many positive roles that NGOs can play in securing rights. And to be aware of the fact that mechanisms are never politically neutral, they are developed by someone, made for someone, using a select method.

Nevertheless, understanding rights as a fundamental pillar of NGO work can help NGOs to develop accountability mechanisms that work in complex political circumstances and help NGOs to sort out what kind of accountability mechanisms are most appropriate for them because rights are always accompanied with responsibilities. In other words, it can help NGOs understand that addressing accountability is a strategic choice. ActionAid's accountability system stemmed directly from a shift in focus and a new understanding in 1999 to a rights-based approach to development. The opposite is true as well. Among elements of the third sector, there is a clear understanding that the solidification of rights for NGOs in part hinges upon a greater articulation of responsibilities. It appears that if NGOs are to retain (or in some cases establish) their legitimacy to do simple things like deliver social services, never mind advocacy activities, they must first articulate their responsibilities to the society and then they may garner rights. When NGOs articulate rights or responsibilities as a basis of their activities, the responsibilities inherent to actualizing rights become much clearer.

A rights framework can help NGOs understand accountability as a strategic choice, and can illuminate the intrinsic value of addressing accountability. One could argue that NGOs should take up the issue of accountability because it is the right thing to do (Edwards, 2002). This argument is not relevant to all NGOs but any NGO that promotes democratic rights (transparency, participation and recourse for minority voices) is going to be more credible if it practices what it preaches. For NGOs that practice aggressive advocacy and are often accused of staking out the moral high ground, undertaking a serious accountability discussion within the organization and actively addressing the level of transparency, knowing which stakeholders are prioritized, and developing accountability mechanisms to bind organizational actions to those stakeholders can help to deflect public attacks on NGO credibility. Without it, an NGO is open to attack. The American Enterprise Institute (AEI), for example, has attacked the entire international NGO sector and in part complained about a lack of transparency. It has set up an NGO Watch website (www.ngowatch.org) which releases documents pertaining to other NGOs' sources of funding and negative press stories relating to their actions. However, AEI, which is itself an NGO, was immediately exposed and criticized because it failed to release similar information about its own activities, identify its primary stakeholders or its financial sources of support. The *International Herald Tribune* and the *New York Times* called AEI's efforts "misguided and ideologically driven" (*New York Times*, 2003; *International Herald Tribune*, 2003).

NGO accountability debates have really only just begun. NGOs are part of a wave of new types of civic associations that operate within and between borders to articulate public interests and serve public needs. When accountability mechanisms are imposed on NGOs from external stakeholders the reactions can be quite defensive; the mechanisms can be divorced from the missions of the organizations, and can jeopardize other important relations that are central to the mission of the NGO. However, when NGOs undertake a serious discourse on accountability the models they develop are often exemplary for the political arena in which they operate. More work needs to be done to help NGOs embrace account-ability as a strategic choice. In the models highlighted in this chapter, two issues were important to the development of solid accountability mechanisms. First, taking into account the context within which NGOs operate, or the arena and its variables, including the recognition of rights in the arena. Second, the development of a rights-based framework can help NGOs to define to whom they are accountable, to define the purpose of addressing accountability, and to develop mechanisms that speak to the mission and the needs of the primary stakeholders.

References

Anthrop, Phil (2001) "NonProfit Results Software: Robust Tracking Power, Civil Liberties Concerns," *NonProfit Quarterly* 8(3), 59.

Arato, Andrew and Jean Cohen (1992) *Civil Society and Political Theory*. Cambridge, MA: MIT Press.

Ball, Colin and Leith Dunn (1995) *NonGovernmental Organizations: Guidelines for Good Policy and Practice*. London: Commonwealth Foundation.

Chapman, Jennifer and Amboka Wameyo (2001) *Monitoring and Evaluating Advocacy: A Scoping Study*. ActionAid, UK.

Ebrahim, Alnoor (2003) "Accountability in Practice: Mechanisms for NGOs," *World Development* 31(5), 813–29.

Edwards, Michael (2002) *NGO Rights and Responsibilities: A New Deal for Global Governance*. London: The Foreign Policy Centre.

Ibrahim, Rustam (2003) "Program of Formulating and Implementing Code of Conduct and Formation of Umbrella Organization for Indonesian NGOs," LP3ES, Unpublished paper prepared for Sawarung Workshop, Indonesia.

International Herald Tribune (22 July 2003) Editorial, "Holding Civic Groups Accountable."

Kovach, H., C. Neligan and S. Burall (2003) *The Global Accountability Report 1: Power without Accountability?* London: Global Accountability Project, One World Trust.

Manheim, Gerald B. (June 2003) "Biz-War: Origins, Structure and Strategy of Foundation-NGO Network Warfare on Corporations in the United States," Unpublished paper presented at the American Enterprise Institute Workshop.

Müller, Kaspar (2003) "Swiss GAAP FER 21: Accounting Standard for Charitable, Social Non-Profit Organisations: The Days after Coming into Force," *International Journal of Civil Society Law* 1(4), 27.

New York Times (21 July 2003) Editorial, "Holding Civic Groups Accountable."

Riggs, David and Robert Huberty (2003) "NGO Accountability: What the US Can Teach the UN," *Foundation Watch*, Capital Research Center, p. 1.

Scholte, Jan Aart (2005) "Civil Society and Democracy in the Global Economy," in A. Mantaha and R. Higgott (eds.) *The Future of International Order: Unilateralism or Multilateralism or What?* Singapore: Asia-Europe Foundation, pp. 206–10.

SGS (Société Générale de Surveillance SA) (July 2002) Brochure: *Certification of Non-Governmental Organizations*.

SustainAbility, UN Global Compact, UNEP (July 2003) *The 21st Century NGO in the Market for Change*. New York: United Nations.

Van Tuijl, Peter (1997) "Responding to Rights at Risk: NGOs in a Disabled Environment, a Preliminary Overview," Unpublished paper prepared for workshop Promoting Three Basic Rights: Towards Greater Freedom of Association, Assembly and Speech in Asia, Thailand.

Websites

Better Business Bureaus Wise Giving Alliance. www.give.org.

Independent Sector. Issues: Ethics and Accountability. www.independentsector. org/issues/accountability/standards.

National Center for Charitable Statistics. www.nccs.urban.org.

Nonprofit Risk Management Center (2003) Pillars of Accountability in the Nonprofit World. www.nonprofitrisk.org.

US Nonprofit Organizations' Public Disclosure Regulations Site. www.muridae. com/publicaccess/accountability.

9   Evaluation and accountability in emergency relief [1]

Coralie Bryant

NGOs are at present challenged as never before to demonstrate *results*. For organizations involved in humanitarian relief work, one reason often given for needing more documentation of results and more accountability is a growing dependence on public money. Ian Smillie's reckoning, for example, is that: "by the early 1990s, 75 percent of British food aid was being channeled through NGOs, and 40 percent of Swedish spending on emergencies and refugees was going through Swedish NGOs. By 1996, 46 percent of French emergency funding was being spent through NGOs, and half of all the EU's European Community Humanitarian Office (ECHO) funding was being spent the same way. Between 1992 and 1997 the United States Agency for International Development (USAID) – with the largest emergency budget in the world – spent over 60 percent of it, not counting food aid, through NGOs" (Smillie and Helmich, 1999, p. 9).[2] Yet some of the NGOs with the strongest accountability cultures are the same ones that are taking the lowest amounts of public money. Thus the motivations or "drivers" for accountability within NGOs are more nuanced and complex than the role of public money; financial drivers are not determinative.

This chapter focuses on evaluation systems in NGOs – how they use evaluation, and how it can both enable and constrain accountability. The chapter draws primarily on the experiences of several well-established international NGOs that are engaged in relief and development work: CARE, Médecins Sans Frontières (MSF), Oxfam (Great Britain and America), PLAN International, Save the Children (UK and US), and World Vision. It discusses the components of accountability that are central to international relief, emergency, and development work: accountability's

---

[1] This chapter is a shortened version of "Accountability, Evaluation and Organizational Learning," in Marc Lindenberg and Coralie Bryant (2001), *Going Global: Transforming Relief and Development NGOs*, Bloomfield, CT: Kumarian Press. Used with permission.

[2] With worries about these relationships, Edwards and Hulme followed up *Beyond the Magic Bullet* (1996) with a second book entitled, *NGOs, State and Donors: Too Close for Comfort?* (1997).

contingent character and complexity, the role of evaluation systems, and the learning process that should emerge through collective reflection on past performance. The focus on evaluation is important because, although it is widely promoted as a mechanism of accountability in NGOs, evaluative practices are often poorly understood and underutilized in terms of how they might best illuminate what works and what doesn't in NGO activities.

The pressure to demonstrate results

The call for accountability is frequently associated with demands for transparency, for demonstrating results, and for giving an answer to constituents about what works. But while accountability is often used synonymously with transparency, there are distinctions between the two. Accountability is providing an account for decisions, actions, and their consequences. Transparency is about providing information – not necessarily an explanation. Although they are interrelated, these concepts are nonetheless separable. Quantities of information may be provided in ways that do not directly address or reveal the connections between decision-makers, decisions taken, and their consequences. Information is essential, but not determinative for achieving accountability.[3]

In addition, while demonstrating results is a popular and worthwhile idea, it can also be interpreted too narrowly, with unintended negative consequences. Michael Edwards and David Hulme point out that for NGOs interested in "empowerment," there is a political dilemma in providing accountability: "If the organization's overt or covert goal is empowerment (making those who have little power more powerful), then transparency on this issue will, at best, make it easier for vested interests to identify what is happening and thus more effectively oppose it, or, at worst, lead to the deregistration and closure of the organization for being subversive" (Edwards and Hulme, 1996, p. 11).

It is not clear that they are right. In the 1970s, many NGOs, including Oxfam GB, were active in Latin America and Central America during the struggles in those countries – doing just what one would have thought not possible: working with opposition groups struggling for more democracy. They were not deregistered, or closed. Moreover, the carefully researched work of Brian Smith in *More than Altruism* documents that several NGOs were successful in reaching and facilitating

---

[3] One of the first major official development sources on these issues was the World Bank's policy paper on *Governance and Development* (1992). This paper argued for three concepts as central to good governance: accountability, transparency, and predictability (rule of law).

alternative paths to influence, and that many of the democratic leaders who emerged later in Central America came out of the NGO movement seeded by this work (Smith, 1990).

Yet in some ways they are right – and their point should be heeded. Empowerment comes through long-term, incremental steps. It is a fragile process, easily uprooted. Demanding "results" can mean either pushing for quick fixes, or insisting upon digging up the seedling to examine its roots before it can bear fruit. Domestic poverty work often is abandoned when narrowly measured results are demanded – and not found. Empowerment is sometimes more tolerated at a distance than it is at home; it seems easier to deal with powerlessness in small countries than with the powerlessness of poor people within Northern post-industrial countries. John Gaventa writes about the speed with which the War on Poverty in the United States in the 1960s was dismantled when it began to be effective (Gaventa, 1998, pp. 50–7).

The "indicator movement" irrevocably changed the way that development theorists and practitioners think about "results." Techniques and skills for the measurement of results have changed in the past three decades. As early as the 1960s, the Yale University Political and Social Data Center was developing social and political indicators to parallel the indicators in use by economists. Knowledge spread that something akin to social accounting (measuring results) was possible. By the 1980s, the multilateral development banks had picked up on performance indicators – and so had managers coming out of business schools. This led in turn to more calls for improved accountability in the public sector. It was only a matter of time until this would be echoed in development work, even though national statistics and census politics in developing countries meant weak databases for measurement.

Multidirectional accountability

As noted in the introduction to this volume and elsewhere, accountability is complicated by an organization's multiple goals, multiple constituencies, and market insulation. Accountability must be *multidirectional* as a result – not only from bottom to top, or from top to bottom. In reality, different parts of any NGO family have to respond to different stakeholders, partners, and people – immediate beneficiaries and others – in order to meet the accountability challenge. Accountability for emergency relief work is different from that of poverty-reducing work, or longer-term development work. As there are weaker links in emergency situations, and different constraints, it is extremely difficult to measure effectiveness. Both public opinion and the donors funding relief work (for example, UNHCR, or the Office of Disaster Assistance) have reporting and auditing requirements that differ from those of ongoing development assistance with a longer timeline. Given the changing context for humanitarian work, however, changed accountability standards will emerge, especially as the borders between relief and development blur. But to date, differences in approach and techniques have meant different reporting and evaluation guidelines as well. In the case of development work, there is longer-term engagement with people and Southern NGOs over a period of time, making possible more participatory and thorough evaluation.

The very volatility of work with internally displaced people and refugees adds dimensions of difficulty to evaluation processes. While generally public opinion has been sympathetic to the added demands of relief work, and thus has lowered expectations for accountability, in the case of Rwanda there was in fact more criticism of NGO work. Peter Uvin has suggested that NGOs should be held accountable, as should the international community, for the structural violence in Rwanda (1998, pp. 17–24).[4] His argument is that NGOs working directly with people at the grassroots had before them all the signals of impending major violence, but that they remained too silent for too long. Enmeshed in their own worlds, they did not blow the whistle. When the violence escalated, and they undertook emergency work, they were often manipulated by terrorists, who outmaneuvered them – for example, by using food programs in refugee camps as foraging places to "refuel" before their next rampage. While some NGOs did decide to withdraw when they became convinced that they were being used by those committed to violence and further bloodshed, others did not decide to withdraw – on equally compelling grounds that the people with whom they were working would be even more immiserated if they abandoned them than if they remained and kept working.

NGO emergency relief work is not likely to be the same in the post-Rwanda world. While the Group of Seven industrial powers was largely focused on the wars in Bosnia and Croatia and later on Kosovo, the numbers killed in those wars, grim as they were, were nowhere near the nearly million lives lost in Rwanda. Nor were NGO staff as deeply at risk.

The sum total of the multidirectionality entailed in these various calls for increased, and differently conceived, accountability and responsibility

---

[4] It is worth noting, however, that the large four-volume study by John Eriksson with contributions from H. Adelman, J. Borton, H. Christensen, K. Kumar, A. Suhrke, D. Tardif-Douglin, S. Villumstad, and L. Wohlgemuth (1996) was one of the first places to discuss the problem of structural violence.

systems has changed the context for NGO senior managers and staff. Since the accountability process is both multifaceted and diverse, conceiving of it in terms of a contingency approach may be helpful. Below we turn to this contingency model for accountability – an approach pointed out to us by, among others, David Brown and Julie Fisher, while discussing NGO accountability with them.[5]

A contingent model for accountability

In all our discussions with them, NGO leaders confirmed that their accountability is both multidimensional and multidirectional. In a discussion on what was involved in strengthening accountability, there was broad agreement when Reynold Levy, CEO, International Rescue Committee, said that accountability to beneficiaries had to be the highest priority. James Orbinski, President, Médecins Sans Frontières International, added that it was hard, however, to prioritize answering to volunteers, beneficiaries, and donors, who were all equally important – creating a circle of accountability. Charles MacCormick, President of Save the Children US, added that one part of the problem is how broadly or narrowly to set aspirations, as it is easier to measure and be accountable for narrower ones.[6] While most perceived their primary responsibility to be towards those directly affected by programs and projects, they added that they must also answer for performance to contributors and donors.

For all of them accountability means adhering to organizational core values, their mission, and performing up to their own standards. The ways to "render an account" range from answering to the collective wisdom of shared values across the NGO family; to using public speeches and public education campaigns to exercise responsible leadership; to providing financial and programmatic data via websites, annual reports, press releases, and documentation. It also means telling people what their operational work is achieving and answering to boards, contributors, beneficiaries, and other stakeholders for their decisions.

One of the implications of multiple and competing audience pulls is that different kinds of information and feedback are needed for different audiences. Therefore accountability is necessarily contingent upon both

---

[5] At a meeting at the Brookings Institution, 29 October 1999, with David Brown, Julie Fisher, Peter Hall, Virginia Hodgkinson, Ray Horten, Steve Smith, Christina Kappaz, and Crispin Gregoire, we discussed, among other issues, the accountability dilemmas, and this model was suggested. It should also be noted that Alan Fowler (1996) uses the same term.

[6] Mark Moore and L. David Brown led this session on accountability in the Seattle NGO Leaders Meeting, 7 May 2000.

the demander and the context of the demand. For example, donors often require formal evaluation reports, while other contributors expect some summary financial reports and annual mailings; beneficiaries, on the other hand, need results – though their own interpretation of favorable results can differ from the interpretations imposed by donors. Thus the contingency model of accountability presented below reflects these differing demands.

The way in which NGO family networks differ within themselves is also part of this contingency model. Moreover, often national members work collaboratively within particular countries when working in, for example, Africa or Latin America. Thus Save the Children UK could be working with Save the Children Sweden in Guatemala – and there is also a Save the Children Guatemala national member. Each of these Saves has different Guatemalan partners and somewhat different objectives in their work (they are, after all, working collaboratively because of their special expertise on a part of the problem at hand). The modalities for holding them accountable within the United Kingdom, or Sweden, or Guatemala are in each case different – as are the kinds of requests made by contributors, donors, or boards to which they need to respond.

The kinds of processes and "products" that NGOs generate inevitably add to the complexity of their accountability systems. Unlike the private sector with its sharp focus on a single bottom line, NGOs, as Mark Moore has said, have two major bottom lines. He points out that for nonprofits, "Mission attainment is calculated in terms that are different from revenue assurance. In this important sense, there are two bottom lines: mission effectiveness and financial sustainability" (Moore, 2000, p. 194). He adds, rightfully, that this makes for greater managerial complexity than a single bottom line.

The internet has both eased and complicated the kinds of reports and data that can be presented. Annual reports are often made available via the internet, easing the mailing costs of getting these to donors. Some contributors can, and do, check websites to find out how projects and programs are progressing. For other contributors, mailings that are less formal than evaluation reports are needed. Because of changes in technology, the total amount of data produced and distributed has increased. The new modalities of communication are of course additional to all of those which senior decision-makers have traditionally used to meet accountability expectations, including meetings and consultations, discussions with key stakeholders, taskforces, and committees. Having an evaluation system, staff tasked to perform that function, and budget resources allocated for evaluation are critical components – but they do not add up to the full range of accountability functions, and may even be a relatively small part of the whole.

In short, it is not easy to account to a diverse set of stakeholders who have different and sometimes conflicting demands. A contingent model of accountability responds to the fact of widely diverse and equally deserving constituencies and multiple modalities for responding to those constituencies. The managerial questions include the who, what, when, and how of giving an account to these dispersed and sometimes competing constituents: To the people in far-flung villages and communities – or refugee camps or settlements – for which they are working? To the foundations or corporations that contribute to their programs? To peer NGOs? To the bilateral aid agencies whose programs they are administering? To the international donors for whom they perform services? And, in the worst case, if it is all of the above, how is this accounting to be sequenced? Since the NGOs most often work through locally based partner agencies, dividing this challenge with those partners is another part of the equation.

Alan Fowler argues that the linear thinking – as exemplified by the logical framework for project design – imposes a presumed certainty that is not the reality at the village level. Like others, Fowler is concerned that the donor agency may force upon an NGO a narrow window through which to view its work. (Of course, lurking in the background for a donor like USAID is the US Congress, which also will want quantifiable evidence of real results for monies disbursed – and Congress's timetable is governed by a short-term election cycle.) Suffice it to say that the emphasis on accountability to donors can lead NGOs to focus on their immediate projects without examining the broader economic, social, and political realities having an impact on communities. In relief work – where little is understood, and less is appreciated, about the relationships between relief and longer-term development – this problem is exacerbated. What will matter over time is not just how many blankets or food rations were distributed, but how community-level problem-solving, for example, began to be reinstated.

All of these questions and criticisms have led to greater insistence on accountability without much clarity about what it is that should be assessed and which of the stakeholders needs what information. NGO leaders have always had to respond – account to – different constituencies. Donors, however, were always more than just another constituency, as they were increasingly implementing programs through NGOs. While much has been written about the possible threats to the long-term mission of NGOs when or if they become more dependent on donor funding, in general the assumption has been that increased donor funding would require more attention to evaluation than had been the case to date in many NGOs. One of the preliminary surprises our interviews surfaced, however, was that the NGOs that are the least dependent on donor funding are in fact the NGOs doing the most about evaluation. It is not yet clear how to explain this counterintuitive finding. A part of the answer, however, may be that donors specify a final evaluation, sometimes hiring their own outside team to conduct it. That evaluation then is to meet donor needs, not the learning needs for the NGO. Often, for example, the NGO simply ensures that the evaluation is done, and does little more than treat evaluation as part of contract compliance – rather than as part of their own ongoing reflection. While it is true that increased donor funding has called into question the role, function, and cost of evaluation, it has not yet become as robust in the process as might have been expected.

Evaluation systems

While accountability is broader than evaluation, accountability drives NGOs to focus more attention on performance, and hence on strengthening their evaluation systems. Monitoring and evaluation processes are, after all, the ways that data is generated on program and project performance. Improving them depends upon staffing and operational budgets, so that strengthening either of these drives up overhead costs. Ironies abound: Donors want to work with NGOs because NGOs' voluntary character means they are less costly than consulting firms. Yet the earlier NGO tradition of voluntarism can be steadily eroded by the same set of actors and factors that led to its initial growth. Now NGOs are often implored to become more "professional." Most donors, however, show little willingness to pay for increased professionalism as it means staff and equipment costs, hence overhead. Support for overhead costs is not available. Professionalism in accountability is not as readily financed as it is demanded.

Monitoring and evaluation systems for large organizations take several different forms, and within the NGO families with which we are concerned, they vary within and among national members. Some are quasi-independent of line operations and report directly to boards. They may be so constituted in order to act as a check or countervailing power to operations, or because a strong executive board wants the evaluation office to have a "watchdog" function. Other organizations – especially smaller ones on lean budgets – integrate monitoring an evaluation so that the two processes can be iterative, with mutual learning of "best practice" through workshops, seminars, conferences, or a wide variety

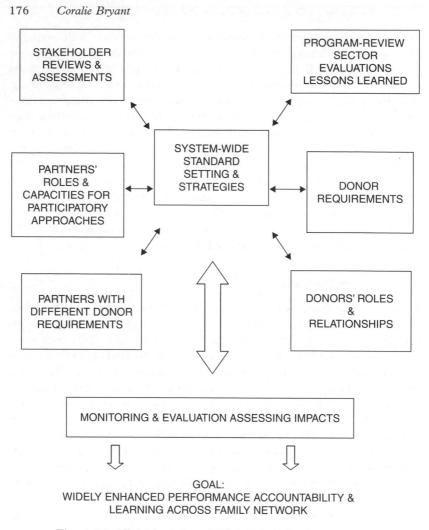

Figure 9.1 Variables in monitoring and evaluation

of other means. The variables within monitoring and evaluation systems
are depicted in Figure 9.1.

Evaluation, like any other function, requires organizational commitment of budget and staff to make it happen. Its advocates are invariably
quick to note that making use of lessons learned will save costly error,
and that investing in evaluation is therefore a sound investment. That
may be, but the question remains of how to undertake evaluation of
programs over time most efficiently as well as effectively. Portfolio
reviews by regions, as CARE has done, make sense. But there are no

easy answers to the questions of how much to invest in undertaking these works, at what intervals, or how often. Coupled with that, when or whether to share the findings from evaluations, and how to do so, is a troubled terrain. Predictably, there will be increased pressure from stakeholders for greater transparency. Transparency taken as a rule can put in place pressures to avoid sensitive areas, and some candor can be lost. Privacy rules and practices are culturally contextual, so that transparency practices in one place put burdens on partners in a different context. There are no right answers to these difficult trade-offs.

The evaluation offices in most Northern NGOs are small, spare in resources, and usually focused on setting guidelines and large parameters for the work that is to be done by either partners, or consultants, or both. Oxfam America and Save the Children US have one or two people fully committed to evaluation in their headquarters offices. These staff members are charged with evaluation responsibility where this means setting guidelines, establishing policy frameworks, assisting with some training for regional offices, and supporting partners. While others may be tasked with aspects of this work, often there is no internal staff to do the work itself. Moreover, since most of these NGOs work with partners, they may ask a Southern partner to manage evaluation research, yet the partner may have even fewer trained staff to do so than the Northern partner. The large bulk of evaluation work that is done for NGOs is done by consultants contracted to undertake various assessments, studies, and impact evaluations. The costs – real and opportunity costs – for undertaking evaluations make them unwelcome demands on the organizational budget. Table 9.1 provides in the matrix an overview of the current state of these NGOs' evaluation systems.

When NGOs work on government contracts, evaluation is generally pre-specified in the contract negotiations – often for a mid-course as well as a final evaluation. Consultants are contracted either by the NGO or by the donor to meet the contract-compliance needs. Most often in contract work, the donor agency's field mission will supervise the evaluation work and be the recipient of the final report (along with the partner field organization, or the field office of the NGO). The evaluation staff in the Northern NGOs' central office often do not see these evaluations – precisely because they go to those most directly involved with having implemented the project at hand.

The constant search for improved ways of doing business, gathering and reflecting upon lessons learned, and measuring impact and consequences require people tasked to do that work. That in turn costs money and comes out of overhead. The challenge for NGOs – who often have to argue that as large a percentage of the funds contributed to

Table 9.1 *NGO evaluation systems*

Organization	Past Practice	Current practice	Drivers for change	Evaluation unit	Learning process
CARE	Largely qualitative and descriptive evaluations done in field for individual projects.	Last five years standard setting for best practice as well as performance developed – now is system wide.	Largely internal; donor requirements had been met in previous system.	Yes. Director of Monitoring & Evaluation position created 1995.	Working towards having a learning system but not in place as an organizational process and system yet.
MÉDECINS SANS FRONTIÈRES	Largely qualitative and descriptive except for quantitative health and medical information.	Done on an as-needed basis to drive internal program needs.	Largely internal; some external (e.g. UNHCR or ECHO requirements).	No. Staff across family network do evaluation based on knowledge and past experience.	Learning for those who most need the operationally relevant findings.
OXFAM GB	Combinations of approaches using participatory data collection. Careful attention to impact assessments.	Learning around impact assessments. Linked to Strategic Change Objectives at global level, Individual projects continue to respond to donor evaluation needs.	Internal and external (partners, stakeholders and donors).	Yes. Under Policy Department. Serves advisory and support role to regions where evaluations are done.	Evaluation results and indicators worked into strategic planning process (?).
PLAN INT'L	System-wide standards reflected in benchmark indicators.	Strong system-wide standards with agreed-upon benchmarks for PLAN priorities.	Largely internal-strong corporate culture of accountability.	Yes. Evaluation unit with emphasis on system-wide indicators. Also strong auditing unit.	No. Process underway to get all members in Plan into corporate-wide standards and measuring performance first.

SAVE THE CHILDREN (UK)	Variety of approaches. Ad hoc, often driven by donor requirements. Reliance on initiative of project managers.	Serious attention to new indicators for each program area. Systematic, global approach linked to strategic planning.	Internal drive to improve on previous ad hoc system to facilitate organizational learning.	Yes. Under Policy and Research Department. Responsible for designing core indicators and supporting project managers in evaluation.	Indicators and change objectives are integral part of programming around core areas. Goal is to use evaluation for learning.
SAVE THE CHILDREN (US)	Donor-required evaluations routinely performed.	Donor-required evaluations done in field with different kinds of teams.	External-donor requirements.	No. A Director of Evaluation sets policy guidance on evaluation.	No. While interested in moving in this direction currently workloads preclude much time available for reflection.
WORLD VISION	Some evaluations done on an as-needed basis.	Increased interest in stronger more systematic evaluations.	Want donor pressure for more systematic data collection.	No. Evaluations done as driven by regional needs.	No. Other internal organizational restructuring kept this from being possible.

them reaches the grassroots as possible – is the real difficulty of financing evaluation. Those who want greatest accountability – meaning narrowly that results are quantified and measurable – are not necessarily those private contributors writing their Christmas checks. Pointing to a stronger evaluation system is, however, not a widely favored way to increase an NGO's popular appeal. It increases the overhead – and annual appeals have to point to low, not rising, overheads.

Program and project evaluation

Interestingly, in spite of all these hurdles, there is a great deal of work underway within most of these NGOs on strengthening their evaluation systems. Let us turn to some of the examples of the changes underway.

Evaluation of projects

While much is written about the shortcomings and the critical reviews of NGO projects, there is equally compelling evidence of many successes. Roger Riddell and Mark Robinson report on, among other things, a major review by the Overseas Development Institute in London of sixteen poverty-alleviating projects in Bangladesh, India, Uganda, and Zimbabwe, several of which were projects supported by Oxfam, Save the Children, and CARE. The aim of the study was "to formulate an approach for assessing not all projects and programs but, more narrowly, those whose purpose was to alleviate poverty and/or improve the living conditions of the beneficiaries, principally people living in rural areas" (Riddell and Robinson, 1995, p. 45). Almost all of the projects and programs reviewed were found to have improved living conditions, or to have raised the incomes of those living in poverty. Riddell and Robinson report on these projects in detail, including their immediate context, country context, and what was learned.

The study is especially noteworthy because it appears to be far less known in the United States than in Great Britain, while in the United States there has been more criticism of NGOs without in-depth empirical research on project and program impacts. But it is also true that evaluation techniques and interest in them spread more rapidly in the United States than in Europe. As Roger Riddell and Mark Robinson pointed out:

For most European NGOs working in the development field, evaluation is still very new and if used at all tends to be more of a one-off affair, most often embarked upon either because things have gone very wrong – the fire brigade approach – or when a particular project is completed but there is a request for future funding, or when a second or third phase of a particular project is to be launched. Indeed, the vast majority of projects and programs funded by British NGOs in developing countries are not subject to any sort of formal evaluation nor bound to specified cycles of expenditure for committed support, as is common with official aid projects. (1995, p. 44)

Yet even as they wrote this in 1995, Oxfam GB, the largest NGO in Britain, had a separate unit for research and evaluation, though Roger Riddell and Mark Robinson added "but even here, no common framework, guidelines, or procedures have yet been adopted. The same is broadly true of current practice among even the largest NGOs in the Netherlands and Germany and among other Northern European NGOs, such as those in Finland and Sweden" (1995, p. 44).

While the absence of common guidelines might have been true in 1995, it was no longer true in 2000 – either for Oxfam GB, or for Save the Children UK. Both of these NGOs, and others, have been rapidly building evaluation capacity and systems appropriate to their needs in the past several years. Save the Children UK improved what it was getting from field-level evaluation by producing its own guide on how monitoring and evaluation might be done – a guide that was publicly available and entitled *Toolkits: A Practical Guide to Assessment, Monitoring, Review, and Evaluation* (Gosling and Edwards, 1995). Their point in this publication was to lay out to field staff and partners the tools for improving how they went about doing monitoring and evaluation.

Subsequently, in 1996–7, Save the Children UK collected 245 reports of Save reviews and evaluations, and, using a sample drawn from that database, summarized the recommendations looking at how institutional and conceptual approaches could be improved. Among the conclusions was that evaluations too often emphasized the achievement of outputs – numbers of children immunized, or wells put in place – but did not address the larger concern: how lives were improved and whether children were healthier. The report pointed out that:

This issue of going beyond counting outputs to address impacts, on how lives are improved is not a narrow issue but one that goes to the heart of institutional change ... Save the Children is already part of this process, developing methodologies for impact monitoring in the field. However this work is currently disparate and great attention needs to be given to integrating evaluation, and its component parts (assessment, planning, monitoring, review, formal evaluation) into program management, providing a strategy for continuous checking, learning, and adjusting within a wider institutional culture of reflective self-criticism. (Mansfield, 1997, p. 9)

CARE USA have also made great strides in strengthening their monitoring and evaluation system since 1995. They too are fully seized of the problem of assessing impacts – not just fulfillment of project activities.

In their case, as there had also been a change internally to a different programming model, the Household Livelihood Security (HLS) system, they could then devise a monitoring and evaluation process keyed to HLS. By the end of 1999, they had developed CARE Impact Guidelines, with a menu of impact indicators for use in light of their goal of strengthening Household Livelihood Security. They are in the midst now of securing across all the CARE national members greater commitment to monitoring and evaluation work in light of these new standards.

Oxfam GB's Chris Roche produced a book, *Impact Assessment for Development Agencies* (1999), that details with clarity how impact assessment might be done. Oxfam GB has housed its evaluation work in different units over time, but it consistently has made evaluation a core function, and was putting into place a new department on policy planning, and evaluation. The earlier, three-volume handbook, *Oxfam Handbook of Development and Relief* (Eade and Williams, 1995), includes several sections on evaluation. Noteworthy throughout these handbooks is their emphasis on participatory evaluation – ways in which those directly reached by a program are engaged in evaluating the program's effectiveness.

Participatory evaluation

Where a Northern NGO has been working through and with a Southern NGO partner, or is working directly through its own local field office, it is likely that participants in a project can be identified to engage in a participatory evaluation process. This depends on the local partnering NGO's perspectives on evaluation, its evaluation capacity, and its willingness to comply readily with an externally hired evaluation consultant. The kinds of data that can emerge from careful participatory evaluations are particularly valuable. If the line of inquiry to be used is planned ahead of time, the kind of data gathered can help both the partner and the funding Northern NGO to learn in ways that may improve future effectiveness. Learning about what happened, how, why, and with what results provides information and insight that can help inform the next generation of projects or programs.

Participatory evaluation is logical and appropriate. The people who experience the impact of relief programs, or of development projects and programs, by definition have first-hand experience with the impact of those projects. and they should have much to say about effectiveness or impact. And, in general, development professionals undertaking evaluation research endeavor to reach and listen to those at the grassroots. There is a large and growing literature on how and why evaluation research must include this kind of qualitative empirical work.[7] But there are severe constraints on ensuring that such work is carried out. It is costly, labor-intensive, and requires skill; it takes time – in several different locations. If it is not well done, the findings are not useful.

The larger the project, the more costly it is to sample and reach those directly affected. Project participants are difficult to track down, and baseline data is often missing: refugees often relocate. It is also true that participants directly impacted will not necessarily be able to provide data on aspects of their situation that are needed in order to put into context the data they do have. For example, they know their income level, but know little about the average income level when the project began and even less about the average for the region. The real strength of qualitative data comes in the insights into *why* something did or did not work. Its weakness comes in its not providing generalizable data. Respondents also may not identify long-term consequences (even for themselves) that the program has had. For example, in evaluating a food-distribution program in a refugee camp, the refugees themselves will not have access to data on nutritional levels, food availability in different locations to appraise the areas of greatest need, or whether and when the percentage of those being fed are in reality terrorists who are "foraging" until the next battle call is sounded.

Evaluation of emergency relief work

It is no surprise that we are most short of evaluation data on emergency relief work. The UNHCR, one of the main international agencies funding NGO work in relief, most generally requests a final financial audit but not an evaluation – in part because of the inherent difficulty of tracking those who benefited from emergency services. The spate of books criticizing NGOs for their roles in Rwanda grew out of nonsampled interviews, anecdotes, and observation drawn not from interviews with large numbers of refugees, but from interviews and recollections from external observers, agency staff, or journalists hazarding guesses about what happened. The more severe the emergency, the less likely it is that the internally displaced people reached through a relief effort are able to help document their perceptions of

---

[7] Participatory evaluation was first promoted in Asia and Africa where it was also often linked with giving people a voice in influencing future policy choices. There was also a Society for Participatory Research in Asia that worked in conjunction with the African Adult Education Association. That approach spread rapidly to Northern industrial countries, and is reflected in much current material on evaluation. See, for example, Kassam and Mustafa (1982) and Jackson and Kassam (1998).

NGO effectiveness. Refugees or internally displaced people voice their issues, the media picks up anecdotes and rumor, and these are beamed rapidly to audiences in distant countries. Systematic evaluation from which cumulative learning can take place is easily available and expensive – and, by the time it is available, it is much less newsworthy.

The importance of strengthening evaluation systems has gained in salience as a result of the increasing pressure for demonstrated effectiveness. Evaluation in development projects and programming has become increasingly skillful in the past decade, but widespread adoption of the cutting-edge techniques is still hindered by logistical and financial barriers as well as barriers stemming from the organizational culture and norms within the nonprofit community. There are significant overhead costs and organizational and staffing implications since evaluation research has grown in sophistication and technique in the past decade. Adoption of evaluation systems has also been affected by the fact that many of the techniques for measuring program effectiveness tend to contradict the inherent organizational culture within most NGOs.

Evaluation through indicators and benchmarking

Data is central to an evaluation system that allows for comparisons across similar kinds of programs or projects. NGOs, and other organizations, have found that the use of indicators, when these are carefully constructed, can be helpful. But getting those indicators, creating a culture of evaluation and learning, and then bringing staff fully on board across a system of national affiliates is an ongoing process – and not a short-term goal that, once achieved, stays in place. Nonetheless, Plan International has been working on doing just that – and appears to be one of the leaders among Northern NGOs for its work on evaluation. It is now beginning to implement an evaluation system for its core areas of work: livelihood, habitat, and health. Plan International went outside to get professional help to come up with indicators for each of the components of these core areas. Wherever it works, it gets baseline data. Of course its operations are long-term and integrated, and it largely operates through programs. Because Plan works in communities for fifteen–twenty years, it can monitor those programs as well.

Performance indicators can be developed to distinguish between measuring inputs, outputs, results, and impacts. Indicator data collected over time provides information critical to learning where attention needs to go to further improvement. Plan International's work in this area has attracted attention from other peer organizations; for example, Novib (the Dutch Oxfam affiliate) turned to Plan in order to strengthen its own system. What is especially noteworthy about Plan's approach is that it is a system-wide approach being used by all of Plan's operational offices. Plan's operational work is undertaken by Southern Plan offices, with much more central coordination and quality control by Plan International in support of those country offices. Plan is, after all, more fully multinational than other Northern NGOs. It is globally structured and staffed with strong coordination across national boundaries. The Plan UK office and Plan US office exist for the purposes of fundraising only; when people within those offices refer to "operations," they mean not field-level operations themselves, but quality control, standard setting, and policy-making vis-à-vis field-level operations. Actual field-level operations in livelihood, habitat, and health are wholly undertaken by Southern Plan International offices and generally wholly by locally hired staff.

Save the Children UK is also in the process of developing a more systematic approach to monitoring and evaluation that will be consistent across its projects. This process builds upon its 1999 strategic review which prioritized Save's work into six core areas (health, education, social policy, food and nutrition, child labor, HIV/AIDS) and four cross-cutting themes (gender, emergencies, disabilities, advocacy). Preliminary indicators (mainly process-oriented) have been identified but much work remains to be done in obtaining baseline data, developing more impact indicators, and in integrating the new approach within country offices.

At CARE, the experience of introducing benchmarking and portfolio-analysis approaches found resistance stemming from the strongly individualistic and independent style of staff and the service culture, which sometimes places a higher value on helping people than on doing things efficiently. Relief situations again accentuate the problem, since the urgent need for action takes precedence over detailed analysis and data collection. Furthermore, the very nature of the work that is being measured is much more ambiguous in relief and development organizations than in the for-profit world. The long-term contribution of any one development or relief effort to the long-term goal of improving people's livelihood is difficult to measure.

An in-depth study of CARE revealed that "in spite of natural barriers, CARE staff were initially receptive to a program impact initiative because there was virtually no CARE-wide data on numbers of projects, beneficiary numbers, costs per participant, and there were few project baselines to compare project performance. CARE staff had a strong personal interest as highly driven professionals in knowing whether their projects were having an impact" (Lindenberg, 2001).

The strategic management process in short led to several things – attention to their mission, incentives, and attention to benchmarking and looking at impacts. It led initially to training on regional impact evaluation. In addition the headquarters technical division was asked to create project data baselines by sector (water, agriculture, health, family planning, micro-enterprise development). The data was even to be collected on a form called the project implementation report. CARE headquarters asked all country offices to approve no new projects without baselines. In an effort to provide different approaches to best practice, three technical approaches were suggested – all of them shared the objective of comparing projects to some performance standard. Staff who believed they had unique projects could do self-comparison, in which staff set performance standards and then monitored for them. For others using a portfolio approach it was possible to use indicators against national standards.

But CARE's extensive work on benchmarking methodologies had mixed results:

[A]lthough top-down external rankings that included good global best practice data were technically strong, they frequently backfired when angry project managers felt they were being ambushed. NGO participative culture made it hard to use external information in a nonthreatening way. In a regional management conference in Asia, project staff members rejected the top-down approach ... Even when participative methods are used, it continues to be a challenge to get field staff members to accept data from global empirical studies and broader evaluations ... [What is more effective is an] overall strategy that includes training in program design and evaluation, standards about project design baseline data, benchmarking, and participative evaluation. (Lindenberg, 2001, pp. 263–4)

CARE staff went on to develop their learning around the development of the household-analysis tool as an example of reconfiguring internal programming approaches in order to improve effectiveness. The household-analysis tool also helped reposition CARE's comparative advantage.

Similarly, World Vision has recognized the need to place greater emphasis on program quality and impact and has begun this process by sharpening the organization's core focus and priorities, developing clearer impact goals and indicators, and establishing new mechanisms for mutual accountability between national offices in its partners. Oxfam GB has also undergone a process of internal review that has resulted in the definition of specific challenges and steps related to a range of issues. To address accountability issues, it will establish a quality-assurance system involving the establishment of quality standards and a system of auditing, and it will develop a new approach to the ways in which it listens to and assimilates the views of its diverse stakeholders.

Given the difficulty of putting in place an integrated evaluation process across all national members of an NGO family, there will always be questions whether this is the best investment in light of the relief and development NGOs' scarce resources and high opportunity costs. While the answer is contingent upon the context and situation of any particular NGO, there is a case for considering how staff are to learn over time, and how organizational learning is to be fostered. An old aphorism teaches us that "While the unexamined life is not worth leading, the overexamined life is not worth writing home about either." That is true of evaluation. While an evaluation system that feeds into and encourages organizational learning is eminently worthwhile, overinvesting in it – given the opportunity costs in a world where more work on poverty reduction and refugee relief cries for attention – is not wise.

That said, most of the NGOs we have looked at have a way to go to improve the quality of their evaluation work. They need to do so in order to understand their own effectiveness. Linking that learning into organizational learning more generally would be meaningful for staff – and helpful in maintaining morale and averting "burnout" as well as increasing productivity. While almost all authors commenting on evaluation start from the assumption that with increased official assistance, organizations will perforce move towards strengthening evaluation, we found in our interviews that two organizations with strong evaluation systems – Oxfam and Plan International – are not accepting significant amounts of official donor assistance. Oxfam America accepts no official development assistance. These agencies therefore moved in this direction in response to internal, rather than external, demands or needs. Further empirical research on the relationships between percentages of budget derived from official development assistance, concern with program impact, and organizational learning would be useful. The implications of organizational learning for staff productivity and morale are significant, and evaluation has a large role to play in a great learning system.

In short, there is a larger case to be made for creating more of an evaluation culture coupled with, and integral to, increased staff learning about effectiveness. An organizational learning process moves towards reestablishing meaning for staff. Learning – especially when self-directed – is intrinsically invigorating. It is worth considering how this process works.

Organizational learning

Organizational learning is one of the intriguing concepts currently receiving significant attention as well as scholarship. Peter Senge, Director of the Center for Organizational Learning at MIT's Sloan

School of Management, works with a large group of professionals on what has become the leading concept in much of the organizational theory and practice field (Senge, 1990; 1995). The core concepts are focused on reinventing relationships, being loyal to the truth, developing strategies for personal mastery, building a shared vision, strategies for team learning and systems thinking, designing governing ideas, and treating organizations as communities. In brief, several schools of thought are at work – mixing and drawing upon the classical work of, for example, Chris Argyris, Russell Ackoff, and Jay Forrester, and incorporating material from, for example, strategic planning, quality management, and the emphasis on excellence. Thus in many ways this current model (and its practice) has long, strong roots and is not dismissible as another management "fad." It is particularly appealing in the context of the development and relief NGOs, since it puts people at the center – thereby building upon the international development management tradition of people-centered development as fostered by David Korten, Louise White, and Robert Chambers.

The core elements of the organizational learning process are rooted in the field of organizational development. By engaging staff working in groups through queries that evoke reflection and analysis on their work, the participants begin to drive the agenda. Oxfam America has gone furthest with organizational learning. Its president, Ray Offenheiser, says that "organizational learning is driving the strategic management of our transformation process. We had to rethink our organizational model . . . the older traditional organization models are gone in light of global changes. Now our core currency is information and organizational learning is our overarching principle" (2001). Oxfam America began by working in groups to develop a strategic plan, and then turned to implementing that plan. To lead off the implementation, it had a week-long workshop at the Goree Institute in Senegal bringing together partners, regional representatives, regional managers, and senior managers to discuss implementation of the theme, "Participation for Equity." It was one of the first times that a large number of managers, staff, and partners had talked with one another systematically about their work. Those who participated conveyed their excitement and commitment to building upon and deepening the process. The Goree week produced a series of guidelines that were then used to guide the management of their strategic planning process. These are still being used: speak with authority and substance on key development issues; invest in knowledge for action; link the local with the global; program outcomes lead to social change; and serve partners and work towards their empowerment.

The core elements in this process are that it focuses on being a learning organization in practice – by breaking down the boundaries between departments, and between center and field and partners; puts people at the center of the organization; and flattens organizational structure. It also – and predominantly from the perspective of operations – creates permeability between planning and taking action. No longer is there a separation between those who plan and those who implement – but these are seen to be, and they become, interchangeable.

Flattening the organizational structure, however, proved to be one of the difficult parts of the process. All the Oxfams are unionized and Oxfam America is no exception. The union (Service Employees International Union) has detailed rules about structure and these precluded giving staff supervisory responsibility. How then could they get to more movement between those who plan and those who implement – a more horizontal organization? Again, this was worked through bit and piece by managers and staff working in groups, devising ways to proceed and yet be in conformance with the union rules. As many union leaders and members experienced organizational learning as empowering, they basically worked their way through a thicket of problems. Some of the old-school union leaders – more accustomed to the fist-fight model of adversarial relationships – had trouble making the change; eventually they lost out in union elections.

Oxfam America drew heavily upon training in what has come to be called interspace bargaining – an approach in which small groups work through competing interests rather than posturing for positions in an argument. This training proved invaluable; staff now knew how to do interest-based negotiating. As the time was approaching for a renewal of the union's contract, this proved important. Instead of drawing upon the older adversarial approaches to union contract issues, groups of staff worked through what needed to be done and drafted side-letters that reflected the agreements reached. Then during the contract negotiations, these side-letter agreements were incorporated into the contract. Now Oxfam America has moved on yet again, moving away from the big bang approach to five-year planning to a more flexible and responsive planning. Organizational learning is firmly driving its planning process, and bringing transformation with it.

There is no doubt that, from the point of view of achieving results, NGOs need an iterative process of engaging staff from top to bottom in identifying and illuminating what is and is not working. It is very easy to be caught up in processes and meeting deadlines, fundraising, disseminating information, and measuring those "inputs" without getting time to reflect and think about the impact or results of this work. Laura

Roper, Oxfam America's director of program planning and learning – the office where setting guidelines and policy on evaluation takes place – told us that there is a real need "to create space and opportunity for staff to reflect." Reflection, especially when informed by data on results or consequences of actions taken to date, leads naturally to learning, or at least identifying what remains to be done. Roper has also recently contracted for assistance to get more quantitative data on program results because she knows that Oxfam's qualitative data from these various processes would be better informed with more quantitative measurement of impact and results.

Conclusions

The international relief NGOs that participated in this study are all committed to accountability and in many instances have also worked to strengthen monitoring and evaluation systems. Few, however, consider these functions their highest priority. For all of the leaders with whom we met, achieving their organization's mission is the uppermost goal; this is what drives them to work on advocacy, on fundraising, and, above all, on programs. Yet they are fully aware that improving performance requires knowing more about that performance. Hence, accountability and its components – monitoring and evaluation systems – are strong intermediate goals.

We must admittedly acknowledge that our data on accountability systems is incomplete. The variations in accountability systems among national members of all the six NGO families in our core group of interlocutors militate against our having a complete dataset on accountability. What we were able to learn is that these variations are real and pervasive. Our timetable did not permit collecting everything that needed to be known within any given family – let alone account for the differences across the different networks. But what we did learn is that there have been significant and serious efforts to improve evaluation systems in the past five to eight years, and that new approaches and learning from them are readily shared across NGO family borders.

What we still know little about, however, is context: how serious differences of perspective within any given NGO family affect how to manage the contingencies in accountability. NGOs' separate country political contexts vary too much for there to be ease with a system-wide approach. For example, Oxfam GB is large enough within the political system of Great Britain that the head of Oxfam GB has ready access to the Prime Minister. Moreover, since a significant percentage of the British electorate uses a payroll deduction system to contribute to

Oxfam, most parliamentarians will listen when Oxfam speaks. That is in marked contrast with the situation of Oxfam America – or of any other NGO based in the United States. As different national members have different constituencies to whom they respond, as well as an array of domestic political and legal forces within the country where they are headquartered, their accountability systems differ more than any other function.

In researching the NGOs on the topics covered in this chapter, it was striking to see how little is actually known about monitoring and evaluation systems within them. Most of the literature takes a very broadbrush treatment of the accountability factors. One of the results of that is a paucity of hard data on exactly what the evaluation systems are within these NGOs. One aspect of that is that the NGOs' leaders are also not very likely to go into details. When probing for this information, one is sent onto others – even when it is said that accountability is a senior management goal.

Of the several trends on the theme of this chapter that warrant further exploration, the one that commands the most attention is the growing interest in understanding the longer-term impact, not just the outputs, of projects and programs. In our interviews, staff expressed a keen interest in that and in having more time for reflection on lessons learned. At the center of this issue is a conundrum: both outsiders and staff would like to know more about when and why NGOs are effective (as many staff believe they are). Replicating that success becomes more possible with such knowledge. Development projects come with hidden surprises and unexpected outcomes – and sometimes beneficiaries most value outcomes that were not planned but happened. Still, more learning is both possible and wanted. Given the scale of the human needs with which these NGOs are struggling, this search for explanations of effectiveness needs further exploration. It is also worth examining why the pressure for such learning sometimes comes more from the field or the staff than from headquarters. It may be that those most immediately engaged in the work are most keen to discover, and document, when they have had an impact.

References

Eade, Deborah and Suzanne Williams (1995) *The Oxfam Handbook of Development and Relief*, 3 vols. Oxford: Oxfam.

Edwards, Michael and David Hulme (1997) *NGOs, State and Donors: Too Close for Comfort?*, London: St. Martin's Press.

Edwards, Michael and David Hulme (1996) *Beyond the Magic Bullet*. Hartford: Kumarian Press.

Eriksson, John (1996) *The International Response to Conflict and Genocide: Lessons from the Rwanda Experience*. [Copenhagen?]: Joint Evaluation of Emergency Assistance to Rwanda.

Fowler, Alan (1996) "Assessing NGO Performance, Difficulties, Dilemmas, and a Way Ahead," in Edwards and Hulme (1996), pp. 169–86.

Gaventa, John (1998) "Poverty, Participation and Social Exclusion in North and South," *IDS Bulletin* 29(1), 50–7.

Gosling, Louisa and Mike Edwards (1995) *Toolkits: A Practical Guide to Assessment, Monitoring, Review, and Evaluation*. Development Manual 5. London: Save the Children.

Jackson, Edward T. and Yusuf Kassam (1998) *Knowledge Shared: Participatory Evaluation in Development Cooperation*. Hartford: Kumarian Press.

Kassam, Yusuf and Kemal Mustafa (1982) *Participatory Research: An Emerging Alternative Methodology in Social Science Research*. Nairobi: African Association for Participatory Development.

Lindenberg, Marc (2001) "Are We at the Cutting Edge or the Blunt Edge? Improving NGO Organizational Performance with Private and Public Sector Strategic Management Frameworks," *Nonprofit Management and Leadership* 11(30), 247–70.

Mansfield, David (1997) *Evaluation: Tried and Tested? A Review of Save the Children Evaluation Reports*. Working Paper No. 17. London: Save the Children (UK).

Moore, Mark (2000) "Managing for Value: Organizational Strategy in For-Profit, Nonprofit, and Governmental Organizations," in Elaine Backman, Allen Grossman, and V. Kasteri Rangan (eds.) Supplement to *NonProfit and Voluntary Sector Quarterly* 29(1), 194. Supplement, Arnova Publication.

Offenheiser, Ray, President, Oxfam America (25 January 2001) Personal Interview.

Riddell, Roger and Mark Robinson (1995) *Non-Governmental Organizations and Rural Poverty Alleviation*. London: Clarenden Press.

Roche, Chris (1999) *Impact Assessment for Development Agencies*. Oxford: Oxfam and Novib Publication.

Senge, Peter M. (1995) *The Fifth Discipline Field Book*. Cambridge, MA: MIT Press.

Senge, Peter M. (1990) *The Fifth Discipline: The Art and Practice of the Learning Organization*. New York: Doubleday Press.

Smillie, Ian and Henny Helmich (1999) *Stakeholders: Government–NGO Partnerships for Development*. In collaboration with Tony German and Judith Randell. London: OECD and Earthscan.

Smith, Brian (1990) *More than Altruism*. Princeton University Press.

Uvin, Peter (1998) *Aiding Violence: The Development Enterprise in Rwanda*. Hartford: Kumarian Press.

World Bank (1992) *Governance and Development*. Washington, DC: World Bank Publications.

10 Towards a reflective accountability in NGOs [1]

Alnoor Ebrahim

The preceding chapters in this volume have laid out two general challenges to our current understandings of accountability in NGOs. First, many of the authors have questioned traditional framings of the concept, especially principal–agent views in which NGOs are primarily seen as the passive subjects of external oversight and punishment. The second challenge posed by the contributors is thus a practical one – to find new forms of accountability which enable, rather than constrain, innovation, creativity, and agency for long-term social change. The purpose of my present chapter is thereby also twofold: 1) to provide a conceptual synthesis and discussion of the key problematics of accountability facing development NGOs; and 2) to offer a practical review of how an accountability system might be shaped to take on a more enabling role, particularly with respect to promoting critical reflection and learning within NGOs.

With respect to the first aim, several contributions in Parts I and II have pointed to two key deficiencies in problematizing the concept of accountability. First, the authors feel stifled by *myopic* conceptualizations of the term and thus argue for more nuanced and visionary framings of accountability. For example, Goetz and Jenkins are dissatisfied with standard mechanisms of "vertical" accountability for holding public agencies and officials to account (e.g., electoral systems and lobbying) and "horizontal" accountability (e.g., public agencies holding one another to account through legislative oversight, auditing, or judicial action). They are troubled by the remoteness of public sector workers from citizens and associations, and by the insulation of bureaucrats from citizens. Brown and Smillie similarly struggle with conventional modes of accountability, particularly in contexts where clear authority and oversight relations do not exist. Lewis grapples with an equally complex challenge – that of

[1] This chapter includes content from work previously published in *Nonprofit Management and Leadership* (Ebrahim, 2003b) and *Nonprofit and Voluntary Sector Quarterly* (Ebrahim, 2005). Used with permission.

positioning accountability in cultural context – and is critical of approaches to accountability that emphasize an "audit culture" model, drawn directly from Western schools of management, and which can weaken organizations "by creating an erosion of trust through the creation of perverse incentives."

In responding to these accountability myopias, each author argues for a new *logic of participation* in which configurations of power enable, rather than impede, the avenues open to citizens in shaping the actions of organizations in society.[2] These are not calls for a single all-encompassing way of thinking about accountability. On the contrary, the authors seek to counter myopic and modernist lenses with multiple, participatory, and postmodern views of accountability. To do so, they turn to innovative examples and case studies for new language and new framings. Goetz and Jenkins identify "diagonal" or "hybrid" mechanisms of accountability that enable greater public influence in agencies intended to serve the public. Brown outlines an approach to "mutual accountability" defined as "accountability among autonomous actors committed to shared values and visions and to relationships of mutual trust and influence." And Lewis, building on insights offered by the Cambridge philosopher Onora O'Neill (2002), proposes nurturing a "trust-based 'intelligent accountability'" that is rooted in NGOs' own cultural realities and perceptions rather than imported managerial models.

Even more concretely, the contributions in Part III devote attention to mechanisms of accountability that are aligned with organizational missions and visions, and which promote critical reflection and learning. Lisa Jordan, for example, provides a poignant set of cases in which a recentering of organizational mission was the driving force behind organizational accountability. Her case of ActionAid (p. 160) shows that "Accountability mechanisms are learning tools for the organization and for its primary stakeholders" and that "assessment is about responsibilities to the mission and to the communities within which the mission is carried out." Coralie Bryant, in her chapter on several large transnational NGOs, similarly argues that processes of organizational learning can help NGOs to devote more attention to the fundamental questions of long-term effectiveness and social change, and that evaluation is an especially important mechanism in this regard.

---

[2] The term "logic of participation" draws from Randall Germain's contribution to this volume, in which he calls for a new accountability that is guided by a logic of participation rather than a logic of compliance. Both his chapter and that of Ngaire Woods examine ways in which increased participation can improve accountability in global governance.

Such "reflective" forms of accountability are a direct response to the problematics of accountability. I elaborate these key problematics below, and then discuss how accountability might be reframed in broader systemic terms. I follow with an argument for placing organizational learning, and especially evaluation, at the core of a more reflective approach to accountability. In closing, I offer a series of propositions on the challenges that NGOs face in enhancing organizational learning while also maintaining accountability to donors.

Problematizing accountability

The ways in which accountability is problematized – how key concerns are framed and prioritized – affect the kinds of solutions that then emerge. If accountability is framed as a problem of insufficient oversight, the resulting solutions are likely to emphasize increased regulation and oversight. If it is problematized as an issue of personal responsibility, the solutions which follow will tend to stress voluntary initiatives and codes of professional conduct. But as the chapters in this book show, there are many ways of framing accountability challenges, some of which may be incommensurable. Nonetheless, the contributions appear to converge on two sets of concerns or problematics: myopias of accountability and logics of participation.

Myopias of accountability

It is inescapable that nonprofit organizations are accountable to numerous actors (upward to patrons, downward to clients, and internally to themselves and their missions). These relations may be said to form a system of accountability. Within this system, the dominant emphasis currently remains largely on accountability of NGOs to donors or patrons. This focus can thus be seen as myopic in two respects. First, it privileges one kind of accountability relation over a broader accountability system. Mechanisms for holding NGOs accountable to funders, for example, can overshadow or marginalize mechanisms for holding NGOs accountable to communities or to their own missions. In other words, this myopia focuses attention on funders and external stakeholder demands rather than on NGO missions and their theories of social change.

The second kind of myopia is normative. What is the purpose of holding an actor to account for its behavior? Is it simply to enforce rule-following behavior, or is it linked to a larger view of public interests? Arguably, accountability mechanisms that emphasize rule-following operational behavior run the risk of promoting NGO activities that are so focused on short-term outputs and efficiency criteria that they lose sight of long-range goals concerning social development and change. Levinthal and March (1993, p. 101) have identified very similar kinds of myopia of learning (rather than of accountability): a tendency to ignore the long run, a tendency to ignore the larger picture, and a tendency to overlook failures.[3]

While there are appropriate uses for conventional mechanisms of oversight and reporting, such approaches to accountability do not promote long-term learning. For a nonprofit or nongovernmental organization that aims to feed schoolchildren a daily warm breakfast, there may be no problem with regular reporting on the number of children fed. But for an organization that aims to address broader public policies concerning urban poverty, such measures of accountability may provide limited useful information on how to tackle long-term systemic change. The challenge for such organizations lies in *finding a balance* between short-term, rule-oriented mechanisms of accountability and more long-term approaches to organizational learning.

Logics of participation

The second problematic of accountability for NGOs concerns *logics of participation*. The forms of participation commonly espoused by public agencies, donors, and many NGOs are based on an assumption that poverty can be eliminated by increasing local access to resources and services. In such cases, stakeholders are able to "participate" through their involvement in project implementation (through consultation or contributions in cash, kind, or labor). Approaches to participatory development are now a basic part of the "toolkit" of development professionals, including community organizers, civil servants, and World Bank teams.

But the benefits of such participation, for purposes of downward and internal accountability, are more imagined than real. In many instances, citizens tend to gain very little decision-making authority, with actual project objectives being determined by NGOs and funders long before any "participation" occurs. This is what Cooke and Kothari (2001) have called a "new tyranny" of participation and what Najam (1996, p. 346)

---

[3] Clearly, these two kinds of myopia do not hold in cases where donors encourage and recognize the need for downward accountability, and in cases where donor commitments and reporting and evaluation requirements reflect a long-term perspective. However, such cases appear to be exceptional rather than usual (Edwards and Hulme, 1996; Riddell, 1999; Smillie, 1996).

has referred to as "a sham ritual" functioning as little more than "a 'feel-good' exercise for both the local community and the NGO." In linking this problem to accountability, Najam argues that "the sham of partici-pation translates into the sham of accountability" because "[u]nlike donors, [communities] cannot withdraw their funding; unlike govern-ments, they cannot impose conditionalities" (Najam, 1996, pp. 346–7). The act of participation or the exercise of "voice" is largely symbolic in such settings; it is not "political action par excellence" (Hirschman, 1970, p. 16). Rarely, in mainstream development practice, has the notion of participation been extended to forms of politicized activity that directly challenge social and political inequities, thus creating benefits that might exceed the costs of exercising voice. These more radical versions of participation stress that poverty is based in power structures embedded in social and political relations. As such, without some mechanism for addressing unequal power relations, participation appears unlikely to lead to downward accountability.

In other words, there is a disjuncture between an imagined logic of participation, which is empowering and enables downward account-ability, and the structural constraints of a real logic of participation that is a disempowering ritual. While participatory methods – such as par-ticipatory rural appraisal (PRA) and participatory learning and action (PLA) – have been part of the repertoire of most development agencies for several years now, the mere use of these tools is inadequate for ensuring downward accountability. For example, a World Bank review of participation in 189 of its projects found that while stakeholder par-ticipation rose from 40 percent of new projects approved in 1994 to 70 percent in 1998, much of the increased participation was narrow in scope, rushed, superficial, or otherwise ineffective (World Bank, 2000, p. vi). Similarly, a study of several participatory impact assessments observed that "participatory exercises in groups can neglect some people's views (for instance, women's or children's) and, moreover, validate and legitimate the views of dominant groups, thus increasing their power vis-à-vis others" (Roche, 1999, p. 148). The author, from Oxfam GB, noted that for participatory tools and methods to reflect differences in power and perspective, they must be part of a more deliberate intervention and research strategy.

It is a search for more empowering forms of participation that moti-vates a number of the case studies of NGOs in this book. Goetz and Jenkins' examination of hybrid forms of diagonal accountability provides an especially rich example of meaningful participation by citizens vis-à-vis public bureaucracies. They show how NGOs and their networks in India played critical roles in inserting citizens directly into oversight functions that were previously controlled by governmental bodies. Public accountability thus took the form of engaged and participatory oversight of public agencies by public citizens, and was institutionalized through various means including legal standing for nongovernmental observers, well-defined protocols for engagements between citizens and public sector actors, structured access to official documentary information, and rights of observers to issue dissenting reports directly to legislative bodies. Lewis' contrasting case of a Bangladeshi NGO offers an even broader look at the embeddedness of accountability practices within wider fields of power and social systems. In that case, the combination of deeply entrenched "patron–client" relations and a "culture of defensiveness" pervaded the organization, thus reproducing social hierarchies and inequalities, while impeding serious participation, organizational learning, and downward accountability.

In short, the two key problematics may be summarized as follows: 1) a myopia of accountability characterized by attention to short-term performance measurement rather than long-term social change, buttressed by a focus on accountability to funders at the expense of accountabilities to clients and mission; and 2) a logic of participation that is often compliance-driven and ritualistic rather than truly about increasing public accountability and power sharing.

What are the implications of these two problematics for rethinking NGO accountability? First, the discussion suggests a need to conceptualize accountability as a *system of relations*, which recognizes the differential power of actors, and the structural limitations on participatory voice. It also suggests a need to distinguish among different types of NGOs in order to better understand how accountability relationships vary among them. Second, it may be helpful to link NGO accountability more explicitly to NGO mission and vision through reflective forms of organizational learning. The remainder of this chapter develops these two ways forward.

Accountability as a system of relations

All organizations inhabit ecosystems with complex webs of relationships and environmental influences. Figure 10.1 depicts the systems and relational nature of accountability for development NGOs. For purposes of clarity, the organizational environment of NGOs is simplified into three primary groups: 1) funders, which may include public agencies, foundations, individual donors, corporate sponsors, international organizations, and Northern NGOs (which support Southern NGOs); 2) sector regulators, which include government agencies as well as self-regulatory

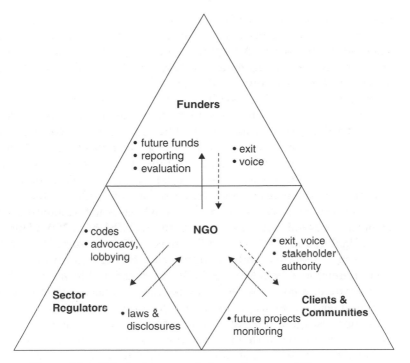

Figure 10.1 Principal–agent relations of accountability

groups that advocate codes of conduct for a particular sector; and 3) clients and communities, such as project beneficiaries, users of services (who may pay for those services), as well as community members who are not directly involved in a project but are indirectly impacted by it.

The arrows in Figure 10.1 point in the direction of accountability. In each relationship, an NGO can serve as both a principal and an agent. *The dominant direction of that relationship is determined by the presence and use of accountability mechanisms to enforce it.*[4] Solid arrows suggest a strong relationship in that direction, whereas dashed arrows indicate a weaker relationship. For example, funders provide money to NGOs in exchange for regular reports and evaluations that confirm the legitimate use of those funds. These reports and evaluations (which include

---

[4] The multidirectional view of principal–agent relations presented here builds on and complicates the unidirectional view articulated by Brown (above, ch. 5). A multi-directional view enables us to examine how NGOs and other actors seek to establish authority, and to operationalize that authority through accountability mechanisms. The limitations of principal–agent models expressed by Brown, particularly in terms of opening up new avenues for mutual accountability, continue to hold.

financial statements, narratives, performance assessments, and monitoring systems) function to hold NGOs accountable to their funders. In other words, the accountability mechanisms position funders as principals and NGOs as agents, as illustrated with a solid arrow between NGOs and funders in Figure 10.1.

What mechanisms allow NGOs to act as principals that can hold their funders to account? For the most part, NGOs are left with two options: exit and voice (Hirschman, 1970). They may exit by refusing donor funds, or they may exercise voice through complaints and efforts to reform their funders. While there are indeed cases of nonprofits challenging their funders, this is likely to be true only in cases where the asymmetry in resources is offset either by the availability of funds from other sources, or in cases where the NGO has a long-established and deeply interdependent relation with its funder (Ebrahim, 2002; Hudock, 1999; Pfeffer, 1987; Pfeffer and Salancik, 1978). In sum, the conventional use of reporting and evaluation as a funder control mechanism serves to reinforce the role of the NGO as an agent of its funders. While the rhetoric of funders and NGOs alike might indicate that NGOs and communities are the true principals, the material reality of accountability mechanisms suggests otherwise. In other words, this is a tightly bounded logic of participation with limited options for downward accountability.

This picture is somewhat more complex with sector regulators. Laws governing nonprofit status and their attendant requirements for information disclosure are generally intended to ensure a minimum level of transparency in NGOs, ostensibly for purposes of ensuring public trust. In this way, they serve as mechanisms of accountability in which NGOs act as agents to some public interest (while recognizing that there are many publics and many interests). Repressive states can, however, abuse powers of regulatory oversight to keep tabs on organizations that are considered subversive. Even in a democratic country like India, the Foreign Contribution Regulation Act of 1976 was enacted shortly after a state of emergency was declared by the government of Indira Gandhi, thus enabling the government to track the flow of foreign funds to NGOs that were critical of it (Sen, 1999). Repressive or not, regulatory oversight nonetheless reinforces the role of NGOs as agents to be monitored or controlled, either in a broad public interest or in a narrow state elite interest.

Another form of sector regulation involves the efforts of NGO networks to develop standards or codes of behavior and performance for themselves. In such cases, NGOs are not simply agents of an external authority, but act as principals in shaping standards for the sector as a whole. Standards and codes have been developed by membership organizations the world over – including by the American Council for

Voluntary International Action (InterAction) and the Better Business Bureau's Wise Giving Alliance in the United States, the Canadian Council for International Cooperation, the Philippine Council for NGO Certification, the NGO Charter in Poland, the Voluntary Action Network India, the Commonwealth Foundation in Britain, and The International Red Cross and Red Crescent Movement and NGOs in Disaster Relief – to name just a few (Ebrahim, 2003a; Schweitz, 2001). Relatedly, information gateways also serve to increase self-regulation and transparency, largely by making information publicly available, such as through the GuideStar website in the United States which provides data on about 850,000 nonprofits recognized by the Internal Revenue Service (www.guidestar.org).

In short, NGOs are linked to sector regulators by accountability mechanisms that position them as agents both of the public and of governments (through externally mandated laws and disclosures) and as collective principals to the nonprofit sector (through voluntary codes of conduct). By virtue of their wider visibility, NGO networks that operate across a sector are also able to exert a policy influence on public officials. Organizations that lobby for policy change act both as agents of the constituents whose voices they seek to represent, and as principals making demands of elected representatives. As such, the arrows linking NGOs to sector regulators in Figure 10.1 are solid in both directions.

The third set of relationships in Figure 10.1 involves clients and communities. Like relations between NGOs and funders, those between NGOs and clients tend to be asymmetric as a result of resource allocations. NGOs engaged in the provision of services – such as education, health care, housing, or rural development – typically provide a predetermined set of services to their clients. To the extent that the interests of clients or "beneficiaries" are congruent with those of the NGO, the services are accepted without conflict. But if clients find the services inadequate or of low priority, their options are generally limited to refusing the service (exit) or to complaining about it (voice). The service-providing NGO, on the other hand, has the powerful option of threatening to withdraw from current or future projects in the event of noncooperation, in the way that a funder can threaten to withdraw funds from an NGO. In addition, cooperation and project implementation are often monitored by NGOs (at the request of funders) to ensure smooth delivery. Under such conditions, NGOs may be viewed more properly as principals, and communities as their agents who accept the services that keep the NGO in business. For this hierarchy to be reversed, client options for voice would have to be considerably stronger, such that the authority over decision-making would rest with beneficiaries.

Stakeholder authority of this nature is unlikely to become common among NGOs primarily engaged in the delivery of services. After all, their survival depends on offering a set of specialized services or products. In such cases, stakeholders are able to "participate" through their involvement in project implementation, but they hold limited authority with respect to decision-making. This is what has already been described as the "sham ritual" of participation (Najam, 1996) or the "new tyranny" of participation (Cooke and Kothari, 2001). On the other hand, NGOs that establish services based on an assessment of community needs are less likely to run into this problem of incongruence, except under conditions where the NGO fails to adapt to changes in community needs and circumstances over time. Nonetheless, it is here that the logic of participation most visibly breaks down, due to the lack of real stakeholder power enabled by it.

In sum, accountability is highly contingent on relationships and on mechanisms put in place to ensure it. Accountability, like any set of relationships, involves a competition among principals. As Coralie Bryant observes in this book (pp. 172–3), "One of the implications for multiple and competing audience pulls is that different kinds of information and feedback are needed for different audiences. Therefore accountability is necessarily contingent upon both the demander and the context of the demand." In addition, this discussion has sought to demonstrate that the dominant direction of those competing pulls is determined by the presence and use of accountability mechanisms to enforce it.

The general lesson here is that any mechanism for improving accountability is myopic unless it is understood in terms of a broader system of relationships, and in terms of its long-term impacts. In response to crises of confidence in NGOs or other organizations, funders and regulators frequently call for more oversight and better reporting and disclosure. Such an approach, however, fails to recognize a broader system of relationships, and addresses only a slice of accountability challenges in that system. In particular, it does little to improve (and may even occur at the expense of) downward accountabilities to communities and stakeholders through meaningful forms of participation, and to enhance accountabilities to NGO missions and values through internal processes of critical reflection, analysis, and organizational learning.

Differentiating accountability among NGO types

The discussion has thus far failed to account for the diversity among nonprofit organizations, and thus how the myopias and participatory logics discussed above might vary with NGO type. Table 10.1 distinguishes

Table 10.1 *Accountability among NGO types*

NGO type	Orientation	Accountability to whom? (Principal)	Mechanisms of accountability	Key accountability characteristics
Membership organization	• self-help development	• member/self	• franchise, reform (voice) • dues (exit)	• member-centered
Service organization	• charitable development	• funders • sector regulators • clients	• future funding, reporting, evaluation and performance assessment • laws and disclosures • codes of conduct • stakeholder authority (voice) • refusal of services (exit)	• contingent • multiple • weak towards clients
Network organization	• issue-based policy change	• individual members • organizational members	• lobbying, litigation, protest, fact-finding, transparency • coordination	• collective and negotiated

between three types of nonprofit organizations: membership organizations, welfare or service-oriented organizations, and advocacy and network organizations. These categories are adapted from typologies offered by Uphoff (1996) and Vakil (1997), and are selected in order to demonstrate central differences in accountability characteristics. I do not distinguish among nonprofits in the North and South which, although situated in dissimilar political and developmental contexts, nonetheless operate in organizational environments with analytical commonalities.

The first column in Table 10.1 lists the three NGO types noted, while the second column describes the orientation of each type. Membership organizations are largely oriented towards serving the interests of their members, and can include organizations as diverse as agricultural cooperatives, savings groups, and interest-based associations such as academic research societies and associations of retired persons. These organizations are often run by and for their members, and might also be called self-interest or self-help groups. They operate on the basis of common interests and pooled resources, and are not always not-for-profit as in the case of agricultural cooperatives (Uphoff, 1996, p. 26).

Much of the discussion in this chapter centers on the second type of organization in Table 10.1 – the service organization. The orientation of such NGOs is charitable in the sense that there is no profit motive, and that the clients and beneficiaries are generally external to the organization. These organizations provide a wide range of services, ranging from health and education to housing and rural development. The clients of service organizations are usually not involved in creating the NGO in the way that members are; they are external actors to the organization and therefore have less voice in shaping its activities and direction.

The third type of NGO includes those that operate through networks which may be regional, national, or transnational in scale. Many such organizations are involved in issue-based policy advocacy work, such as the campaign to ban blood diamonds described by Smillie in this book. I distinguish between two kinds of networks based on the composition of their membership: those made up of organizations and those made up of individuals. The first type typically brings together a number of organizations to pool resources on a focused policy issue. Some of these networks are fairly well established and formalized such as the global anti-dam movement which has linked organizations in the North and South for many years (Khagram, 2000). Others, like the anti-war movement that has formed around the US-led war in Iraq, are more recent, less formalized, and akin to a fluid coalition in which many members are likely to be involved for only a short time. In many cases, such networks rely on new information technologies to communicate, and on the exercise of a collective voice in order to be effective. The second kind of network involves a single organization that joins *individuals* from dispersed locations around a common cause. This kind of network is exemplified by membership organizations such as Amnesty International and the Sierra Club which have highly dispersed memberships that care about a specific set of issues (such as human rights or the environment). Such NGOs are distinct from conventional membership organizations because they do not display the characteristics of direct self-help and accountability common to membership organizations like cooperatives.

For accountability purposes, each of these three types of NGOs can be differentiated in two respects: *to whom they are accountable* (that is, their principals) and the *mechanisms they employ* for ensuring accountability. For service organizations, these principal–agent links and mechanisms have already been depicted in Figure 10.1. The context for membership organizations, however, is not accurately illustrated in that figure. Membership organizations are accountable largely to their own members and, as such, do not distinguish between the organization and its clients. They are both their own principals and agents. The mechanisms of accountability available to members include franchise (voting for the organization's leaders), revoking membership and dues (and joining another cooperative, for example), and attempting to reform the organization either by influencing leaders or by running for a leadership position. As with service organizations, all of these options involve either exit or voice but they have more impact in membership organizations because the members/clients are internal to the organization. In this way, membership organizations combine internal accountability (to members of the organizations) with downward accountability (to clients, who are members). In short, the challenges of accountability myopia and participation can be expected to be much less acute in such organizations because of the structural equality between principals and agents, and the significantly greater potential of exit and voice options.

Service organizations offer much less powerful forms of voice and exit to their clients, except in highly competitive contexts where clients have multiple service-providers from which to choose. The clients or beneficiaries of an NGO, by virtue of being buffered from the organization, "cannot hold it accountable in the same direct way that members can. Clients and beneficiaries of NGOs are in a 'take it or leave it' relationship, quite similar to that of customers and employees of private firms" (Uphoff, 1996, p. 25).

Network organizations pose new challenges to the above perspectives on accountability. They display characteristics that are common to membership as well as service organizations, and also characteristics that are unique. For example, NGOs like the Sierra Club and Amnesty International both have individual members who pay dues and thus have the option of taking their dues elsewhere should the organization fail to satisfy their interests. But they are not self-help organizations in the way that cooperatives are, and most members do not have direct access to organizational decision-making or even to other members (nor do they necessarily desire such access), despite the fact that they elect board members. They are more like clients of service organizations. In other words, while their options for exit (e.g., franchise, and revoking membership dues) are potentially powerful, their actions are likely to be remote and isolated. Such organizations are not without their problems of accountability. For example, the first report of the Global Accountability Project (Kovach et al., 2003), based in the United Kingdom, notes that a number of international NGOs fare very poorly in providing public access to information about how they spend their money or how well they are achieving their aims.

On the other hand, these NGOs attract members by virtue of their policy advocacy work – thereby seeking to hold policy-makers and public officials accountable to the views of their members. From this perspective, the members are principals who, through the services of NGOs, seek to hold agents (elected officials and political actors) accountable for policy-making at regional, national, or even global levels. The mechanisms of accountability available to them are advocacy-oriented (voice), including lobbying, litigation, protest, negotiation, fact-finding, and demanding transparency in the reporting of information and events. These actions may be considered legitimate in a pluralistic society to the extent that they represent certain principles or the collective voice of a group of people. Networks in which the members are organizations, rather than individuals, involve an additional layer of accountability that depends on negotiation and coordination among member organizations. Accountability is collective in the sense that it depends on reliable coordination and pooling of resources among key players (for examples, see the cases discussed by Brown and Smillie, above, chs. 5 and 6, as well as Fox and Brown, 1998; Khagram et al., 2002).

In summary, the diversity among nonprofit organizations suggests that accountability relationships and mechanisms necessarily vary with NGO type. Mechanisms of accountability to clients, for example, are quite different in membership organizations (where clients or members are internal to the organization) than they are in service organizations (where clients are external). Accountability in membership organizations may be characterized as being largely member-centered, whereas it is multiple and contingent in service organizations. Advocacy networks represent still another type of NGO, with accountability being negotiated and collective in nature.

Reflective accountability: linking evaluation and learning

The purpose of the first half of this chapter was to problematize accountability in NGOs, both in terms of identifying common myopias of accountability, and with respect to framing it as a system of relations. Accountability mechanisms, as such, vary with relations among actors (between NGOs, communities, funders, and sector regulators) and with NGO type (membership, service, and network). However, despite these distinctions, all NGOs arguably face a common accountability challenge: creating mechanisms of accountability that are aligned with organizational missions and visions, and which promote critical reflection and learning. It is to this problem that I now turn.

Following Coralie Bryant's cue in the previous chapter, my focus here is primarily on the use of *evaluation* as a mechanism of accountability commonly employed by NGOs and their funders. Given that systems of accountability involve numerous mechanisms and actors, this focus on evaluation covers only a slice of these broader systems.[5] Evaluations, however, merit special scrutiny not only because they are widely used for explicit purposes of accountability, but also because they provide a critical link between accountability and organizational learning. As such, a look at evaluative practice offers a window through which to view reflective practice more generally.

Linking evaluation to learning

The link between evaluation and learning is both practical and normative: in order for evaluations to be of use to the organizations being evaluated, it is necessary to find systematic ways of feeding that information back into decision-making. Organizations can be seen as learning "by encoding inferences from history into routines that guide behavior" (Levitt and March, 1988, p. 320) or, in broader terms, by "improving actions through better knowledge and understanding" (Fiol and Lyles, 1985, p. 803). Learning, as such, involves generating knowledge by processing information or events and then using that knowledge to cause behavioral

---

[5] For a review of several additional mechanisms, see Behn (2001), Bovens (1998), Ebrahim (2003a), Kearns (1996), and Najam (1996).

change. Simply generating knowledge is not enough. Evaluations such as impact assessments can thus be said to contribute to learning only when they lead to behavioral change in an organization.

The notion that learning can be a deliberate and somewhat systematic process for changing organizational behavior is only now beginning to take hold among nonprofit and nongovernmental organizations, over a decade after its popularization in the business world by Peter Senge's (1990) *The Fifth Discipline*. Argyris and Schön (1996) have suggested that learning occurs at two basic levels in an organization – single-loop or double-loop. The former is "concerned primarily with effectiveness: how best to achieve existing goals and objectives, keeping organizational performance within the range specified by existing values and norms" while the latter involves "inquiry through which organizational values and norms themselves are modified" (Argyris and Schön, 1996, p. 22). Both single- and double-loop learning involve an iterative process in which information is processed in order to affect decisions.

It is important to note that relationships of power and accountability among organizations shape learning processes. Evaluations that reward success while punishing failure (e.g., through revocation of funds or additional conditions on funding) are unlikely to engender organizational learning since they encourage NGOs to exaggerate successes, while discouraging them from revealing and closely scrutinizing their mistakes. Smillie (1996, p. 190) has suggested that many donor countries, including the Netherlands, the United States, and Canada, generally use evaluation "more as a control and justification mechanism . . . than as a tool for learning or for disseminating findings."

In more recent years, the nonprofit community in the United States (and increasingly elsewhere) has begun to shift its attention from measuring outputs as indicators of progress towards measuring outcomes. The link between accountability, outcomes, and learning is plainly expressed on the website of the United Way of America, which has been one of the leaders in this move:

Although improved accountability has been a major force behind the move to outcome measurement, there is an even more important reason: *To help programs improve services*. Outcome measurement provides a learning loop that feeds information back into programs on how well they are doing. It offers findings they can use to adapt, improve, and become more effective. (United Way of America, 2002, emphasis in the original)

Evidence from practice, however, reveals a much more ambiguous relationship. The United Way's own survey of 391 agencies engaged in outcome measurement found that while an overwhelming proportion of organizations found the process useful for communicating results and identifying effective practices (84–88%), as well as for helping to improve service delivery of programs (76%), a significant number also reported that implementing outcome measurement has led to a focus on measurable outcomes at the expense of other important results (46%), has overloaded the organization's record-keeping capacity (55%), and that there remains uncertainty about how to make program changes based on identified strengths and weaknesses (42%) (United Way of America, 2000).

The muddle of outcome measurement, as one consultant puts it, is that while it appears to be "a good tool to help funders see what bang they're getting for their buck" it runs the risk of being counterproductive in the long run, both by drawing precious resources away from services and by putting too much emphasis on outcomes for which the causal links are unclear (Glasrud, 2001, p. 35). In addition, not only are most nonprofits ill-equipped for complex social science research (given that it is much more difficult to assign causality to outcomes than to outputs), but the emphasis on immediate results and gratification has not been ameliorated by the shift to outcomes. Outcome measurement, as such, appears to reflect more of an obsession with upward accountability to funders, than an interest in actually finding ways of improving services and results (Torjman, 1999, p. 5). In other words, while outcome measurement can assist organizations in identifying effective practices as well as question-able ones, it does not necessarily help in translating that information into systematic changes in organizational routines and behavior.

To be fair, outcome measurement does sometimes help NGO staff to think in terms of broader impacts rather than simply in terms of outputs, while also catalyzing staff energy towards important goals (Torjman, 1999; United Way of America, 2002). Nonetheless, case studies of thirty-six nonprofits conducted by the Independent Sector and the Urban Institute noted that only about half of these organizations undertook some form of data analysis to help improve programs (Morley et al., 2001). The report recommended increasing attention to analyzing results, including identifying reasons for outcomes so as to improve staff awareness about factors believed to have affected perfor-mance. Noting that the most common audiences for outcome reports were boards and funders, the report recommended distributing outcome data regularly to field-level staff and holding brainstorming sessions to identify possible program modifications. Similarly, The James Irvine Foundation's efforts to assist nonprofit agencies in California to improve systems for gathering and assessing data on performance outcomes concluded that "establishing these systems alone was not good enough.

In the end, the project's success had less to do with whether measurement systems were developed and more to do with whether the organizations were able to create a culture that valued the process of self-evaluation" (Hernández and Visher, 2001, p. 2).

In short, it is easy to overstate the potential benefits of evaluation, and particularly in the form of outcome measurement. Proponents contend that it can enable both single- and double-loop learning, noting that it "provides knowledge of the effect of programs in the external environment, providing superior information" as part of a system in which "Information is fed back into planning systems, and goals and strategies are changed accordingly to effect learning" (Buckmaster, 1999, pp. 192–3). The problem is that most NGOs have neither the resources nor the social science expertise to invest in complex information systems and analysis.

There are some inspirational exceptions which involve multiple constituency approaches to evaluation (D'Aunno, 1992). For example, a research group based at the City University of New York has been working since 1990 with dozens of community-based organizations to survey residents of inner-city neighborhoods in order to identify "practical truths" that support action. Their evaluations and surveys involve city residents at multiple stages of the process, and lead not only to assessments of outcomes or impacts, but to reassessment of the desirability of those very outcomes. Inspired by the writings of Gramsci and Freire, the evaluators note that "Instead of measuring community life against standards set externally, participatory research can allow communities to find their personal and shared realities and desires that can be both negotiated and contested. The outcome is not to uncover a stable reality, but to generate dynamic knowledge that can be used to discover, debate, and fulfill the wishes of the community" (Saegert et al., 2004, p. 55).

As Lisa Jordan has pointed out (above, ch. 8), an ambitious NGO effort in multi-stakeholder evaluation is currently being undertaken by ActionAid, a transnational organization that works on issues of injustice and inequality that underlie poverty. As part of a broad series of strategic changes to create a rights-based approach to accountability, ActionAid has eliminated its requirement for country offices to submit annual reports to its headquarters! Instead, it has instituted "annual participatory review and reflection processes" (PRRPs) which aim to improve programs by examining and sharing successes as well as failures through engagement with stakeholders at all levels – including poor people, partners, donors, and peers – to analyze and critique programs (ActionAid, 2000). Multi-stakeholder evaluations such as these are also beginning to receive more attention, sometimes described as "360-degree evaluation and accountability" (Behn, 2001, pp. 196–217), and often included to some extent in social auditing standards (e.g., AccountAbility, 1999). These manifestations of evaluation hold considerable promise for promoting both single- and double-loop learning, especially in organizations where stakeholders' views on performance vary considerably. For the time being, however, examples of persistent use of such evaluations remain rare.

The challenges of integrating various forms of evaluation (such as outcome measurement and participatory reflection) with learning are thus manyfold. First of all, linking evaluation to learning requires explicit attention to how information generated from evaluations can find its way into decision-making processes. In addition, it necessitates a look at how relationships of power influence (and might be modified to encourage) a scrutiny of failure, particularly among multiple constituencies. Finally, and more broadly, a learning approach to evaluation suggests a need for a perceptual shift from seeing evaluations as report cards of performance to a means of improvement.

In actually integrating evaluation with learning, however, NGO managers inevitably confront the power and attitudes of their funders. In cases where donors are focused on short-term goals and demonstrations of funds well spent, one might expect evaluations to be used largely for purposes of upward accountability. But in cases where NGOs and their donors are more attentive to long-term goals and the difficulties of social change, one might anticipate an orientation towards organizational learning as well as downward accountability.

Observers of the international development funding context, and particularly of bilateral funders, suggest that the former situation is the norm – where donors tend to emphasize short-term quantitative targets for purposes of control and justification rather than as part of a system directed towards complex learning and long-term change (Edwards and Hulme, 1996; Riddell, 1999; Smillie, 1996). This is one kind of accountability myopia discussed earlier in this chapter, characterized by a short-term vision of accountability as rule-following behavior rather than as a means to longer-term social change. A second kind of myopia involves a tendency to see accountability as a set of binary and unconnected relations rather than as a broader system of relations. As Bryant notes in her chapter on international emergency relief NGOs (above, p. 173), each set of actors expects different accountabilities: "donors often require formal evaluation reports, while other contributors expect some summary financial reports and annual mailings; beneficiaries, on the other hand, need results – though their own interpretation of favorable results can differ from the interpretations imposed by donors." The subtext of Bryant's observation concerns "power" although she does not describe it as such. Arguably, accountability mechanisms such as evaluations that focus on short-term and quantifiable results strengthen the hand of donors whose own reputations rely on measuring results and demonstrating success over annual budget cycles, while weakening the hands of communities where effective social change may result only over longer time frames.

In summary, if accountability is about relationships between organizational actors, then accountability mechanisms (such as evaluations) cannot properly be understood without some consideration of for whom and for what purpose they are employed. A central challenge for non-governmental organizations, as such, is to find a *balance* or a mix between mechanisms that respond to the upward accountability concerns of donors, and those that meet the needs of staff and communities (i.e., internal and downward accountability), while also leading to positive changes in organizational behavior. For many NGOs, finding this balance will require a reorientation towards learning processes and accountability to mission, in order to place upward-driven evaluation reporting in proper perspective. The key point is that accountability, like power, is a relational concept and the effects of its mechanisms can thus only be understood when placed in context. In cases where funders share a long-term perspective with NGOs, this balancing can be expected to occur with less difficulty. But in cases where donor priorities emphasize short-term results at the expense of long-term learning, this mismatch can lead to conflicting accountabilities.

Research propositions: balancing learning and accountability through evaluation

In order to understand better the links between evaluation, learning, and accountability, a number of factors for further investigation stand out. Improved organizational learning and responsiveness to mission do not have to occur at the expense of upward accountability to donors. The list of seven factors below suggests that evaluation is crucial to mediating the relationship between upward accountability and learning. These factors should be treated as propositional and thus subject to systematic empirical validation in further research.

Prioritization of accountabilities

While upward accountability to donors is clearly important, its domination of NGO information and reporting systems can occur at the expense of accountability to clients or to organizational mission. Reporting and information systems designed to track progress towards organizational goals and objectives can, in the long run, also satisfy donors and clients. The problem, of course, is that donors often operate on short time frames and are thus able to skew NGO priorities towards "demonstrating results" over annual budget cycles. In addition, accountability oriented towards organizational processes is more likely to facilitate critical self-evaluation than accountability focused on outputs and outcomes (Lerner and Tetlock, 1999). The contingent and relational nature of accountability necessarily requires a prioritization of accountabilities. In Lisa Jordan's words (above, p. 155), "addressing accountability can be a strategic choice rather than a punitive process divorced from the mission of an NGO."

> Proposition 1: Organizational learning is more likely if internal accountability to mission, rather than upward accountability to donors, guides information and reporting systems.

This proposition is foundational to the others that follow because it requires NGOs to reappropriate accountability for themselves, so that it might enable and drive social change rather than impede it.

Perceptions about learning

Perceptions of organizational members influence the degree to which learning is taken seriously in an organization and also affect who is involved in learning. Tools and processes that can contribute both to learning and to accountability, such as evaluation and outcome measurement, are often viewed by NGO staff as tasks set aside for special monitoring units or for outside "experts." They are seen as being separate from the "real work" of the organization (Edwards, 2002, pp. 334, 339; Riddell, 1999). This perception is particularly true of processes that concern the development of organizational strategy and long-range planning. Lower-level staff (e.g., field staff) are excluded from such discussions, either because managers do not see them as having relevant expertise, or because they are themselves hesitant to overstep their role boundaries. This is despite the fact that field-level staff frequently possess the most experience with respect to implementation of the "real work" of the organization. Unless learning is a deliberate and conscious part of organizational strategy, it is unlikely to become habitual at all organizational levels (Denton, 1998).

> Proposition 2: Organizational learning is more likely if staff perceive evaluation as central to their own work, rather than as a task only for managers and outside experts.

Perceptions about failure

How staff think about failure is an important determinant of how NGOs deal with problems or with discordant information. Relationships between NGOs and funders are particularly important in this regard, in that relationships based primarily on funding encourage a hiding of failure (Edwards, 2002, p. 336). Bryant (above, ch. 9, pp. 169–70) expresses concern about increasing calls from donors for accountability that is centered on pushing for quick fixes, noting that "Domestic poverty work often is abandoned when narrowly measured results are demanded – and not found." In addition, while NGOs do seem to admit minor failures or those in the distant past, there is limited evidence that they actually welcome learning from failure (Smillie and Hailey, 2001, p. 76). Negative perceptions of failure can lead organizations to become defensive or secretive in the face of potential criticism. Arguably, openness to criticism or bad news at the highest levels of an organization, while difficult, is essential (Garvin, 1993, p. 87). Learning from failure may thus be possible where the threat of sanction is minimized. Otherwise, an embracing of error can carry high organizational and personal costs. Moreover, learning from failure is necessary for avoiding the same problems in the future. In other words, learning requires that error be embraced as an opportunity rather than as a mistake to be hidden (Chambers, 1994; Edwards, 2002, p. 334).

Proposition 3: Organizational learning is more likely if error is embraced as opportunity and the threat of sanction is minimized.

Organizational visions of the future

A view towards the future, particularly in terms of environmental stability, also affects attitudes and approaches to learning. Developing a vision, and especially one that is shared at different levels in an organization, is one of the key "disciplines" of a learning organization (Denton, 1998, p. 93; Senge, 1990, p. 209; Smillie and Hailey, 2001, p. 89). Organizations that inhabit stable environments tend to concentrate on refining their existing activities without anticipating possible changes in their environment (Levinthal and March, 1993; March, 1991; March and Olsen, 1988). In an international development context, the environment is rarely stable, as it is subject to various changes including those involving funding, the physical environment, public policies and regulations, and a rapid transformation in industrial and agricultural economies. Development organizations which only monitor very selective aspects of their work and environment (such as meeting financial targets) risk deceiving themselves into thinking that their environment is stable. On the other hand, organizations that attempt to anticipate future uncertainties (e.g., by conducting strategic reviews or scenario planning which involve various levels of staff in strategic discussion, and which may require alliances with other organizations such as research institutions, funders, and even competitors) may be better positioned to recognize and respond to environmental change. The experience of ActionAid is particularly instructive in this regard, as an organization that rethought its vision through a critical review of its role in the broader policy environment (Jordan, above, ch. 8).

> Proposition 4: Organizational learning is more likely if organizational capacities are built to anticipate and respond to environmental instability.

Reporting and communication structures

Control-oriented structures enable routine error-correction and quality control (i.e., single-loop learning), but tend to discourage fundamental forms of change and innovation (i.e., double-loop learning). Highly departmentalized organizations with tight role boundaries can support learning within a department, but inhibit the spread of ideas across departmental boundaries as well as across the organization as a whole. On the other hand, structures that maintain strong feedback loops between field staff and managers as well as across departmental units, as part of standard operating procedures and teamwork groupings, build in opportunities for examining impacts of field-level and cross-departmental change.

Poor vertical communication and coordination, note Beer and Eisenstat (2000), are part of a series of "silent killers" of strategy implementation and organizational learning. They note the importance of communication structures, both formal and informal, not only for learning upwards from staff to management but also for effective downwards implementation of strategy. Denton (1998, pp. 92, 196) adds that a flexible structure which enables cross-functional teamwork can help generate and spread new knowledge and learning in an organization. This presents advantages for small organizations that have the benefit of less hierarchy and greater flexibility, although they may lack in training and experience. Contrary to popular conception, good communication does not necessarily require that organizations be entirely horizontal or non-hierarchical in structure, since hierarchies can sometimes serve as efficient clearinghouses for knowledge, especially under conditions where that knowledge is new and of uncertain relevance

(Schultz, 2001). A potentially powerful barrier to learning across hierarchies, however, can arise from the anxiety of managers who fear a loss of status or power by decentralizing knowledge and its dissemination and use (Smillie and Hailey, 2001, p. 87).

> Proposition 5: Organizational learning is more likely if internal reporting structures maintain strong feedback loops between field staff, managers, and directors.

Job roles and incentives

Reporting and communication are related to job roles and incentives provided to individuals to engage in learning. Learning can, for example, be built into job descriptions and performance appraisals, so that staff are rewarded for critically reflecting upon their own work and for coming up with new ideas, rather than being penalized for "taking time out" to think. Stepping back from one's work, observing it and analyzing it, are difficult skills to acquire and can be supplemented through staff workshops and training on basic learning and information skills (Garvin, 1993). Where such incentives are not in place, staff may see learning as being someone else's responsibility, particularly if they are rewarded for implementation and for demonstrating success (rather than assessing and reflecting on failure). Providing learning incentives is particularly important at the level of field staff since, in development NGOs, this is often a very experienced and stable population in the organization (i.e., it has low personnel turnover) and is thus an important component of the memory of the organization.

In a summary paper on learning experiences in NGOs, Edwards (2002, p. 339) has argued that "experiential learning among fieldworkers is the foundation for other learning linked to good practice, policy and advocacy work. If learning is not taking place at grassroots level, then other layers in the learning system will be defective." Ironically, international donors show little desire to pay for the overhead costs necessary for supporting field-level learning (e.g., staff, training, and equipment) even though they demand professionalism in accountability. In some cases, however, NGOs are taking on evaluations for purposes of learning even without donor support. Coralie Bryant's chapter (above) suggests that those organizations least dependent on donor funding are actually the most active in evaluation. This counterintuitive finding may partly be explained by the observation that donor evaluations often involve outside teams hired largely for the purpose of performance assessment, whereas internally motivated evaluations are more likely to be engaged for learning purposes. But she also observes that creating an evaluation and learning culture among staff of an NGO requires "an iterative process of engaging staff from top to bottom in identifying and illuminating what is and is not working" (p. 189). In other words, an analysis of lessons learned and reflection on impacts requires hiring people for these tasks or allocating time and resources to existing staff. Otherwise, the opportunity costs of engaging in evaluation and learning can be high, particularly where budgetary allocations for such activities are low.

Proposition 6: Organizational learning is more likely if job descriptions and performance appraisals reward staff for analysis and innovation, supported by resources of time and training.

Information systems

The relevance of information which is gathered by an organization is also important to learning and accountability. There is typically a gap between the originators of information and the users of that information. For example, NGOs sometimes collect information because funders require it, but do not actually use that information because they do not see it as being relevant to their own needs. It is difficult to get staff to use this new knowledge unless, as Edwards (1994, p. 123) puts it, they see "that by using it they will be able to improve the quality of their work and increase the benefits enjoyed by the subjects of the work in question." Organizations can increase the relevance of information (or at least its perceived relevance) by involving the originators of information in its analysis. This step involves a shift from perceiving field-level workers simply as implementers to also seeing them as foundational problem-solvers.

The issue of relevance is closely related to systems for accessing, storing, transferring, and disseminating information and knowledge throughout the organization. Overly complex information systems can form just as large a barrier to learning and accountability as poorly developed ones. NGOs and donors tend to overemphasize formally documented knowledge, information storage, and dissemination (Edwards, 2002, p. 336). But since development NGOs and nonprofits are primarily focused on implementation rather than research and analysis, simple and flexible systems that are seen as being relevant to NGO needs are more feasible than elaborate or highly technical systems that can overwhelm NGO staff. While some proponents of outcome measurement and evaluation have advocated for improving the capacity of nonprofits to conduct rigorous and sophisticated assessments (Buckmaster, 1999; Hoefer, 2000), few nonprofits have the resources to be able to do so. In addition, many NGOs have a surfeit of information that is counterproductive in promoting learning (Smillie and Hailey, 2001, p. 85).

A more practical approach may be to develop simpler systems that are congruent with existing resources and which can be built up if resources increase. NGO members, especially at the field level, have neither the time nor the inclination to write analytical reports or to develop computerized databases. If they are to be encouraged to use information in order to reflect on their own work, it must be made available in forms that are accessible and culturally meaningful (e.g., workshops, newsletters, meetings, discussion, video, theatre, etc.). In their study of nine highly regarded South Asian NGOs, Smillie and Hailey (2001, pp. 78–9) found that a combination of formal and informal processes of learning and dissemination were apparent. They also noted that Northern NGOs have much to learn from the experiences of successful Southern NGOs – since the latter have actually invested more in research, staff training, and learning than have their Northern counterparts. In addition, as the experience of large NGOs such as Save the Children has borne out, forging alliances with universities and research organizations may be more productive and useful than creating extensive in-house research units (Edwards, 2002, p. 343).

> Proposition 7: Organizational learning is more likely if information systems are simple and flexible, rather than elaborate or rigorous, and where the distance between information originators and users is minimized.

The seven propositions outlined above suggest that balancing accountability and learning requires not only changes in formal structure and information systems, but also shifts in basic perceptions about learning and failure, as well as a commitment to forging inter- and intra-organizational relationships that foster inquiry, experimentation, and critical reflection. The broader value of such integration lies not simply in improving existing practices, but in building the capacities of nonprofits to achieve their missions. Conscious learning processes can help NGOs critically to assess and guide their strategies of social development, so as to increase their leverage in influencing public policies and practices. It is in affecting these larger forces of social change that learning can be most powerful (Fowler, 2002).

Conclusions: implications for NGO–funder accountabilities

The focus of the above propositions is largely on internal change in nongovernmental organizations rather than on their larger external environments. But if accountability is to be viewed as being embedded in relations of power, then what use is internal organizational change for altering this relational and political context? The subtext of these seven propositions is that internal change in NGOs is a vehicle towards altering their interactions with external stakeholders. Each proposition suggests a shift away from relations of patronage between NGOs and funders, towards a more negotiated set of interactions that includes not only funders but also other stakeholders such as communities. This is most obvious in the case of prioritization of accountabilities (proposition 1), where internal accountability to mission would necessarily require NGOs to renegotiate reporting to funders – so that it enables progress towards mission and responsiveness to clients or communities, rather than simply satisfying donor data needs. Relatedly, if information and reporting systems in NGOs are to be simpler, more flexible, and coherent (propositions 5 and 7), this will require that donors ease off on onerous and rigid upward reporting that draws scarce resources away from internal organizational learning. This is not to say that donors should not receive regular reports – indeed they have a right to know that funds are being well spent – but they will need to reconsider the balance between reporting systems designed for short-term accountability and those that can enable longer-term change through organizational learning.

The propositions also imply shifts in the nature of capacity building supported by donors. First, funders may need to enhance their own capacities (rather than just those of NGOs) for better understanding what kinds of information systems and communication structures better enable learning (propositions 5 and 7). To their credit, many donors already encourage nonprofits to engage in periodic strategic reviews, particularly if they work in unstable environments (proposition 4). However, funders less frequently support overhead costs required for creating a culture of learning, that is, for the training, rewards, and time needed by NGO staff (or even their own staff) to analyze lessons learned and to reflect on the impacts of past work (proposition 6).

Perhaps the greatest challenges, for nonprofits and funders alike, are perceptual. If NGO staff are to perceive evaluation as central to their own work, rather than as a task only for managers or outside experts (proposition 2), it will also be necessary for funders to support evaluations that engage staff at all organizational levels. This would require a move away from the predominant approach to external evaluation used by funders (although this would still be necessary on occasion, especially for strategic reviews), towards one that builds an internal culture of assessment and reflection. Moreover, if NGOs are to begin to perceive "failures" as opportunities for learning, this will only be possible if funders minimize sanctions for reporting those failures (proposition 3). Indeed, such a change might require funders to take some responsibility for failures by their NGO partners, particularly if the errors arose from inadequate capacity building provided by the funders. In more courageous funders, such a perceptual shift would logically extend to involving NGOs in evaluating the funders themselves.

In sum, current myopias of accountability have arisen from the privileging of upward relationships of NGOs with funders and regulators, and have become a structural feature of the international development landscape. Arguably, there is a need for greater attention to mechanisms of accountability that are aligned with organizational missions and visions, and which promote, rather than constrain, critical reflection and learning. A related normative challenge concerns a reassessment of participatory logics as contributing to downward accountability. In practice, it appears that participation is frequently structured to reproduce inequalities while limiting the actual decision-making influence of participants. A reframing of accountability as a system of relations requires a look at participatory mechanisms that are empowering rather than ritualistic and symbolic. Each of the seven propositions offered above implies a shift in the very nature of NGO–funder dynamics, and might equally be applied to community–NGO relations. Even if all of the propositions tested true, this would not necessarily diminish upward accountability to funders – because the very notion of accountability would be reframed in terms of valuing and measuring long-term learning and change, and multiple accountabilities to mission, clients, and donors.

Finally, in making a case for long-term learning as a corrective lens for accountability myopia, one runs the risk of romanticizing learning in the place of accountability. After all, how can learning be anything but good? Indeed, this is the very problem that practitioners and scholars alike face, with learning coming to mean all things to all people. A cautionary note is warranted. Levinthal and March (1993, p. 110) in their inspirational paper on "The Myopia of Learning," candidly note that learning processes are imperfect and don't easily lead to improvements in organizational behavior:

The imperfections of learning are not bases for abandoning attempts to improve the learning capabilities of organizations, but they suggest a certain conservatism in expectations. Conservative expectations, of course, will not always enhance the selling of learning procedures to strategic managers, but they may provide a constructive basis for a realistic evaluation and elaboration of the role of learning in organizational intelligence. Magic would be nice, but it is not easy to find.

In a world of complex and systemic problems of poverty and social inequity, it is tempting and perhaps natural to look for "quick fixes." But a key message for organizations involved in complex processes of social change is that neither accountability nor learning are panaceas.

References

AccountAbility (1999) *Accountability 1000 (AA 1000) Framework: Standard, Guidelines and Professional Qualification*. London: Institute of Social and Ethical Accountability.

ActionAid (2000) *ALPS: Accountability, Learning and Planning System*. London: ActionAid.

Argyris, C. and D. A. Schön (1996) *Organizational Learning II: Theory, Method, and Practice*. Reading, MA: Addison-Wesley Publishing.

Beer, M. and R. A. Eisenstat (2000) "The Silent Killers of Strategy Implementation and Learning," *Sloan Management Review* 41(4), 29–40.

Behn, R. D. (2001) *Rethinking Democratic Accountability*. Washington, DC: Brookings Institution Press.

Bovens, M. (1998) *The Quest for Responsibility: Accountability and Citizenship in Complex Organisations*. Cambridge University Press.

Buckmaster, N. (1999) "Associations Between Outcome Measurement, Accountability and Learning for Non-Profit Organisations," *The International Journal of Public Sector Management* 12(2), 186–97.

Chambers, R. (1994) "All Power Deceives," *IDS Bulletin* 25(2), 14–26.

Cooke, B. and U. Kothari (eds.) (2001) *Participation: The New Tyranny?* London and New York: Zed Books.

D'Aunno, T. (1992) "The Effectiveness of Human Service Organizations: A Comparison of Models," in Y. Hasenfeld (ed.) *Human Services as Complex Organizations*. Newbury Park: Sage, pp. 341–61.

Denton, J. (1998) *Organizational Learning and Effectiveness*. London and New York: Routledge.

Ebrahim, A. (2005) "Accountability Myopia: Losing Sight of Organizational Learning," *Nonprofit and Voluntary Sector Quarterly* 34(1), 56–87.

Ebrahim, A. (2003a) "Accountability in Practice: Mechanisms for NGOs," *World Development* 31(5), 813–29.

Ebrahim, A. (2003b) "Making Sense of Accountability: Conceptual Perspectives for Northern and Southern Nonprofits," *Nonprofit Management and Leadership* 14(2), 191–212.

Ebrahim, A. (2002) "Information Struggles: The Role of Information in the Reproduction of NGO-Funder Relations," *Nonprofit and Voluntary Sector Quarterly* 31(1), 85–113.

Edwards, M. (2002) "Organizational Learning in Non-Governmental Organizations: What Have We Learned?" in M. Edwards and A. Fowler (eds.) *The Earthscan Reader on NGO Management*. London and Sterling, VA: Earthscan, pp. 331–46.

Edwards, M. (1994) "NGOs in the Age of Information," *IDS Bulletin* 25(2), 117–24.

Edwards, M. and D. Hulme (1996) "Too Close for Comfort? The Impact of Official Aid on Nongovernmental Organizations," *World Development* 24(6), 961–73.

Fiol, C. M. and M. A. Lyles (1985) "Organizational Learning," *Academy of Management Review* 10(4), 803–13.

Fowler, A. (2002) "An NGDO Strategy: Learning for Leverage," in M. Edwards and A. Fowler (eds.) *The Earthscan Reader on NGO Management.* London and Sterling, VA: Earthscan, pp. 353–60.

Fox, J. A. and L. D. Brown (eds.) (1998) *The Struggle for Accountability: The World Bank, NGOs, and Grassroots Movements.* Cambridge, MA: MIT Press.

Garvin, D. A. (1993) "Building a Learning Organization," *Harvard Business Review* 71(4 (July–August)), 78–91.

Glasrud, B. (2001) "The Muddle of Outcome Measurement: Be Careful How You Measure Programs," *Nonprofit World* 19(6), 35–7.

Hernández, G. and M. G. Visher (2001) *Creating a Culture of Inquiry: Changing Methods – and Minds – on the Use of Evaluation in Nonprofit Organizations.* San Francisco: The James Irvine Foundation.

Hirschman, A. O. (1970) *Exit, Voice, and Loyalty: Responses to Decline in Firms, Organizations, and States.* Cambridge, MA: Harvard University Press.

Hoefer, R. (2000) "Accountability in Action? Program Evaluation in Nonprofit Human Service Agencies," *Nonprofit Management and Leadership* 11(2), 167–77.

Hudock, A. (1999) *NGOs and Civil Society: Democracy by Proxy?* Cambridge, MA: Blackwell.

Kearns, K. P. (1996) *Managing for Accountability: Preserving the Public Trust in Nonprofit Organizations.* San Francisco: Jossey-Bass.

Khagram, S. (2000) "Toward Democratic Governance for Sustainable Development: Transnational Civil Society Organizing Around Big Dams," in A. M. Florini (ed.) *The Third Force: The Rise of Transnational Civil Society.* Tokyo and Washington, DC: Japan Center for International Exchange and Carnegie Endowment for International Peace, pp. 83–114.

Khagram, S., J. V. Riker and K. Sikkink (eds.) (2002) *Restructuring World Politics: Transnational Social Movements, Networks, and Norms.* Minneapolis: University of Minnesota Press.

Kovach, H., C. Neligan and S. Burall (2003) *The Global Accountability Report 1: Power without Accountability?* London: Global Accountability Project, The One World Trust.

Lerner, J. S. and P. E. Tetlock (1999) "Accounting for the Effects of Accountability," *Psychological Bulletin* 125(2), 255–75.

Levinthal, D. A. and J. G. March (1993) "The Myopia of Learning," *Strategic Management Journal* 14, 95–112.

Levitt, B. and J. G. March (1988) "Organizational Learning," *Annual Review of Sociology* 14, 319–40.

March, J. G. (1991) "Exploration and Exploitation in Organizational Learning," *Organization Science* 2(1), 71–87.

March, J.G. and J.P. Olsen (1988) "The Uncertainty of the Past: Organizational Learning under Ambiguity," in J.G. March (ed.) *Decisions and Organizations*. Cambridge, MA: Basil Blackwell, pp. 335–58.

Morley, E., E. Vinson and H.P. Hatry (2001) *Outcome Measurement in Nonprofit Organizations: Current Practices and Recommendations*. Washington, DC: Independent Sector.

Najam, A. (1996) "NGO Accountability: A Conceptual Framework," *Development Policy Review* 14, 339–53.

O'Neill, O. (2002) *A Question of Trust: The BBC Reith Lectures 2002*. Cambridge University Press.

Pfeffer, J. (1987) "A Resource Dependence Perspective on Intercorporate Relations," in M.S. Mizruchi and Michael Schwartz (eds.) *Intercorporate Relations: The Structural Analysis of Business*. Cambridge University Press, pp. 25–55.

Pfeffer, J. and G.R. Salancik (1978) *The External Control of Organizations: A Resource Dependence Perspective*. New York: Harper and Row.

Riddell, R.C. (1999) "Evaluating NGO Development Interventions," in D. Lewis (ed.) *International Perspectives on Voluntary Action: Reshaping the Third Sector*. London: Earthscan, pp. 222–41.

Roche, C. (1999) *Impact Assessment for Development Agencies: Learning to Value Change*. Oxford: Oxfam GB.

Saegert, S., L. Benitez, E. Eizenberg, T. Hsieh and M. Lamb (2004) "Participatory Evaluation: How It Can Enhance Effectiveness and Credibility of Nonprofit Work," *The Nonprofit Quarterly* 11(1), 54–60.

Schultz, M. (2001) "The Uncertain Relevance of Newness: Organizational Learning and Knowledge Flows," *Academy of Management Journal* 44(4), 661–81.

Schweitz, M.L. (2001) "NGO Network Codes of Conduct: Accountability, Principles, and Voice," Paper presented at the International Studies Association Annual Convention, Chicago, II, February.

Sen, S. (1999) "Some Aspects of State–NGO Relationships in India in the Post-Independence Era," *Development and Change* 30, 327–55.

Senge, P.M. (1990) *The Fifth Discipline: The Art and Practice of the Learning Organization*. New York: Currency Doubleday.

Smillie, I. (1996) "Painting Canadian Roses Red," in M. Edwards and D. Hulme (eds.) *Beyond the Magic Bullet: NGO Performance and Accountability in the Post-Cold War World*. West Hartford, CT: Kumarian, pp. 187–97.

Smillie, I. and J. Hailey (2001) *Managing for Change: Leadership, Strategy and Management in Asian NGOs*. London: Earthscan.

Torjman, S. (1999) *Are Outcomes the Best Outcome?* Ottawa: Caledon Institute of Social Policy.

United Way of America (2002) "Outcome Measurement Resource Network," website at http://national.unitedway.org/outcomes/resources/mpo/why.cfm. 21 October 2002.

United Way of America (2000) *Agency Experiences with Outcome Measurement: Survey Findings (Report 0196)*. Alexandria, VA: United Way of America.

224   *Alnoor Ebrahim*

Uphoff, N. (1996) "Why NGOs are Not a Third Sector: A Sectoral Analysis with Some Thoughts on Accountability, Sustainability, and Evaluation," in M. Edwards and D. Hulme (eds.) *Beyond the Magic Bullet: NGO Performance and Accountability in the Post-Cold War*. West Hartford, CT: Kumarian, pp. 23–39.

Vakil, A. C. (1997) "Confronting the Classification Problem: Toward a Taxonomy of NGOs," *World Development* 25(12), 2057–70.

World Bank (2000) *Participation Process Review*. Washington, DC: Operations Evaluation Department (OED), The World Bank.

Global accountability frameworks and corporate social responsibility

The contributions in this final section shift our attention to accountability in the corporate world. One of the primary responses of the private sector to growing calls for accountability has been "corporate social responsibility" (CSR), operationalized largely through certification systems, codes of conduct, and the production of social and environmental reports. The three chapters in Part IV all examine corporate accountability efforts at network and structural levels; that is, rather than focusing on individual cases, they set their sights on analyzing regimes such as CSR, and the networks involved in creating and implementing them.

Michael MacLeod employs a social constructivist lens to chart the "rise and nature" of CSR as "an alternative, non-state source of authority in international affairs" and especially its subset of socially responsible investing (SRI) instruments. He finds that there is as yet very little evidence that links CSR to changes in corporate behavior or to improved financial performance, and argues instead that the strategic advantages of adopting CSR practices lie in a "logic of appropriateness" where companies wish to be seen as doing the right thing by global consumers, NGOs, and regulators.

Kate Macdonald concurs, and adds empirical skepticism. She finds that, in the transnational garment industry, codes of conduct selectively address concerns of consumers in the global North, while often failing to address the real interests of Southern workers. CSR efforts represent only a partial institutionalization of an accountability based on "complex reciprocity." She thus develops a "plurilateral" accountability framework that more accurately describes the interdependence among players, premised on reconfigurations of power among states, NGOs, workers, and consumers. In so doing, she brings us back to the notion of "public" accountability raised in Part I, which she argues is no longer about states or binary principal–agent interactions, but about core principles of empowerment in systems of global production and governance.

Weisband, too, returns us to public accountability and multilateralism in his critique of CSR. His survey of seven CSR frameworks finds that many foster internal reflection and learning in corporate actors, but most fall short of enabling global accountability because "of the absence of external benchmarks and their recursive influence on internal dynamics of learning." This conclusion for the corporate sector is similar to Ebrahim's for the NGO sector – that accountability relies on a linking and balancing of internal learning with benchmarks. But while Weisband observes that corporate accountability lacks sufficient external benchmarks, Ebrahim finds that NGO accountability falls short on internal learning. This is where multilateralism matters, contends Weisband, for in the interactions between governments, corporations, and civil society organizations, it is possible to craft tough benchmarks and monitoring systems as well as support for internal learning. Such "tripartite multilateralism" is embodied in the International Labour Organization's accountability structures for international labor standards. It is an example of the logic of participation in structured form, and is thus simultaneously local and global.

This brings us to the concluding chapter of the volume, in which Edward Weisband revisits and elaborates a postmodern conception of accountability, suggesting a need to embed the discussion of accountability in larger frames that include both network analysis and discourses over the future character of public ethics. While accountability concerns might initially be grounded in suspicion and mistrust, it is perhaps more crucial to recognize that, in an increasingly interdependent world, accountability must constantly be renegotiated among global and local actors. In this landscape, networks and networking become the vehicles for forging a more participatory and pluralistic praxis of accountability, for citizen activism, and for nurturing trust.

11 Financial actors and instruments in the construction of global corporate social responsibility

Michael R. MacLeod

Introduction

A great deal of attention has been paid in recent years to the increasing role and power of multinational corporations (MNCs) and the apparent lack of accountability they have to the international community at large. There has been a tremendous growth in the numbers of these large companies and an acknowledgment of their critical importance to the global economy (Koenig-Archibugi, 2004). In terms of influence, one familiar argument is that such firms are criticized for the power they have over economic policies: states compete with each other to attract foreign investment capital, the so-called "race to the bottom" thesis in which legal and regulatory standards are purportedly compromised in this competition.[1] A related and increasingly common line of criticism is that the advent of global capitalism has not been matched by the development of governance mechanisms that can adequately oversee if not restrain the excesses of its primary agents, i.e. transnationally active firms. Indeed, holding such corporations accountable for actions (or inactions) that harm (or are perceived to harm) society has become a focal action point.[2]

Many people thus believe that the central nexus in the debate over the future of capitalism itself surrounds the extent to which corporate interests can and should be made more accountable, if not subservient, to broader societal interests. The extreme views on this issue are clear: those who call for more extensive national and international regulation of corporate behavior versus those who argue that business should have nothing or very little to do with social systems and stick to maximizing

---

[1] See Spar and Yoffie (1999) for an excellent overview of the "race to the bottom" debate.
[2] See Barnet and Cavanagh (1994) for a typical analysis of this renewed attention in the 1990s.

profit only. Since the early 1990s, however, the discourse has been joined by more moderate views emphasizing, first, the need for a "sustainable" capitalism in light of some of the more painful externalities of globalization and, second, that business–society relations are indeed changing, and multinational corporations in particular, given their critical importance, need to become more responsive and accountable to the environments in which they operate. George Soros, one of the world's wealthiest individuals who benefited directly from liberal investment regimes associated with economic globalization, has now become a staunch critic of its direction and effects, arguing that "the main failing of global capitalism is that it is too one-sided; it puts too much emphasis on the pursuit of profit and economic success and neglects social and political considerations" (Soros, 2000, p. 179).

The future of global capitalism has become intertwined with what has become known as corporate social responsibility (CSR), the extralegal obligations and commitments that businesses have to the society(ies) in which they operate involving consideration of factors beyond profit maximization, i.e. the environment, human rights, and labor issues. Although CSR is not a new concept, there is a developing consensus that in its modern manifestation it has developed into a "movement" which may be reconstituting business–society relations on a global scale. One analyst argues that "there is no denying the existence of such a movement, given the increasing public, political and business attention it receives on a daily basis" in Europe, the Americas, and Australia (Jonker, 2003, p. 425).[3] Indeed, even those most opposed to CSR within the business community itself are critical that there has been a significant change in philosophy of how business should be done, as evidenced by the work of, and apparent widespread support by, leading firms on CSR in such forums as the World Economic Forum (WEF) in Davos and the World Business Council for Sustainable Development.[4] Comments by business leaders that in order for capitalism to survive corporations "must consider social and environmental issues, even if it means rejecting profitable business opportunities" are becoming quite common.[5] Some go so far as to argue that there is a degree of "institutionalization" of CSR taking place within and among firms that will have long-lasting effects on the international community (Moon, 2002).

---

[3] See Ougaard (2002) for a more nuanced assessment.

[4] Henderson (2001) calls CSR a "misguided virtue."

[5] The quotation is by a spokesperson for the Group Board, Deutsche Bank, at the debate "From Business Leaders to Global Leaders," World Economic Forum Annual Meeting, 3 February 2002. Available at www.weforum.org.

The emergence of modern corporate social responsibility poses a number of theoretical and empirical questions for scholars of international relations. Among those most interesting are: what is the nature of the relationship between this contemporary CSR movement, global capitalism, and global governance – the latter being "the processes through which rules (broadly conceived) are constructed/maintained/evolve in political spaces that lack central authority"? (Hoffmann, 2002, p. 2). To what extent does the definition or understanding of corporate social responsibility vary across countries, i.e. to what extent is a "global" CSR movement affected by domestic politics and the varieties of business–society relations? Or is there evidence of a global convergence of expectations for the behavior of multinational corporations and what are the drivers for this? And what is the relationship between corporate responsibility and the increasing global demand for corporate accountability, i.e. are these the same thing? The analysis here attempts to answer some of these questions by offering a theoretical perspective on CSR and providing empirical evidence of its relevance as an emerging mechanism of accountability in world politics.

In this chapter, I first proceed to analyze corporate social responsibility by setting the theoretical context, arguing that CSR is best viewed through the lens of social constructivism, which is an increasingly utilized approach in international relations theorizing particularly well suited for assessing social processes and the agents behind them. I then present an assessment of the extensiveness of the contemporary CSR movement, how and why it has evolved, and its representation in various national and international settings, all of which reveal the degree to which greater social responsibility by multinational corporations appears to be central to emerging societal governance. The third and final element of the chapter is a review of one set of factors that has been relatively under-explored in international relations scholarship and deserves more attention: the relationship between financially related actors and instruments and the behavior of multinational corporations. Specifically, I examine the recent evolution of CSR-related initiatives in the financial services sector, the impact of socially responsible investing (SRI), and the degree to which governments (nationally and internationally) are leveraging corporate social behavior via financial and related incentives or legislation. Identifying and evaluating the extent to which financial institutions (private banks, institutional investors, public agencies, development banks, and so forth) have influenced and/or are driving the development of CSR is an overriding goal here. In focusing on these financial actors and instruments, I argue that we gain the advantage of "unpacking" some of the dynamics behind how corporate social responsibility is becoming constructed and institutionalized trans-nationally. The chapter concludes by offering some comments on the CSR movement and its relationship to global corporate accountability.

Conceptualizing corporate social responsibility

In international relations theorizing, constructivism emphasizes the socially constructed nature of world politics and arguably has gone further than other approaches exploring the impact of, and authority wielded by, non-state actors and emerging governance structures. The focus, however, is not on actors per se but on their interactions. In any continuous interaction within a given issue-area, constructivism posits that relevant actors – states, NGOs, corporations, or combinations thereof – interact to produce a convergence of expectations and a set of common understandings (intersubjectively held) that give rise to a set of legitimate norms, rules, values, and procedures associated with this issue. This approach emphasizes the importance of authority and legitimacy instead of power and capabilities, and compliance with decisions tends to be voluntary rather than enforced through coercion (Wolfish and Smith, 2000). Thus, constructivism is conducive to explaining the rise and nature of alternative, non-state sources of authority in international affairs; in particular, scholars have recently examined several areas in which the private sector, including corporations, took the lead in estab-lishing norms, rules, and institutions that guide the behavior of actors and affect the opportunities open to them (e.g., Cutler et al., 1999; Hall and Biersteker, 2002).

Explaining and understanding global corporate social responsibility from a constructivist approach involves a focus on the development of "norms," a norm being a set of intersubjectively held expectations of proper behavior by an actor (Finnemore and Sikkink, 1999). According to the insights from social constructivism, actors in world politics are said to base their behavior on a "logic of appropriateness" – rule-guided behavior in which actors try to determine what rule of course of action is appropriate (doing the "right thing") given their identity, rather than maximizing or optimizing their given preferences through strategic beha-vior, a "logic of consequences" (March and Olsen, 1989). Multinational corporations are no different in this from other actors: they are deeply embedded in and affected by the social institutions in which they act, attempting to discern, follow, and recreate social norms and rules. The argument by some is that the modern CSR movement has become so prolific and embedded within different social structures and the actors themselves that corporate social responsibility should be understood as an emerging socially constructed norm in world politics, i.e. that we are witnessing a convergence of expectations around what constitutes proper behavior for corporations in society, whether domestically or globally.[6] It is speculated that in terms of the stages of development of the norm life cycle – emergence, cascade, and internalization – that CSR is either close to, or fell over, the "tipping point" whereby a "critical mass" of agents has accepted the norm as appropriate (Finnemore and Sikkink, 1999; Hoffmann, 2003). The evidence of these changed expectations is argued to be manifest in changing public opinion worldwide, the numerous codes of conduct adopted over the past decade by corporations, and the extent and breadth of financial actors and instruments utilizing CSR-related criteria, all of which are discussed further below.

But whether CSR constitutes a new and clearly identifiable norm (or series of norms) is secondary to what I would argue is the distinct theoretical advantage of constructivism: its focus on social change, "the emergence of new constitutive rules, the evolution and transformation of new social structures, and the agent-related origins of social processes" (Adler, 2001, p. 102). In other words, social constructivism is explicitly a theory of process, one that asks how interactions (persuasion, coercion, and socialization) lead to the emergence and reification of rules, norms, and institutions. It focuses on social learning and habitualization that lead an actor to internalize new norms and rules of appropriate behavior and redefines their interests and identities accordingly (Borzel, 2000, p. 13). Relatedly, constructivism argues that "norm entrepreneurs" – agents who advocate different ideas about appropriate behavior from organizational platforms that give their ideas credence – are critical elements in building new ideas of appropriate behavior for actors in world politics.

With respect to the evolving CSR movement, examining the processes behind its development, and the agents involved, reveals complex and fluid dynamics. There are a multiplicity of actors and instruments participating in the construction of corporate behavior. States remain powerful influences since they can and do shape the environment in which corporations operate, even if not through direct regulation. As is discussed below, governments (individually or intergovernmentally) have rarely been leaders in forwarding the contemporary CSR movement, though they may remain important in supporting its evolution via indirect methods.[7] More likely, states influence (and more so *are*

---

[6] For example, Risse (2004) asserts that CSR is a "new transnational norm that appears to follow the norm life cycle ... for international norms in general" (p. 12).

[7] Some argue that the role of governments and public policy in CSR is in fact critical. For example, see Aaronson and Reeves (2002) and Aaronson (2003).

influenced) via global public policy networks devoted to building CSR in the international community; these are issue-based alliances of activists, civil society, businesses, and governments that work to frame, negotiate, monitor, and manage a more socially responsible behavioral norm for corporations, especially multinationals.[8] The advent of socially responsible investment (SRI) initiatives is an example of CSR agents in action as they persuade and frame a norm of responsible behavior of corporations by using market and ownership pressures. The phenomenon of SRI highlights how complex CSR-related processes have become as multinational corporations face intense attention and new pressures from the financial services sector – commercial and investment banks, asset management institutions, reinsurance and direct insurance groups – about their activities. Before we examine in detail financially related developments in corporate social responsibility, the next section offers an outline of the evolution and manifestations of the modern CSR movement.

The contemporary CSR movement

There is a deepening interest in corporate responsibility and accountability in business, academia, and government. In part, this has been provoked by criticism of the lack of external accountability of multinational corporations, largely by transnational social movements that had previously focused their concern over the negative externalities of economic globalization against states and international organizations. "External" accountability refers to people or groups outside the acting entity who are nevertheless affected by it. The concept of accountability "is useful because of its actor-centredness," i.e. it allows us to identify the particular responsibilities of corporate actors involved in transnational governance (Risse, 2004, p. 7). In the case of international business operations, their very legitimacy has become increasingly identified with the values (norms) of global environmental stability, respect for human rights, and social issues in general. It seems axiomatic now that a) multinational corporations are under the light of public attention as never before, and b) that more is expected of them as a result. How did we get here?

It is argued by some that modern corporate social responsibility originated as far back as the late 1960s, partly due to rising social awareness

---

[8] Reinicke and Deng (2000) develop the term "global public policy network" to denote conglomerations that link together interested individuals and institutions from diverse countries and sectors of activity (levels of government, MNCs, and civil society).

in the West of the power of multinational corporations and their impact on the developing world (e.g., Branson, 2002; Davies, 2003). Throughout the 1970s, public opinion across Western countries in particular showed a clear increase in the belief that large companies should have a wider responsibility to the community than profit making alone, that business had a moral obligation to help other institutions achieve social progress (Carroll, 1999; Hopkins, 1999).[9] Yet there was little indication within the business world itself that CSR was something to be seriously considered or operationalized, especially in the business-friendly environment nurtured in the core Reagan–Thatcher years of the 1980s. Promoting a more expansive business accountability to society ran headlong into a consolidating neoliberal economic ideology emphasizing deregulation and more unfettered opportunities for corporations. Nevertheless, concerns about environmental sustainability and the role of business also blossomed in this period, and a few organizational initiatives such as the UK-based interest group Business in the Community were formed promoting CSR against a background of high unemployment, collapsing traditional industries, and inner-city riots ("Business in the Community," 2001).

By the 1990s, the CSR concept had transitioned into a number of alternative themes, most notably the idea that in contrast to the dominant shareholder view of responsibility, businesses have a variety of "stakeholders" in society that must be accounted for in the modern corporation's decision-making and practices. The stakeholder approach carries forward the aforementioned idea of a wider responsibility to mean a larger number of relationships that must be taken into consideration, expanding the list of relevant actors beyond shareholders to include employees, local and global communities, consumers, suppliers, and interest/advocacy groups.[10] In doing so, CSR in practice requires attention to the issues stakeholders care about, usually considered to be the three central "pillars": environmental sustainability, human rights, and labor concerns.

The extent to which a stakeholder perspective has taken hold in practical business considerations of MNCs is highly debatable. What is more certain is that the vast majority of large Western corporations have increasingly publicly acknowledged some form of social responsibility to a wider constituency beyond direct shareholders, and operationalized this in various ways. They do it by producing annual corporate social

---

[9] Carroll (1999) and Hopkins (1999), citing surveys in the US and UK.
[10] See Carroll (1999) and Post et al. (2002) for contributions on the stakeholder perspective.

responsibility reports, by increasingly creating senior management positions devoted to CSR, or by creating company codes of conduct (or participating in codes created elsewhere). In 2003, one estimate was that 98 percent of the top fifty UK companies reported on CSR via their websites and most had a formal social or environmental report usually externally authenticated (Moon, 2003, p. 266).

Although codes of conduct date back a hundred years, they have grown to number in the hundreds in less than a decade and virtually all multinational corporations (at least those based in the West) have signed on to at least a few of them.[11] Two recent international studies identified 132 and 246 separate codes of conduct across various industries and sectors, and over 2,000 companies voluntarily reporting their environmental, social, and financial performance and practice (Kolk et al., 1999; Gereffi et al., 2001). The most comprehensive compendium of ethics codes and instruments of corporate responsibility identified, as of mid-2003: sixteen comprehensive codes, fourteen industry-specific codes, four country-specific codes, and a multitude of company-specific codes, principles for public officials, national and international CSR-related standards initiatives, among others.[12]

Internationally, the organizations and associations dedicated to pushing CSR are legion. There are religiously motivated groups (the Interfaith Center on Corporate Responsibility), standards organizations (Social Accountability International), exclusively private sector groups (the World Business Council on Sustainable Development and the US-based Business for Social Responsibility), and exclusively nongovernmental groups (CorpWatch), among many others. The most popular vehicles to encourage CSR are the aforementioned numerous codes of conduct or monitoring efforts managed by some of the above groups, such as the "Global Sullivan Principles," "SA8000," and the "Global Reporting Initiative."[13]

In terms of corporate views and adoption of CSR, on the one hand we have apparent evidence of substantial differences on CSR and its place in business operations among even advanced Western economies. For example, a 2001 survey of the top 500 companies in Australia showed that only 7 percent saw corporate social responsibility as central to the strategic direction of their businesses, with firms there "way behind" in

---

[11] In discussions with a leading financial services Canadian MNC, I was told that there is such a glut of codes of conduct available that there is growing reticence among businesses to get involved for fear of committing the company to standards far beyond what it could realistically achieve, and also a fear of "watering down" a serious attempt to change corporate values and behavior.

[12] *Compendium of Ethics Codes and Instruments of Corporate Responsibility* (2003).

[13] See Andriof and McIntosh (2001), "Introduction."

environmental sustainability reporting and performance (cited in Newman, 2001). Conversely, in the United States and the United Kingdom there seems to be considerably more appreciation of CSR by business and greater adoption of related principles into company strategic planning and operations. In the US, up to 85 percent of large companies now have codes of conduct, while in the UK, 70 percent of large companies voluntarily publish formal environmental reports.[14] On the other hand, there is also considerable evidence of a cross-national convergence among businesses worldwide. An August 2002 on-line survey by Environics of 212 leading business officials across fifty countries revealed a strong consensus on the issue of sustainable development, a key tenet of CSR: 92 percent said the benefits of commitment outweigh the costs while 76 percent strongly agreed that global companies have a vital role to play in solving developing world problems (cited in Gardiner et al., 2003, p. 69).

What is driving multinational corporations to take into account stakeholders, to adopt codes of conduct and other CSR practices? Why does a Shell Oil executive comment that "we now have to be responsible for things we could never have imagined would be our responsibility"? (cited in Greeno, 1998, p. 36). Why bother with socially responsible concerns such as human rights on a *voluntary* basis – the modus operandi of CSR practices?[15] Is it simply to stave off external criticism from nongovernmental organizations (NGOs) and the threat of regulation or interference by government? There has always been a case for CSR but why has it become something greater in recent years? As Bateman (2003) persuasively argues, CSR has become more than an idea; it is arguably also increasingly a mainstream movement embracing business people, business associations, academics, NGOs, international institutions, and the media. One can read CSR material in dedicated magazines and journals, take CSR courses in schools of business and management, visit myriad websites and read dozens of books on the subject.[16]

---

[14] Andriof and McIntosh (2001), ch. 4 on "Global Corporate Citizenship in a Dot.Com World."

[15] For instance, US-based oil and gas MNC Unocal, under fire for its operations in Burma (Myanmar), has recently admitted/declared that "human rights are not just a matter for governments" (see www.unocal.com/responsibility/humanrights/hr.l.htm). See also Addo (1999).

[16] One study on media coverage in the US shows a significant increase in the number of articles written about CSR: from 236 in 1990, 313 in 1995, to 427 in 2000 (Sims, 2003). My search (in March 2004) using a popular on-line bookseller, Barnes & Noble (www.barnesandnoble.com), found at least 318 titles concerned with corporate social responsibility, with a significant number (107) published in the past five years (since March 1999).

Part of the answer to the puzzle of the rise of CSR is globalization, the compression of time and space, the mobility of nonhuman factors of production, and greater awareness of the part of global citizenry (Bateman, 2003). The expansion of international business has created a complex web of production networks, outsourcing, and commodity chains that have increased the potential for externalities (Gereffi et al., 2001). At the same time, technological innovations, especially in communication technology, give the consumer and society-at-large much more information about their environment; people know more and they know it more quickly (Bateman, 2003, p. 5). Connected to this are the public policy vacuums or governance gaps that have emerged with the rise of globalization and the neoliberal trends of deregulation and privatization. With decreasing faith in the ability of government to bring forth positive change, it is argued by some that the (large) corporation is recognized as the most powerful social construct of the present era and, most importantly, that businesses that are responsive to societal concerns are more likely to be rewarded (Andriof and McIntosh, 2001). Some speculate it is the quid pro quo for trade liberalization, that with the dominance (since the 1980s) of pro-market policies of governments and international organizations such as the World Bank, society "expects" corporations to accept growing responsibilities (Drohan, 2000).

At the same time, specific, high-profile incidents involving or associated with multinational corporations in the past two decades – among them, the toxic poisoning of thousands of people in Bhopal, India in 1984, the *Exxon Valdez* oil spill in Alaska in 1989, the killing of Nigerian writer and activist Ken Saro-Wiwa, and the public reaction to the proposed disposal of the Brent Spar oil-storage buoy in 1995 (both associated with Shell Oil) – have served to sensitize people to the dramatic consequences of corporate *ir*responsibility.[17] They focus our attention, in other words, on the rules and norms of behavior that do and do not bind such private actors to behave in particular ways. Public attitudes towards corporate social responsibility do seem to be consistently strong across a diverse set of countries. Two comprehensive surveys in 2000 both found that two in three people want business to go beyond its traditional role of making a profit and obeying laws.[18] Another survey in

---

[17] For the companies involved in these particular incidents – Union Carbide, Exxon and Royal Dutch/Shell – and their industries, the ramifications of these events were far-reaching and continue to this day. Sklair (2001) outlines these in chs. 6 and 7. See Schwartz and Gibb (1999), ch. 3, for a case study on Royal Dutch/Shell's experiences in 1995.

[18] The "Millennium Poll on Corporate Sustainability," conducted by Environics in 2000, surveyed 25,000 citizens in twenty-three countries on six continents, and Market &

2002, this time of citizen attitudes around the world on the changing role of business, found a "continuing upward trend on the public's focus on the social responsibility of companies."[19] It also found that an increasing number of people "self-reported punishing a company because of their perceptions that it wasn't fulfilling its social responsibilities seriously."[20] Between 2001 and 2002, this number went from 43 to 58 percent in the US with similarly dramatic increases in Canada, the UK, Germany, Italy, and France as well (Gardiner et al., 2003, p. 69).

On the surface, the resonance that CSR seemingly has with the public contrasts sharply with the lack of action by governments. International conventions among states on corporate behavior are generally criticized as weak, with the International Labour Organization (ILO) and Organization for Economic Co-operation and Development (OECD) having created codes of conduct for MNCs that are voluntary and not regulatory in nature. The OECD's Guidelines for Multinational Enterprises, for example, created in 1976 and updated in 2000, is considered the primary model of a voluntary code of conduct yet is viewed as containing weak obligations and criticized for not being legally enforceable (Ratner, 2001).[21] However, other intergovernmental-based mechanisms have recently been enacted that are explicitly designed to build momentum around corporate social responsibility; while voluntary, they have the potential ability, it is argued, to persuade and reframe corporate behavior. The recently created (in July 2000) United Nations "Global Compact" (UNGC) is given as a prime example of this, being an atypical IGO-led effort with primarily MNC membership; corporations declare their intention to abide by ten principles found in existing UN agreements such as the UN Declaration of Human Rights, and report back on their efforts, primarily via their internet websites. Nongovernmental organizations are invited to be members as well, ostensibly to monitor whether the Compact's MNCs are in fact adhering to these principles.[22] On the one hand, one of the Global Compact's architects promotes the Compact as a network-based (as opposed to hierarchical) structure created simply as a mechanism for multinationals

---

Opinion Research International (MORI) poll surveyed 12,000 Europeans across twelve countries. See *Government and Corporate Social Responsibility: An Overview of Selected Canadian, European and International Practices* (2001).

[19] Cited in "CSR is Here to Stay" (2002).   [20] "CSR is Here to Stay" (2002).

[21] Interestingly, Vernon (1998) is more positive on the long-term ripple effect of the OECD guidelines; he argues that, among other things, the OECD code informed the US Congress in the 1970s when it enacted the Foreign Corrupt Practices Act, which in turn informed several anti-corruption initiatives in the 1990s (see pp. 183–6).

[22] See Tesner (2001), ch. 2, for a positive assessment of the UNGC, Paine (2000) for a highly critical view, and Hurd (2001) for a more nuanced perspective.

to exchange information on CSR "best practices." Yet, on the other hand, he is also cautiously optimistic that the UNGC might be able to "close the proliferating governance gaps that are generated by globalization" (Ruggie, 2000a; 2000b). It is for this reason that the Compact is considered by some to be a fairly significant milestone in the development of a global consensus on CSR.

In terms of country-specific actions by governments, certain countries have acknowledged the importance of corporate responsibility in a variety of ways. National CSR standards are at various stages of development in the UK, France, Australia, Israel, Mexico, and Brazil (Rotherham, 2003). The United Kingdom was the first (and so far only one) to appoint a Minister for Corporate Social Responsibility to provide coordination on CSR issues across various departments, and there are over sixty government initiatives related to the promotion of CSR within British industry as well as two all-party groups related to CSR in Parliament. France has passed a law that requires all publicly listed companies to publish sustainability reports (Rotherham, 2003). Denmark has created a Social Index to determine to what degree a company lives up to its social responsibilities and funds, and established the Copenhagen Centre, the only governmental effort of its kind, designed to coordinate domestic and international activities on CSR. The European Union (EU) as a whole has recently apparently taken a serious interest in CSR, developing in 2001 a CSR Green Paper and announcing its intention to promote a partnership involving companies, public authorities, and stakeholders to "build a model of corporate social responsibility on European values."[23]

This brief overview of the modern CSR movement gives a good indication as to its extent and influence on setting the global agenda. The context for the emergence of the idea of corporate responsibility is, at the broadest level, an intensifying debate over how business–society relations must evolve in light of economic globalization and the devolution of political authority away from national governments. The emergence of private authority and the recognition that modern governance is complex and multilayered has encouraged more attention to the participation of corporations. In particular, how and why they behave and the extent to which processes of change in corporate accountability are developing are just beginning to be assessed by scholars of world politics (Cutler et al., 1999; Hall and Biersteker, 2002). It would seem that there is sufficient evidence to argue that there has been a shift in societal expectations in support of greater responsibility by

[23] Available at http://europa.eu.int/comm/employment_social/soc-dial/csr/greenpaper_en.pdf.

corporations, and that CSR is indeed increasingly central to emerging systems of societal governance (Moon, 2002).

There are, as noted, a multitude of drivers involved in the institutionalizing of CSR into the realm of global governance. Galvanizing incidents, NGOs and advocacy networks, information technologies, and the work of some public agencies have certainly contributed. On the one hand, multinational corporations are motivated to adapt CSR-related objectives by a "logic of consequences," i.e. the instrumental/strategic concerns of minimizing risk and liability, and especially the need to promote and safeguard their reputation (Ruggie, 2003; Haufler, 2001). The link between "reputational capital" and liability considerations is central to a corporation's ability to attract investment, hence the role of financially related "inputs" would seem critical. On the other hand, as the discussion below indicates, there is also a "logic of appropriateness" – the need to be seen "doing the right thing" – underlying the motivations and actions of financially related actors and the use of financial instruments to affect the behavior of multinational corporations. What are these financial inputs and how they interact and influence corporate behavior is the subject of the next section.

The role of financial actors and instruments

Many nascent governmental initiatives involving corporate social responsibility are inching their way into public policy via the financial backdoor. The UK government recently legislated (from July 2000) requirements for pension fund managers to state (but not necessarily to direct) whether they considered environmental, ethical, and social issues when making their investment decisions. This type of mandate has potentially interesting effects on funds and the companies whose stock is in those funds, since neither the fund managers nor the companies wish to be seen as irresponsible.[24] Some business executives in the UK say that their firm's initial involvement in CSR was triggered by this legislation; "the change in pension funds legislation raised the debate" (Keeler, 2002, p. 23). Similar legislation on pensions was enacted in Belgium, Germany, and Sweden in 2001. France has a similar law that applies to companies listed on the Paris stock exchange instead of pension funds. In 2003, the UK government announced plans for a proposed Operating

---

[24] The UK group Social Funds reported recently on a study of the effects of the law, finding that 59 percent of the UK pension funds surveyed, representing 78 percent of total assets, incorporate SRI into their investment strategies. Only 14 percent of funds, representing 4 percent of total assets, stated specifically that social concerns will not be taken into account (see www.socialfunds.com).

and Financial Review (OFR) for large companies to allow for greater disclosure of nonfinancial performance.[25] A 2004 assessment of the OFR argues that, despite its voluntary nature, it will fundamentally reshape and refocus corporate reporting because it specifies how companies should assess the company's impact on the wider community and environment, give an account of key stakeholder relationships, and enact policies and performance reviews on reputational issues.[26]

Government agencies such as export credit and insurance operations (ECAs, which are now found in virtually every industrialized nation) are increasingly being called upon to ensure that public money is not used to support problematic international business ventures, i.e. those that appear to violate CSR-related norms or standards. Many ECAs are developing or have developed social and/or environmental criteria within their overall project finance assessment procedures. Part of the impetus is coming from agreements reached under the auspices of the OECD which supports the benchmarking of projects against international standards. Even without these, international operations involving some sort of governmental ECA funding are increasingly scrutinized and made tenuous by any appearance, justified or not, of violation of the common good. For example, the UK export credit agency withdrew support to the engineering firm Balfour Beatty in 2002 for the construction of a dam in Turkey because of, among other factors, the public reaction to reports of flooding of rare archaeological sites (Rotherham, 2003, p. 4).

At the broadest intergovernmental level, international financial institutions (IFIs) – i.e. multilateral development banks such as the World Bank Group and regional banks such as the European Bank for Reconstruction and Development (EBRD) – increasingly stipulate CSR-related criteria for investment projects and specifically access to capital (Kelly, 2000, p. 2). As of late 2003, for example, the World Bank was in the middle of a review of its engagement in extractive industries (oil and gas, mining) and is likely to expand the growing practice of integrating social and environmental criteria into investment decisions (Rotherham, 2003, p. 4). The lending arm of the World Bank, the International Finance Corporation, is considering including human rights in its sustainable development safeguards, a move that could have implications for private sector banks that finance projects in developing countries.[27]

---

[25] *Investing in Responsible Business* (2003). The OFR legislation was unexpectedly dropped by the government in late 2005 after pressure from the lobby group Confederation of British Industry.

[26] *CSR and the Financial Community* (2004).

[27] *Financial Times*, 4 November 2003, p. 6.

Many private sector banks and insurers have attained a degree of convergence with development banks on CSR, partly because the due diligence process required for project finance projects has become increasingly complex and necessitated better risk-assessment procedures.[28] Relatedly, in June 2003 ten of the world's leading project finance banks adopted the "Equator Principles," a set of voluntary environmental guidelines covering investments in major projects specifically modeled on the IFC's criteria pushed by the World Bank itself. The first eighteen banks that signed the Principles covered 74 percent of all project financing loans.[29] One part of the banks' motivation for this specific change was the desire to create a "level playing field" by banding together as an antidote to sponsors with sensitive projects gravitating to institutions with lax standards (Glasgow, 2003). But they also have reputational concerns and pressure coming from activists and the development banks to "do the right thing." Some senior bank officials have argued that participation in the guidelines was only partly determined by strictly short-term business criteria; a "significant motivation" is their perception that "times have changed" and social and environmental concerns have to be given more normative weight than before.[30]

A financial intergovernmental project has been developed by the United Nations Environment Programme (UNEP). The UNEP FI (Finance Initiative) was launched in 1992, ostensibly to engage financial firms and institutions in a dialogue on economic development, environmental protection, and sustainable development. Businesses that join the initiative sign on to a statement by the UNEP on environment and promoting sustainability in their operations. The collaboration involved, as of mid-2004, 300 commercial and investment banks, insurance and reinsurance companies, fund managers, multilateral development banks, and venture capital funds. Like the UN's Global Compact, the UNEP FI is voluntary and does not enable verification of implementation of the statement by the signatory financial firms. While some argue that peer pressure has not taken place as expected – meaning that it is difficult to deal with free riders – others argue that the initiative has grown in both numbers and scope and offers a way to generate norm-building momentum in a key area related to corporate responsibility.[31]

Multinational corporations are also facing financially related pressure from the growth in what is called "socially responsible investing" (SRI),

---

[28] *Investing in Stability* (2003).   [29] Stichele (2004).
[30] Based on the author's preliminary discussions with senior management in charge of CSR in two participating institutions.
[31] Stichele (2004).

which can be simply defined as "financial investment which takes account of social, ethical and environmental criteria thereby considering a social as well as a financial return" (McCann et al., 2003, p. 32). SRI is, in essence, a process of identifying and investing in companies that meet certain standards of corporate social responsibility.

Like CSR, modern SRI's roots extend back to the early 1970s in the US when the first modern ethical fund, the Pax World Fund, was created to exclude from its portfolio any company with links to the arms industry (Stewart, 2002, p. 47). This "negative" screening approach has been used to filter out investments in tobacco companies, for example, or avoid business activity in Burma, or the best-known example, the divestiture from companies doing business in South Africa to support the anti-apartheid movement. While such avoidance screening is still the basic SRI strategy, "positive" screening to identify companies with "best practices" in CSR is increasingly utilized, establishing benchmarks for corporations to achieve in terms of addressing social and environmental criteria.[32] In addition to positive and negative screening, other approaches to SRI include engagement (dialogue between investors and boards or other management of companies to alter corporate behavior) and/or shareholder activism (the use of shareholder powers at company annual general meetings in support of SRI-related resolutions). The issues associated with SRI have changed and broadened over time and now commonly include climate change and environmental systems, human rights and supplier codes of conduct, and genetically modified organisms, among many others.[33]

The use of SRI has increased worldwide, nowhere more so than in the United States where, from 1995 to 2005, assets involved in social investing grew 40 percent faster than all professionally managed investment assets. About $2.1 trillion of portfolio assets in the US (more than 1 in 9 dollars under professional management) are subject to some SRI-related criteria, up from just $40 billion in 1984 (Lobe, 2003). Social investors can include individuals, businesses, universities, hospitals, foundations, pension funds, religious institutions, and other nonprofit organizations. But the biggest drivers in this increase are institutional (as opposed to individual, also referred to as "retail") investors, those investors "with money under professional management in an organization that invests on behalf of a group of individuals, another organization or a group of organizations" (Brancato, 1997).[34] Public companies in the

---

[32] *Socially Responsible Investment Among European Institutional Investors* (2003), p. 10.
[33] *2003 Report on Socially Responsible Investment Trends in the United States* (2003).
[34] In the US, the most important investors are mutual funds and pension funds.

US (and Europe) are "now facing systematic institutional investor questions on CSR-related issues and increasingly sophisticated tools and measures" (Davies, 2003, p. 314). Some believe that such institutions could prove to be the crucial lever that shifts CSR into the mainstream and a central element of normal business operations for their clients' multinational corporations. As financial institutions buy into MNCs and/or finance their projects because they are corporately responsible, it induces companies to behave in that way because otherwise their shares (hence, reputations) will be out of favor with institutions (investors) and ultimately the market (Keeler, 2002, p. 22).

In Europe, the overall presence of SRI has also recently increased, with over 300 SRI market funds available to investors as of mid-2003, up 20 percent in just eighteen months.[35] The absolute size of the European SRI market in 2003 was about $400 billion, or about 20 percent of the American market, but has grown at about the same pace recently, and is especially strong in the UK, the Netherlands, and France. Moreover, more than three-quarters of European fund managers believe that interest in SRI will continue to grow.[36] In the UK, recent evidence shows that about 80 percent of pension scheme members require a SRI policy as part of the pension's corporate governance (Solomon et al., 2002, p. 43). Moreover, there is some evidence that British institutional investors are becoming more aggressive in their dealings with corporations on some issues; for example, in May 2004, representatives from a consortium of public pension funds announced their intention to attend the general meetings of a number of FTSE 100 companies to persuade them to report on their carbon emissions, due to an increasing concern among investors (persuaded by social activists) of the importance of addressing global warming.[37]

In Japan, where SRI has been much slower to develop than in Europe and North America, the first SRI pension fund was launched only in 2003. But its significance lies in the source: similar to CalPERS (California Public Employees' Retirement System) in the US and the UK Universities Superannuation Scheme (USS), the Mutual Aid Association for Tokyo Metropolitan Teachers and Officials is the largest public pension fund in Japan. Its decision to eventually commit 10 percent of its pension portfolio to SRI-related strategies has been linked to changed behavior on the part of some Japanese MNCs, such as

---

[35] *Green, Social and Ethical Funds in Europe 2003* (2003).
[36] *Investing in Responsible Business* (2003).
[37] "Global Warming Heats up at UK Shareholder Meetings," 4 May 2004 (see www. srimedia.com).

Canon holding an investor relations meeting for institutional investors on its environmental initiatives in June 2003, apparently one of the first times that a Japanese company has explained its environmental policies to investors. Moreover, a Japanese expert in corporate planning sees SRI as merging with mainstream investment in the long term, such that SRI-related strategies will become integrated and considered as elemental in institutional investment (cited in Baue, 2003).

Socially responsible investing is reflected in the development of CSR-related market indices such as the FTSE4Good index in London, the Jantzi Social Index (which tracks sixty socially responsible Canadian companies on the Toronto stock exchange), and the Dow Jones Sustainability Index (DJSI). These have been added recently by newer, more complex, issue-specific attempts such as the Climate Leadership Index established by the Carbon Disclosure Project, which is a collection of ninety-five institutional investors worldwide accounting for $10 trillion in assets claiming to be the world's largest CSR initiative. The index is specifically designed to make more global companies acknowledge their responsibility in relation to climate change, reporting their status and developing coherent strategies. The chairman of the Project says this is an example of the investment community "showing a profound new awareness of its fiduciary responsibility relating to climate change, and sending an unmistakable message to corporations that their investors will no longer tolerate a lack of accountability about their exposures and practices."[38]

In part, the trend to SRI on the part of investors is driven by an increasing number of these institutions factoring in the prospects/risk of litigation into their decision-making processes. Insurers now demand social risk analysis; for example, the Association of British Insurers, which controls $2 trillion in investment funds, issued guidelines in October 2001 calling on companies to disclose in their annual report that they have identified the major risks to their international business arising out of social, environmental, and ethical issues (Hertz, 2004, p. 205). Institutional investors are partly motivated into adopting SRI strategies because of their perceptions of the importance of reputation risk arising from corporate misbehavior. Indeed, CalPERS, the largest and most influential investment institution in the US, has opted to apply social criteria to all its investment decision-making, stating that: "equity in corporations with poor social and ethical records could represent an excessive fiduciary risk because such firms court boycotts, lawsuits, or

---

[38] "Business Respect – CSR Dispatches 74," available at www.mallenbaker.net.

labor activity" (qtd. in Solomon and Solomon, 2004, p. 214). The head of SRI at a leading UK financial institution subtly remarks "we want to invest in companies which are able to answer CSR questions with more confidence and which we are comfortable with at board level."[39]

A significant aspect of the SRI trend is of course increased specific pressure from NGOs. Environmental groups turned their attention to commercial banks in the late 1990s on the grounds that they were increasingly funding controversial projects avoided by public institutions such as the World Bank. Many of the biggest banks have yielded to pressure, keen to protect their reputations after recent financial scandals.[40] In 2003, over 100 advocacy groups signed the Colleveccio Declaration, calling on financial institutions to implement more socially and environmentally responsible lending policies.[41] In the same year, a major environmental group declared a ceasefire in its three-year campaign against Citigroup, the world's largest financial institution, after new commitments by the bank to adopt more responsible social and environmental policies in deciding what projects to finance. The Rainforest Action Network had targeted Citigroup for being, among other things, the top lender to both the coal industry and fossil-fuel pipelines around the world.[42] Moreover, SRI-related shareholder activism, partly inspired by various NGOs, is increasing and having an impact on corporate behavior. In addition to the aforementioned great increase in the number of corporate codes of conduct (for individual companies and often sectorwide), there has been a great rise in the number of companies producing stand-alone social and environmental reports, many in connection to receiving a social audit of their business operations. In just two years, from 2002 to 2004, the percentage of FTSE 100 companies producing such reports jumped from 49 to 80 percent (cited in Owen, 2004, p. 4).

Clearly, the variety of financial actors and instruments that are concerned with promoting CSR-related behavior is broad and increasing. Moreover, given that many of these have an increasingly global orientation (for example, institutional investors have less restrictions on the foreign content of equities, tend to search out opportunities in foreign markets, etc.[43]), there is increasing evidence that despite national differences in, for example, the amount of socially responsible investing

[39] *CSR and the Financial Community* (2004).
[40] "Greening of Financial Sector Gathering Speed," *Financial Times*, 4 June 2004.
[41] "Four Banks Adopt IFC Agreement," *Financial Times*, 7 April 2003.
[42] "Citigroup Yields to Pressure from Environmentalists," *OneWorld US*, 17 April 2003.
[43] *The Global Investor and Corporate Governance: What do Institutional Investors Want?* (2003).

among various Western nations (or the mixture of involvement by mutual funds versus pension funds), such practices tend to be rapidly converging (Owen, 2004). In part this is likely due to the highly globalized nature of financial markets and especially financial institutions; for example, large banks from numerous countries are involved in complex project finance deals requiring extensive due diligence and risk assessment, and with social and environmental risk becoming a greater concern, incorporating these elements into financial agreements with multinational corporations is now commonplace.

Conclusion

I have argued in this chapter that the behavior of multinational corporations is best understood utilizing a social constructivist approach that emphasizes the need to unpack the dynamics behind the emergence of a norm (or series of them) of corporate social responsibility in world politics. The contemporary CSR movement was shown to be extensive and manifest in a variety of settings, in domestic and international politics, in the attitudes and practices of business and other actors, including reflected in the evolution of financial actors and instruments. I would further argue that these financial and related actors – institutional investors, public agencies, activists, and corporations – represent an emerging global public policy network loosely formed to address and rein in the adverse effects of markets by using the tools of markets themselves to do so. This community of agents – "norm entrepreneurs" to use the social constructivist term – seeks to instill and encourage business acceptance and compliance with an emerging norm of corporate social responsibility using the instruments of financial investment and related ownership tools.

Many (if not most) of these agents of change attempt to persuade multinational corporations that business behavior in line with CSR norms and principles actually makes good business sense. The overt argument is based on the rational expectation ("logic of consequences") that investors and management make about protecting and growing the assets of companies. However, since there is as yet very little definitive link between CSR and improved financial performance of corporations (as well as pension funds and similar instruments), the strategic advantages of adopting CSR-related business strategies is arguably about both protecting "reputational capital" in the global community and also simply to be seen doing the right thing – behaving properly (the "logic of appropriateness") – according to changing norms (expectations of behavior) that people worldwide have of international business. As one author explains: "if you want to be a socially accepted 'global player' these days, you better subscribe to at least some international human rights and environmental standards and you better report about your efforts at implementing these norms" (Risse, 2004, p. 11).

Finally, some comments about the relationship between corporate social responsibility and corporate accountability are required – especially for a volume that is explicitly concerned with "global accountabilities"! One perspective sees the two terms as identified with very different perspectives on the same problem of the externalities associated with the growing influence of multinational corporations. Accordingly, there are those who believe that the power of multinational corporations is something to be challenged, to be removed, reduced, or redefined. Thus, the corporate accountability 'movement' – associated with the anti-corporate, anti-globalization social movement evident at the 1999 Seattle World Trade Organization meeting protests – requires going beyond current governance mechanisms to empowering societal stakeholders via regulatory and similar reforms and generally confronting corporate power whenever possible (e.g., Richter, 2002). Then there is the corporate social responsibility movement, argued to be identified with those who more or less accept corporate power as inevitable in the current environment and consider it to be an opportunity to engage multinationals, seen, for example, in the development of such emerging governance mechanisms – voluntarist in nature – as the previously described UN Global Compact and others. In this perspective, therefore, corporate accountability clashes with corporate responsibility as apparently quite incompatible views.

However, I would argue that it is more enlightening to view the two terms as simply two sides of the same coin and not incompatible. As noted earlier in this chapter, multinational corporations are facing increasing questions over their (lack of) external accountability since the decisions and actions of these large companies have huge consequences for people around the world. The rise of the contemporary social responsibility movement in all of its manifestations is at its heart very much about *increasing* the external accountability of MNCs and other firms. The various emerging arrangements and mechanisms described earlier – from private–public partnerships to self-regulation to the use of financial instruments such as equity market indices or socially responsible investing strategies – all reflect the growing awareness that multinational firms face an accountability problem in the global capitalist economy. Perhaps the most important task in the days ahead is to identify which processes, actors, and instruments are critical in making corporate social responsibility an effective tool in changing the behavior of multinational corporations and transforming the accountability of these powerful actors in world politics.

References

2003 Report on Socially Responsible Investment Trends in the United States (2003). Washington, DC: Social Investment Forum.

Aaronson, S. (2003) "CSR in the Global Village: The British Role Model and the American Laggard," *Business and Society Review* 108(3), 309–38.

Aaronson, S. and J. Reeves (2002) *Corporate Responsibility in the Global Village.* Washington, DC: National Policy Association.

Addo, M. (ed.) (1999) *Human Rights Standards and the Responsibility of Transnational Corporations.* The Hague: Kluwer Law International.

Adler, E. (2001) "Constructivism and International Relations," in W. Carlsnaes, T. Risse, and B. Simmons (eds.) *Handbook of International Relations.* London: Sage, pp. 95–118.

Andriof, J. and M. McIntosh (eds.) (2001) *Perspectives on Corporate Citizenship.* Sheffield: Greenleaf Publishing.

Barnet, R. and J. Cavanagh (1994) *Global Dreams: Imperial Corporations and the New World Order.* New York: Simon and Schuster.

Bateman, T. (2003) "Thinking About Corporate Social Responsibility," available at www.iintegra.infotech.sk.

Baue, W. (2003) "The Sun is Rising on SRI in Japan" and "Attitudes and Actions Behind the Growth of SRI in Japan," available at www.socialfunds.com.

Borzel, T. (2000) *Private Actors on the Rise? The Role of Non-State Actors in Compliance with International Institutions.* Bonn: Max-Planck-Projektgruppe Recht der Gemeinschaftsgüter.

Brancato, C. (1997) *Institutional Investors and Corporate Governance: Best Practices for Increasing Corporate Value.* Chicago: Irwin Professional Publishing.

Branson, D. (2002) "Corporate Social Responsibility Redux," *Tulane Law Review* 76(5/6), 1207–27.

"Business in the Community" (4 December 2001) *Financial Times Supplement.*

Carroll, A. (1999) "Corporate Social Responsibility: Evolution of a Definitional Concept," *Business and Society* 38(3), 268–95.

Compendium of Ethics Codes and Instruments of Corporate Responsibility (2003). Toronto: York University.

CSR and the Financial Community: Friends or Foes? (2004). London: Echo Research.

"CSR is Here to Stay" (October 2002) *CSR Magazine.*

Cutler, C., V. Haufler, and T. Porter (eds.) (1999) *Private Authority and International Affairs.* Albany: State University of New York Press.

Davies, R. (2003) "The Business Community: Social Responsibility and Corporate Values," in J. Dunning (ed.) *Making Globalization Good: The Moral Challenges of Global Capitalism.* Oxford University Press, pp. 301–19.

Drohan, M. (2000) "With Power Comes Corporate Responsibility," *The Globe and Mail*, 6 July, p. A12.

Finnemore, M. and K. Sikkink (1999) "International Norm Dynamics and Political Change," in P. Katzenstein, R. Keohane, and S. Krasner (eds.)

Exploration and Contestation in the Study of World Politics. Cambridge, MA: MIT Press, pp. 247–77.

Gardiner, L., C. Rubbens, and E. Bonfiglioli (2003) "Research: Big Business, Big Responsibilities," *Corporate Governance* 3(3), 67–77.

Gereffi, G., R. Garcia-Johnson, and E. Sasser (2001) "The NGO-Industrial Complex," *Foreign Policy* 125, 56–65.

Glasgow, B. (July 2003) "A Point of Principle," *Global Finance Magazine.*

Government and Corporate Social Responsibility: An Overview of Selected Canadian, European and International Practices (2001). Toronto: Canadian Business for Social Responsibility.

Green, Social and Ethical Funds in Europe 2003 (2003). Milan: Avanzi SRI Research.

Greeno, J. (ed.) (1998) *Making Business Sense of Sustainable Development.* Cambridge, MA: Arthur D. Little.

Hall, R. and T. Biersteker (eds.) (2002) *The Emergence of Private Authority in Global Governance.* Cambridge University Press.

Haufler, V. (2001) *A Public Role for the Private Sector: Industry Self-Regulation in a Global Economy.* Washington, DC: Carnegie Endowment for International Peace.

Henderson, D. (2001) *Misguided Virtue: False Notions of Corporate Social Responsibility.* London: Institute for Economic Affairs.

Hertz, N. (2004) "Corporations on the Front Line," *Corporate Governance* 12(2), 202–9.

Hoffmann, M. (2003) "Entrepreneurs and the Emergence and Evolution of Social Norms," unpublished manuscript. Newark, DE: University of Delaware.

Hoffmann, M. (March 2002) "Global Governance: Conceptual Clarity or Conceptual Confusion?" Paper prepared for the Annual Meeting of the International Studies Association, New Orleans.

Hopkins, M. (1999) *The Planetary Bargain: Corporate Social Responsibility Comes of Age.* London: Macmillan.

Hurd, I. (August 2001) "Assessing the UN's Global Compact Program: A Hard Life Between the 'Anarchist Turtle People' and the 'Merchants of Global Death,'" Paper prepared for the American Political Science Association Meetings, San Francisco.

Investing in Responsible Business (2003). Brussels: Report produced by CSR Europe, Deloitte, Euronext.

Investing in Stability (2003). New York: UNEP Finance Initiative.

Jonker, J. (2003) "In Search of Society: Redefining Corporate Social Responsibility, Organizational Theory and Business Strategies," in J. Batten and T. Fetherston (eds.) *Social Responsibility: Corporate Governance Issues.* Oxford: Elsevier Science, pp. 423–40.

Keeler, D. (2002) "Spread the Love and Make It Pay," *Global Finance* 16(5), 20–5.

Kelly, M. (2000) "Note on Financial Instruments and Incentives," Contributing paper, prepared for Thematic Review III.2: International Trends in Project Financing, World Commission on Dams.

Koenig-Archibugi, M. (2004) "Transnational Corporations and Public Accountability," *Government and Opposition* 39(2), 234–59.

Kolk, A., R. van Tulder, and C. Welters (1999) "International Codes of Conduct and Corporate Social Responsibility: Can Transnational Corporations Regulate Themselves?," *Transnational Corporations* 8(1), 143–80.

Lobe, J. (2003) "Church Groups Launch Global Corporate Code of Conduct," Inter Press Service.

McCann, L., A. Solomon, and J. Solomon (2003) "Explaining the Growth in UK Socially Responsible Investment," *Journal of General Management* 28 (3), 32–53.

March, J. and J. Olsen (1989) *Rediscovering Institutions: The Organizational Basis of Politics*. New York: The Free Press.

Moon, J. (2003) "Socializing Business," *Government and Opposition* 38(2), 265–73.

Moon, J. (2002) "The Social Responsibility of Business and New Governance," *Government and Opposition* 37(3), 385–408.

Newman, P. (2001) *Regulation and the Triple Bottom Line: An Australian Perspective*. Institute for Sustainability and Technology Policy, Murdoch University, Perth, Australia.

Ougaard, M. (2002) "The CSR Movement and Global Governance," Paper for the International Conference on Business–Social Partnership: Beyond Philanthropy. Calcutta, 4–7 December 2002.

Owen, D. (2004) *Corporate Social Reporting and Stakeholder Accountability: The Missing Link*. Nottingham: International Centre for Corporate Social Responsibility.

Paine, E. (2000) "The Road to the Global Compact: Corporate Power and the Battle Over Global Public Policy at the United Nations," available at www.globalpolicy.org.

Post, J., L. Preston, and S. Sachs (2002) *Redefining the Corporation: Stakeholder Management and Organizational Wealth*. Stanford: Stanford University Press.

Ratner, S. (2001) "Corporations and Human Rights," *The Yale Law Journal* 111(3), 443–545.

Reinicke, W. and F. Deng (2000) *Critical Choices: The United Nations, Networks, and the Future of Global Governance*. Report on the United Nations Vision Project on Global Public Policy Networks.

Richter, J. (2002) *Holding Corporations Accountable*. London: Zed Books.

Risse, T. (2004) *Transnational Governance and Legitimacy*. Berlin: Center for Transatlantic Foreign and Security Policy, Otto Suhr Institute of Political Science.

Rotherham, T. (2003) "Implications for Canadian Industry of International Standards on CSR Management," *IISD Executive Brief*. Geneva: International Institute for Sustainable Development.

Ruggie, J. (2003) "Taking Embedded Liberalism Global: The Corporate Connection," in D. Held and M. Koenig-Archibugi (eds.) *Taming Globalization*. Cambridge: Polity, pp. 93–129.

Ruggie, J. (20 November 2000a) "Globalization and the Global Community: The Role of the United Nations." The J. Douglas Gibson Lecture, School of Policy Studies, Queen's University, Kingston, Canada.

Ruggie, J. (2000b) "Globalization, the 'Global Compact' and Corporate Social Responsibility," *Transnational Associations* 6, 291–4.

Schwartz, P. and B. Gibb (1999) *When Good Companies Do Bad Things: Responsibility and Risk in an Age of Globalization*. New York: John Wiley.

Sims, G. (2003) *Rethinking the Political Power of American Business: The Role of Corporate Social Responsibility*. Department of Political Science, Stanford University.

Sklair, L. (2001) *The Transnational Capitalist Class*. Oxford: Blackwell.

Socially Responsible Investment Among European Institutional Investors (2003). Paris: European Sustainable and Responsible Investment Forum.

Solomon, J. and A. Solomon (2004) *Corporate Governance and Accountability*. Chichester, UK: John Wiley & Sons.

Solomon, J., A. Solomon, and S. Norton (2002) "Socially Responsible Investment in the UK: Drivers and Current Issues," *Journal of General Management* 27(3), 41–54.

Soros, G. (2000) *Open Society: Reforming Global Capitalism*. London: Little Brown.

Spar, D. and D. Yoffie (1999) "Multinational Enterprises and the Prospects for Justice," *Journal of International Affairs* 52(2), 557–79.

Stewart, J. (2002) "Is Your Money in Safe Hands?" *Geographical* 74(8), 47–53.

Stichele, M. (2004) *Critical Issues in the Financial Industry*. Amsterdam: SOMO Financial Sector Report.

Tesner, S. (2001) *The United Nations and Business: A Partnership Recovered*. New York: St. Martin's Press.

The Global Investor and Corporate Governance: What Do Institutional Investors Want? (2003). New York: The Conference Board.

Vernon, R. (1998) *In the Hurricane's Eye: The Troubled Prospects of Multinational Enterprises*. Cambridge, MA: Harvard University Press.

Wolfish, D. and G. Smith (2000) "Governance and Policy in a Multicentric World," *Canadian Public Policy* 26 (Supplement 2), S51–S72.

12 Public accountability within transnational supply chains: a global agenda for empowering Southern workers?

Kate Macdonald

In recent years, one of the central claims promoted by critics of "globalization" has been that the existing system of global economic governance is being undermined by the emergence of "accountability deficits." According to this widespread view, the expanding power of multinational companies to influence the lives of workers in the global South, in the absence of adequate accountability mechanisms, is leading to increasing exploitation of Southern workers. Partly in response to such perceptions, a range of non-state actors have begun to explore new strategies that attempt to hold companies within transnational supply chains directly accountable for their impact on the lives of workers. In this context, both the seriousness of existing accountability deficits, and the effectiveness of non-state initiatives designed to confront them, remain the subject of widespread debate.

This chapter presents an analysis of these debates with reference to a case study of workers in Nicaraguan garment factories, and the production chains that connect them into the global structures of the garment industry.[1] It maps current changes to institutions of governance and accountability within the garment industry, and evaluates the impact of these changes upon the "empowerment" of Southern garment workers.[2] The garment industry offers an ideal case for exploring transformations of public accountability within transnational economic structures, since it is both extensively globalized and highly politicized. Its transnational supply chains connect some of the world's poorest

---

[1] This particular case is used here simply for illustrative purposes. For a more detailed account of the dynamics of change within structures of power and accountability in the global garment industry, and of the examples referred to in the present discussion, see Macdonald (2004).

[2] The concept of empowerment is elaborated below. It provides the conceptual framework through which the implications for Southern workers of transformations in global governance are then analyzed and evaluated.

workers with affluent and powerful consumer markets and corporate entities in the global North, and it has been prominently politicized in recent years by coalitions of non-state actors promoting a global agenda of "core labor standards." The present analysis draws on field research conducted at all levels of the supply chain, including the production phase in Nicaragua, consumer markets in the US, and the actions of investors and civil society advocates spanning the US, Europe, and East Asia.

The chapter begins by reviewing the central concepts deployed in the subsequent analysis; it then maps the broad patterns of change currently evolving within institutions of public accountability in the global economy. The discussion takes as its point of departure the structures of the state-based governance system and the "binary" relations of accountability that underpin it and describes how these structures are being challenged by the emergence of new agendas, which I characterize as "transformative" and "external" accountability. The extent to which these different forms of accountability are serving to empower Southern workers is then evaluated, drawing on examples from Nicaragua-based garment supply chains. It is concluded that in order to institutionalize the empowerment of Southern workers more effectively within transnational production chains, it will be necessary to develop a more complex "plurilateral" approach to the design of global institutions of public accountability.

Governance and public accountability

What is accountability, and why does it matter?

The central concept underpinning the present discussion is that of "accountability," which I define as a property of an institutionalized relationship in which the exercise of power by one set of actors is constrained subject to some requirement of *responsiveness* to those over whom their power is exercised. This conception of accountability can be usefully decomposed into two functional dimensions: *transparency* in the exercise of power (entailing either formal reporting requirements or some alternative information transmission mechanism), and *enforceability* of the principle of responsiveness (generally via provision of some means by which sanctions can be imposed on powerholders in cases where their behavior breaches some common understanding of "acceptable" standards) (Woods, 2000; Keohane and Nye, 2001; Keohane, 2002; Newell and Bellour, 2002).[3] While accountability

---

[3] In the complex institutional environments that are necessary to facilitate global structures of production, accountability relationships can involve divisions of labor in

relationships can exist between the bearers and objects of power within any institutionalized relationship, debates surrounding "accountability deficits" in institutions of global governance are concerned more narrowly with accountability for the exercise of what is considered to be "public" power. The following analysis therefore focuses specifically on the concept of "public accountability." I use this term to refer to answerability for the exercise of power over "publicly relevant" outcomes, understood as that range of outcomes in which shared or competing interests are significantly implicated.[4]

Structures of accountability provide those actors who are subject to the exercise of power with an institutionalized means of redress through which they can express dissatisfaction with the actions of powerholders. Such structures can therefore be understood as comprising an institutionalized form of *countervailing power*. Considered in this light, the concept of accountability makes little sense unless it is analyzed with reference to the structures through which *primary* sources of public power are distributed. Publicly relevant power is traditionally conceptualized as being exercised and regulated through state institutions; however, much of this chapter will focus on structures of public power and accountability that are emerging *beyond* this state-centered realm. The concept of "governance," referring to the processes through which an organization or society steers and coordinates itself, offers a framework through which the distribution of such broader sources of power can be analyzed (Rosenau, 2000; Scholte, 2002).[5]

which those who are entitled to demand answers from powerholders are not necessarily the same actors as those in charge of determining and imposing penalties (Goetz and Jenkins, 2002). For example, information regarding a firm's activities which is exposed by an NGO or provided to a regulatory agency can, when made public, stimulate the imposition of a sanction in the form of a consumer boycott. Some important implications of these pluralistic divisions of labor within accountability structures are discussed below.

[4] This definition of publicly relevant power encompasses both a liberal concern for power that constrains other social actors' autonomy (Keohane, 2002; Held, 2004), and an understanding of public power as that advancing a general or common interest. The sphere of public interest is thus defined according to the extent to which interests are interdependent – either common or competing. Of course, what we define as being publicly relevant is itself politically contested, and dominant relations of power will be reflected in its construction (Cutler, 2002, p. 34).

[5] I therefore use the term "governance" to refer to activities backed by shared goals that do not necessarily derive from legal and formally prescribed responsibilities, or rely on police powers to attain compliance (Smouts, 1998; Stoker, 1998). Instead, governance operates through a combination of institutions, organizations, and networks in which publicly relevant power is exercised – not only through formally sanctioned systems of law, but also through the construction of meanings, identities, and norms, and through diffuse as well as centralized enforcement mechanisms (Rosenau, 1992; Rosenau, 2000; Detomasi, 2002; Lipschutz and Fogel, 2002; Woods, 2002).

Institutions of governance and accountability can then be understood as mutually constitutive dimensions of an overarching institutional complex that I refer to as a "governance system." The structure of accountability relationships in a governance system is of central importance in determining the way in which roles, responsibilities, and powers are distributed between actors, and the mechanisms through which the exercise of power is constrained.[6] Put simply, accountability mechanisms are designed to *equilibrate power and responsibility* within a governance system. This requires first that power and responsibility are distributed such that identifiable actors have responsibility for publicly relevant outcomes, and those with responsibility also have the capacity to steer and regulate these outcomes. Second, it requires that a degree of countervailing power is placed in the hands of those over whom the primary power is wielded, thus enabling the responsibilities of powerholders to be effectively enforced. By facilitating and constraining the exercise of power, the operation of accountability mechanisms is often crucial in determining patterns of "winners" and "losers" that emerge within the governance system as a whole.

Why is the existing state-centered system of accountability and governance being challenged by new agendas of accountability?

To make sense of how and why new forms of global accountabilities are emerging, we must first identify the ways in which changes in the global political economy are challenging the effectiveness and legitimacy of the preexisting state-based system of governance and accountability. Within this existing system, we tend to take for granted the distribution of power and accountability through what I refer to as a *binary* structure, in which responsibilities for publicly relevant outcomes are assigned primarily to centralized state institutions, and public accountability is then constructed as a binary relationship between a territorially constituted state and members of its constituent "public."[7] There is widely shared understanding and agreement regarding the core principles through

---

[6] A similar point is made by Newell and Bellour (2002).

[7] The logic of this binary accountability structure is not incompatible with the fact that individual companies also wield direct power over "publicly relevant" outcomes experienced by workers; clearly, such power has always been a feature of capitalist economic systems. Rather, this logic assumes that such forms of corporate power are framed and sustained by the overarching regulatory power of the state, and thus that the location within the state of centralized responsibility for protecting working conditions is matched by state capacity to steer and regulate outcomes.

which public power and associated responsibilities are thus distributed, in which the exercise of countervailing power by constituent members of the territorial public (both individuals and collective non-state actors) functions to *legitimize* privileged sources of state power by institutionalizing their limits, subject to an expression of consent by the governed. Because the legitimacy of prevailing power distributions are thus conditional upon the operation of these binary accountability relations, such mechanisms of "legitimizing accountability" serve to strengthen and reproduce the existing governance system, maintaining its stability over time.

Because these binary relations are constructed between a *territorially bounded* public and state, the ongoing legitimacy of existing accountability structures is contingent upon the premise that power to determine publicly relevant outcomes remains subject to territorial control. However, within the global garment industry the legitimacy of this state-centered governance system is being undermined by the increasing exercise of direct power over Southern workers by extraterritorial corporate actors controlling global supply chains. Within these "buyer-driven" chains, Northern brands and retailers are able to control marketing and design activities, which in turn enables them to wield extensive power over decision-making throughout the global chain (Gereffi, 1999).

According to the principles of the state-centered governance system, the direct power exerted by Northern brands and retailers over Southern workers should be regulated by each state within which affected workers are located. In fact, the high degree of territorial mobility of these buyer-driven production chains undermines the effectiveness of such state-based regulatory structures, resulting in misalignment between systemic distributions of responsibility and outcome-producing power that has increasingly undermined the capacity of national governments to discharge effectively the regulatory responsibilities that continue to be vested in them.

The weakened capacity of the state to discharge its assigned responsibilities as a result of these changes in the global economy is clearly exemplified by the case of Nicaragua. While Nicaragua's constitution and labor laws codify extensive safeguards of working conditions and other entitlements of workers (CENIDH, 2003, p. 16), the Nicaraguan government's performance in monitoring and enforcement of these rules has demonstrated significant weaknesses. Ineffective state enforcement can be attributed primarily to a lack of resources and penalties available to inspectors within the Ministry of Labor. According to the Ministry's own records, they have carried out only seventy-five inspections in the country's sixty-two free-trade-zone factories over a period of four years, despite rules requiring periodic visits (CENIDH, 2003,

p. 62).[8] The penalties themselves are also very weak, with the maximum fine payable by companies that violate the labor laws being only 10,000 *cordobas* (approximately US$630). This absence of strong coercive mechanisms dilutes the impact of the enforcement regime, even in those cases in which penalties are imposed.[9]

This failure to effectively enforce state-based labor standards, in particular the absence of adequate penalties, can to a large extent be attributed to a lack of political will at the highest level of Nicaraguan government, as illustrated by the National Assembly's failure to pass a bill initiated in 1999 by the women's organization Maria Elena Cuadra; this organization had sought to have tax exemptions made conditional upon compliance with labor standards – a change that would have provided a more strongly coercive mechanism to enforce labor laws (CENIDH, 2003, p. 15). Such lack of political will is in turn attributable at least partly to the direct pressure placed on governments by investors, who enjoy considerable mobility with respect to production locations due to the labor-intensive nature of assembly production, and who openly express their preference for investing in countries where labor legislation will not cause them "problems."[10] Such pressure from investors is exerted upon host governments not only in relation to the overall legislative framework of the labor law, but also in the context of specific labor disputes.

This increasing misalignment between regulatory power and distributions of responsibility is often characterized as reflecting a shift in power from "states" to "markets" or "corporations," each conceived as a generic category. However, analysis of the garment industry suggests that in fact much of the shift in regulatory power is not away from the state-based system as a whole, but rather from states in which production and workers are based, and towards consumer states (and to a lesser extent, investor states) located higher up the chain of buyer-driven production. At a structural level, this reflects a redistribution of power towards the governments of countries in which are located those stages of economic activity that are characterized by greater barriers to the exit of capital.[11] Shifts of power between individual states that are positioned

---

[8] These inspection requirements are outlined in Article 14 of the Ministry's *Reglamento de Inspectores del Trabajo*, 20 February 1997.

[9] Source: Interview by the author at MITRAB, Managua, 13 November 2003.

[10] Source: Interview by the author at Nien Hsing head office, Taipei, 10 March 2004.

[11] This is consistent with the idea that deregulation of capital movements has "altered the power of capital by creating a greater number of 'exit' options in relation to both labor and the state" (Held, 2000, p. 396; Strange, 2000; Koenig-Archibugi, 2004). However, it goes further in that it highlights the direct correlation between the magnitude of this

differently within global production chains are less commonly identified as a source of emerging accountability deficits than are shifts in power between "states" and "corporations."[12] However, such an analysis draws attention to the important fact that when we speak of "powerful actors" being unaccountable to the workers whose lives they affect, this should be understood as referring not only to extraterritorial corporate actors, but also to extraterritorial *states*.

This point is illustrated by the processes through which the wages and working conditions experienced by Nicaraguan garment workers are directly influenced by the priorities and decisions of investor and consumer states.[13] Investor states retain some ability to exert leverage over outgoing garment investors, often by placing conditions on the provision of assistance. For example, the Taiwanese government channels assistance to garment investors through its "Plan to Subsidize Industries Investing in Diplomatically Tied Countries," which supports garment companies investing in countries that recognize Taiwan's sovereign status, such as Nicaragua; similarly, the US government provides assistance to foreign investors via the Overseas Private Investment Corporation (OPIC). Both US and Taiwanese decision-makers consistently choose to deploy such support to promote nationally defined interests, rather than to defend the labor standards of workers outside their own territories. The Taiwanese subsidies take no account of a company's record on labor standard compliance (Nee, 2002), and while assistance through OPIC is nominally conditional upon the host country being in compliance with internationally recognized worker rights,[14] in reality this condition is applied with considerable discretionary bias shaped by prevailing US economic and foreign policy considerations (Méndez and Koepke, 2001).

Because consumer markets represent the only component of the global commodity chain that cannot be territorially relocated, sovereignty over territory in which final consumer markets are located bestows regulatory power that is not eroded by the mobility of global

---

effect and the position of a given state and force within the globally disaggregated production process.

[12] A notable exception is Keohane (2002), who places great emphasis on the lack of accountability of "powerful" states.

[13] Acknowledgment of the importance of decisions taken by states other than the one in which the affected workers are located reflects the idea that "decisions taken by representatives of nations and nation-states profoundly affect citizens of other nation-states – who in all probability have had no opportunity to signal consent or lack of it" (Held, 1995, p. 139).

[14] See www.opic.gov.

capital. Accordingly, the greatest regulatory power is structurally located at the level of consumer states, which in the case of Nicaraguan garment production means the US government, since almost all garments produced in Nicaragua's free-trade zones are destined for US consumer markets. Although the US has a range of unilateral policies linking imports to labor standards,[15] such regulations, as with labor provisions within OPIC, are administered through political processes in which protectionist or broader foreign policy objectives are generally accorded higher priority than the protection of foreign workers. Thus, although the position of consumer and (to a lesser extent) investor states gives them some *capacity* to regulate wages and working conditions of Southern workers within transnational supply chains, *responsibilities* to defend labor standards are exclusively constructed at the level of states in which workers are territorially located. This generates a disjuncture within the global political system, which contributes to the increasing ineffectiveness of state-based structures of governance and accountability in discharging the responsibilities they have been assigned for the protection of working conditions in the global South.

Challenges and transformation to the state-based system of governance and public accountability

Accountability directed to actors beyond the state

These structural weaknesses within the traditional state-based governance system have contributed to the increasingly widespread view that the current system is failing effectively to regulate the impact of transnational corporate actors upon the lives of Southern workers. Accordingly, public accountability claims are being directed towards powerful actors beyond the centralized apparatus of the state: in particular, towards powerful "corporate" actors. Goetz and Jenkins (2002) identify this shift away from a narrow conceptualization of accountability as relating exclusively to the accountability of public sector institutions, and argue that a broader accountability agenda has been building momentum in recent years:

The failure of democratic institutions and the decline of national sovereignty have combined to generate pressure for new ways of making powerful actors,

---

[15] The most notable among these are the Generalized System of Preferences, the Caribbean Basin Initiative, bans on imports of goods produced using prison labor or forced child labor (Tsogas, 2001), as well as broader forms of "diplomacy" conducted through the International Labor Affairs Office and the Special Representative on Labor Affairs.

within and beyond the state, accountable for the impact of their actions on poor people ... The result has been the emergence of "The New Accountability Agenda". Existing mainly in fragments of conceptual innovation and practical experiment, the basic features of this agenda are nevertheless increasingly visible. (Goetz and Jenkins, 2002, pp. 3–4)

Such new agendas of accountability represent a broad challenge to deeply established ways of conceptualizing and institutionalizing power, responsibility, and accountability. As new agendas develop, they are contributing to the creation of more layered and composite structures of accountability that incorporate not only the binary structures of legitimizing accountability discussed above, but also what I refer to as "transformative" and "external" accountability, both of which are elaborated in greater detail below.

Transformative accountability

I use the term "transformative accountability" to describe those practices that have emerged, as actors seeking to transform the existing system reject the core principles through which power is distributed and legitimized within the existing governance system, demanding instead that institutions of power and accountability be structured in accordance with a redefined set of principles. In contrast to practices of "legitimizing accountability" described above, transformative accountability demands function to *delegitimize* the existing governance system, and thus to contest the authoritative basis of existing structures of power. Transformative accountability claims therefore signal the *denial* of consent, not just to particular acts of power but to the fundamental structure of institutions through which power is distributed and legitimized.

Those issuing transformative accountability demands do more than challenge the legitimacy of the prevailing system. They also attempt to hold powerful actors accountable to the rules of a transformed governance system that does not yet formally exist. Under such circumstances, it is usual for powerholders to be unwilling – at least initially – to participate in these new accountability relations by voluntarily providing information or accepting sanctions. Development of functional accountability mechanisms in the absence of the consent of powerholders therefore requires the construction of independent networks to facilitate the transmission of information regarding the activities of powerful actors, as well as independent mechanisms through which sanctions can be imposed unilaterally upon those powerholders who violate specified transformative principles. The imposition of these new accountability mechanisms thus contributes to the construction of a transformed system – both by directly forcing changes in the activities of targeted actors, and by reshaping constitutive discourses in ways that characterize prevailing power structures as illegitimate. These processes thereby contribute to developing a broader "public" in which norms, identities, and beliefs adapt to a transformed set of principles.[16] In this way, the continued imposition of transformative accountability demands gradually opens new political spaces in which transformed institutions of governance can be imagined, constructed, and legitimized.

The "anti-sweatshop" campaigns that emerged within the global garment industry during the 1990s provide a clear illustration of the mechanisms through which agendas of transformative accountability have been advanced. Through such campaigns, networks of human rights and labor advocates have attempted to improve working conditions and raise wages for workers in developing countries via a series of publicity campaigns directed towards "powerful" clothing brands and retailers in the United States and Europe.[17] One commonly employed strategy has been the exposure of abuses within specific factories (a tactic sometimes referred to as "naming and shaming"), drawing on individual cases to support broader campaigns. In Nicaragua, for instance, the National Labor Committee in late 1997 launched a consumer campaign directed against Walmart, Kmart, and JC Penny via a documented "exposé" of conditions within Nicaraguan factories, screened on the US *Hard Copy* television program (Elliott and Freeman, 2000).[18] Anti-sweatshop campaigns are also commonly based on the "international solidarity campaign" model, in which international "solidarity" networks comprised of non-state actors such as labor unions and NGOs are formed to support the demands of local unions in specific factories. A clear example of this is the campaign launched in 2001 in support of workers at the Taiwanese-owned Chentex factory in Nicaragua's Las Mercedes Free Trade Zone (Macdonald, 2004).

In launching such campaigns, non-state actors reject the traditional claim that regulation of labor standards is the exclusive responsibility of the governments of producing countries, pointing to the erosion of the regulatory capacity of such governments in the face of internationally mobile capital. Instead, they demand that companies be held directly accountable for the impact of their activities upon Southern workers,

---

[16] I use the term "principle" in the sense defined by Braithwaite and Drahos (2000).

[17] Of the forty-three US-based groups identified by Elliott and Freeman (2000) as working on sweatshop issues, just over half were formed in the 1990s, and nearly 80 percent have existed only since 1980. Harrison and Scorse (2003) similarly document a 400 percent increase in the number of newspaper articles focusing on sweatshop activities during the 90s.

[18] See www.sweatshopwatch.org/swatch/headlines/1997/nica_dec97.html.

framing their demands within principles of "core labor standards," "universal human rights," and "opposition to corporate power." Transformative demands thereby seek to reconstruct fundamental roles and responsibilities in ways that delegitimize existing arrangements in which a range of private sector actors wield important forms of publicly relevant power without accepting associated public responsibilities. They then demand that "private" actors should accept increased responsibility for the well-being of Southern workers within the transnational supply chains that they control.[19]

Imposition of these new accountability demands has required the groups that issue them to construct mechanisms via which information can be transmitted and sanctions imposed without the consent of the companies concerned. In the short term, increased consumer awareness and concern regarding working conditions in offshore factories facilitates the strategic mobilization of consumer action, and its deployment as an independent coercive weapon able to be wielded in support of campaigners' demands.[20] Such sanctioning mechanisms operate both through direct consumer boycotts, and through deeper processes of socialization manifested as broader reputational damage to company brands.[21] The significant sanctioning power generated by such strategies is illustrated by the fact that many companies participating in Nicaragua-based production chains reported that damage to their reputation represented a greater threat than the primary state-based sanctioning mechanism – that is, government-imposed fines.

The fines are very small and aren't really a big issue – the much bigger concern is the bad image of the company that being given a fine produces, and the impression of not complying with the law of the country. This is the real threat. For us Nien Hsing is a big company, and our reputation is very important. The fine doesn't worry us; rather it is being colored with the label of being a violator of rights. It is the prestige and not the money that we are worried about.[22]

---

[19] In many cases, however, their discourses are constructed in *opposition* to any shift in the location of public power, with many arguing that both responsibility and power should ideally remain with the state. To this extent, these challenges to identities and responsibilities associated with the categories of public and private are regarded by some as a second-best solution.

[20] The importance of reputational effects is reflected in the statement in 1994 by the then CEO of Levi Strauss, Bob Haas, that "In today's world a TV exposé on working conditions can undo years of effort to build brand loyalty" (Jenkins, 2001, p. 7).

[21] Reputation is important not only with respect to concerned consumers, but also regarding a range of business relations on the production side, including relations with current and potential employees, business partners, and government (Haufler, 2001; Ruggie, 2001).

[22] Interview by the author at Chih Hsing, Managua, 4 November 2003.

Senior government officials appeared very conscious of this reality, seeking to harness non-state sanctioning mechanisms in support of their own laws in cases where firms were repeatedly failing to comply with state regulations.

In reality, what we have to do is have someone senior ring them up and threaten them with what will happen if they don't comply: we say that we're going to pass the information about what is going on in their firms on to the media. They are very scared of this, much more than of the fines, so then they can be made to comply.[23]

In these ways, anti-sweatshop campaigns have constructed independent information transmission and sanctioning mechanisms through which powerful corporate actors can be pressured to accept increased responsibility for their impact upon the well-being of Southern workers. The transnational solidarity networks formed to support factory-based campaigns have provided further direct mechanisms through which information can be deployed and sanctions imposed in support of these transformative demands. The solidarity campaign based around the Chentex factory was able to exercise countervailing power by deploying the communicative and coordinating capabilities of their transnational networks to construct complex webs of influence that exerted pressure at strategic nodes of decision-making power. Within the private sector sphere, network participants in each country exerted pressure on the companies based in their territory, utilizing the mass media where possible. In Taiwan, the participating coalition of labor activists (the Taiwan Solidarity for Nicaraguan Workers) exerted pressure on the Taiwanese owner of the Chentex factory (the Nien Hsing consortium) by protesting outside the stockmarket and at the company's annual meeting. In Nicaragua, the Sandinista-based Chentex union placed direct pressure on local management via widespread protests and strikes. In the US, labor campaigners organized consumer boycotts and protests at retail outlets across the country, directed against major clients of the Chentex factory. Pressure was thereby exerted directly at each major point of decision-making within the global production chain, in the hope that pressure at the higher levels would be passed down to the factory level via the chains of command internal to the supply chain. There is evidence that this strategy functioned unevenly, but with considerable effectiveness.

The unions called CEOs of our customers at 2 in the morning to bother them and so then they called us and said settle it down ... The brands were under lots

---

[23] Interview by the author with representative of Corporacion de Zonas Francas and MITRAB, Managua, 4 November 2003.

of pressure and were very concerned about their reputation – they said to us that we had to settle down the problem or they would give our orders to others ... Some other brands were more supportive though, and said just ignore it. Different brands responded differently.[24]

While the vast majority of anti-sweatshop campaigns have directed their delegitimizing campaigns primarily towards corporate power-holders, in some cases, such as that of Chentex, solidarity campaigns have also placed coordinated pressure on the powerful, extraterritorial, investor, and consuming *states*, demanding that they also must accept responsibility for the conditions of Southern workers. In the case of Chentex, pressure was placed on individual members of the US Congress, who in turn signed letters of protest addressed to both President Clinton and the Taiwanese President.[25] Labor groups also pressured the US Trade Representative to write to the Nicaraguan Minister of Foreign Affairs, warning that Nicaragua's Caribbean Basin Initiative preferences might be threatened if the dispute was not resolved.[26] In addition, a legal action was launched in the US against Nien Hsing under the Alien Tort Law, alleging violations of the human rights of Chentex workers.[27] Various forms of pressure were brought to bear in Taiwan: labor groups placed pressure on the state-owned Labor Insurance Fund, which owns about 5 percent of the shares in Nien Hsing; they also placed pressure on the Ministry of Foreign Affairs, suggesting that assistance provided through the "Plan to Subsidize Industries Investing in Diplomatically Tied Countries" should be denied to companies violating labor standards in offshore factories (Nee, 2002); further, a parliamentary hearing on the conflict was held in the Legislative Yuan.[28] Nicaraguan unions attempted to place pressure on the Nicaraguan Ministry of Labor, and utilized judicial proceedings to challenge the union-busting activities of

---

[24] Interview by the author at Nien Hsing head office, Taipei, 10 March 2004.

[25] Letters signed by sixty-four members of Congress were sent to both President Clinton and the Taiwanese President Chen Shui-bian on 21 July 2000, following a delegation to Nicaragua led by Congressman Sherrod Brown.

[26] US Trade Representative Charlene Barshefsky wrote to the Nicaraguan Minister of Foreign Affairs Eduardo Montealegre on 3 October 2000 expressing concern regarding rights violations in the Chentex and Mil Colores factories, and stating that "failure to achieve an improvement in this situation could place part or all of Nicaragua's CBTPA trade preferences in jeopardy".

[27] US District Court, Central District of California, *Gladys Manzanarez Tercero, Zenayda Torez Aviles, Harling Bobadilla, and Felix Rosales Sanches*, Plaintiffs, v. *C&Y Sportswear Inc., Nien Hsing Textile Co. Ltd. and Chentex Garments, SA*, Defendents, Case No CV 00–12715 NM (CTx).

[28] E-mail from Professor Hsin-Hsing Chen to US members of the solidarity network, 1 April 2000, "Report on Taiwan Legislative Yuan Hearing on the Chentex Case."

Chentex management. They also appealed to the ILO,[29] attempting to deploy its formal complaints mechanisms to place additional pressure on the Nicaraguan government. By coordinating action at these multiple, state-based pressure points, in addition to targeting multiple decision-making nodes within transnational production chains, anti-sweatshop campaigners attempted to mobilize their independent information transmission and sanctioning capabilities to demand that not only powerful companies but also extraterritorial states must accept greater responsibility for the well-being of Nicaraguan workers.

External accountability

Over time, as transformative accountability claims have continued to be directed towards new categories of powerful actors, some of these powerholders have begun to respond, at least superficially, to the transformative challenge. As they have begun to acknowledge increased responsibilities for their impact on an expanded set of "external" stakeholders, such actors have established a range of institutional mechanisms through which limited forms of answerability to certain categories of such stakeholders can be facilitated. These institutions, which I refer to as institutions of *external accountability*, therefore represent the partial institutionalization of transformative demands in which previously unacknowledged responsibilities and accountabilities are constructed.[30]

The emergence of external accountability mechanisms is often characterized as offering a potential solution to the emergence of accountability deficits within the existing system of global governance. However, the concept of external accountability – defined by Keohane (2002, p. 14) as "accountability to people outside the acting entity, whose lives are affected by it" – remains underspecified in two crucial ways.[31] First, the attempt to present a coherent definition of external accountability relations based on membership of an "acting entity" serves to circumvent rather than resolve the key source of the accountability deficit: that is, the contestation of social and political boundaries, and thus the

---

[29] "Complaints against the Government of Nicaragua presented by the Jose Benito Escobar Trade Union Confederation of Workers and the International Textile, Garment and Leather Workers' Federation," Report No 324, Cases Nos 2092 and 2101.

[30] The concept of "external accountability" is very close to the more commonly used "stakeholder accountability."

[31] This does not reflect a weakness specific to Keohane's definition; rather, it reflects deeper limitations of the concept of external accountability, and of the set of institutional practices with which the concept has been associated.

underlying disagreement regarding who or what constitutes the "acting entity" in the first place. Discourses of external accountability have emerged precisely because the boundaries between multiple and over-lapping social and political "entities" are not clear or agreed, so incor-porating this term into the definition as though its meaning were self-evident serves not to clarify but simply to obscure the underlying systemic conflict from which the concept of "external accountability" has emerged.

Second, this definition in itself tells us nothing about appropriate normative criteria of "affectedness," on the basis of which we might seek to define the boundaries of new forms of external accountability. While more extensive responsibilities to external stakeholders are acknowledged, there is no agreed definition of who new relationships of responsibility and accountability should be constructed between, or precisely what these responsibilities should entail. In practice, the var-ious corporate practices that are subject to constraint via mechanisms of "external" or stakeholder accountability therefore emerge as a product of pragmatic political compromise, and remain largely discretionary in scope and substance. The concept of external accountability is useful insofar as it implies some acknowledgment of the *problem* of contested legitimacy of prevailing power relations. However, without resolution of the underlying sources of normative contestation, external account-ability cannot in itself constitute a *solution*.

The implications of such ongoing normative contestation for the kinds of institutions and practices that have emerged are reflected in the most prominent example of external accountability structures within the gar-ment industry: codes of conduct. These codes have emerged as a key means by which firms have responded to the sustained pressure exerted on them by the transformative accountability demands of the anti-sweatshop movement. A diverse range of models have been developed, including "corporate" codes of conduct (the most common variety in Nicaraguan garment factories), industry association codes such as Worldwide Responsible Apparel Production (WRAP), multi-stakeholder codes such as that of the Fair Labor Association (FLA) and NGO-driven codes such as SA8000. A range of monitoring systems have also been developed to enhance the effectiveness and credibility of these codes, including private sector monitoring systems conducted by companies such as PricewaterhouseCoopers, monitoring systems operated in-house by retailers, brands, or their contracted trading companies, and independent monitoring procedures conducted by local NGOs.

By implementing a code of conduct, firms institutionalize within this formal structure some acknowledgment of the power that they already wield within transnational supply chains and, at least nominally, they accept increased responsibility for the conditions of workers participating within these structures. Because the codes have emerged at least partially in response to anti-sweatshop campaigns, they institutionalize to some extent the transformative demands of external stakeholders. However, the primary motivation of the firms establishing such codes is to respond to the specific demands that they perceive as most strongly delegitimizing their activities in the eyes of the Northern consuming public. They therefore tend to respond only to those elements of the demands that they consider most vital to protecting their reputation among consumers,[32] and continue to contest the legitimacy of more extensive demands. Such codes therefore represent only a *partial* institutionalization of transformative accountability demands, and the principles embodied within the codes then continue to compete for legitimacy with the more radically transformative principles advocated by anti-sweatshop campaigners.

Within this fundamentally contested structure of governance and accountability, labor organizations are faced with two choices. They can support external accountability structures by conducting monitoring of compliance with the codes, thereby strengthening and legitimizing the code-based structures. Or they can continue to work outside the code-based governance system, seeking to delegitimize and further transform it through the ongoing application of transformative accountability claims. This strategic dilemma has generated significant divisions among labor campaigners, with different groups making different judgments regarding which strategies are capable of most effectively empowering workers. Some NGOs and unions have been deeply involved in developing codes (Jenkins, 2001), while others have opposed them vehemently, regarding such schemes as co-optive public relations exercises that threaten to crowd out union and other grassroots participation. In this context of ongoing contestation, in which neither the scope nor the substance of legitimate relationships of power and responsibility have been agreed, external accountability mechanisms remain incapable of offering more than a partial and contested institutionalization of emerging demands for new and transformative forms of public accountability.

---

[32] Such demands commonly refer to measures such as bans on the use of child labor, and health and safety measures to prevent publicly conspicuous accidents such as mass poisonings and factory fires. These demands for responsibility tend to be those based on clear demonstration of a direct imposition of harm (commonly considered to be the strongest normative basis for a claim of responsibility).

The empowering capacity of new agendas
of public accountability

Our interest in these new forms of public accountability extends beyond the desire to understand the dynamics through which they have emerged; it also encompasses a concern for their *distributional* implications. While practices of public accountability are most commonly evaluated in terms of their role in advancing the agenda of democratic governance,[33] the goal of this chapter is to evaluate the implications of changing institutions and practices for the well-being of a *specific* group of disadvantaged actors: workers in the global South. An evaluative framework focusing on the "empowerment" of this particular group of actors enables us to shift our focus away from the conventional concern with empowering a "public," imagined as some kind of coherent or unitary entity, and towards concern for the empowerment of specific disadvantaged individuals and groups within the wider society or public.[34]

The concept of empowerment is widely used, but rarely defined rigorously. I define empowerment as an advance in the well-being of a disadvantaged or vulnerable individual or group with respect to their *material welfare* and/or their *agency*, where "welfare" refers to the fulfillment of basic material needs, and "agency" is defined as both an individual and a collective concept referring to freedom and capacity to act in pursuit of self-perceived interest. The concept of agency has been employed variously to denote the ability to exercise choice, to participate in social and political processes, and to effect social transformation.[35] While at times it is helpful to distinguish between different dimensions of "agency," often the achievement of these varying dimensions requires essentially the same sets of capacities: choice, freedom, deliberative, and

---

[33] This is particularly the case where accountability is examined within discussions of global governance. See for example Keohane and Nye (2001), Newell and Bellour (2002), Keohane (2003), and the special issue of *Government and Opposition on Global Governance and Public Accountability* (Spring 2004) 39(2).

[34] More broadly, this goal is increasingly relevant in the context of a global "public" that is characterized by pluralism, fragmentation, and often extreme inequality.

[35] Giddens (1984), Rahman (1984), Rahman (1993), Held (1995), Nelson and Wright (1995), Schneider (1999), Kabeer (2000), and World Bank (2002). Sen, for example, uses the term "agency" in all these ways. He employs it to denote transformational capacity when he defines an agent as "someone who acts and brings about change" (Sen, 2001, p. 19), as choice in the context of his discussion of freedom (Drèze and Sen, 2002), and as participation in reference to political and social organizations (Sen, 2001, p. 284). He even uses it in a fourth sense, distinguishing it from living standards and well-being to denote freely chosen actions *in conflict* with the agent's welfare (Saith, 2001).

critical capacities, and the ability to translate these into action within the external institutional environment.[36]

As applied to workers in the Nicaraguan garment industry, the *welfare* dimension of empowerment can be understood primarily in terms of income and working conditions. Key indicators of the *agency* dimension of empowerment include workers' control over their movements within the workplace (such as unconstrained access to the bathrooms or to visit doctors); control over hours worked; freedom to unionize; access to information regarding entitlements and obligations; access to an effective complaints procedure; and the ability to participate in rule-making institutions that affect them, through both direct involvement in short-term decision-making and the ability to initiate and direct underlying agendas of institutional reform.

How then has the emergence of new forms of global accountability affected the capacity of workers to realize these multiple dimensions of empowerment? From a long-term, industrywide viewpoint, such campaigns have contributed positively to the welfare-related empowerment of Southern garment workers by helping to modify dominant industry norms and practices towards closer compliance with core labor standards. Significant improvements for many workers have been achieved as a result of the dramatic changes in the supply chain management policies of well-known retailers and brands that are most vulnerable to targeting by such campaigns. The changes introduced as a result of prominent campaigns against Nike, Liz Claiborne, the Gap, and Levi illustrate clearly this process.[37] The transformation of dominant practices and norms among both consumers and industry players has generated an increasing expectation that brands and retailers should accept responsibility for labor standards within their supply chains (Spar and Burns, 2000). This contributes to greater empowerment at a structural level, since it represents the first steps towards more effectively aligning distributions of responsibilities with those of regulatory capabilities. However, empowering effects at the factory level, achieved by factory-based campaigns, have been much more limited. In the Chentex case, for example, the protracted dispute achieved only nominal concessions, most of which have not been sustained.[38]

---

[36] Freire (1985), Chambers (1998), Kabeer (2000), Pimbert and Wakeford (2001), Brock and McGee (2002), and VeneKlasen and Miller (2002).

[37] Spar and Burns (2000) document the case of Nike, which is perhaps the best known of successful activist campaigns, producing dramatic changes in supply chain practices.

[38] In the end, a negotiated settlement was reached in which all legal actions were dropped and four union leaders reinstated. However, within a month they had all been forced to

The partial institutionalization of some elements of these demands in the form of codes of conduct can also make some contribution to empowerment. As mechanisms of external accountability, codes provide a direct institutional means via which evolving norms and practices can be transmitted along supply chains to global production sites. They can also be a powerful coercive mechanism through which norms and practices can be enforced (by the threat to cut off contracts in cases of persistent code violation), thereby facilitating responses to social demands that empower workers. Garment firms unanimously emphasize the importance of complying with codes if contracts with major brands are to be retained.

They have monitors that watch very closely and if you don't fulfill the standards then they take the orders away. If there are always problems then there are no orders.[39]

In the past, the firings of Chentex and the international campaign that followed have meant that now there are more visits and the codes are more severe. The firms are afraid of these, as the contracts can be cancelled if they don't comply. There are different buyers, so a couple of times a month there are inspections, and all the firms are involved in this.[40]

Evidence from factory owners, investors, and some union representatives also suggests that the imposition of these code-based regimes has led to significant improvements in some basic working conditions,[41] thereby empowering Nicaraguan workers in terms of core welfare criteria.

They did an inspection in October, and in Fortex and in Sino Nica, they put in many things – fans, comfortable seats, they hung extinguishers in the dining areas, washed the dining area, put out protective masks, put soap and toilet paper in the toilets – a whole heap of things. The Chinese owners don't use these things generally, but the brands have done inspections, and there have been many changes.[42]

However, the empowering potential of these new accountability practices is significantly limited by the fact that the countervailing power

---

resign, and there is still no CST (Sandinista) affiliated union operating in the Chentex factory.

[39] Interview by the author at Nien Hsing head office, Taipei, 10 March 2004.

[40] Interview by the author with representative of CPT ("management") union, Managua, 2 December 2003.

[41] Evidence from other countries also supports the claim that codes of conduct can lead to improvements in certain aspects of working conditions. Jenkins (2001) for example presented evidence from Vietnam, El Salvador, and Honduras showing that concrete improvements have resulted from the imposition of codes.

[42] Interview by the author with representative of CST (Sandinista) union, Managua, 13 December 2003.

they wield is no longer simply a direct counterbalance to primary sources of power, as envisaged within the binary state-centered accountability system; rather, such forms of accountability have entailed the diffusion of power between actors, and the emergence of an increasingly fragmented and multilayered distribution of power. Within this pluralistic structure, firms exercise power over workers, information flows from workers through NGOs to consumers, and consumers (together with broader social actors in the global North) may then impose sanctions upon firms.[43] Mechanisms of power, countervailing power, information transmission, and sanctioning are thus becoming more fragmented, functionally disaggregated, and diffuse. Increasingly, outcomes are determined not within centralized and privileged sites of political power, but as the product of interactions between multiple layers of actors: states, firms, consumers, and a range of non-state actors spanning multiple levels of transnational production structures. In this context, a demand to "hold powerful actors accountable *for* their actions" does not necessarily translate into an outcome in which powerholders are held accountable *to* those affected. The emergence of what is effectively a whole new category of "intermediaries" within accountability relationships creates two related problems.

First, there is an implicit conflation of those subject to power and those demanding accountability, so that power relations between those impacted by the primary source of power and those making accountability claims are often obscured, and these secondary power relations between intermediaries and workers are not themselves constrained by effective accountability mechanisms. This problem is clearly illustrated by the power dynamics that emerged during the Chentex factory campaign within the non-state networks through which transformative accountability demands were advanced. Although solidarity campaigns are nominally driven from the bottom up, campaign structure tends to reflect the structure of global production chains. Accordingly, the "transnational advocacy networks" through which many of these campaigns are conducted themselves embody asymmetric power relations in which it is often Northern participants rather than workers themselves who play the dominant decision-making roles. The most powerful sources of leverage over US brands, consumers, and government are concentrated in the hands of US members of the network, since it is they

---

[43] These new geographies of power then interact with binary structures of power and accountability that continue to operate (albeit in more limited ways) within state-centered governance systems located in each territory participating in the global production chain.

who can most easily access these sites of power, and they possess disproportionate access to financial resources and communication technology. Power is also exercised asymmetrically in the initial construction of network membership, as the disproportionate ability of Northern participants to control network membership gives them significant discretionary power to decide which local groups to include and which to exclude, leaving little scope for conflicting voices at the local level to be mediated within the processes of forming campaign goals and strategies.

Despite the significant degree of power wielded by Northern actors within these networks, such actors are generally not accountable to workers for the way this power is exercised.[44] The lack of accountability to workers whose "stories" are being deployed as weapons has meant that campaign design has often failed to give top priority to the direct interests of the workers immediately involved, which significantly reduces the potential of such campaigns to empower workers. Indeed, some anti-sweatshop campaigns have generated outcomes that have caused direct harm to significant numbers of workers. The screening on US and Nicaraguan television in 1997 of the *Hard Copy* program "exposing" sweatshop conditions in Nicaraguan garment factories was followed by the firing of workers directly involved with the program, job losses due to the cancellation of some contracts by targeted firms, and the firing of hundreds of workers under eighteen (despite the labor code allowing workers from the age of fourteen) as firms attempted to avoid the charge of using child labor.[45]

This failure to appropriately distinguish the interests and preferences of workers from those of the Northern actors dominating the campaigns creates a second, closely related problem as accountability relations between companies and their critics begin to be institutionalized within structures of external accountability such as codes of conduct. In many cases, external accountability mechanisms are constructed between inappropriate sets of actors, as firms are made accountable to Northern NGOs, consumers, and "independent" monitors rather than directly to affected workers themselves; this problem is reflected clearly in many of the discourses surrounding codes of conduct. The World Bank, for instance, explicitly uses the language of external accountability in explaining the emergence and functioning of corporate codes of conduct, but its only mention of individual workers and their families – who are those most directly affected by such codes – is under the label of

---

[44] This is a similar point to that made by Keohane (2002) when he refers to a disconnect between legitimacy and accountability.

[45] See www.nicanet.org/115laborpanel.html.

"organized labor," despite the majority of global garment workers not being organized in any way:

External stakeholders, including students, human rights organizations, organized labor, religious institutions, consumer advocates, universities, representatives of local, state and federal governments around the world, and the Secretary General of the UN have demanded greater transparency and accountability by corporate institutions with respect to business decisions that have a social and environmental impact ... corporate leaders have recognised that the success of their brands is tied to whether their business is conducted in a manner acceptable to those affected by it. (World Bank, 2003, p. 1)

Even this reference is buried in a long list of external stakeholders from the global North, the majority of whom are those participating in accountability relations through their role in information transmission and sanctioning, rather than as those affected by corporate decisions. The disappearance from the picture of those who are supposedly the ultimate "principals" of these new structures of "external" accountability has significantly undermined the effectiveness with which such codes have empowered Southern workers. This appears to be due primarily to the multiple ways in which the exclusion of workers from these structures has weakened code enforcement. Significant barriers to the participation of workers and their organizations in monitoring code enforcement include the absence of adequate formal consultation processes within the inspection process, the absence of complaints procedures, a failure to effectively inform workers about code content,[46] and the extreme lack of transparency regarding monitoring procedures and findings.[47] In part as a result of such weaknesses, Nicaraguan workers speaking with Prieto and Bendell (2002, p. 7) claimed that the codes "are for decoration, as the workers don't see them being implemented." The lack of accountability to workers within the processes through which codes are initially formulated further undermines their empowering potential, as the formation of codes is driven primarily by a perceived need to be accountable to consumers. This has resulted in codes being driven by top-down consumer-focused agendas, thus producing a disproportionate emphasis on issues – such as underage labor – that have a high profile among Western consumers and are therefore considered by firms to be the most potentially damaging (Jenkins,

[46] Source: author's discussion with Nicaraguan factory workers at MEC workshop, 23 November 2003.
[47] Target, for example, claims that "The procedures used by our Corporate Compliance area are considered proprietary," personal communication, Target Guest Relations, 28 November 2003. It is also very rare for the content of monitoring reports to be revealed either to workers or to the wider public.

2001). This focus often comes at the expense of issues identified by workers themselves as higher priorities.[48]

Conclusions: new forms of accountability and the empowerment of Southern workers – from transformative to plurilateral accountability

The emergence within transnational supply chains of these new agendas of public accountability has already produced substantial changes within targeted transnational production chains. The impact of these changes thus far suggests that they have significant potential to further advance the empowerment of Southern workers within the governance structures of the global economy. However, these agendas remain limited by the persistence of *binary* discourses of accountability, which are no longer appropriate within an environment increasingly characterized by pluralistic structures of power. As described above, a binary view of accountability results in the implicit conflation of those actors who are subject to power with those who are demanding accountability, which significantly constrains the capacity of existing accountability mechanisms to empower Southern workers. In order to entrench principles of empowerment at a structural level within a transformed global governance system, and thus to provide a systemic basis of countervailing power for Southern workers, there is a need for some far-reaching changes in how we conceptualize public accountability structures and their relationship to the ordering of publicly relevant power. This will entail moving from the distorted and contested structures of transformative and external accountability to a reconstructed governance system in which accountability structures can once again function to legitimize and reproduce systemic power distributions through a stable set of reconstituted principles. To enable these changes, new forms of institutional innovation will be required.

I argue that such innovations should be based on a central principle of "plurilateral" accountability: that is, pluralistic structures of accountability that mirror and equilibrate the pluralistic distributions of power within the prevailing governance system.[49] Concepts of "plurilateralism"

---

[48] Workers interviewed by Prieto and Bendell (2002, p. 8) reported a number of their priorities to differ from those appearing in official corporate codes. Commonly mentioned concerns included health and safety issues related to pregnancy, transport home from work, and restrictions on overtime which some workers considered inappropriate given the insufficiency of their standard wages.

[49] The case for the development of plurilateral mechanisms of accountability rests primarily upon *institutional* arguments, which must be separated from the normative concerns I raised above in relation to concepts of external accountability. The

and "hybridity" are commonly deployed in the analysis of structures of global governance (Cerny, 1993; Vayrynen, 2003), but little attention has been given to how we might construct parallel pluralistic structures within our discourses and institutions of accountability. To this end, I suggest that it is helpful to imagine a plurilateral system of governance and accountability that is structured according to the central principle of "complex reciprocity." Instead of dichotomizing governors and the governed (or agents and principals), and simply holding the former accountable to the latter, such a system would be characterized by a layered, horizontal structure in which each category of actors, performing disaggregated functions and exercising differentiated forms of power, is held accountable to each other, supporting the emergence of a system-wide equilibration of power and responsibility.

The idea of a plurilateral accountability structure implies a radical change in how we conceptualize accountability – more so than would occur simply by moving from a single binary accountability relationship between a state and a public to a seriality of vertical and binary relationships in which each agent is linked to an expanding number of external principals. Although the idea of "complex reciprocity" may appear largely consistent with many features of an accountability structure comprised of serial binary relations, it has been demonstrated above that the ongoing dominance of such binary discourses appears to be supporting significant distortions within emerging institutions of external accountability. These distortions are undermining the capacity of these institutions to empower Southern workers, which means that there is a practical as well as a theoretical imperative to consider more seriously how we might progress from the binary structures of "external" accountability towards the construction of a balanced, plurilateral system of public governance and accountability.

It is beyond the scope of this chapter to speculate in depth about specific institutions via which the central principle of plurilateral accountability could be materially entrenched. However, building from the central principle of re-articulating power and responsibility by means of a systemic structure of complex reciprocity, it is possible to suggest several key features that such an accountability system would need to embody, in order to empower Southern workers most effectively. Considering each major category of systemic actor in turn, *firms* should be

development of an effective and legitimate system of plurilateral accountability would require not only the development of workable institutional mechanisms, but also the specification of an agreed set of normative principles to define the legitimate relationship between power and responsibility.

held accountable through structures of information transmission that are linked directly to workers, and that are backed up by sanctions imposed at overlapping levels by consuming and producing states, by NGOs, and by consumers.[50] At the same time, *states* need to be held accountable not only to NGOs, workers, firms, and consumers within their own territory, but also to workers and other stakeholders located outside these physical boundaries. *Non-state actors* within the transnational networks that promote agendas of transformative accountability must themselves become more accountable to the workers whose interests they claim to represent, through the construction of more durable and accountable network structures and more effective engagement with the range of competing views at the local level during the process of constructing network membership.

Currently, the global garment industry remains characterized by governance structures in which key decisions affecting Southern workers are controlled by Northern brands and retailers, and by the governments and populations of the countries in which these powerful Northern actors are located. The transformative accountability agendas that are being pursued by transnational networks of non-state actors have achieved some initial progress towards placing countervailing power in the hands of Southern workers and their supporters, and external accountability initiatives have partially institutionalized the core principles of this transformative agenda. However, a new agenda of "plurilateral accountability" must now be developed and implemented to enable core principles of empowerment to be more effectively embedded within the institutional system that governs global production, in which Southern workers play such a fundamental role.

References

Braithwaite, J. and P. Drahos (2000) *Global Business Regulation.* Cambridge University Press.

Brock, K. and R. McGee (2002) *Knowing Poverty: Critical Reflections on Participatory Research and Policy.* London: Earthscan.

CENIDH (2003) *Maquila en Nicaragua ... ¿Una esperanza? Conflictividad laboral en la maquila: un análisis desde la práctica de los derechos humanos.* Managua: Centro Nicaragüense de Derechos Humanos.

---

[50] Different actors are able to impose sanctions of different kinds. Sanctions imposed by consumers and NGOs are able to distinguish more effectively between firms, thus supporting efforts of industry leaders to expand the boundaries of socially responsible best-practice, while state sanctions based on the uniform imposition of minimum standards are particularly important for regulating the conduct of "laggards." Overlapping layers of sanctions can thus be complementary, providing greater flexibility and strength to the accountability system as a whole.

Cerny, P. G. (1993) "Plurilateralism: Structural Differentiation and Functional Conflict in the Post Cold War Order," *Millennium: Journal of International Studies* 22(1), 27–51.

Chambers, R. (1998) "Paradigm Shifts and the Practice of Participatory Research and Development," in I. Guijt and M. K. Shah (eds.) *The Myth of Community: Gender Issues in Participatory Development*. London: Intermediate Technology Publications.

Cutler, A. C. (2002) "Private International Regimes and Interfirm Cooperation," in R. B. Hall and T. J. Biersteker (eds.) *The Emergence of Private Authority in Global Governance*. Cambridge University Press.

Detomasi, D. (2002) "International Institutions and the Case for Corporate Governance: Toward a Distributive Governance Framework?," *Global Governance* 8(4), 421–42.

Drèze, J. and A. K. Sen (2002) *India: Development and Participation*. Oxford University Press.

Elliott, K. A. and R. B. Freeman (2000) "White Hats or Don Quixotes? Human Rights Vigilantes in the Global Economy," NBER Conference on Emerging Labor Market Institutions. At http://papers.nber.org/papers/W8102.

Freire, P. (1985) *Pedagogy of the Oppressed*. Harmondsworth: Penguin.

Gereffi, G. (1999) "A Commodity Chains Framework for Analyzing Global Industries." Available at www.ids.ac.uk/ids/global/valchn.html.

Giddens, A. (1984) *The Constitution of Society: Outline of the Theory of Structuration*. Cambridge: Polity.

Goetz, A. M. and R. Jenkins (2002) "Voice, Accountability and Human Development: The Emergence of a New Agenda," Background paper for the Human Development Report 2002 ("Voice and Accountability") (Paper prepared for the meeting of the UNDP HDR Advisory Panel, 5–7 November 2001).

Harrison, A. and J. Scorse (2003) "The Impact of Globalisation on Compliance with Labor Standards: A Plant-level Study," Paper presented at Brookings Trade Forum.

Haufler, V. (2001) *A Public Role for the Private Sector: Industry Self-Regulation in a Global Economy*. Washington, DC: Carnegie Endowment for International Peace.

Held, D. (2004) "Democratic Accountability and Political Effectiveness from a Cosmopolitan Perspective," *Government and Opposition* 39(2), 364–91.

Held, D. (2000) "Regulating Globalization? The Reinvention of Politics," *International Sociology* 15(2), 394–408.

Held, D. (1995) *Democracy and the Global Order: From the Modern State to Cosmopolitan Governance*. Cambridge: Polity.

Jenkins, R. O. (2001) *Corporate Codes of Conduct: Self-regulation in a Global Economy*. Geneva: UNSRID.

Kabeer, N. (2000) *Discussing Women's Empowerment: Theory and Practice*. Stockholm: Swedish International Development Cooperation Agency.

Keohane, R. O. (2003) "Global Governance and Democratic Accountability," in D. Held and M. Koenig-Archibugi (eds.) *Taming Globalization: Frontiers of Governance*. Cambridge: Polity.

Keohane, R. O. (2002) "Global Governance and Democratic Accountability." Available at www.poli.duke.edu/people/Faculty/docs/millpaper.pdf.

Keohane, R. O. and J. S. Nye (2001) "Democracy, Accountability and Global Governance," available at www.ksg.harvard.edu/prg/nye/ggajune.pdf.

Koenig-Archibugi, M. (2004) "Transnational Corporations and Public Accountability," *Government and Opposition* 39(2), 234–59.

Lipschutz, R. D. and C. Fogel (2002) "Regulation for the Rest of Us? Global Civil Society and the Privatisation of Transnational Regulation," in R. B. Hall and T. J. Biersteker (eds.) *The Emergence of Private Authority in Global Governance.* Cambridge University Press.

Macdonald, K. (2004) "Emerging institutions of Non-state Governance within Transnational Supply Chains: A Global Agenda for Empowering Southern Workers?" American Political Science Association, Chicago, 2–5 September.

Méndez, J. B. and R. Koepke (2001) *Mujeres y Maquila. Respuesta a la globalización: organización de mujeres centroamericanas en medio de la competencia y la cooperación transnacional en la industria maquilera.* San Salvador: Fundación Heinrich Böll.

Nee, G. (2002) "The Political-Economic Analysis of the Nien Hsing/Chentex Campaign," in Y. C. Chen and M. Wong (eds.) *New Bondage and Old Resistance: Realities and Challenges of the Labour Movement in Taiwan.* Hong Kong: Hong Kong Christian Industrial Committee.

Nelson, N. and S. Wright (1995) "Participation and Power," in N. Nelson and S. Wright (eds.) *Power and Participatory Development: Theory and Practice.* London: Intermediate Technology Publications.

Newell, P. and S. Bellour (2002) "Mapping Accountability: Origins, Contexts and Implications for Development," IDS Working Paper 168. Sussex: Institute of Development Studies.

Pimbert, M. and T. Wakeford (2001) "Overview – Deliberative Democracy and Citizen Empowerment," in M. Pimbert and T. Wakeford (eds.) *Deliberative Democracy and Citizen Empowerment, PLA Notes* 40. London: International Institute for Environment and Development.

Prieto, M. and J. Bendell (2002) *If you Want to Help us then Start Listening to us! From Factories and Plantations in Central America, Women Speak out about Corporate Responsibility.* Bristol: New Academy of Business.

Rahman, M. A. (1993) *People's Self-development: Perspectives on Participatory Action Research: A Journey through Experience.* London: Zed Books.

Rahman, M. A. (ed.) (1984) *Grass-roots Participation and Self-reliance: Experiences in South and South East Asia.* New Delhi: Oxford and IBH in collaboration with Society for Participatory Research in Asia.

Rosenau, J. N. (2000) "Governance in a Globalizing World," in D. Held and A. G. McGrew (eds.) *The Global Transformations Reader: An Introduction to the Globalization Debate.* Cambridge: Polity.

Rosenau, J. N. (1992) "Governance, Order and Change in World Politics," in J. N. Rosenau and E. O. Czempiel (eds.) *Governance without Government: Order and Change in World Politics.* Cambridge University Press.

Ruggie, J. G. (2001) "global_governance.net: The Global Compact as Learning Network," *Global Governance* 7, 371–8.

Saith, R. (2001) "Capabilities: The Concept and its Operationalisation," QEH Working Paper Series (No. 66).

Schneider, H. (1999) "Participatory Governance for Poverty Reduction," *Journal of International Development* 11, 521–34.

Scholte, J. A. (2002) "Civil Society and Democracy in Global Governance," *Global Governance* 8, 281–304.

Sen, A. K. (2001) *Development as Freedom.* Oxford University Press.

Smouts, M.-C. (1998) "The Proper Use of Governance in International Relations," *International Social Science Journal* 50(155), 81–9.

Spar, D. and J. Borns (2000) *Hitting the Wall: Nike and International Labor Practices.* Buston: Harvard Business School.

Stoker, G. (1998) "Governance as Theory: Five Propositions," *International Social Science Journal* 50(155), 17–28.

Strange, S. (2000) "The Declining Authority of States," in D. Held and A. G. McGrew (eds.) *The Global Transformations Reader: An Introduction to the Globalization Debate.* Cambridge: Polity.

Tsogas, G. (2001) *Labor Regulation in a Global Economy.* New York: M. E. Sharpe.

Vayrynen, R. (2003) "Political Power, Accountability and Global Governance," Paper prepared for the Joint Sessions of the European Consortium for Political Research, Edinburgh.

VeneKlasen, L. and V. Miller (2002) *A New Weave of Power, People and Politics: The Action Guide for Advocacy and Citizen Participation.* Oklahoma City: World Neighbors.

Woods, N. (2002) "Accountability in Global Governance," Background paper for the Human Development Report 2002 (Occasional Paper 2002/21).

Woods, N. (2000) "Accountability, Governance and Reform in the International Financial Institutions," available at www.g24.org/woods.pdf.

World Bank (2003) *Company Codes of Conduct and International Standards: An Analytical Comparison.* Washington, DC: World Bank.

World Bank (2002) *Empowerment and Poverty Reduction: A Sourcebook.* Washington, DC: World Bank.

13 Tripartite multilateralism: why corporate social responsibility is not accountability

Edward Weisband

Multilateralism and global accountabilities

Multilateral institutions and regimes operate in a world politically dominated by sovereign nation-states. On the other hand, transnational capital, multinational business enterprises, and international markets generate diverse effects that intrude on national societies in a wide variety of ways, from unprecedented wealth to unconscionable poverty, from growth and prosperity to atrophy and marginalization. Together, these and similar anomalies produced across the global fault-lines of wealth and power, have stimulated renewed emphasis on global accountabilities as a means of collective action to counter a broad array of problems, from political violence and economic injustice to social disintegration and environmental degradation. As we have seen throughout this volume, global accountabilities provide relief but no panacea. They carry costs and they create their own tensions and contradictions, even as they supply the elements necessary for effective governance.

Such is the case when one begins to examine the relationship between global accountabilities and multilateralism, in particular the role and effectiveness of multilateral institutions and regimes, intergovernmental organizations (IGOs), transnational business enterprises, and civil society organizations (CSOs) or nongovernmental organizations (NGOs) that function across borders. Multilateralism might well be perceived as an indispensable factor in managing global affairs and in promoting global accountabilities. Instead, multilateral institution-building, particularly the development of reporting and monitoring procedures and of regulatory mechanisms on behalf of institutional accountability, provokes skepticism and, in many instances, outright hostility. To some, it reeks of the specters of a global bureaucracy and thus the trappings of a panopticon society anticipated by an array of authors, from Kafka and Orwell to Foucault. Alternatively, critical perspectives derived from the doctrines of sovereign autonomy and state-centric realism cast doubts with respect to the efficacy of the United Nations, its specialized agencies, and thus over the capacity of all international bureaucracies involved in policy issues such as world finance and trade, nuclear proliferation, intellectual property, environmental enhancement, protection of human rights, promotion of labor standards, pursuit of safe and sound immigration policies and practices, etc., to achieve accountability without incurring the cost of technocratic intrusion on political decision-making.

When viewed through the limited perspectives of states, markets or, even, firms, multilateral forms of governance and accountability often appear hardly worth the transaction costs they generate. The neoliberalism of the Reagan–Thatcher era that places faith in free-flowing competitive or heteronomous markets, and state-centric realism that stresses state power and the international order that follows from its exercise, both tend to denigrate multilateral institutions in at least two ways: first, in terms of their internal accountability, that is, in terms of their capacity to monitor and to reform themselves; and, second, in terms of their ability to promote internationally acceptable standards and to promote normative expectations with them. In short, multilateral institutions and organizations, especially in the public sector, are often alleged to be anti-democratic, self-aggrandizing, and more expensive than they are worth.

In a political climate shaped by such assumptions, multilateral solutions appear to become the problem. At the point when the gains of intensified global accountabilities loom on the horizon as a kind of global public goods, multilateralism, the very approach that would generate such goods, suffers from widespread indifference and political disdain. This triggers the initial assumption grounding the arguments of this chapter: multilateralist forms of accountability are beset by public skepticism and massive disenchantment, precisely at a time when they are needed the most. The question becomes, then, how to reverse this? How might multilateralist approaches to global accountabilities contribute to the reciprocated fulfillments of each other? If multilateral institutions and regimes are to generate wide public acceptance and political support, they must provide evidence of their *internal accountability*. This can only be sustained through administrative mechanisms that enhance openness, accessibility, transparency, independent review, and, ultimately, institutional learning and bureaucratic reform.

Such represents one path to legitimacy. But this avenue runs into the problem provoked by the need for measurable parameters across sovereign and institutional boundaries. The dynamics of learning and openness, if effective, should facilitate multilateral forms of *external accountability.* These should work to promote practices on the part of constituent actors, including sovereign states, designed to encourage adherence to international or global normative expectations, obligations, rules, and principles, particularly those benchmarked to accountability standards. Optimally, internal and external modes of accountability drive each other in tandem, thus empowering the virtuous cycles that weld multilateralist designs to global accountability frameworks and vice versa. But reality does not always conform to such optimal ideals.

The basic issue for students of multilateralism and global account-abilities is, therefore, one of how to align internal learning with external standards and benchmarking. I suggest that the multilateral frameworks functioning in areas of global accountability must operate recursively. They should foster feedback linkages between sets of outcomes bench-marked to externalized standards, on the one hand, but tied to internal processes of organizational learning, on the other. The formula is easy to outline in theory, but difficult to implement in practice. Multilateral institutions should learn how to promote and advance global account-abilities through experience. And these experiences and the lessons learned from them should enable them to function internally in ever more effective ways. Greater external impacts, improved internal operations, should be the recursive dynamics of multilateral organizations as they balance the tensions between learning and benchmarking. Herein lies the distinction between corporate social responsibility and corporate global accountability. The former is content to conceive and implement internal methodologies for learning alone. The latter implies not only processes of learning but feedback loops that indicate the presence of externalized standards of measurement and evaluation. Why is so much of what goes by the way of corporate social responsibility not global corporate accountability? The answer is the absence of external benchmarks and their recursive influence on internal dynamics of learning.

The dynamics of recursivity set the stage for examining corporate social responsibility against the need to define corporate global accountability in terms that imply agential willingness to comply with recognized and recognizable standards. To be sure, these can serve as chilling effects that impede internal processes of learning. The result is that a vicious cycle replaces the virtuous cycle born of recursivity: in such instances, bench-marks and measurable standards inhibit internal processes of organiza-tional learning; simultaneously, internal learning is severed from the realities of external organizational effects and regime influences. Arguably, therefore, institutional and organizational forms of learning are values that must be synergistically realized – but relative to externalized practices and norms. In this sense, the promotion of standards is ultimately the true test of learning. And learning ultimately results in the successful promotion of normative standards and expectations. Otherwise, global accountabilities within the context of multilateral frameworks and structures as well as corporate social responsibility could not become deepened.

Tripartite channels and "intermestic" networks in global accountabilities

What, then, are the primary features of global accountabilities regimes, structures, and processes, particularly those that might serve to strengthen the legitimacy of multilateralism in an era of widespread criticism and doubt? No single answer or approach responds to every contingency. But the point of this chapter is to present "a best practice argument" in favor of multilateral venues that establish and maintain *tripartite* representative interactions among governments, businesses, and CSOs. A logical extension of this argument is that those forms of global accountabilities that are most likely to prove valuable in the long term are those that ensure the active engagement of tripartite stakeholders from across the spectrum of public and private agencies. I call such modalities, *tripartite multilateralism*. And I argue that this approach is strategically important to the future advance of global accountabilities. In so doing, I seek to contrast the character of a global *accountabilities* regime, properly so-called, from that of a corporate *social responsibility* regime. This contrast is based precisely on the degree of presence or absence of this crucial dynamic between externalized benchmarks recursively linked to internal dialogues on which learning depends through feedback mechanisms.

In previous chapters, several authors underscored the importance of bringing government and CSO representatives together in efforts to create a new logic of participation (see especially the contributions in Part I). Here I would emphasize the role of tripartite representative structures organized around the profit and rent-seeking pursuits of transnational business enterprises as well as the activities of governments and CSOs. My argument simply broadens the theoretical scope adumbrated by the notion of domestic stakeholder partnerships. These have attracted considerable academic interest as vehicles for determining locally grounded environmental policies and practices. Stakeholder partnerships, in conceptual terms, operate from the "bottom up," as well as from the "top down." They first facilitate dialogue (bottom-up) among interested stakeholders in the design of programmatic solutions; second, they serve to galvanize the efforts of participants (top-down) to become directly involved in the process of implementing the very policies recommended as a result of deliberations among stakeholders.

Charles Lindblom (1977) once observed that what counts in the liberal soul of interest-group pluralism is policy-making that emphasizes "the trip rather than the arrival." So too is this the case with stakeholder partnerships. In theory, at least, they bring together self-regarding agents that entertain diverse personal or professional backgrounds, different institutional identities, and, often, conflicting policy interests. The purpose is to forge acceptable notions of "the common good" on the basis of "common ground" through their deliberative discourse including those that entail value and policy disagreements. Environmentalists may want strict air regulation; employers may argue that such a regulatory environment is counterproductive to growth and jobs. Workers and their representatives may find themselves caught in between. But the point of stakeholder partnerships is to set in motion a deliberative process, one that battles out local policy solutions, communal standards, and collective regulations. The key is to balance such interests and values in ways reflective of the overall interests of the community, as perceived and interpreted by stakeholder representatives themselves. Programs and policies are not imposed "top-down," rather they reflect a consensus initially stemming from "bottom-up" procedures and deliberations.

The question arises: can such a locally instilled approach ever be made to inspire global-to-local forms of accountability? First, the problem of "representativity" arises: who selects whom to represent what sets of interests? Second, how are representative channels established in the name of global accountabilities? This suggests the essential role of tripartism as an approach to global accountabilities: to permit multi-lateralism to proceed in ways leading to the design of opportunities for the "deep" structuring of tripartite modes of interactions; and to allow these in turn to strengthen the legitimacy of multilateralism. The key lies in the authorization and/or empowerment of tripartite "intermestic" networks or constituencies, partially domestic, partially international. Kahler has suggested, for example, that intermestic networks cultivate "compliance constituencies": social and political networks willing to submit domestic conflicts to international and transnational tribunals for purposes of review and resolution. "Transnational dispute resolution," he states, "empowers compliance constituencies in two ways. It grants access to nonstate actors, expanding the pool of those who may attempt to obtain compliance." But it also raises the cost of infraction. "Governments that do not comply face a new calculus: in addition to the international costs of breaching a legalized commitment, they must now face the much more serious reputational and political costs of breaching legal commitments before their own citizens" (Kahler, 2000). Kahler's focus is on judicial frameworks, but compliance networks and constituencies remain relevant when extrapolated into the context of global accountability. By creating a myriad of new institutionalized entry-points, intermestic channels embolden domestic networks and constituencies to use the mechanisms of global accountabilities regimes in bottom-up as well as in top-down ways. Thus the role, and certainly the aspiration, of compliance constituencies become focused on the need not only to participate in the activities of global accountabilities but also to promote the legitimacy of tripartite multilateralism as an approach to global governance.

Multilateral public institutions, including UN specialized agencies, have a special role to play in this regard. They are in a position of being able to bring governments, transnational business enterprises, and CSOs together in international settings that encourage diverse *and divergent* constituencies across many societies to engage in discourses with respect to common concerns. To achieve this, IGOs are finding that they must assume increasingly less hermetic and thus more porous administrative forms than those traditionally modeled by the classical Weberian paradigms or conceptions of organizational boundaries. Business firms have learned the advantages of openness and concentric divisions of labor oriented to task or goal-specific forms of networking. Similarly, rigid hierarchies and centralized or vertically structured kinds of managerial control are under attack within the universe of IGOs. Thus, as part of this wave of new institutionalism, IGOs might further learn how to incorporate tripartite discursive frameworks into their operations in order to become more effective at gleaning the advantages of stakeholder participation. Such openness to external networks would augment the legitimacy of public multilateral institutions, as previously stated, by sustaining the virtuous cycles that reciprocally promote tripartite multilateralism, legitimacy, and internal learning as well as externalized forms of accountability.

Recent controversy concerning globalization has tended to revolve around the primacy of state power relative to transnational capital and business enterprise. An additional issue concerns the putative impacts of liberalized markets and of intensified forms of international civil society on international politics. But casting the arguments in this way leads to a zero-sum kind of rationalization. The dynamics of global governance are not manifestations of political, economic, and social power organized as separate integers. The question is not the demise of the state relative to capital. From the perspectives of global governance, the question presented by the interface between states and firms is how to embed the interactions among them, as well as the structures of power and wealth that each represents, in normative frameworks that regulate practices, especially within international markets.

In this, global accountabilities frameworks, structured along tripartite lines to include CSO intermestic representatives, might play a crucial role in the "taming" of states and firms. How? Tripartite multilateralism operates in ways that help bind states within a networked web of accountability relationships so that Grotian kinds of normative obligations can work to attenuate Hobbsian realist excesses in the exercise of power. Assayed against the theorized perspectives of realism and neo-realism, intermestic tripartism might well cut into the proverbial "billiard ball" of unitary state action and effectively erode the putative "anarchy" of international relations. Similarly, tripartism facilitates the evolution of liberal institutionalism. It fosters "intermestic" activities up the ladder of subsidiarity from local to global. Seen from the vantage points of functionalism and neo-functionalism, it could well promote recognition by self-regarding agents of the essential role played by multilateral forms of collaboration in the pursuit of self-interests, whether defined in security or rent-seeking terms. From the perspectives of social constructionism, finally, tripartite multilateralism might permit a recasting of the social identities of agents through a re-envisioning of the discursive relationships in which they see themselves embedded.

One should enter a disclaimer here. This is not to argue that tripartite multilateralism is some version of a *deus ex machina* that leads inexorably to the success of global accountabilities. On the contrary, its methods and mechanisms are always fragile and subject to enormous risks of failure, especially when it comes up against the power of entrenched interests, as it inevitably must. Nonetheless, tripartite multilateralism reconstitutes the political universe in which states, firms, and CSOs pursue their visions of preferred reality. Its dynamics solidify "intermestic" linkages among deliberative or discursive stakeholder partnerships and networks of global accountability. Tripartite intermestic networks legitimated through feedback between internal learning and external forms of accountability are the essential features of global accountability regimes and frameworks oriented to multilateralism in an era of partial globalization, imperfect liberalization, and resistant nationalism.

Models of global accountabilities and the template of the ILO

Where do we discover concrete examples of how and in what ways tripartite multilateralism might become implemented and thus institutionalized for purposes of global accountabilities? The basic model has historically been derived from that institutionalized by the International Labour Organization (ILO), headquartered in Geneva, Switzerland. The ILO is governed through a tripartite plenary system of representation that brings together delegations selected by governments, employers', and workers' organizations. The ILO, with its tripartite governance structures, and with its "top-down, bottom-up" approach to the formulation, ratification, and monitoring of substantive labor standards, provides a concrete case study directly relevant to an analysis of how tripartite multilateralism has worked in the past, how it operates today and how it might function in the future. To recount the rudimentary elements of ILO tripartism and to demonstrate how it functions as a global accountability regime, permit one to examine in a systematic and comparative fashion seven major global accountabilities frameworks operating in international society today. ILO tripartite multilateralism is especially relevant since these global accountabilities regimes historically reflect in isomorphic fashion the administrative template originally provided by the ILO itself. There are those who would see irony in this. The ILO is often portrayed as an example of a failed multilateralism; and yet, its accountability structures, specifically its supervisory monitoring procedures with respect to international labor standards, represent the basis for several of the major global accountability frameworks.

This is demonstrated by a brief examination of "justiciability," the capacity to sanction failures to comply with standards through legal or judicial means, in the context of the ILO "special complaints" regime. This ILO "special complaints" regime takes tripartite multilateralism and institutionalizes it around the trappings of law, litigation, courts, and judicial decision-making, hence the term, "justiciability." Furthermore, the special complaints procedures of the ILO require intermestic networking, that is, bottom-up as well as top-down deliberations and decision-making. The ILO special complaints regime thus provides an example of a global accountability framework concentrating on "special complaints" armed with the features of a court of law or judiciary. Swepston, for example, inquires about the general features of global accountability mechanisms based on ILO forms of tripartism and justiciability.[1] He suggests the following:

- ILO standards are drafted by tripartite actors comprised of employers', workers', and government representatives;
- multilateral standards are translated directly and incorporated into national law in ways readily evoked in courts;

---

[1] At the time of writing, Lee Swepston served as Chief, Equality and Human Rights Coordination Branch, International Labour Office.

- clear procedural rules with respect to freedom of association labor standards and allegations of violations;
- precise conclusions or findings, as underlying standards allow;
- reasonably rapid;
- domestic findings influence future regime operations and application of standards at multilateral levels (Swepston, 2000).

This outline punctuates the "top-down, bottom-up" intermestic approach at the core of any administrative form of tripartite multilateralism. Swepston stresses the role of judicial proceedings, given the jurisprudential character of ILO international labor standards. Other global account-abilities frameworks and regimes, however, may not possess the full complement of such judicial or legalized procedures. Rarely, if ever, do global accountability regimes, including those examined in this chapter, convey the full weight of formal or positive international law. Instead, global accountability frameworks in today's climate of international rela-tions tend to seek "to encourage" or "promote" rather than "to enforce compliance." Thus they function more as "producers of guidelines" rather than as the purveyors of legally sanctioned obligations. That said, the ILO special complaints regime appears to have generated similarities among the major global accountability regimes examined below. Thus, the discussion below focuses on the ILO special complaints regime. This regime monitors what is known in labor law as freedom of association rights and principles. It does so in ways that are intermestically networked. Thus the ILO special complaints structure is amenable not only to bottom-up, top-down com-munications and networking but also, as we shall now see, to recursive forms of feedback between learning and benchmarks.

By the year 2002, the ILO had adopted 184 labor Conventions and 195 Recommendations. These cover the broad range of international legal issues concerning labor and work, from employment, environment, health and safety to social security, labor administration, and protection of "special groups," such as indigenous and tribal peoples to workers in specific sectors. At the base of this normative jurisprudence rests a set of core ILO international labor standards. These establish fundamental freedoms and human rights within the realm of international labor law in the form of eight ILO Conventions divided into four subcategories of worker and trade union rights. The nucleus of core international standards is identified in two freedom of association Conventions. Throughout its history, the ILO has subscribed to freedom of association principles as the very basis for its existence: in the Preamble to its Constitution; in its 1944 Declaration of Philadelphia, a reaffirmation of principles concluded near the end of World War II; and most recently, by the ILO Declaration of

1998 on Fundamental Principles and Rights at Work. Featured in Article 23 (4) of the Universal Declaration of Human Rights (UDHR), the principles of freedom of association are reiterated in Article 22 of the International Covenant on Civil and Political Rights (ICCPR), as well as in Article 8 of the International Covenant on Economic, Social and Cultural Rights (ICESCR) (see ILO, 2000).

Freedom of association principles work to guarantee the promotion of democratic institutions along the lines of social and economic justice. They attempt to promote linkages among civil and political rights and the rights of workers to become organized, to represent themselves and their interests, and to undertake collective action, particularly within collective bargaining or industrial relations systems. The expression of freedom of association rights requires that the workplace serve as a site for democratic practices and demands the availability of laws and mechanisms that permit the participation of workers and their representatives in workplace decision-making. Admittedly, trade unionism and corporatist forms of collective bargaining appear less and less attractive to more and more workers in advanced or post-industrial economies recast by service sector activities or by entrepreneurial structures subjected to the decentralizing, sometimes destabilizing, influences of information technology and globalization. Nonetheless, freedom of association principles, practices, and procedures remain essential for many who work under economic or social conditions of poverty, injustice, or exploitation as well as for those in certain industrial sectors or in the public sector of advanced economies.

ILO member states continue to ratify freedom of association Conventions in overwhelming numbers. ILO Conventions Nos. 87 and 98, the basic pillars of freedom of association rights, are among the most widely ratified. As of the year 2000, the two freedom of association Conventions had been ratified respectively by 127 and by 145 of 174 ILO member states. The Freedom of Association and Protection of the Right to Organize, 1948 (No. 87) Convention recognizes the right, "freely exercised," of workers and employers, "without distinction" to form and to join organizations of their own choosing in order "to further and defend their interests." Subsequent provisions underscore the right of worker associations "to draw up their own constitutions and rules" and, "to organize their administration and activities and to formulate their programs." In particular, worker associations retain the capacity to acquire "legal personality" in unrestricted ways. The Right to Organize and Collective Bargaining, 1949 (No. 98) Convention in upholding the rights to free collective bargaining, additionally establishes the validity of complaints and claims arising from anti-union discrimination or prejudicial acts against individuals as a result of their trade union affiliation. This sets the stage for the activities of the ILO special complaints regime embodied in the form of the ILO Committee on Freedom of Association (CFA) (ILO, 2004).

As suggested earlier, the ILO tripartite system of representation confers equal voting privileges on delegations representing workers' associations and employers' associations as well as on those representing governments. This tripartite representative structure shapes the political character of the ILO. In particular, it fosters the emergence of principles of freedom of association as the normative foundation for institutional values. Since the 1950s, the CFA has functioned as a judicial tribunal empowered with the authority to determine cases and complaints brought before it by means of the special complaints procedure that is both intermestic and tripartite in character. The CFA possesses an array of judicialized prerogatives appropriate to a court of law. It is armed, for example, with the mandate to review complaints involving alleged ILO member state violations; with the capacity to evaluate the facts relevant to each complaint; and with the power to define jurisprudential implications through legal inferences contained in reports officially promulgated as case law. Overall the responsibility of the CFA is "to consider" whether or not "cases are worthy of examination by the Governing Body." CFA legal findings revolve around a basic issue: whether or not the complaints forwarded to it deserve, in the lexicon of the CFA, "further examination." Complaints are assessed in terms of the form in which they are conveyed, as well as in terms of their substance, particularly the extent to which complaints appear to be appropriate given the labor issues involved. But each is initially reviewed to determine whether it will be considered for further examination according to receivability thresholds designed to ensure that bottom-up complaints are valid and deserving of CFA examination top-down.[2] The intermestic character of the CFA as an accountability regime is demonstrated by its bottom-up receivability procedures that set in motion its subsequent top-down decision-making process.

CFA complaint procedures entail precise methods for the filing of complaint allegations and for the presentation of supporting forensic documentation. Receivability criteria emphasize "the status of complainant organizations, the form in which the complaints are communicated, and whether or not particular complaints have been previously submitted to the CFA." Receivable allegations, for example, must come from "a national organization directly interested in the matter, by international

---

[2] For a comprehensive outline of ILO Committee on Freedom of Association standards and procedures, see: Tajgmen and Curtis (2000); ILO (1996); and ILO (2005).

organizations of employers or workers having consultative status with the ILO, or other international organizations of employers or workers where the allegations relate to matters directly affecting their affiliated organizations." In recent years, the CFA has acted to recognize fledgling organizations by occasionally classifying certain complaints as receivable even though they may originate from an organization that has not "deposited its by-laws, as may be required by national laws," or from those without official recognition in instances "when it is clear" that the organization in question has at least a de facto existence. This too has helped to expand bottom-up channels. In addition, CFA procedures require that complaints be written, signed, and supported by evidence of specific infringements of workers' or trade union freedom of association rights. Finally, complaints repeatedly submitted, especially in instances where the CFA has communicated final recommendations to the Governing Body, are deemed irreceivable except when "new evidence was adduced and brought to its notice" (ILO, 1996).

CFA rules of evidence require that documentation be provided concerning how and under what auspices complaints were first communicated from first-party complainants; how second party or plaintiff governments initially replied to the allegations contained in complaints; whether or not steps have been taken to remedy the situation outlined in the original complaint, etc. CFA published reports outline the allegations contained in complaints and the replies that the CFA has (or has not) received from the various parties involved. Episodes of repeated failure on the part of second-party member states to supply the CFA with required documentation are considered serious infractions. CFA guidelines do not mince words on this account. "If the procedure protects governments against unreasonable accusations, governments on their side should recognize the importance for their own reputation of formulating, so as to allow objective examination, detailed replies to the allegations brought against them." The CFA is armed with a capacity to identify and isolate a member state found to be in serious dereliction of its obligations. The CFA thus reserves the right to "deplore" instances of continued failures by defendant governments to supply requested information in official CFA reports. Myanmar has recently been the subject of such CFA opprobrium.

From corporate social responsibility to global accountability frameworks: feedback and recursivity

I now proceed to examine the following major seven regimes that implement – in the name of corporate social responsibility – global accountabilities standards and procedures against the background established by my outline of the procedural framework of the ILO Committee on Freedom of Association. The thrust of this comparative analysis is that the frameworks that have recently arisen to promote accountability in the form of corporate social responsibility do not satisfy the requirements of global accountabilities in terms of recursivity in the way that the CFA does. Only three of them may be considered to have even the basic dimensions of reciprocated dynamics between external benchmarks and learning. As such, they fail to meet the accountability standards associated with the CFA.

In a sense, global accountability frameworks operating in the field of corporate social responsibility represent exercises in the production of knowledge. At their core, they represent programs in the epistemological promotion of information, its meanings, modes, and methods. The essential objective of these global accountability frameworks is to establish the normative grounds of knowledge and information. They accomplish this through the development of discrete categories of understandings regarding either common standards or benchmarks or the particularized forms of learning they advance. Typically, they do this within specific domains of economic or social activity and specialization.

Another way to frame this set of propositions is to suggest that global accountability procedures within the domain of corporate social responsibility identify and, ultimately, promulgate particular forms of discourse. Each framework, on behalf of its own brand name in the marketplace of competitive ideas, advertises and, in a certain sense, "sells" its own "epistemological products." Global accountabilities frameworks thus vie for a place within the language games of multilateralism. To the extent that any are successful, more and more networks of actors and agents adopt the taxonomies and standards that each promotes. Here, again, success has tended not to be measured in zero-sum terms where the gains to one have appeared to represent an equivalent loss for all the others. Arguably at least, all have gained through the recognition that any one of them is valid and legitimate. Global accountabilities frameworks applied in terms of corporate social responsibility differ from each other in their content or analytical focus. But contrasts in their substantive orientation are ultimately less significant than how they differ from each other in their approach to the relationship between process and results. Some emphasize externalized benchmarks and standards as a result or outcome; while others stress the importance of internalized learning as a process. They also differ on how they handle the problems of top-down, bottom-up communications. The key issue comes down to how each attempts through process and procedure to generate the positive kinds of feedback each seeks by ways of results and outcomes.

The presence or absence of feedback mechanisms, however, enables us to draw a key contrast between two kinds of regimes: global corporate accountability and corporate social responsibility. Feedback processes are rarely distant from the structures of accountability, but they hardly appear anywhere the dynamics of corporate social responsibility can be found. A set of analytical issues derive from this: how do results or outcomes alter processes and procedures; and how are processes and procedures, in turn, changed or affected by results? In analyzing physical as well as the behavioral dynamics said to involve feedback, from thermostats and turbo engines to student evaluations, from ecological sustainability to the vectors of poverty, the essential dimension of feedback is its recursivity. How are the results or outcomes of a process fed back into the process itself; and how does this feedback regulate the future process? Such dynamics of feedback require linking results and outcomes. In the case of global accountabilities, the connection between benchmarked standards and processes of learning becomes crucial. The presence of regular or routinized forms of feedback, from outcomes to process and from process to outcomes, provides, therefore, the sufficient and necessary dimension to any structure that purports to be one of global accountability.

It is thus not entirely surprising that whenever corporate citizenship is represented, the term of choice in recent years has become "corporate social responsibility" rather than "corporate social accountability." Sound corporate citizenship fulfills the promise of corporate social responsibility to the extent that it fosters dialogue among stakeholders, shareholders, and corporate executives, and to the degree that it promotes corporate learning. But corporate social responsibility, however desirable, does not require nor necessarily promote realization of corporate social accountability. More is needed. The reasons refer to feedback dynamics: how learning must be pressed into the service of standards and benchmarks; how benchmarks are measured and verified; and, finally, how the process of benchmarking and verification contribute to greater human capital within the firm and thus towards corporate forms of learning.

From this perspective, the frameworks below tend to fall into the category of corporate social responsibility frameworks or regimes. As such they do not measure up to full-scale global accountabilities frameworks. Clearly, the SA8000 framework of Social Accountability International (SAI) as well as the Global Reporting Initiative (GRI) evidence to the greatest extent the features and dimensions of a global accountabilities framework. The AA1000 system of the Institute of Social and Ethical Accountability also manifests the basic elements of a global accountabilities framework but seems to require further development between the relationships linking verified outcomes and processes of learning.

The others, including the Global Sullivan Principles, the Global Compact, the ISO 14001, and the OECD Guidelines, play an important role in the firmament of corporate social responsibility. They sponsor various methods for the promotion of corporate global citizenship and responsibility. All emphasize tripartite forms of stakeholder dialogue with elements of bottom-up, top-down communication. Thus all require some form of learning among their participants. They do not constitute global accountability regimes, however. Recursive dynamics grounded in accountability feedback remain for the most part absent. The result is that standards and benchmarking do not necessarily feed back into organizational learning. Such learning, encouraged and even registered through multilateral questionnaires, remains constrained. They are specifically delimited by the dynamics of "responsibility," that is, dynamics constituted to avoid accountability standards benchmarked to accountability frameworks that promote learning.

The listings below, designed to outline certain defining features of the following "responsibility" frameworks, are presented in order *of least to most*, that is, from regimes that *least* demonstrate global accountability to those that do so the *most*.

The Global Sullivan Principles

- The Global Sullivan Principles follow the historic pattern established initially by the Sullivan Principles on South Africa; these played a role in efforts to eliminate apartheid; the reputation of the Global Sullivan Principles reflects the personal stature of Reverend Leon Sullivan who died in 2001;
- They identify principles deemed appropriate to corporate social responsibility; they ask corporations as well as cities to sign on to them; participants are henceforth required to provide regular progress reports on the manner and extent to which the principles have been implemented; freedom of association rights are not included in the Global Sullivan Principles;
- Most of the companies involved are located in the United States, giving rise to the suspicion that this is essentially an American initiative;
- The future of the Global Sullivan Principles as an international or transnational regime in corporate social responsibility is in doubt.[3]

---

[3] For a fuller description see www.globalsullivanprinciples.org/principles.html.

The Global Compact

- Unique among global accountabilities frameworks in that it was initiated by the office of the UN Secretary-General; it provides sovereign states and their governments with multilateral mechanisms to promote corporate social responsibility with respect to three basic international policy domains: environment, labor, and human rights;
- The Global Compact represents a tripartite multilateral structure of "networks within networks comprised of governments, firms and civil society organizations";
- Corporations become signatory to it by agreeing to adhere to the Compact's nine major principles; the nine principles trace their origins to the Universal Declaration of Human Rights, the ILO Fundamental Principles and Rights at Work, and the Rio Declaration on Environment and Development;
- Member corporations must make three commitments: 1) they explicitly endorse Global Compact principles in corporate publications, including in annual reports in order to publicize the Compact's nine principles; 2) they post or file progress reports on the Global Compact website at least once a year listing concrete measures taken to fulfill the Compact's principles; they are also enjoined to provide details regarding negative experiences in order to nurture a global or regional discussion among a range of interested or involved parties regarding sound practices and how or how not to implement them; the Global Compact website may thus be represented as a resource location for information regarding best practices and thus for global, regional, or local forms of corporate learning; and 3) member corporations participate in partnership projects allied to localized attempts in sustainable development particularly in areas suffering from economic marginalization and rampant poverty;
- The Global Compact embraces the interests and values of a vast range of actors and agents; thus it suffers from a lack of epistemological precision with respect to its managerial strategies, analytical categories, and measures for assessing implementation or evaluation; established to foster "bottom-up" dialogue, it promotes the convening of conferences and meetings but often in ways criticized as mere "talking-shops";
- On the basis of experience thus far, the question arises: does the Global Compact comprise an exercise in public diplomacy rather than a framework for global accountabilities, one that grafts tripartite multilateralism onto a recursive framework tailored to the needs of the business community seriously seeking verification of standards as well as the development of human capital or learning among its personnel?;

- The potential of the Global Compact remains important; it represents an extensive exercise in tripartite multilateralism; its activities are structured around an expanding network that includes, besides government and corporate representatives, the five UN offices involved in the Global Compact, i.e., the Office of the Secretary-General, the ILO, the UN Environment Programme (UNEP), the UN Development Programme (UNDP), and the Office of the UN High Commissioner for Human Rights (OHCHR); in addition, a wide range of labor and environmental organizations participate in its activities; these include the International Confederation of Free Trade Unions (ICFTU) and the International Trade Secretariats (ITSs), peak labor organizations throughout the world, as well as business and employer organizations such as the International Chamber of Commerce (ICC) and the International Organisation of Employers (IOE), as well as the World Business Council for Sustainable Development (WBCSD).[4]

OECD Guidelines for Multinational Enterprises

- The primary objective promoted by this regime is designed to guide transnational corporate policies within the locales where they operate in ways that promote sustainability and positive social effects; OECD Guidelines thus represent a unique framework for the pursuit of corporate social responsibility in that they seek to establish the creation of "local national contact points" to permit more open dialogue between corporate and civil society representatives;
- OECD Guidelines are comprehensive in that they deal with competition, finance and investment, taxation, employment, industrial relations, environment, science and technology; since 2000, they have included core ILO standards;
- Governments are asked to promote OECD Guidelines within the private sector; since the OECD allows governments to accept and apply the Guidelines on a promotional basis alone, this framework fails to generate strategies, methods, procedures for holding specific companies accountable to international benchmarks or normative standards;
- Thus, OECD Guidelines stress sustainable development, local capacities by means of training and enhancement of human capital expansion, as well as bottom-up practices; but overemphasis on local

---

[4] See www.unglobalcompact.org; The Global Compact is a global, multi-stakeholder and multi-issue network comprised of more than forty regional and national "sub-networks"; networking is thus a key to its modus operandi.

or bottom-up practices comes at the price of top-down cross-border standards; for example, OECD-compliant employers are required to adopt labor practices less favorable or less attractive than other employers in the same country; but such employers are not obliged to introduce practices in conformity to normative standards bench-marked to international or transnational criteria; OECD Guidelines thus readily lead to a relativist approach to normative standards rather than one pegged to international or transnational criteria;

- OECD Guidelines promote consensus exclusively oriented to sub-national, localized, and thus bottom-up forms of learning without top-down forms of measurement or evaluation, and they proceed in the absence of explicit cross-border or international or transnational standards or benchmarks.[5]

ISO 14000 series

- By means of its ISO 9000, ISO 14000, and subsequent series, the International Organization for Standardization promotes standards relating to corporate social responsibility with respect to environmental "quality" as well as health and safety; since ISO standards are applied globally by virtually thousands of enterprises, it represents the most widely adopted of all corporate responsibility regimes; ISO 14001, part of the 14000 series, was initiated in 1996 to serve as a framework for firms in the private sector seeking to pursue environmentally sound policies and practices conducive to sustainable development;

- ISO 14001 emphasizes managerial systems in terms of learning, not benchmarks, outcomes, or results; thus the key objectives fostered by ISO 14001 series standards focus on how firms and corporations manage environmental impacts; they stress methods aimed at improving company environmental performance by delineating pedagogical methods, training techniques, and approaches to instruc-tion for purposes of enhanced managerial awareness with respect to the environmental impacts of enterprise operations;

- ISO 14001 does not mandate changes in company policies or executives' performance once ISO standards have been applied; ISO 14001 underscores the importance of executive learning and human capital development in the field of environmental policies; in particular, it identifies methods for determining procedural changes

---

[5] See www.oecd.org/department/0,2688,en_2649_34889_1_1_1_1_1,00.html. OECD Guide-lines pertain specifically to environment, technology, science, taxation, labor rights, and national contact points.

with respect to documentation and managerial systems in five areas of learning: environmental policies; evaluation and assessment procedures of environmental policies; examination of statutorily required and voluntary obligations; managerial systems; and bottom-up reports to senior management based on regular internal audits;

- Thus, the hope is that environmental standards become embedded within corporate "cultures" by concentrating on managerial processes of learning; the presumed benefit provided by full implementation of ISO 14001 process or procedural standards is that they influence corporate decision-making and company or enterprise cultures; the major weakness, however, remains the virtual exclusion of performance standards;
- ISO 14001 certifications thus testify to excellence in managerial learning systems rather than excellence in environmental outcomes or results; recursivity between managerial learning procedures and environmental impacts are assumed rather than verified.[6]

AccountAbility 1000

- Launched in 1999 under the auspices of the Institute of Social and Ethical AccountAbility (AccountAbility), AA1000 seeks to infuse the dimensions of social, ethical, and environmental auditing and reporting into the mainstream of corporate managerial and accountability practices; it is oriented to the need to establish process or procedural standards that promote corporate accountability in areas that are not necessarily quantitative or financial but rather are social and qualitative in their character and consequences;
- The AA1000 framework identifies five stages: planning, accounting, auditing and reporting, embedding, and stakeholder engagement; these stages emphasize the relationship between corporate citizenship, learning, and professional development; in this they are similar to OECD Guidelines;
- AA1000 emphasizes the essential role of stakeholder dialogue and promotes corporate engagement with extended numbers and kinds of stakeholders; a key objective is to promote strategies for effective bottom-up, top-down communication by companies seeking to report on activities and results in transparent and verifiable ways;
- The nexus between learning and communication becomes explicit within this framework; it advances corporate–civil society partnerships

---

[6] See www.iso.ch/iso/en/prods-services/otherpubs/iso14000/index.html.

designed to initiate and nurture implementation of initiatives that advance social, ethical, and environmental auditing and reporting;

- As a global accountabilities framework, its stress on auditing, reporting, and performance standards sets it apart from the orientation established by the OECD Guidelines; on the other hand, AA1000 constructs a framework that defines process and procedural standards for pursuing business–stakeholder partnerships;

- AA1000 is concerned with the need to establish the epistemological grounds for managerial templates of best practices aimed at the promotion of corporate social responsibility; its design includes a series of strategic stages that an organization or business firm may adopt in developing such best practices; these again stress the central significance of stakeholder participation and continuing corporate engagement with these constituencies; such stages include a commitment to social, ethical, and environmental auditing and reporting (SEEAR); identification of stakeholders' issues; constant review and reexamination of the scope of SEEAR in partnership with stakeholders;

- AA1000 outlines the processes that attend implementation of sound SEEAR procedures; according to AA1000 such procedures must be inclusive, complete, material, and regular; other essential principles advanced by AA1000 include quality assurance, accessibility, comparability, reliability, relevance, and comprehensibility of information; in this, AA1000 is the most explicitly epistemological in its orientations;

- Although AA1000 does promote the full adoption of best practices in areas of social, ethical, and environmental reporting and auditing and also advances the full engagement of stakeholders, its emphasis on systems of learning prevents it from mandating the kinds of recursive feedback systems that embed benchmarking;

- AA1000 is amenable for use in a range of markets and economic settings but its stress on bottom-up discourses, admirable as they are, inhibits development of top-down standards that can be measured, compared, and verified across companies, sectors, and economies, and applied recursively to sustain future learning;

- Subsequent iterations of AccountAbility standards may embrace methods for developing business–civil society partnerships designed to promote and embed best-practice SEEAR processes and procedures but within structures of accountability oriented to verifiable benchmarks and transparent standards across markets and economies.[7]

---

[7] For a range of materials and introduction to the AccountAbility 1000 framework, see www. accountability.org.uk. Perhaps it should be noted that Theodore Kreps (1897–1981),

Global Reporting Initiative (GRI)

- Conceived by the Boston-based Coalition for Environmentally Responsible Economics (CERES) in collaboration with the Tellus Institute, the GRI is an independent organization and a constituent agency of the UNEP Collaborating Centre; the GRI represents an epistemological exercise in that it develops a series of questionnaires that were initially adopted and field-tested in 1999, and which are subsequently subject to regular periods of review and revision; GRI Guidelines provide elaborate forms of guidance, assistance, and instructions on how to respond to the questionnaire relative to an elaborate set of reporting criteria on all aspects of a company's performance;
- By establishing a single multiplex questionnaire, the GRI seeks to promote a common set of framework standards and benchmarks with respect to environmental and social performance;
- The GRI stresses a bottom-up approach by emphasizing the role and status of the very negotiations it establishes among the participating parties to whom questionnaires will ultimately be sent; the questionnaire is the focus as well as the result of dialogue and learning among those who design it and who are ultimately expected to apply it to themselves; by means of systematic inquiry and methodological investigation, the GRI encourages corporations to enter discussions with stakeholder groups; GRI does this by means of its questionnaires that provide guidance on how corporate representatives might (should) communicate with stakeholder groups and on what matters or sets of concerns;
- Based on social partnerships between non-state or civil society agents that include businesses, NGOs, and accounting firms, the GRI promotes targets and benchmarks by encouraging them: 1) to set targets or benchmarks; 2) to attempt to meet them; and 3) to explain in GRI questionnaires whether and to what extent they have been met and why;
- On account of its dialogical approach that culminates with an agreed common framework based on template questionnaires targeted to performance indicators identified by corporations and organizations as the most relevant to themselves, the GRI strikes a middle ground between internal processes of learning and externalized forms of benchmarking; it promotes learning among corporate decision-makers,

a Stanford University Business School Professor, first coined the term, "social audit," during the 1940s.

investors and shareholders, stakeholders, and the public-at-large, but it fosters performance measures amenable to benchmarking, monitoring, and, ultimately, third-party verification; in this, the GRI framework is anchored by the feedback proposition: the outcome of the process, that is, the GRI questionnaire, regulates the process;

- Thus, the GRI global accountability framework goes from learning and bottom-up dialogue to benchmarking and from benchmarking to enhanced reliance on the capacity of corporations and CSOs to apply the questionnaire as a guide to best practices and thus as a guide to learning; herein lies feedback at the heart of the process; it is an exercise in recursivity.[8]

Social Accountability 8000

- Created by Social Accountability International (formerly, the Council on Economic Priorities Accreditation Agency) in collaboration with a range of NGOs, trade unions, and business firms; the content of SA8000 benchmarks and standards originates with ILO labor conventions, as well as other UN agencies and the management systems of the International Organization for Standardization (ISO);
- Initially the vast majority of companies that adopted SA8000 were in the apparel and footwear industry or engaged in the manufacture of toys; there is increasing interest among companies within the electronics and agricultural sectors; SA8000 certification thus appears especially popular among corporations in the retail sector seeking to protect against reputational forms of risk; Toys R Us has been a major corporate sponsor; nonetheless SA8000 and its promoters seek to have it applied in all national settings by making its applications relevant to any economic sector and to any corporate enterprise, company, firm as well as any supplier or producer chain;
- SA8000 converts international labor standards and workers' rights into an auditable framework for global benchmarking that includes procedures for accreditation of companies and personnel certified to conduct inspection and verification;
- Of all global accountabilities frameworks under review, it is most oriented to externalized forms of global benchmarking; it stands in stark contrast to the OECD global accountabilities framework;
- The key objective in SA8000 inspections is to enable a company or a supplier and producer chain to ensure the verifiability of its claims

---

[8] See www.ceres.org/our_work/principles.htm. Also, www.globalreporting.org/guidelines/2004.asp and Global Reporting Initiative (2002).

that workers' rights and labor standards are protected and promoted; the *key means* for achieving this is for a company to engage the services of SA8000 certified auditors authorized to conduct inspections;

- The *key instruments* are SAI accredited "certification firms"; SAI thus accredits certification firms and NGOs to audit, report, and ultimately to certify company or chain compliance or conformity with labor standards and workers' rights;
- SA8000 and subsequent versions promote learning by providing certification firms and companies seeking to be certified with the necessary epistemological/analytical tools; it advances the concepts and categories relative to labor standards and workers' rights; it provides guidance on how to develop management systems capable of applying SA8000 categories in ways subject to review and inspection by qualified SA8000 certified inspectors;
- But the strength and unique contribution of SA8000 as a framework of global accountabilities is that it consists of a globally applied auditable set of standards that requires inspections by qualified personnel whose certification is designed to guarantee not only company certification, but verification of company claims as well.[9]

Conclusion

This has been an examination of global economic governance at a time when speed and spatiality combine to send waves of turbulence through markets on a global scale. State and governmental regulators, firms, large and small or multinational and national, producers and buyers at all levels of market leverage, as well as the coordinators of now globalized assembly chains, up and down the "value" ladders of production and retail, along with the widest conceivable range of CSOs, all have had to respond to the challenges of post-industrial modes of production. These responses have been made more challenging by post- and meta-Fordist modalities of information technology, niche marketing and just-in-time inventories that propel world production and distribution systems today. A world capitalist economy organized by speed, space, and delivery portends change and threatens stable order in many ways. States, governments, firms, organizations routinely struggle to meet the challenges of innovation, competitiveness, and market-share. It is a battle for survival at the specific centers of rent and profit within the sites

---

[9] See www.sa-intl.org/SA8000/SA8000.html.

of an economic swirl punctuated by place but denominated by economies of scale and scope.

In such an era of partially realized globalization, issues of trust and fairness become salient. Fairness enters center stage because the outcome of international market forces and interactions has significant domestic impacts within many societies, segments of which tend to be systematically disadvantaged by the structure of competition; and trust because the entire lattice of information guiding service delivery and commodity production is constructed on notions of contract and obligation. Fairness, however defined, and trust, however conceived or performed, represent cultural values that sustain and yet challenge market agents as they participate in the economic activities influenced by globalization.[10] In the absence of some elements of trust, markets and firms could not operate; without some appearance of fairness, states could not preserve institutional legitimacy. As Adam Smith so sagely foresaw, modern markets thrive on prudential economic reasoning grounded in notions of mutual trust and societal fairness.

But as Oliver Williamson has more recently observed (1985), markets also encourage the anomic behaviors of guile and opportunism. Such market temptations readily generate incentives for defection from standards on the part of market agents, for disloyalty among those that are party to contractual exchange, for structural disequilibrium across economies that rewards in the short term the proverbial race to the bottom. A theory of contract viewed from the perspectives of transaction-cost economics stresses the importance of asset specificity in preventing defection, disloyalty, and disequilibrium. And it is this very component, asset specificity, that suggests the reasons why multilateral networking has become so important as a form of economic governance.

This chapter has confronted the phenomenon of networks and of networks within networks, as the basic mechanisms for generating global accountability. In large measure, the reasons originate in transaction-cost economics, that is, the need to contribute specific sets of informational or productive assets astride complex policy and decisional domains – and to do so in a world economy defined by immediacy across a limitless universe. Networks arise precisely on account of their efficiency and effectiveness in providing asset-specific forms of information and

---

[10] For a statement that links trust, human rights, and the responsibilities of business enterprises see, *Norms on the Responsibilities of Transnational Corporations and Other Business Enterprises with Regard to Human Rights*, www1.umn.edu/humanrts/links/commentary-Aug2003.html.

learning in the face of increasing complexity within market and production niches. They are efficient in the sense that they reduce or severely limit the budgets of centralized or vertically integrated organizations and hierarchies; they are effective because they are fast moving and dynamic as well as concentrated. They move where the economic "action" moves and can thus advocate or deliver services wherever and however they are needed. In a sense, therefore, networks combine the advantages of firms and of markets. They offer some degree of organizational continuity, but without the carrying costs of hierarchical firms. They also introduce the elements of markets, in terms of agile exchange and mobile interactions, but without providing the same set of incentives that reward defection or disloyalty. Networks offer the strengths of non-hierarchical forms of leadership and organizational continuity in order to allow a combination of analytical talents and infrastructural assets to come together or to disband as the need for them arises and/or dissipates.

This chapter demonstrates that global corporate accountability is not a luxury to be occasionally indulged, nor a game to be left to chance. Global corporate accountability is now an essential component of transnational economic activity and thus a key to doing business in the modern world. One can proclaim this on ethical grounds alone: trust and fairness are profoundly ethical in nature. But the justification for global accountabilities is and remains crucially economic. Global accountabilities promote levels of trust necessary for contractual relationships in a world economy characterized by deepening forms of market interdependence based on transnational divisions of labor and global structures of financial intermediation.

Furthermore, with the increasing economic power of large economies beset by enormous populations consisting of largely marginalized and immiserated workers, as in the case of Brazil, Indonesia, and Nigeria, fairness is also a central tool of pragmatic international economic policies and trade practices. But the point here is that the very nature of the global accountabilities regimes, frameworks, and CSO networks that we have studied throughout this book, allows them to serve the purposes of trust, contract, and, ultimately, fairness. They do this more inexpensively and possibly with greater effectiveness than any other kind of global economic governance. For this reason alone, global accountability networks are economically as well as ethically justified within the markets of the world economy. Simply stated, they contribute assets that meet the exigencies of corporate productivity and competitiveness. Herein is the significance of *tripartite multilateralism*. Tripartite multilateralism represents an approach to accountable networking. As we have seen, it advances the cause of multi-stakeholder dialogue bottom-up and thus contributes to dialogical processes among varying stakeholder communities. Global accountabilities regimes and frameworks may thus be likened to networks that expedite conversations among those endowed with specialized forms of information. But they function in ways that allow them to generate learning to the general benefit of all through the application of benchmarked standards. Accountability begins to reign once such benchmarked standards promote trust and equity in a world society where too little of each exists. Corporate social responsibility fosters the kinds of internal learning that is crucial as a first step. But without recursive forms of feedback benchmarked to external standards, social, ethical, and environmental frameworks of assessment become devoid of genuine forms of global corporate accountability.

References

Global Reporting Initiative (GRI) (2002) *Sustainability Reporting Guidelines.* Boston: GRI.

ILO (2005) *ILO Law on Freedom of Association: Standards and Procedures.* Geneva: ILO.

ILO (2004) *Summaries of International Labour Standards.* Geneva: ILO.

ILO (2000) *Your Voice at Work: Global Report under the Follow-Up to the ILO Declaration on Fundamental Principles and Rights at Work.* Geneva: ILO.

ILO (1996) *Freedom of Association: Digest of Decisions and Principles of the Freedom of Association Committee of the Governing Body of the ILO,* 4th rev. edn. Geneva: ILO.

Kahler, M. (2000) "The Causes and Consequences of Legalization," *International Organization* 54(3), 661–83.

Lindblom, C. (1977) *Politics and Markets: The World's Political-Economic Systems.* New York: Basic Books Inc.

Swepston, Lee (2000) "Justiciability and ILO Freedom of Association Conventions," Unpublished paper.

Tajgmen, D. and K. Curtis (2000) *Freedom of Association: A User's Guide – Standards, Principles and Procedures of the International Labor Organization.* Geneva: ILO.

Williamson, Oliver E. (1985) *The Economic Institutions of Capitalism: Firms, Markets, Relational Contracting.* New York: The Free Press.

Websites

AccountAbility 1000. www.accountability.org.uk.

Global Reporting Initiative. www.ceres.org/our_work/principles.htm and www.globalreporting.org/guidelines/2004.asp.

Global Sullivan Principles. www.globalsullivanprinciples.org/principles.html.

ISO 14000 Series. www.iso.ch/iso/en/prods-services/otherpubs/iso14000/index. html.

OECD Guidelines. www.oecd.org/department/0,2688,en_2649_34889_ 1_1_1_1_1,00.html.

Social Accountability 8000. www.sa-intl.org/SA8000/SA8000.html.

United Nations Global Compact. www.unglobalcompact.org.

14 Conclusion: prolegomena to a postmodern public ethics: images of accountability in global frames

Edward Weisband

Incommensurability and accountability interpretivism

Inevitably, at the conclusion of a volume such as this, the question arises as to whether the experiences recounted, the narratives told, the conclusions enumerated, and the meanings derived, contribute to the development of an integrated framework. Such a framework would purport to allow us to ground broad generalizations of either practical use or theoretical value. The chapters included here stand together, however, in opposition to the construction of a neat package of conclusive findings and definitive lessons. Our very emphasis on *global accountabilities* broadcasts our antipathy towards modernist presumptions that project meta-narratives onto local histories, cultural traditions, and participatory or institutional practices. Suggesting, for example, that accountability involves "transparency," "answerability," "compliance," and "enforcement" in "account-giving," is appropriate in certain circumstances. But to assume from this that common understandings exist – either with respect to the applied meanings of this lexicon or with regard to the values served by their application across a range of diverse political communities – runs the risk of fixating the viewer's understanding of accountability *before* one has examined who "performs" accountability and how, where, why, under what conditions, and with what effects.

Such an analytical stance, grounded in a priori assumptions that tend to reduce cultural significations to axiomatic and homogenized generalizations, has afflicted the study of global accountability in comparative contexts. An essential task of this volume and of each of its chapters is to help remedy this by enhancing our capacity to interpret the dynamics and meanings of accountability in global frames calibrated to cultural and organizational differences and distinctions. At the end of the day, our contributing authors have held to the task of avoiding the traps of shallow "universalizability." They have done so in order to forge a sense of global accountabilities viewed from analytical perspectives anchored to the buoys of difference, incommensurability, and value-pluralism.

Does this necessarily commit us to the irresolute notions of value-relativism in which all practices are deemed equally valuable? Alternatively, does this mean that each and every experience in global accountabilities is radically unique in hermetic ways? Clearly not. Global accountabilities embrace certain common aspirations and retain their distinct character amenable to comparative analysis. We remain beholden, however, to the requirements of a value-pluralism that denies the validity of rationalistic measures on which to base judgment of global accountabilities as a singular, let alone identical, set of practices or procedures across localities. Universal appearances notwithstanding, global accountabilities tend to be molded by distinct cultural "exemplars." Applications of social scientist and value-neutral units of analysis infused by modernism tempt us into disregarding the cultural and linguistic ensembles that presuppose ethnological comparative analysis.[1] For example, we have repeatedly confronted the tension between accountability conceived as a set of participatory practices that serves the values of internal, subjective, or organizational forms of learning, on the one hand, as opposed to accountability conceived as formal evaluative frameworks and procedures linked to objective parameters imposed on agents or agencies held to account. The issue of incommensurability is further exacerbated by the fact that the contributing chapters do not establish any clear global, regional, or institutional pattern with respect to learning, benchmarking, and other kinds of applied accountability.[2]

---

[1] David Wong (1989) describes three forms of incommensurability within philosophy of science and comparative methodology: 1) the failure to translate concepts and meanings across cultural traditions; 2) epistemic contrasts within cultures that prevent analytical alignments or congruence; and 3) absence of rational grounds for determining rules of evidence or the grounds of "decidability." Alasdair MacIntyre (1977; 1991) has argued in favor of a "comparison of comparisons" by suggesting that philosophy and science require a theoretical vantage point combined with cultural admission of ever-present possibilities of fallibilism.

[2] The methodological implications of incommensurability, theoretically enunciated by Thomas Kuhn, Paul Feyerabend, and others, resound sonorously but implicitly across this book given its emphasis on the differing dynamics and meanings of global accountabilities. When specifying what global accountabilities has meant within the discrete settings where it occurs, contributing authors have applied diverse methods and divergent methodologies. In so doing, they have responded analytically to the issues that attend incommensurability.

Incommensurability as a methodological problem in scientific or formal analysis arises as a result of this and the similar tensions identified throughout this volume. The conceptual and analytical language applied in each of our cases derives from local and institutional meanings, values, and interpretations. Global accountabilities are first and foremost about social relationships, and the nature of what is in "the between" or "among" such relationships requires an imagination deep enough and sensitive enough to comprehend and interpret them on their own terms. And this is precisely what our contributors have attempted to do in this book. Incommensurability with respect to the examination of comparative global accountabilities, therefore, is not only a matter of comparing apples and oranges; the analytical problem that besets global accountabilities as a consequence of this intrinsic incommensurability stems from the difficulties of comparing apples with apples and oranges with oranges – that is, phenomena that lend themselves to common forms of categorization but which nonetheless maintain highly distinct characteristics, if not their unique character.

All this obligates us to frame our overall conclusions in terms denominated by the modifications of incommensurability and value-pluralism. The core lesson that our contributing authors construct points to irreconcilable tensions that arise across the contested terrains where global accountabilities are said to occur. Incommensurability, within the analytical domains of linguistic philosophy and contemporary philosophy of science, as well as within the study of meta-ethics, stresses the absence of any rational method for resolving theoretical and philosophical conflicts over moral or ethical norms where heuristic comparisons do not lend themselves to common metrics or grounds. Incommensurability underscores the necessity of protecting against formulaic applications of the term "accountability" especially in ways that appear conceptually consistent but which also give rise to false extrapolations and fraudulent certainties.

For these reasons, the roles, characters, and meanings of global accountabilities on display here do not yield overarching conclusions, singular political or legal requirements, or universal social and ethical compulsions. Given their incommensurability, they offer little in the way of justifying themselves *to each other*. Accountability practices and the values that guide them do not provide arguments for determining why or on what basis one such experience is somehow better than any other. Each form or standard of accountability stands primarily for itself. Each, in all of its complexity, is valuable in and of itself in that it speaks to the nature of the community and/or organizational agency that embeds each set of accountability practices, policies, procedures, frameworks, outcomes, and consequences. Incommensurability in our examination of global accountabilities thus serves to inhibit our willingness to draw glibly "global" conclusions, especially those based on notions of "comparative best practices." On the contrary, incommensurability admonishes us to avoid indicating which set of practices should prevail in all circumstances for all time since, as we have seen, global accountabilities serve many purposes and objectives and do so in ways that can only be justified for incommensurable but equally significant reasons – culture to culture, community to community, agency to agency.

Again, we must ask, does this acquiescence to incommensurability set us adrift on a sea of relativism? As the late political theorist Isaiah Berlin reminded us some years ago, however, value-pluralism and value-relativism are not identical. Liberty and social justice tend to provoke irreconcilable tensions between them, tensions exacerbated by the pluralist nature of the democratic objectives they serve.[3] These cannot always be rationally adjudicated, since all such values are worthy and compelling on normative as well as political grounds. Nonetheless, they nurture conflicting collective choices and sustain conflicting standards in democratic societies where normative polarities require not so much relativism or irresolution but deliberation and debates over value conflicts in ways that make participatory decision-making what it is. Are we thus condemned to a kind of evaluative agnosticism that asserts that global accountabilities are simply what their structures and dynamics are and that, as a result, all must be considered equal in weight and merit? Does this in turn not pander to the kinds of positivist inferences that would aver that global accountabilities are merely what social practices make of it and seek to go no further towards theoretical understanding? Is there not a heuristic device or method that allows us to approach global accountabilities both as an individuated series of micro-paradigms but simultaneously as a macro-universe subject to an all-inclusive inquiry into the nature of global accountabilities across the spectrum of its value polarities and structural articulations?

One possible method for resolving this conundrum inheres in legal hermeneutics, specifically the methodological framework of legal interpretivism, especially that developed by Ronald Dworkin.[4] Dworkin emphasizes the fundamental significance of legal interpretation and the

---

[3] For a fuller exposition of Berlin's approach to value-pluralism, see Berlin (2002).

[4] Ronald Dworkin has elaborated a theory of interpretivism in several seminal studies beginning with his *Taking Rights Seriously* (1977). Perhaps his most comprehensive outline on interpretivism may be found in ch. 7 of his *A Matter of Principle* (1985). Also see his *Law's Empire* (1986). For a recent commentary on Dworkin and interpretivism, see Hershovitz (2006).

role played by those who interpret the law, such as lawyers, judges, and legal philosophers. Contrary to the tenets of legal positivism, Dworkin rejects the amoral notions that law and legal norms exist as the neutral artifacts of social practices derived through neutered time and institutional traditions. He does so for a reason. He seeks to reestablish law as an idealized intellectual and social enterprise, one that is undertaken self-consciously by those who wish to attach rights and duties in a given community to what grounds them and thus ultimately to the social and political ideals that inform the way and manner legal and normative principles are validated and justified.

This is what Dworkin takes to be the meaning and function of *interpretation*. Interpretation turns on legal and judicial responses to disagreements over matters concerning rights and duties when the search for answers aspires to the "right" or "best" responses in terms of the theories, principles, or doctrines that fit and justify the law as a whole within any political community. Interpretation in any given instance of contested law over rights and duties is thus an interpretation of the purposes, values, and ideals to which the law is taken to serve. And the key modality is how and in what ways laws and legal norms are justified. For Dworkin, legal interpretation is always about what, how, and on what basis legal justifications are themselves justified. Legal interpretivism thus points to an ultimate form of accountability, that is, how justifications of legal norms and practices become validated within the cultural frames and institutional fabrics of each political community. Legal interpretivism grafted onto the heuristics of global accountabilities thus promotes a kind of bimodal analytical sensitivity, first, in relation to the nature of concrete accountability practices, but second, and crucially, with respect to the values, principles, or ideals to which such practices are deemed to serve – *within the frames of each culture of accountability*.

This approach allows us to speak of *accountability interpretativism*, one that would proceed in tandem with legal interpretivism. Such a method calls on those who study accountability to become consistently engaged in the development of self-reflective understandings of the doctrines, laws, or values used to justify and validate accountabilities' schemes and practices. This too represents a core objective of this book: to interpret accountability practices in terms of what justifies them, not as phenomena universally given, but within the contexts of the specific political communities or organizations or inter-institutional and interagency fields in which accountability relationships arise. Accountability interpretivism would hold that accountability norms and standards exist not as political facts or practices alone, but rather as *"interpretive"* facts reflective of the scheme of doctrines that justifies political practices within the political community. Accountability interpretivism, as implicitly evidenced in the chapters above, focuses, first, on actual political and normative practices within accountability relationships, but, equally, on the doctrines, theories, values, and normative propositions used to justify them. This provides a way of reconciling a structuralist view of accountability as a set of disciplinary techniques (in Foucauldian terms) and a normative view of accountability as a force for value-driven change.

As such, the interpretivist quest is not merely to identify accountability practices and the values that justify them. In addition, the function of accountability interpretivism is to seek rationales for and/or to elaborate how best to justify the very values that accountability practices are assumed to serve within the global frames of specific political communities or organizational cultures. The objective of accountability interpretivism, then, is to explore ultimate rationales for accountability practices by examining the values presumably served by means of the obligations established by and through the required practices. The interpretivist quest thus entails analysis of practices, of the values considered served by such practices. And crucially, it seeks to advance the development of a rationale of justification that validates such values against a global interpretation of the entire fabric of legal and normative practices that help shape and make a political community what it is. Global accountabilities assayed from the perspective of accountability interpretivism thus encourages progression of a theoretical discourse in which accountability becomes not only a set of objective practices to be observed, and not only a mechanism for the advancement and support of certain values such as rights and certain values like duties, but, in addition, the subject of its own rationale in terms of what constitutes it, how, and why. Accountability interpretivism would thus promote an exegetical conversation in global accountabilities designed to ensure that the values taken to be constitutive of accountability practices were in fact the case. Such a discursive exercise would remain sensitive, in keeping with Dworkin's methodological interpretivism, to what he calls the "fit" between practices and the values that suffuse them within each and every instance of global accountabilities. But, and this is the crucial dimension, it would also seek to interpret the standards, rationale, and justifications that ground global accountabilities within the scheme of rights and duties nurtured by political communities that ground such communities and make them amenable to accountability practices in the first place.

The central lesson of this study cast in light of interpretivism is, therefore, that comparative study of global accountabilities strengthens our capacity to examine and understand the rationales and organizing doctrines that ground accountability practices in democratic values and participatory practices. Such rationales and justificatory schemes are not necessarily derived from the practices themselves. Rather they evolve from self-aware considerations promoted by those who operate within as well as from outside accountability structures. The contributing authors have sought *ipso facto* to act as interpreters of the ways in which different cultures and communities justify accountability practices. The scales of evaluation and worth that would apply to these examinations must thus be framed by recognition of the nature of such an effort. Each exercise in global accountabilities is thus unique, but comparative merit, if it is to be assessed, must thus be based on an interpretation of how well and the extent to which each instance of accountability is justified in terms not only of any given political community and/or organization – but also in terms of what each community takes accountability to mean, that is, in terms of its own conceptions of rights and duties writ large.

This emphasis on rights and duties should not be taken to mean that the objective of any accountability scheme is limited to any specific set of "uses" in a utilitarian sense or that it promotes specific ethical values or normative principles in any deontological sense. On the contrary, as we have seen repeatedly, the structures and dynamics of global account-abilities have increasingly tended to be organized around the promotion of participatory practices designed to frame a wide range of dialogues contingent upon context, culture, competing accountability demands, symbolic values, and semiotic or knowledge systems, etc. One feature that stands out is the plethora of networks and networking that has emerged across global accountabilities some of which appear to be successful in advancing public confidence as much as they seem effec-tive in promoting normative or ethical accountability as such. There may be wisdom in this. Any conclusive summary based on the experi-ences of global accountabilities examined here must include an exam-ination of networking as a phenomenon relevant to postmodernist frames of global accountabilities. I suggest that networking provides a virtual platform, a stage for the postmodernist theatres of global accountability to be played out in ways designed to demonstrate virtue in an aretaic ethical sense. And it is to these topics that I now turn in bringing our volume to conclusion.

Accountability networks in neo-Wilsonian frames: exercises in neo-idealism

Much is written in the study of global politics and international relations concerning networks and networking as a key dimension of global civil society. But few understand their sources in economics or society.[5] The exponential expansion of functional networks operating at every level of governance provides a lesson in transactional efficiencies and effectiveness, especially when networks contribute to risk and cost reductions in transaction or exchange. Networks struggle against entropic pressures of instability and dissolution that threaten their viability, their efficiency, and their effectiveness. Why, then, have networks become so predominant in global civil society? The answers that are often enumerated include the roles and influences of information technology and communication. But a deeper probe yields an analytical interpretation grounded in transaction-costs economics. The implications point towards: the dynamics of risk in processes requiring divisions of labor; standards of efficiency in distributing assets or organizing skills; and effectiveness in providing leadership to achieve goals and to secure objectives over time.

Divisions of labor in world society have increasingly become organized by means of networks. This leads some observers to associate contemporary society with the logics of networking. Networks represent a metaphor for the present-day conditions of mature capitalism. In examining post-industrialism, Ulrich Beck, among others, dwells on the notions of "risk society" to dramatize the linkages between networks and late capitalism (Beck, 1992).[6] Similarly, Manuel Castells in his analysis of "the rise of network society" portrays global production from machinofacture to cybernetic as divisions of labor driven by network hubs and nodes (1997). Hardt and Negri (2000) in their fulminations over empire envision the challenges of social transformation during the remainder of this century in terms of networks that are socially organized but politically invisible. As Hardt and Negri suggest, what binds governance to legal jurisdiction is political power, and power tends to become more not less entrenched when threatened with the dissolution of structures that support it. For such reasons, an alternative approach

---

[5] Perhaps the most sustained recent discussion of the roles and impacts of networks in international relations is Keck and Sikkink (1998) who argue that the most important instrumentalities of networks reside in the capacities to cull and collate information and to muster it where it can be most "persuasive."

[6] Beck (1992) emphasizes the concept of "reflexive modernization" to interpret the relationship between social structures and social agents, in particular the transformations of modernity favoring "individualization" and fostering "risk"; see his ch. 6, "Standardization of Labor" (pp. 139–50) for observations regarding work, divisions of labor, flexibilization, and networking in postmodernity. For other pertinent discussions of risk and its significance for an understanding of postmodernity and mature capitalism in a number of economic and sociological contexts, see Bernstein (1998), Ericson and Haggerty (1997), and Hood et al. (2001).

has emerged as the mainstay of postmodern attempts to reckon with global accountability deficits: networks and networking. Networks have tended to be presented almost as sui generis, that is, as a self-evident autonomous phenomenon driven by information technology and global communication systems. Networking is alternatively viewed as a strategy, a framework, as a form of informal organization that characterizes and explains the shift from government to governance. Contributing authors to this volume have attempted to pierce through the fog of heuristic assumptions that surround networking in order to establish why and how networks foster accountability and participatory practices.

The widespread lack of analysis on network and networking relevant to economic governance and global divisions of labor has thus served as an implicit theme throughout this book. Although many observers count on networks to pursue a wide range of objectives in transnational governance, as often as not they tend to fall into the traps of neo-Wilsonian forms of neo-idealism by refusing to specify the conditions under which networks might fail or falter. Such authors do not take into account the factors that help us to explain why accountability networks emerge and how they succeed. Content to observe that networks exist in a broad variety of fields, domains, and policy areas, such treatments fall into a kind of exhortation over the importance of networking with respect to cross-boundary forms of governance and global accountability deficits. But absent is a sustained analysis with respect to what networks are and how they operate in different cultures and by means of certain organizational structures, that is, their raison d'être.

Benner et al. (2004),[7] for example, outline a set of "ideal-typical" features of accountability networks that include "interdependence" or cooperation, "flexibility" in terms of learning, and "complementarity" or asset specificity on the part of contributing members (p. 196). Benner et al. also identify five accountability "mechanisms" that networks require to work effectively and to ensure their own accountability: professional/peer, public reputational, market or consumer, fiscal/financial, and legal. They conclude their analysis by suggesting that postmodern public ethics demands networking aimed at "naming and shaming." In this, they refer back to the hyper-realities of postmodernist images. In cases of states, firms, brands, other civil society organizations, they write, "loss of credibility is one of the most effective negative sanctioning mechanisms"

---

[7] Benner et al. (2004, p. 197) describe networks as "mechanisms that facilitate the transfer and use of knowledge and other resources of various actors in the global public policy-making process. They also offer a new mechanism that helps to bridge diverging problem assessments and interest constellations via political debate and mediation."

(p. 200). But their analysis provides little basis for allowing us to evaluate how a network devoted to the pursuits of accountability sustains itself over the long term, nor do they suggest ways for evaluating the impacts of "naming and shaming." We are left to wonder why networks rather than some other organizational form are best suited to the counter-accountability deficits. And thus, despite their clear commitment to a world of collective due process, their analysis provides little basis for grounding a postmodern public ethics on networking.

Slaughter (2004), too, trumpets the importance of making governments accountable on a transnational basis as a step towards postmodern global governance. Hers is a neo-Wilsonian perspective on the moral economy of a postmodern public ethics. She envisions the possibilities of nationalist and parochial boundaries becoming porous. In her scheme, political decision-making within the international society comprised of sovereign states becomes not only trust-based but "dualistic" and thus organized by networks in addition to states. Slaughter's brand of dualism represents a bow towards postmodernism in that she draws a distinction between government and governance. Her aim is clear: "First is to develop a concept of dual function for all national officials – an assumption that their responsibilities will include both a national and a transgovernmental component," she writes. Her protocol involves five strategies for etching governing networks onto the geopolitical maps of states. For example, she calls for the following: "a concept of dual function for all government officials"; extension of "visibility and accessibility of government networks"; expansion in the number of "legislative networks"; greater attempts by governments to "mobilize nongovernmental actors"; and "customized solutions" by domestic constituencies relative to accountability. This leads to what Slaughter calls "disaggregated sovereignty" and the mapping of a global "virtual public space" for monitoring all decision-making processes.[8] How networks foster the kinds of accountability intrinsic to her notions of disaggregated sovereignty and how disaggregated forms of sovereignty will arise to promote a postmodern public ethics linked to public international law in her analysis remain open questions.

The contributions in this book have sought to avoid the failings of those who assume that networks arise as a "natural" or "universal" organizational form rather than as a reflection of the cultures and societies in which they are embedded. Thus the task we have imposed on the authors in this book necessarily reasserts itself: explanations of

---

[8] See especially pp. 163, 171–2, and 175–85 in Slaughter (2004).

networks must pierce through the veil of organizational form or structure if we are to understand why networks and accountability together comprise a basis for a postmodern public ethics. Therefore, our conclusions may be formulated as follows:

- a postmodern public ethics linked to accountability requires the development of meaningful participatory practices (i.e., where participants have influence and not simply voice);
- the ethical implications of global interdependencies are realized in practical terms by means of accountability networking as an organizational form;
- transaction-cost efficiencies gleaned from networking and accountability contribute to governance in ways appropriate to the dynamics of postmodern civil society;
- participatory practices must reflect diverse cultures and divergent institutional settings appropriate to the problematics of accountability measured in terms of the benefits of inter-subjective learning as well as benchmarked deficits.[9]

These propositions encapsulate much of what we have understood in examining the case studies outlined in this volume. What remains is the need to specify the requirements of a moral economy relevant to a postmodern public ethics based on accountability networks and networking.

Hierarchy, heteronomy, and networking: towards the moral economy of a postmodern public ethics

Networks, along with governments, markets, firms, and institutions, each provide opportunities for the resolution of a central problem in economic governance, that is, how to coordinate divisions of labor.[10] Adam Smith was the first to recognize that economic productivity required labor to divide its tasks and functions. He famously observed

---

[9] On debates regarding the moral relevance or significance of global interdependencies, see Simon Carney (2004). Carney argues that global interdependencies do not bear "on the scope of justice or the appropriate distributive principle but they do indicate that global interdependence possesses moral relevance because it affects people's duties to uphold the rights of others."

[10] For a relevant discussion of networks and networking from the perspectives of economic sociology, see Powell and Smith-Doerr (2004, pp. 368–402). One of the major analytical issues for economic sociology concerning networks is the extent and manner that networks are technical instrumentalities as opposed to organizational forms embedded in cultural and sociological relationships.

that distributions of task in a pin factory contributed to greater volume of output at less cost per unit of labor input. Classical and neoclassical economics have reaffirmed this in countless ways ever since. Neoclassical microeconomics emphasizes consumer preferences as the basis for measuring the market efficiencies that determine divisions of labor. This underscores the relationship between production costs and consumer use values at the "margins" of social choice and economic decision-making. Often the guide to efficiency in division of labor is assessed in terms of the macroeconomic efficiencies of price mechanisms or against the curves of market equilibrium measured by swings in supply and demand. But the efficiencies that derive from divisions of labor require a larger calculus than cost reductions or increasing labor productivity. The reason points to the phenomenon of risk. Wherever divisions of labor occur, so does risk arise as a consequence of the interdependencies demanded of those elements that must become specialized in the performance of task or function.

Division of labor is a kind of distribution based on specialization or asset specificity, one that depends of the concentration of tasks, skills, or capacities. This sets in motion the dynamics of risk, the risks that embed relationships grounded in interdependence, particularly in instances of social collaboration such as division of labor. Divisions of labor, interdependencies, and structural risks, together comprise the triadic operational elements driving the engines of economic processes. The dynamic remains functionally constant with respect to the relationship between risk and growth: as the vectors of economic growth proceed by means of divisions of labor, the depth of social interdependence and thus the magnitude and complexity of risks expand. In the wake of such effects, the efficacy of networks and networking as a form of economic governance becomes critical to the management of risk and thus a key to postmodern forms of governance.

There exist two basic governance methods or modes in modernism to resolve the problems that accompany the risks stemming from divisions of labor and subsequent interdependence: hierarchy as in states or firms, and heteronomy as in consumer and business-to-business markets. Networks, as I suggest below, represent a hybrid of both, but based on reciprocated trust and virtue displayed according to notions of aretaic ethics.[11] This is

---

[11] Virtue ethics or aretaic ethics refers to perspectives or approaches in normative philosophy that focus on human character, specifically the qualities, features, or dimensions that enable us to define what a virtuous person is. Virtue ethics, as an ethical system, typically stands both in contrast to deontological ethics – such as Kantian systems that emphasize the importance of rules and duties, that is, "right actions for the right reasons" – and in opposition to utilitarian or consequentialist traditions that stress

the key to their viability and to the linkages between the moral economy of a postmodern public ethics and accountability networking.

The sites where divisions of labor are coordinated by means of hierarchy or heteronomy are so familiar they often appear to be sui generis rather than artificially contrived methods for risk reduction in the face of division of labor and interdependence. States and firms as examples of hierarchy, and markets an example of heteronomy, cushion the risks that accompany divisions of labor based on specialization. They do so in a variety of ways and to varying degrees of success. But their capacities have recently been challenged. Globalization in production structures, liberalization of international markets, regionalization in political and economic dynamics, each generates different sets of influences that together have tended to erode fixed notions of boundary, legitimacy, and jurisdiction.

In other words, the quest for legitimacy and accountability today encounters a central challenge: nebulous or uncertain boundaries of governance. These result from the dynamics of information technology and electronic communication, transportation, global production chains and delivery systems as well as open international markets. The speed, intensity, and extensity of exchange of all kinds transform firm boundaries into porous membranes and overlapping managerial sites. What is foreign becomes familiar. Changing densities of contact and connectivity confront demarcations of separation and notions of proximity. Divisions of labor are taking shape in myriads of new ways across the globe. As we have seen in the chapters contributed to this book, governance structures necessary for the coordination of increasingly interdependent agencies are now assuming hybrid forms: multilateralized interagency arrangements within different sectors; transectoral networks linking public institutions, businesses, and nongovernmental organizations; transnational business

---

"good" and "bad" as measures of utility that enable us to evaluate social practices as well as collective outcomes or conditions. Although virtue ethics enjoys a distinguished pedigree that predates Aristotelian teleology, its impact has been limited. In recent years, however, it has gained philosophical stature on account of its emphasis on supererogatory forms of charity, compassion, or benevolence, not only as forms of action in the face of social suffering, but as practices that ennoble human character. Virtue ethics is often associated with phronesis or practical wisdom, or eudaemonia or happiness and success. The relevance of virtue or aretaic ethics to the study of global accountabilities stems from its philosophical emphasis on excellence of character as a virtue to be socially displayed for itself as an end in itself. Thus aretaic virtues are virtues to be displayed for the purposes of demonstrating virtue in human character. Global accountabilities in encouraging participatory practices that serve as virtuous ends in themselves may thus be considered as aretaic. For a sampling of sources, see Slote (2001), Hursthouse (1999), Galston (1991), Driver (2001), and Foot (2001). Of particular relevance to democratic accountability is Slote (1993).

firms, both agglomerated and dispersed; civil society organizations that include nongovernmental organizations, transnational advocacy networks, and social movements.

The loss of fixed jurisdictional terrains and anchored traditions contributes an additional source of insecurity in governance. Governance today occurs in a time and space warp often heralded by shibboleths such as the "end of distance" and the global "near." The English language places one suffix on multiple words to refer to these processes: "*ization*." As a result, we speak of "global-*ization*," "regional-*ization*," "liberal-*ization*," etc. The impacts of such processes vary, but perhaps it is safe to suggest that conceptions of political boundaries and economic geography are being altered. Political sentiments may remain anchored to national, communal, and sectarian traditions. But the cultural constructions of collective identity no longer embrace universalized sovereignty as an immutable given. The standard "vessels" of government and the state, the inclusiveness of citizenship and of national membership, and the exclusiveness of class and culture, are becoming hollowed out the longer they are beset by pressures and dilemmas beyond their immediate control. The peculiarities of the English language denote the concentric cartographies of globality by means of a series of prefixes: sub-, inter-, supra-, super-, and trans-. The irony of postmodern conditions again emerges: where pre-*fixes* and suf-*fixes* seek to "*fix*" boundaries of governance, the boundaries become strangely elusive. This is at once fundamental to the inspirations of postmodernism, and critical to the calls almost everywhere for greater and greater accountability.

Governance faces a new crisis, one that is set in motion by the lack of congruence between the impacts of decision-making and the political, legal, and managerial jurisdictions in which decision-making occurs. Governance has become besieged by non-congruence between issue areas and jurisdiction. This element generates the problem central to the role of accountability in postmodern governance once examined in global frames: *global accountability deficits*. David Held, for one, tackles the concept of global accountability deficits. He first defines "the equivalence principle"[12] to the effect that benefits and losses stemming from production of public goods and their distributions "should be matched with the span of the jurisdiction in which decisions are taken on that good" (Held, 2004). Held's argument is straightforward: political geography should circumscribe the impacts generated by the processes of decision-making. "At its simplest," Held writes, "the principle

---

[12] In defining the equivalence principle, Held credits Kaul et al. (2003, pp. 27–8).

suggests that those who are significantly affected by a global good or bad should have a say in its provision" and thus in its recompense. Held stresses the "mismatch" in global political and economic geography to stress the significance of "spillovers." He does so to demonstrate that those who pay the costs of decisions are often distant or alienated from the structures or processes in which such decisions are made. Many pay the price for a few. They do so in numerous ways including in terms of ecological and bio-atmospheric degradation. Thus the equivalence principle as advanced by Held appears to represent a recasting of the concept of economic externalities whereby the overall costs of a good or service are not included in market prices at the margins. The result is that society as a whole or government or a third party must compensate for market failures as in the case of the social costs of automobile pollution or traffic congestion. This underscores the relevance of accountability in reflecting on global accountability deficits.

But how does one settle on fair compensation in the absence of what Held describes as the "matching circles of stakeholders and decision-makers"? Held wrestles with the notion of "significantly affected" and would benchmark this according to three levels of impact: vital needs, life chances, or life style. He concludes with the proposition that cosmopolitan multilateralism based on the principles of global subsidiarity must be developed. Held's vision of global accountability thus combines a kind of participatory praxis with a call for fluid concentric circles of governance to ensure inclusiveness, subsidiarity, and, by implication, greater accountability. The structural consequences would be real. "If diverse peoples beyond borders are effectively stakeholders in the operation of select regional and global forces, their de facto status as members of diverse communities would need to be matched by a de jure status." Realizing this in any practical way remains difficult, however. For in many cases, social cartography would have to transform political and economic geography. Lack of congruence in governance across multiple legal zones and municipal jurisdictions no doubt will continue to assail governing institutions into the future. Held's notions of political malleability may serve to exacerbate the very problem he seeks to resolve with respect to the discontinuities between rule and policy impacts, on the one hand, and participatory practices, on the other.

The consequence is that the standard or modernist methods for limiting and containing risks, particularly those attached to hierarchical structures and heteronomous social orders, now confront the unprecedented boundary problems associated with postmodernism. Globalization and liberalization, in particular, challenge the coordinating capacities of governments, markets, and firms in relation to the risks provoked by intensifying interdependencies locally to globally. Coordination of division of labor and risk management becomes especially arduous for governments and markets to perform given the boundary problems of mismatch and spillover that assail global society. It is as if cascades of interaction based on specialization and division of labor are over-whelming modernist organizational competences thus requiring new forms of economic governance appropriate to the new boundary conditions of postmodernism.[13]

Networks, therefore, have emerged as mechanisms to coordinate divisions of labor in a postmodern environment defined by porous boundaries and the intensification of risk brought on by the densifying complexity of specialized relationships at all levels of economic asso-ciation and political formation. Networks and networking now stand equally alongside states, markets, and firms as methods of choice for risk reduction and for reciprocated trust whenever divisions of labor require coordination or social collaboration. This, however, again leads to the question of why and how networks provide for strategic or managerial resolutions to the problems of risk.

One set of answers peals back to the theoretical contributions of Ronald Coase, who famously inquired whether or when either firms or markets were more efficient in coordinating divisions of labor for purposes of "mitigating hazards" (Coase, 1991). Coase and Oliver Williamson have since developed transaction-cost economics as an analytical perspective on risk, "bounded rationality," and organization structure. "This is the world with which transaction cost economics is concerned," Williamson has written. "The organizational imperative that emerges in such cir-cumstances is this: *Organize transactions so as to economize on bounded rationality while simultaneously safeguarding them against the hazards of opportunism*" (Williamson, 1985, p. 32; 1990; 1996).

A constant theme that has informed the chapters in this volume is the need to observe in ethnological fashion how different network clusters confront the challenges raised by various demands of specialization as a form of bounded rationality, on the one hand, and how they deal with and suppress the risks of guile or opportunism that are present as a consequence. In a sense, the authors of our chapters have all been speaking the language of transaction-cost economics but without fully

---

[13] For example, the sovereign nation-state, theorized by classical realism as a unitary rational actor operating according to the dictates of the "billiard ball" model, now becomes subjected to various pressures that undermine its capacities for boundary control and closure. Similarly, the boundaries of firms become highly porous as transnational firms become transmogrified into the postmodern firms of many firms, the enterprise of many enterprises. Other examples abound.

acknowledging it. Nonetheless, standard definitions of transaction costs tend to employ an analytical logic closely calibrated to the integers of accountability and the costs and benefits of economic regulation. One such definition reads as follows: "Transaction costs are all the expenses resulting from negotiating, monitoring, and enforcing activities that are necessary for a firm to accomplish its distribution tasks through exchange. Transaction costs also involve the cost of arranging, monitoring, and enforcing contracts. Transaction costs can be contrasted with production costs, which are the costs associated with executing a contract" (Pelton et al., 2004, pp. 359–60). Such logics favor firms, markets, or networks under differing conditions shaped by such a mix of factors. But it is here, at this critical juncture, where the economic logic and utilitarian rationales of networks and networking explain why global civil society is functioning the way it does. This also illustrates why accountability has become the code equivalent of legitimate governance everywhere.

The heuristic keys point to the comparative costs of coordination and to the relative gains stemming from hierarchical structures of decision-making as opposed to heteronomous or market structures. Within states, governments, firms, institutions, and organizations, for example, coordination and risk reduction operate through hierarchical structures typically denoted by the arrangements of offices, authority, rank, echelon, pecking orders, etc. Within divisions of labor coordinated by markets, risk reductions occur through heteronomous exchanges, that is, by means of countless decisions of market agents, both large and small, acting in defense of self-interest or in pursuit of egoistic forms of self-maximization. Markets promote heteronomous decision-making that tests agent capacities for risk reduction and thus for social cooperation.

There are those who glory in hierarchy or heteronomy as the preferred method for risk reduction and coordination of divisions of labor. Neoliberals, for example, revel in market heteronomy and thereby celebrate the dynamics of the "invisible hand" in generating the kinds of discipline that sustain mutual dependence absent governmental or hierarchical regulation. On the other hand, there are those who rely on governments or hierarchical forms of planning to temper the structural excesses of size or privilege that sometimes grow out of unregulated markets. Varieties in economic systems produce variations in the mix between hierarchical and heteronomous forms of economic governance depending on the degrees of regulation and planning present in economic exchange and regulation.

From the perspectives of accountability, the combinations of hierarchy and heteronomy become *forged*, as emphasized by the title of this book, by means of networks and networking that bring together certain dimensions of hierarchy and certain elements of heteronomy. This may be encapsulated in the following way:

Networks and networking emerge for purposes of risk reduction as a hybrid between: hierarchy and heteronomy; vertical and horizontal forms of coordination; centralized and decentralized decision-making; bounded and unbounded divisions of labor; trust and non-trust in interdependent economic arrangements.[14]

In a strict sense, networks are not hierarchical institutions or heteronomous markets, but rather *both* simultaneously. They are combinations of vertical and horizontal, centralized and decentralized, and bounded as well as unbounded forms of organization, and coordination. They partake of the features of hierarchy, but they can successfully avoid the dysfunctions that such arrangements sometimes entail. These include bureaucratic inertia, ossified decisional processes, poor resource management, nonproductive cost structures, and declines in human capital. Similarly, networks incorporate features of heteronomy but in ways that can avoid the dysfunctions of markets or of the kinds of market failures, especially those that require regulation to fix.

Market conditions sometimes encourage guile, opportunism, or collusion, for example as demonstrated by both transaction-cost economics and models of the Prisoner's dilemma or rational choice. Heteronomy as a form of economic governance requires contractual arrangements and reciprocated obligations in order to promote exchanges, especially those that ground competition and competitiveness. On the other hand, heteronomy can lead to anomic or psychologically irrational behaviors that would threaten the viability of heteronomous markets themselves. In episodes of heteronomous decision-making the temptations of opportunism or collusion can resemble rational strategies for reward, especially to those seeking gain but at the risk of disloyalty or defection from standards. One hardly needs to think in terms of collusion or corruption, furthermore, to grasp how heteronomous structures of decision-making can tempt competitive or self-regarding agents to act in ways that ultimately defeat the trust-based interdependent relationships that all

---

[14] A way to describe how transaction-cost reductions can lead to hybrid organizational forms in business firms is as follows: "Other transactions can occur *within* the firm (a hierarchy). Traditional economic theory suggests that firms should continue to expand (within the hierarchy) until the marginal cost of an extra transaction is greater than the cost of a market transaction. Markets and hierarchies represent the extremes on a continuum of exchange. In between these extremes are hybrid exchange types that are neither wholly market nor wholly hierarchical. Examples of hybrid exchange types are franchise systems and buying groups" (Pelton et al., 2004, pp. 359–60). For our purposes, such examples represent networking within the private profit-seeking sector.

competitive markets require. For this, one need only refer to monopoly, monopsony, oligopoly, cartels, mergers and acquisitions, and "competitive capture," etc., terms that depict various dysfunctional market structures or failures in heteronomous forms of governance. These failures may appear to work to reduce risk but they do so at the cost of suppressing open choice and competition. Thus they suppress the very factors sought by means of heteronomous market structures. In such instances, the role of governmental regulation and thus of hierarchical intrusion becomes logically appropriate, even when controversial.

From our perspectives on forging global accountabilities, however, networks carve out a middle ground in economic governance between hierarchy and heteronomy. They provide a means for encouraging participatory practices, one that works to diminish the primacy of hierarchical rank or authority, but in ways that also weaken heteronomous structures organized around individualistic forms of economic egoism.[15] Networks are hybrids that embrace the dimensions of heteronomy. They function openly to reduce the incentives that reward guile and opportunism and they enhance the dynamics of trust and common purpose that is the key to effective network coordination. Networks also reduce the carrying costs of vertical integration, but they do not necessarily dispense with vertical management or control. They operate in ways that diminish the incentives that reward dysfunctional market behaviors. But they can and do support structures of heteronomous decision-making amenable to competition and/or subsidiarity.

Networks and networking are thus a form of hybrid economic governance that contributes to postmodern moral economies and to the rise of global civil society. Accountability networks can be efficient and inefficient, effective and ineffective. Much depends on the cultures they develop and how these cultures of accountability function. This too we have seen throughout this book. But cultures of accountability cannot proceed in the absence of active participation by groups of citizens and specialists alike. Ultimately, effective forms of accountability require citizen activism. Networks and networking depend on divisions of labor

---

[15] In discussing the mixes between heteronomy and hierarchy in the theoretical framework of transaction-cost economics, Williamson comments: "The fact that hazards can take many forms has been recognized only gradually as transaction cost economics has moved beyond from its initial preoccupation with vertical integration to consider related contractual transactions (labor, finance, vertical market restraints, and other forms of nonstandard contracting, regulation, trust, and the like) and to push beyond governance (markets, hybrids, hierarchies, bureaus) to consider the influence of the institutional environment (the political, legal, and social rules of the game)" (1996, p. 14).

based on specialization and trust. How to transform citizen activism into specialized skills or assets and how to ground network relationships in reciprocated forms of trust and/or aretaic displays of civic virtue represent the great challenges of networking in the development of a postmodern public ethics true to global accountabilities.[16]

Deconstructing ourselves through reciprocated ontologies: the dynamics of reversible accountability

The import of networks for envisioning new forms of emergent accountabilities is twofold. First, as demonstrated, networks can enable a hybridization of heteronomy and hierarchy, thus opening up new forms of governance and accountability among actors. In doing so, they suggest how actors in a network might be accountable *to one another* rather than simply *one to the other*. And second, networks offer a view of a postmodern public ethics that goes beyond epistemology, veering instead towards an ontology that emphasizes reciprocity and mutuality in the process of deconstructing power relations.

This is revealed in the chapters above that have consistently emphasized the importance of inter-subjective forms of participatory practices and the "flows" of reciprocity or mutuality as organizing principles of governance. A postmodernist "take" on public ethics embedded in notions of accountability, therefore, tends to stress that agents who *do* accountability in one context must become *subject* to accountability procedures in another and, if possible, held to account by those whom they had previously held accountable. It is such patterns of reciprocated routines and the mutual reiterations of inter-subjective exchanges that allow for the development of a postmodern public ethics oriented to accountability. In this sense, reciprocal inter-subjectivity in the regimes of governance is what a postmodern public ethics linked to accountability is all about. In the morality plays of postmodernist ethics, agents become accountable to principals, but principals become accountable to agents. Monitors monitor other monitors, but on an inter-subjective and reciprocated basis. Thus certifications become subjected to verification,

---

[16] Keck and Sikkink (1998) describe networks as "sets of strategically linked activities in which members of a diffuse principled network (what social movement theorists would call a 'mobilization potential') develop explicit, visible ties and mutually recognized roles in pursuit of a common goal and (generally against a common target)" (p. 6); such a definition stresses the persuasive substantive orientation of politically motivated networks and civil society organizations, but avoids the sociological and economic dimensions of networking activities across borders.

while verification procedures become monitored and mutually certified. Under the regime of such reciprocated accountability practices, it is this very sense of the vice versa, the converse, this process of mutual certifications and verifications, that conduce towards the deconstructions of power. This, in turn, helps to support the lattice of reciprocated accountability that permits inter-subjective learning to grow through participatory practices. Such is what makes postmodernist global accountabilities, *postmodernist*. And it is these factors that open up to the possibilities of establishing a postmodern public ethics, particularly based on aretaic displays of virtue through the dynamics of accountability networking.

Our authors have attested to this by focusing on how the obligation to hold others to account closely parallels obligations to act accountably. Under such conditions, the social identities of agents become reciprocally exchangeable. From this point of view, postmodernist public ethics built on notions of accountability emphasizes the importance of *"othering ourselves"* so that our social identities become mutualized through reciprocated participatory practices. By means of the reciprocal vocabularies we adopt, we communicate the cartographies of our political being. What makes accountability a special form of political language is its capacity to encourage a process of identity construction that depends on reversible agency or learning based on inter-subjective mutuality. Thus it is through the language of reciprocated accountabilities that we construct our social or collective identities in ways connected to the progression of a postmodern public ethics. And this becomes a key to the display of virtue or aretaic ethics through accountability practices and relationships.

Mulgan, among others, is aware of the need to conceive of accountability relationships in terms of reversible ontologies, but he does so in terms of abuse of power or malfeasance rather than in terms of role reversal for purposes of accountability. Those delegated with power and authority, such as government officials, police officers, utility companies, etc., may act abusively towards those on whose behalf and behest they have been empowered to act. In such instances, he writes, "the servant becomes the master and the master the servant. How is such a reversal of roles to be prevented?" (2003, p. 8). The ultimate answer resides in the exercise of rights on the part of account-holders down to individual citizens. In Mulgan's scheme, the qualitative measure of accountability is not "voice" or "answerability" alone, but whether or not and to what extent sanction or enforcement is present. Thus, reversible ontology in accountability is not so much an exercise in reverse consciousness. It involves a specific form of reversal, one that might be likened to a dialectical reversal in that roles or positions among principals and agents become reversed. In such a manner, those armed with power and the capacities of decision-making become themselves subjected to the authority of the rectification procedures they had previously applied.

Accountability discourses as constructed by our authors, however, provide theoretical justifications for expanding the modernist forms of reversibility in favor of identity constructions where the counterpart images of the self and others are reciprocally exchanged. Such a reversible ontology intrudes, impedes, and, ultimately, subverts fixed notions of reified identity in ways congruent with postmodernist notions of governance. Accountability practices can preserve a sense of "ontological presence," but presence becomes diffused and inter-subjectively mediated through reversibility and, ultimately, by means of virtue displayed. The vernaculars of accountability are thus more than a practical program of applied epistemological categories and utilitarian meanings. They represent the vehicles for the expression of collective self-identification in postmodernist contexts that establish new possibilities for public ethics grounded by displayed virtue.

This points towards the relevance of civic virtue and aretaic ethics in postmodernist considerations of global accountabilities that would reconnect ethics to virtue displayed by means of participatory practices advanced through networking. Accountability networking, after all, promotes access. Access, in turn, permits the rise of participatory engagements that serve, in principle at least, to counter exclusion and marginalization. Such activities require "political theatres" and "rhetorical performances" that function in the name of discursive power. As a consequence, one can begin to outline the emergence of a new vocabulary of accountability, a method for its analysis, and a new normative approach to justifying its practices. These point neither to specific normative or ethical standards in any deontological sense, nor to utilitarian objectives as such, but to the dynamics of displayed virtue on the part of responsible and informed citizenries enabled by their capacities for aretaic forms of ethical virtue and empowered by the exigencies of performance and display to participate in accountability networking.

Herein arises a kind of "irony of ironies": accountability as an expression of political value and displayed virtue is geared to empirical and ethical skepticism, but the assumptions that inform the narratives adumbrated in our chapters also appear to presume the necessity of a supportive moral order or aretaic moral community whenever accountability relationships need to be nurtured. Where there is doubt and suspicion so too is there the need for social trust and virtue as an antidote. Thus, accountability discourses are cast within the cultural frameworks of trust, obligations, contract, promissory commitments, normative expectations, and virtue – all the very substance of public ethics. In this, we return to the morality plays of inter-subjective, reciprocated, or reversible identities. Dubnick and Justice (2004, p. 12) state, "What is distinctive about the accountability genre ... is its reliance on the existence of a 'moral community' that shapes (and is shaped by) the expectations, rules, norms, and values of social relationships." Wherever accountability practices operate there exists a culture of appropriateness to guide social and institutional interactions. To understand participatory practices requires consummate sensitivity to the ethnological idiosyncrasies of unique cultures. So the question becomes how do ethical impulses in collective life and action become attached to the laces and ligatures of accountability within governance structures across diverse cultural settings?[17]

The answer in the democratic accountability literature is often to stress the need to preserve or protect the "public right to know." The presumption here is that from information comes "truth," and that exposure to truth creates accountable restraints on power, especially in societies that seek to hold decision-makers to account in complex policy environments where specialized forms of knowledge might advantage the few unfairly. But such assumptions "smack" of modernism. From the vantage point of our analysis, decision-making in specialized contexts requires a substratum of legitimacy to operate effectively, and notions of legitimacy imply more than the right "to know." *The dynamics of legitimacy demand a collective consensus or a commonly understood cultural sense of what right is in any given instance of governance.* It is this ineluctable ingredient of consensus that makes accountability so endlessly alluring as a perspective on governance. For it speaks to collective meanings, indeed, to the influences and impacts of culture and collective conscience, as well as to how public interests come to be formulated, implemented, and, eventually, evaluated. Legitimacy grows out of the participatory practices that inform postmodernist notions on perspectivism. But even beyond

---

[17] Dubnick and Justice graft a kind of political ontology onto the dynamics of accountability through postmodernist frames of analysis imbued with Foucauldian analysis. The essential feature of such an approach is to attempt, first, to go beyond formal epistemology, that is, conceptions of accountability as cognitive and, as such, oriented to learning and scientific, technical, operational, or administrative rationales, and, in addition, to ground accountability in notions of political ontology that, in particular, reveal how and in what ways aretaic forms of civic virtue suffer from the defects of power and governmentality. The implications of Foucauldian understandings are thus clearly defined: aretaic virtue or ethics displayed in the name of accountability practices can never fully escape the ravages of power and control exerted through the mechanisms of governmentality; see Dubnick and Justice (2004, p. 14).

this, the forging of global accountabilities demands public displays of virtue as practices designed to bind moral communities together.

For these reasons, public ethics reflective of shared or collective understandings as to authoritative legitimacy, on the one hand, and participatory forms of accountability, on the other, proceed along the same political and cultural tracks. And the discursive meanings of accountability arise or are perhaps best appropriated in situations where serious public deliberation occurs over the nature of public ethics. This is especially apt when such dialogue focuses on the meanings of legitimate governance and/or the legitimate mechanisms necessary for accountability, first, as a general prescription for consensus building, as well as a proactive antigen against substandard behaviors on the part of principals and agents alike. Again, it would appear that a kind of language game appropriate to postmodernism is at work here: governance is accountable when it is legitimate; it is legitimate when it is accountable. Practitioners of accountability are legitimated by culture, values, or social strictures, and the cultural values and social strictures that affirm the validity of accountability mechanisms do so in the name of consensus building over the nature of public ethics and its legitimacy. More than even this, however, public displays of virtue through the schemes and routines of accountability networks facilitate the formations of moral community across the shifting boundaries of governance.

Global civil society and postmodernism: citizen activism and civic virtue "all the way down"

Networks and networking reveal and reinforce the dynamics of a global civil society characterized by the permeability of political boundaries and the extensity of policy domains. Networking inheres in cyberspatial communication critical to globalization, post-industrialism, and postmodernism. Global civil society networks and organizations are both product and cause of postmodernist conceptions of space, time, and boundaries. In varying degrees, they are open and participatory, unbounded and accessible, and extensive across political municipalities. They often survive and sometimes thrive by means of networking that allows them to encourage participatory forms of activism. This speaks to the nature of their core rationale: to coordinate participatory practices in ways that contribute to a public ethics under the conditions of postmodernism. They thus address requirements of civil society that demands citizen participation "all the way down." Herein lies the true significance of accountability as a political agenda. Accountability networks are both vehicles for and the expression of citizen activism and virtue displayed.[18] But citizen activism and aretaic ethics are not only a means; in a very real sense they are ends in themselves. Through accountability networks and networking, citizens can exert specialized forms of knowledge, skills, and capacities. And beyond this, they are able to exert not only skilled forms of excellence but ethical excellence as well in keeping with the dictates of civic virtue and aretaic ethics. In this, the ultimate advantages of networking for purposes of accountability reside in the displays and activities oriented to learning that it promotes among an activist and "virtuous" citizenry.

The requirements of learning raise many questions. These must be historically mediated site to site, place to place, through the dynamics of politics and culture. Kuper speaks of "the sites of governance," and asks, "At which levels and loci of power should governing institutions be situated so that they are stable, enabling office-holders and citizens to operate in these justifiable ways on an on-going basis?" (2004, p. 192).[19] He argues that, "sovereignty can and should be dispersed horizontally and vertically, to multiple levels and loci of authority, each exercising distinct and determinate power over kinds of human practice and resources." He inquires about "political participation" and asks, "To what extent and in what ways can and should non-office-holders make political judgments and decisions, as well as control the actions of those office-holders and institutions?" These are germane to accountability networks and how they might promote a postmodern public ethics. Kuper implicitly underscores the importance of networking strategies by stating, "Plurarchic sovereignty is, however, limited on functional grounds by needs for efficacious coordinated action and democratic inclusion – needs that give rise to Principles of Distributive Subsidiarity and Democracy" (2004, p. 197). Such principles connect the lines between citizen activism, networks, accountability, and postmodern public ethics.

Networks do not provide a panacea against all forms of harm, but they can and do facilitate the kinds of subsidiarity that fosters greater degrees of social involvement and citizen participation. That both justice and democracy are served by an engaged and active citizenry is a given. What is questionable and difficult to assess are the capacities of networks in coordinating citizen activism to encourage the kinds of learning

---

[18] For purposes of the present analysis, I have taken networks and civil society organizations to be synonymous. For a discussion that provides a taxonomic scheme of civil society organizations and networks, see Arts et al. (2002), esp. ch. 2, and Reinalda (2002, pp. 11–40).

[19] Kuper raises these questions by ways of outlining "ten dimensions" of theories of global justice and democracy.

that leads to more complex forms of division of labor and thus increasing forms of specialization, deeper interdependencies, and thus greater need for reciprocated forms of trust and civic virtue. Hardly a language exists to analyze accountability networks from such a perspective on learning. In true Derridean fashion, the questions that arise are "double-sided": how to make networks accountable at micro-levels of governance where subsidiarity intersects with participation; second, how to study the participatory practices of accountability networks according to standards of learning and civic virtue.

Hirschman anticipated such an inquiry by delineating three alternate strategies available to those seeking organizational influence and policy change. The metaphors he used have stood the test of time: "exit," "voice," and "loyalty."[20] Each carries the freight of ethical considerations in policy disputes and political decision-making relevant to aretaic notions of displayed virtue in contexts of accountability. To "exit" is to leave an organization, to want to change it by means of departure, and/or to join another organization or to find a workable substitute that would permit one to pursue the objectives or values in dispute. "Voice" consists of public expression of beliefs, aims, goals, values, preferences, or objectives. It allows individuals as well as groups to make claims, to assert preferences, and to exert influence on the wide boulevards of debate and contention over political and policy issues. Voice can play an important role in articulating citizen interests, in aggregating those interests in the form of social movements or advocacy groups, and in mustering influence on authoritative agencies, particularly regarding services such as health and education and their delivery, as well as with respect to the protection of rights and the distribution of entitlements. "Loyalty" inclines those who are dissatisfied or discontent to remain within the organization in order to fight within it another day and in other ways on behalf of policy change or reform.

Exit, voice, and *loyalty* are personal risks that individuals face within organizations and within networks as well when challenges in collective action arise. As such, aretaic strategies become relevant to accountability, first, because they represent ways of galvanizing networks to perform, but, additionally, because they permit citizens to assess the range of options they face as they seek to conform to the demands of accountability. If networks are to function in ways that are *both accountable and hold others to account* they must establish cultures that

---

[20] See Hirschman (1970); on "voice" and "loyalty" in the context of public ethics and the public right to know, see Weisband and Franck (1975); also see, Dobel (1999), esp. chs. 5 and 6.

associate *individual exit strategies with social learning as a form of displayed virtue*. If those in dispute, on the basis of knowledge or access to policy debates, cannot exit in ways that contribute to network or social learning, the purposes served by exit remain individualistic rather than collective. For such reasons, resignations-in-protest and whistle-blowing represent important instruments of accountability and vehicles for social learning and demonstrated forms of virtue. They inform and help to mobilize citizenry in the name of what Dobel calls "public integrity." If voice is to be expressed effectively, it must find ways to have *impact*, to make a difference by means of discipline and information: discipline because political influence in networks so often requires time and hard work; information, given the specialized nature of many policy or administrative issues confronting accountability networks.

And, finally, if loyalty is to guide citizen participants in their efforts to form and to use network organizations, *benchmarks and measurable standards* become essential requirements. *Exit with learning, voice with impact or influence, and loyalty with benchmarks* – these together demonstrate the vitality of accountability in networks and within civil society organizations (Omelicheva, 2004).[21] In the absence of these, one cannot know whether and/or to what extent citizen participation is meaningful. Citizen networks can readily become "talking clubs," ones that may encourage preaching to the converted but as a consequence foster and promote accountability standards in the loosest manner possible. These represent traps that assail citizen activism whenever internal divisions of labor fail to promote interdependencies through learning. The lesson is clear: without information, specialized skills, and knowledge based on learning, divisions of labor cannot proceed; and in the absence of divisions of labor, the dynamics that generate risk, demand trust, and call out for civic virtue do not produce the kinds of collective action that promote global accountabilities.

The enhanced role and impact of citizen groups pursuing accountability represent one of the positive developments that lends hope to the aspirations for a global civil society capable of cultivating a postmodern public ethics. Goetz and Jenkins (2002) duly note, for example, the phenomenon of newly extended quasi-professional roles played by citizens in numerous political settings that deal with accountability issues; they note as well the proliferation of citizen networks devoted to accountability that, in turn, have become "themselves" accountable

---

[21] Omelicheva (2004, pp. 18–19) found high levels of agreement among civil society organizations and their members regarding their mission, objectives, roles, and methods with respect to accountability and transparency.

(p. 39). They also detect the emergence of a "new accountability agenda" that includes, "the interplay of *many* voices," ones that they describe as "the means by which societies collectively evolve the standards of justice and morality against which the actions of the powerful are to be held accountable." They conclude, "It is this 'constructive role' for voice – a second type of instrumental value – that has been particularly evident in the emergence of a new accountability agenda" (p. 10). Such a new accountability agenda represents an emancipatory praxis based on networking appropriate to the moral economy of a postmodern public ethics.

But the danger is that citizen participation and activism will consort with postmodernist images in ways that would serve the interests of "virtuality" rather than virtue by addressing the exigencies of a global society subjected to overlays of pressure and disarticulation from a vast array of sources. Citizen activism would proceed in chimera rather than according to the logics of divisions of labor appropriate to the public spaces of collective action and to participatory practices reflective of a postmodern public ethics.

It remains necessary, therefore, to inquire where the analytical field of accountability leaves us as we turn to the future in light of the institutional problematics and participatory practices that loom on the horizons of global accountabilities going forward. Several contributing authors have investigated how, across varied cultural environments and institutional settings, accountability tends to be viewed as a mechanism that supports citizen participation in the decisions that influence or alter the quality of their lives. More than this, accountability has been sometimes represented as a means for the construction of citizen identities through the constellation of roles and responsibilities that derive from their participation in networks devoted to accountability. Yet the ethical affirmation and political legitimacy often bestowed upon accountability, along with its regimes and frameworks, provoke a nagging sense of doubt regarding its core nature, as a pragmatic strategy, and as a philosophical discourse or analytical approach. Such misgivings represent a pervasive incertitude regarding the challenges of governance that infect institutional and political relations wherever power structures exist today.

Postmodernism and global accountabilities as congruent dramaturgical textualities

Such political insecurities cast shadows over the contemporary era, one that I have characterized as postmodern. Postmodernism, as an interpretative perspective on the present, tends to cast doubt about society's uncritical embrace of accountability. There is a sense of "hyper-reality" about accountability – a nagging conviction that the discourses of accountability are partially about civic virtue and learning, but that they also represent an elaborate façade, a series of images that obscure rather than enlighten. At times, the ironies of postmodernism seem to be unrelenting. The more the very "presence" of accountability, the greater is the uncertainty, doubt, and skepticism over its capacity to remedy or ameliorate. Accountability thus devolves into a kind of postmodern morality play, one, as we have seen, that is rehearsed across the dramaturgical stages of governing institutions or power structures, but with diverse and often diffusive effects. Postmodernist sensibilities would have us recognize, therefore, the inbred circularity that accompanies the logics of accountability: the more the realities of power become discursively discounted, the more the effects of knowledge materialized through the appearances of accountable governance become philosophically relativized.

Our authors have examined how institutions, organizations, and networks have sought to "frame" accountability around the appearances of probity, transparency, answerability, culpability, enforceability, etc. In so doing, they have provided a series of snapshots which, collectively, articulate a postmodernist array of images. In depicting how participatory practices and accountability frameworks operate within comparative contexts and across numerous jurisdictional lines, our chapters have outlined the sites and discursive locations where accountability structures, processes, and policies operate. What these interpretative analyses vividly advance, therefore, is our understanding of how accountability practices may be conceived as a kind of a postmodern text written about appearances. In a metaphorical sense, we are carried along in a stream of images across diverse locations and policy domains. Appropriately enough, however, we remain seized by questions concerning the realities "behind" appearances. For such reasons, we are obliged finally to speak of the postmodernist *problematics* in accountability.

Postmodernism is grounded by suspicion. It is permeated by wariness towards modernism, with its ontological fixities, epistemological confidence, and conceptual certainties. What makes accountability as a textual discourse so compatible with postmodernism – indeed, what renders postmodernism and accountability "*congruent textualities*" – is that both arise as reactions to the dismal failure of modernism. This is first and foremost a failure born of and derived from the many political failures to resolve the problems that modernism had promised to fix, from genocide to economic exploitation, from social or cultural marginalization and poverty to environmental degradation. The inability of modernism to get its social "house" in order established the political and philosophical conditions that have contributed to the conjoining of postmodernism and accountability as complementary themes. Both adhere to a set of profound commitments to reconsider public ethics and to reconfigure collective action around the standards of learning and civic virtue.

For these reasons, postmodernism and global accountabilities both dethrone arrogations of vanity associated with universal reason, or the allures and enchantments of technology, as well as of any kind of cultural or political supremicism grounded in fixed categories or certainties. Postmodernism passes beyond modernist politics in its intensity of philosophical, especially epistemological, skepticism. This sets the stage for global accountabilities. For postmodernism is suffused with philosophical rejection of what it avers is the subservience to power in modernism. It underscores the capacities of structures of power to define truth, knowledge, or reality, a capacity based on modernism's meta-narratives of universalized forms of "totality." Global accountabilities as a form of discursive practice and deconstruction permit an understanding of the pervasive and so often the perverse relationship that obtains between truth and power. In postmodernist moments of global accountabilities all manner and form of "philosophical essences" are denied; the very notion of political "*presence*" as the reality of governance is discarded. In place of the certitudes of political realism and philosophical materialism, comes the postmodernist focus on deconstruction of modernist forms of realism and materialism in order to heighten the visibility of those aspects of power and of power relationships that tend to be invisible.

To see accountability as the conversion of what is invisible into what is visible provides validation for all that global accountabilities represent, a set of potentially subversive representations of totalizing forms of power and truth that call out for the remedies grounded in postmodern notions of deconstruction. For postmodernist accountability is rightly preoccupied by the possibilities of trust and the promises of moral community and public ethics that deconstruct power realities into dramaturgical cultures of participatory action and aretaic meanings. To deconstruct power structures and relations in the name of accountability is to underscore the significance of collective action based on trust, ethical practices, and, even, civic virtue. How then do we, as students of accountability, hold ourselves to account in the spirit of postmodernism? Our response is to embed accountability in the development of a postmodern public ethics grounded in value-pluralism and accountability interpretivism oriented to learning and through learning to trust and civic virtue displayed across the diverse settings of governance. Such an approach forges global accountabilities in the name of civility and collective action.

References

Arts, Bas, Math Noortman, and Bob Reinalda (eds.) (2002) *Non-State Actors in International Relations*. Burlington, VT: Ashgate.

Beck, Ulrich (1992) *Risk Society: Towards a New Modernity*. Trans. Mark Ritter. London: Sage.

Benner, Thorsten, Wolfgang H. Reinicke, and Jan Martin Witte (2004) "Multisectoral Networks in Global Governance: Towards a Pluralistic System of Accountability," *Government and Opposition* 39(2), 191–210.

Berlin, Isaiah (2002) *Freedom and Its Betrayal: Six Enemies of Human Liberty*, ed. Henry Hardy. Princeton University Press.

Bernstein, Peter L. (1998) *Against the Gods: The Remarkable Story of Risk*. New York: John Wiley & Sons.

Carney, Simon (2004) "The Global Basic Structure: Its Nature and Moral Relevance," Paper presented at the annual meeting of the American Political Science Association, Chicago (2–5 September).

Castells, Manuel (1997) *The Information Age: Economy, Society and Culture*, Vol. I: *The Rise of the Network Society*, and Vol. II: *The Power of Identity*. Cambridge, MA: Blackwell Publishers.

Coase, Ronald H. (1991) "The Nature of the Firm: Origin, Meaning, Influence," In Oliver Williamson, and Sidney Winter (eds.) *The Nature of the Firm: Origin, Evolution, Development*. Oxford University Press.

Dobel, J. Patrick (1999) *Public Integrity*. Baltimore: The Johns Hopkins University Press.

Driver, Julia (2001) *Uneasy Virtue*. Cambridge University Press.

Dubnick, Melvin J. and Jonathan Justice (2004) "Accounting for Accountability," Paper presented at the annual meeting of the American Political Science Association, Chicago (2–5 September).

Dworkin, Ronald (1986) *Law's Empire*. Cambridge, MA: Harvard University Press.

Dworkin, Ronald (1985) *A Matter of Principle*. Cambridge, MA: Harvard University Press.

Dworkin, Ronald (1977) *Taking Rights Seriously*. London: Duckworth.

Ericson, Richard V. and Kevin D. Haggerty (1997) *Policing the Risk Society*. University of Toronto Press.

Foot, Philippa (2001) *Natural Goodness*. Oxford: Clarendon Press.

Galston, William (1991) *Liberal Purposes: Goods, Virtues and Diversity in the Liberal State*. Cambridge University Press.

Goetz, Anne Marie and Rob Jenkins (2002) "Voice, Accountability and Human Development: The Emergence of a New Agenda". Unpublished. United Nations Development Programme, Human Development Report Office. Background Paper or HDR.

Hardt, Michael and Antonio Negri (2000) *Empire*. Cambridge, MA: Harvard University Press.

Held, David (2004) "Democratic Accountability and Political Effectiveness from a Cosmopolitan Perspective," *Government and Opposition* 39(2), 364–91.

Hershovitz, Scott (2006) *Exploring Law's Empire: The Jurisprudence of Ronald Dworkin*. Oxford University Press.

Hirschman, Albert O. (1970) *Exit, Voice and Loyalty: Responses to Decline in Firms, Organizations, and States*. Cambridge, MA: Harvard University Press.

Hood, Christopher, Henry Rothstein, and Robert Baldwin (2001) *The Government of Risk: Understanding Risk Regulation Regimes*. Oxford University Press.

Hursthouse, Rosalind (1999) *On Virtue Ethics*. Oxford University Press.

Kaul, I. et al. (2003) "How to Improve the Provision of Global Public Goods," in I. Kaul, P. Conceição, K. Le Goulven, and R. U. Mendoza (eds.) *Providing Global Public Goods*. Oxford University Press.

Keck, M. E. and K. Sikkink (1998) *Activists Beyond Borders: Advocacy Networks in International Politics*. Ithaca, NY: Cornell University Press.

Kuper, Andrew (2004) *Democracy Beyond Borders: Justice and Representation in Global Institutions*. Oxford University Press.

MacIntyre, Alasdair (1991) "Incommensurability, Truth and the Conversation Between Confucians and Aristotelians about the Virtues," in Eliot Deutsch (ed.) *Culture and Modernity: East–West Philosophic Perspectives*. Honolulu: University of Hawai'i Press.

MacIntyre, Alasdair (1977) "Epistemological Crises, Dramatic Narrative and the Philosophy of Science," *Monist* 60, 453–72.

Mulgan, Richard (2003) *Holding Power to Account: Accountability in Modern Democracies*. Hampshire, UK: Palgrave Macmillan.

Omelicheva, Mariya (2004) "Global Civil Society: An Empirical Portrayal," Paper presented at the annual meeting of the American Political Science Association, Chicago (2–5 September).

Pelton, L., D. Strutton, and J. R. Lumpkin (2004) *Marketing Channels: A Relationship Management Approach*. New York: McGraw-Hill Co.

Powell, Walter W. and Laurel Smith-Doerr (2004) "Networks and Economic Life," in Neil J. Smelser and Richard Swedberg (eds.) *The Handbook of Economic Sociology*. Princeton University Press.

Reinalda, Bob (2002) "Private in Form, Public in Purpose: NGOs in International Relations Theory," in Arts et al. (2002).

Slaughter, Anne-Marie (2004) "Disaggregated Sovereignty: Towards the Public Accountability of Global Government Networks," *Government and Opposition* 39(2), 159–90.

Slote, Michael (2001) *Morals from Motives*. Oxford University Press.

Slote, Michael (1993) "Virtue Ethics and Democratic Values," *Journal of Social Philosophy* 14, 5–37.

Weisband, Edward and Thomas M. Franck (1975) *Resignation in Protest: Political and Ethical Choices between Loyalty to Team and Loyalty to Conscience in American Public Life*. New York: Viking Press.

Williamson, Oliver E. (1996) *The Mechanics of Governance*. Oxford University Press.

Williamson, Oliver E. (ed.) (1990) *Organization Theory: From Chester Bernard to the Present and Beyond*. Oxford University Press.

Williamson, Oliver E. (1985) *The Economic Institutions of Capitalism: Firms, Markets, Relational Contracting*. New York: The Free Press.

Wong, David (1989) "Three Kinds of Incommensurability," in Michael Krausz (ed.) *Relativism: Interpretation and Confrontation*. Notre Dame University Press, pp. 140–59.

Index